Sew Simple

A step by step guide to dressmaking

English Sewing Ltd

Hutchinson
London Melbourne Sydney Auckland Johannesburg

Hutchinson & Co. (Publishers) Ltd
An imprint of the Hutchinson Publishing Group
17–21 Conway Street, London w1p 5hl

Hutchinson Group (Australia) Pty Ltd
30–32 Cremorne Street, Richmond South, Victoria 3121
PO Box 151, Broadway, New South Wales 2007

Hutchinson Group (NZ) Ltd
32–34 View Road, PO Box 40–086, Glenfield, Auckland 10

Hutchinson Group (SA) (Pty) Ltd
PO Box 337, Bergvlei 2012, South Africa

First published 1980
Reprinted 1981 (twice)

© English Sewing Ltd 1980
Illustrations © English Sewing Ltd 1980

Printed in Great Britain by The Anchor Press Ltd
and bound by Wm Brendon & Son Ltd
both of Tiptree, Essex

British Library Cataloguing in Publication Data

English Sewing Ltd
  Sew simple.
  1. Dressmaking
  I. Title
  646.4'3'04   TT515

isbn 0 09 143610 9 cased
      0 09 143611 7 paper
      0 09 145611 8 schools edition

Contents

Introduction

The Education Department of Dewhurst, the Home of Sewing, first published this manual in ring-bound form under the title *Learning about Sewing*. It was designed to aid the students of needlework in schools, colleges and further education centres by presenting carefully researched and illustrated dressmaking instructions in a manner that was both easy to understand and enjoyable to read.

It proved to be so popular that we decided to satisfy the many requests that we have it published in book form, thereby increasing its usefulness by giving all home sewers and dressmakers the chance to benefit from the wealth of material it contains.

We would like to express our grateful thanks to Janet Harvey, the well-known home economist, who acted as our Consultant Adviser during the production of the manual, and worked many long hours ensuring that the form it took was right from the standpoint of both teaching and learning.

Our thanks go equally to Terry Evans, an artist in much demand for his fashion and sewing illustrations, whose drawings were used throughout to illustrate each section clearly and attractively.

We feel sure that *Sew Simple* will help to give readers many hours of enjoyable, rewarding sewing — for, after all, sewing should be a pleasure.

Hazel Chapman
Education Adviser
English Sewing Ltd

Metric Measurements

1. **Metric Units**
2. **Fabrics**
   Widths
   Lengths
   Quantities needed
3. **Haberdashery**
   Zip lengths
   Sewing machine needles
   Stitches per inch/centimetre
   Knitting yarns
4. **Pattern and Body Measurements**
5. **Sewing Measurements**
6. **Clothing Sizes**
   Women's wear
   Men's wear
   Children's wear
7. **Continental and American Sizes**
   Women's wear
   Men's wear

The uncertainty of the final changeover date to the metric system in this country has complicated the task of dressmakers, since not all items are yet sold in metric quantities. Children learning only the metric system will have no problem in future, but those who were taught in imperial units will need to use conversion tables for some time. Do not despair! The final garment will be almost exactly the same even if a little more thought has to be given to the measurements. Many purchases will be marked with both imperial and metric sizes for some time, but where this has been discontinued use the following tables of *equivalents*. (Exact conversions can be too complicated e.g. 1 inch equals 2.54 centimetres). Buy a good quality tape measure marked with both sets of measurements and use it frequently to get used to the new lengths.

1. Metric Units
A millimetre (written "mm") is the smallest metric measurement of length. Use it for lengths of less than an inch. A centimetre (written "cm") is used a lot in dressmaking. 2.5 cm is about 1 inch. A metre (written "m") is the basic metric length measurement. Use it for lengths of fabric.
10 mm = 1 cm, 100 cm (or 1000 mm) = 1 m.
Use 2.5 cm for 1 inch. 30 cm for 1 foot
1m for 1 yd 3 in (39 ins).

2. Fabrics
Widths
36 in is equivalent to 90 cm (or 900 mm)
42 in is equivalent to 107 cm (or 1.07 m)
45 in is equivalent to 115 cm (or 1.15 m)
48 in is equivalent to 122 cm (or 1.22 m)
54 in is equivalent to 140 cm (or 1.40 m)
56 in is equivalent to 142 cm (or 1.42 m)
60 in is equivalent to 150 cm (or 1.50 m)
68 in is equivalent to 172 cm (or 1.72 m)
72 in is equivalent to 182 cm (or 1.82 m)

Lengths
Lengths of fabric will normally be cut in the shop to the nearest 10 cm (about 4 in). The usual conversion of fractions of a yard are shown here, and it may be necessary to decide whether to round the required fabric length up or down to the nearest 10 cm.
$\frac{1}{8}$ yd is about 10 cm
$\frac{1}{4}$ yd is about 20 cm
$\frac{3}{8}$ yd is about 30 cm
$\frac{1}{2}$ yd is about 40 cm
$\frac{5}{8}$ yd is about 50 cm
$\frac{3}{4}$ yd is about 60 cm
$\frac{7}{8}$ yd is about 80 cm
1 yd is about 90 cm
Remember that most shops will have conversion charts available and if you are still in doubt ask for advice.

Quantities needed
Some idea of the amount of fabric to buy can be seen below:
Using 140 cm wide fabric:
A coat will need about 2.80 m.
A sleeveless dress will need about 1.4 m.
A dress with sleeves will need about 2.00 m.
A suit will need about 2.10 m.

3. Haberdashery
Not all items have yet been marked with metric measurements.
Zip lengths

4 in	10 cm	10 in	25 cm	22 in	55 cm
5 in	12 cm	12 in	30 cm	24 in	60 cm
6 in	15 cm	14 in	35 cm	26 in	66 cm
7 in	18 cm	16 in	40 cm	28 in	70 cm
8 in	20 cm	18 in	45 cm	30 in	76 cm
9 in	23 cm	20 in	50 cm		

Sewing machine needles

Sizes — British	Continental
7	60
9	70
11	75
12	80
14	90
16	100
18	110
19	120

Stitches per inch — stitches per centimetre.	
8	3
10	4
12	5
14	6

Knitting yarns
Now packed in 20, 25, 40 or 50 gramme packs. 25 grammes is slightly less than 1 ounce. New knitting patterns use metric measurements for quantity of yarn and size of garment. Heavy wools are usually packed in 25 and 50g packs; synthetic and blended yarns in 20 and 40g packs.

4. Pattern and Body Measurements
Body measurements and fabric amounts are usually given in both metric and imperial units. Compare actual body measurements with those in the pattern book and buy the nearest size. (See the chapters of Body Measurements, and on Choosing a Pattern for details.)

5. Sewing Measurements
Equivalents are more useful than exact conversion.

$\frac{1}{16}$ in	2 mm	$1\frac{1}{4}$ in	3.2 cm
$\frac{3}{8}$ in	3 mm	$1\frac{1}{2}$ in	3.8 cm
$\frac{1}{4}$ in	6 mm	$1\frac{3}{4}$ in	4.5 cm
$\frac{3}{8}$ in	10 mm	2 in	5.0 cm
$\frac{1}{2}$ in	13 mm	4 in	10.0 cm
$\frac{5}{8}$ in	15 mm	5 in	13.0 cm
$\frac{3}{4}$ in	20 mm	6 in	15.0 cm
$\frac{7}{8}$ in	22 mm	7 in	18.0 cm
1 in	25 mm (2.5 cm)	8 in	21.0 cm

6. Clothing Sizes
Women's wear
The usual sizes (10, 12, 14, 16, 18) are still used but the bust, waist and hip measurements will be shown in metric measurement. Measure the figure with a metric tape measure and round up or down to the nearest centimetre.

Size		10	12	14	16	18
Bust	cm	81	86	91	97	102
	in	32	34	36	38	40
Waist	cm	56	61	66	71	76
	in	22	24	26	28	30
Hips	cm	86	91	97	102	107
	in	34	36	38	40	42

Men's wear
Chest and waist

cm	76	81	86	91	97	102	107	112
in	30	32	34	36	38	40	42	44

Metric Measurements

Inside leg

cm	74	76	79	81	84
in	29	30	31	32	33

Collars

cm	33	34/35	36	37	38	39/40	41	42	43
in	13	13½	14	14½	15	15½	16	16½	17

Children's wear

From 2 – 12 years — based on height and approximate age.

Height cm	91	97	102	108	114	121
in	36	38	40	42½	45	47½
cm	127	133	140	146	152	
in	50	52½	55	57½	60	

Approx. age	2	3	4	5	6	7	8	9	10	11	12

Chest

cm	53	55	56	58	61	63	66	69	72	76	79
in	21	21½	22	23	24	25	26	27	28½	30	31

7. Continental and American Sizes

Women's wear

British	32	34	36	38	40	42	44
Continental	38	40	42	44	46	48	50
American	8	10	12	14	16	18	20

Men's wear

British	36	38	40	42	44	46
Continental	46	48	50	52	54	56
American	36	38	40	42	44	46

Length comparison

feet & inches	centimetres (cm)
2 in	5
3 in	10
6 in	15
	20
9 in	25 ($\frac{1}{4}$m)
12 in (1 ft)	30
	40
18 in	
	50 ($\frac{1}{2}$m)
24 in (2 ft)	60
27 in	70
	75 ($\frac{3}{4}$m)
	80
36 in (3 ft)	90
	100 (1m)

yards	centimetres (cm)
$\frac{1}{8}$	10
$\frac{1}{4}$	20
	30
$\frac{3}{8}$	40
$\frac{1}{2}$ yd	50cm
1 yd	1m
1½ yd	1.5m
2 yd	2m
2½ yd	2.5m
3 yd	3m
3½ yd	

Equipment for Sewing

There is no doubt that all good craftsmen know the importance of having and using the right equipment for each job. It is only the inexperienced beginner who tries to make do and then finds that the finished results are disappointing. The very wide range of sewing aids on the market can be rather confusing, so it is wise to begin with a single basic set of good quality equipment and add to it later. The cost of the basic equipment is soon covered by the savings on making clothes instead of buying them. It is very rewarding to maintain a neat, well-stocked workbox, instead of the jumbled bin of blunt scissors, rusty pins and tangled threads so often seen;

it is probably also an economy in the long run, as little is wasted. Consider too, the area of the home in which sewing will take place, and how the equipment will be stored. These factors are very important, as trying to make a garment in a cramped, untidy corner will be tiring and give poor results; the irritation of not being able to find a vital implement at the right moment can make sewing a chore rather than a pleasure. Good working habits should be practised from the very beginning as it is difficult to overcome a bad start.

1. The Sewing Area

Few of us can have a special sewing room set aside at home, and even if this is possible, careful planning is still necessary. Dressmaking processes can be rather untidy and usually the work is spread over several sessions, so that working in the main living room is unlikely to be the best place. For occasional mending tasks or embroidery, a small box of equipment that can be carried around is probably sufficient, but for any one who will be dressmaking regularly there are many considerations in choosing and planning a suitable place:

1. Time and effort are saved if the work in progress does not have to be unpacked and packed away each time.

2. Good natural and artificial light is important as it is easy to make mistakes and to tire the eyes in a poor light. Avoid blocking the light during sewing and use an "Anglepoise" type lamp for detailed work. When there is no source of daylight, the type of lamp needed for working indoors is the "high intensity" lamp, and the brilliant colour-balanced fluorescents. Always view fabrics, threads and buttons in daylight in the first instance.

3. The cutting-out space should be large and flat and may, as a last resort, have to be the floor. Ideally, use a table at normal working height and position it so that it can be used from all four sides. Folding, cutting-out boards are available and these are also marked with a useful grid of lines.

4. Keep a small, clean dustpan and brush in the area together with a large wastebin.

5. Electrical sockets are needed for the sewing machine, iron, etc. It may be necessary to use an extension flex if existing outlets are too far away; take care that this is positioned safely, and do not overload sockets with adaptors.

6. A table or bench is needed for the sewing machine and this should be at a comfortable working height, in a good light. Have enough space round the machine to place the fabric and tools.

7. A comfortable chair that supports the back when hand-sewing or machining is vital — dressmaking can be very tiring otherwise.

8. Some hanging space is useful for unfinished garments, and flat storage space is needed for fabrics and small pieces of work.

9. Adequate and suitable storage for haberdashery and sewing tools must be arranged nearby to save time, effort and temper! (See below for details).

10. Use a small, personal workbox containing a few essentials to carry around to other rooms for fitting, mending, embroidering, etc.

11. Space is needed for pressing, either on a bench or on a portable ironing board.

12. It is essential to use a full length mirror in a good light for fitting. A three-section mirror is a luxury, except for those who will do a great deal of fitting.

13. Sewing can be misery in a cold room, yet if it is too hot the hands become moist and sticky, marking the fabric. Suitable heating and ventilation are, therefore, important.

14. Remember that the noise of a sewing machine may disturb sleeping children or anyone who may be working or studying.

Equipment for Sewing

Suggested sewing areas

An alcove or large cupboard in a bedroom cut off by a curtain or screen.
A corner of a room, hidden by a curtain or free-standing screen.

A fold down, flap table fitted into a cupboard.
A large cupboard in the children's playroom can be unlocked at night to provide a suitable space.

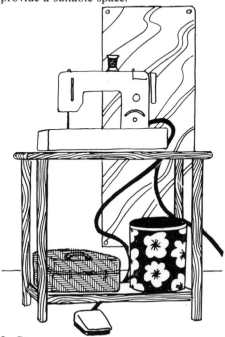

2. Storage

As well as the tools used, other items of equipment such as fabrics, haberdashery, paper patterns and your "Learning about Sewing" manuals all need storage space. It is sensible to plan this in advance, even if only a few things are bought to begin with. It is not always necessary to set aside special storage if plenty of drawer and shelf space is available. Otherwise, a group of strong cardboard boxes obtained from a supermarket will be better than nothing, and will at least keep the place tidy.

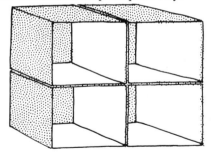

Consider each item needing storage and try to use something exactly right — cuphooks, open shelves, pegboard, shallow drawers, deep drawers, open bins, large brown envelopes, hanging rails, drawstring bags, etc. Old filing cabinets, bought secondhand, can be repainted to make excellent storage, or consider a filing trolley on casters.

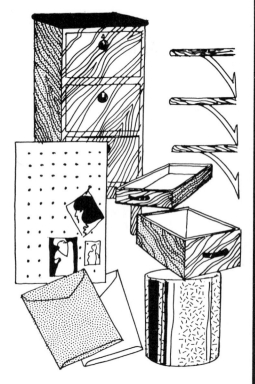

For tools, a good sewing box is very useful but can be very expensive if bought from a shop. Why not consider adapting a cheap wicker basket or large sponge-bag, or cover some small cardboard boxes with pretty paper and stack them to form open cubbyholes. Even a cheap cutlery tray will help to keep equipment in good order; or spend a little more on a sectioned plastic box with a transparent lid. Special plastic boxes are available in which reels of thread may be stacked, but a cheaper alternative is a strip of wood studded with nails. Small, sturdy cigar boxes or tobacco tins can be painted and labelled for keeping small items.

Equipment for Sewing

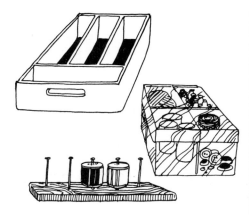

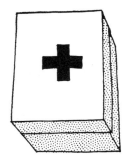

3. Equipment
One absolute must for sewers to have at the ready is an emergency medical kit!

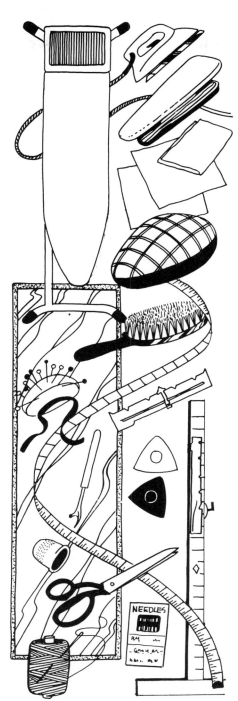

When using stitch rippers, pins, needles, scissors, etc. — however careful you may be there is bound to be an occasion when you cut or prick yourself and the resulting bloodstains can ruin fabric if not dealt with immediately — as well as the risk of infection if a cut is not suitably treated.

It is not practicable to draw up a list of tools suitable for every needlewoman but a suggested basic list is given below as a guide. Details of many other sewing aids follow after that. In every case, buy the best quality (not necessarily the most expensive) as it will have a very long life if looked after. Spend time looking around before buying, and test each item to be sure that it is right for your needs, then keep it in good working order ready for use. Be particularly careful when thinking of buying new "gadgets" as they can prove very disappointing.

Basic items of equipment

Sewing Machine

Pressing equipment
Iron and ironing board
Sleeve board
Pressing cloth
Tailor's ham

Measuring and marking equipment
Tape measure
Transparent ruler
Metrestick
Hem gauge
Tailor's chalk or pencil
Pins and pincushion

Cutting equipment
Cutting out shears
Paper cutting scissors
Embroidery scissors
Stitch ripper

Needles and threads
Selection of needles for hand and machine
Needlecase
Needle threader
Tacking thread
Sylko and Star thread

Miscellaneous
Mirror
Magnet
Thimble
Adhesive plasters

Detailed descriptions and additional items
(*Basic equipment marked**)
Sewing Machines *
There are now four basic categories of sewing machine (the second, third and fourth categories having the most to offer).
Straight stitch —
Sews forwards and backwards. Feed may be covered or lowered to facilitate darning or free embroidery. Very limited in use.

Equipment for Sewing

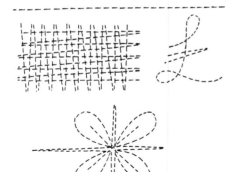

Zig-zag or swing needle —
In addition to straight stitching the needle moves from left to right. Can produce simple decorative patterns when set to satin stitch, by manual manipulation of the stitch width control.
Sews buttonholes — attaches buttons — overcasts. Sews simple, stretch seams. Free embroidery is possible.

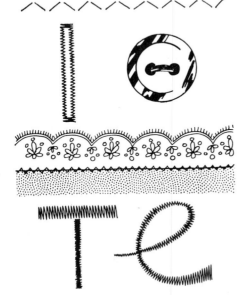

Automatic —
This category covers both the so-called semi-automatic and automatic machines. Those described as semi-automatic generally have a small selection of carefully chosen, practical stitches —

straight stitch and zig-zag, plus stepstitch for mending and overcasting, blind hemstitch for woven fabrics, stretch blindstitch for jersey fabrics and perhaps two to four more for finishing and stretch sewing purposes. The automatic models have, in general, the same potential as the semi-automatic models plus a number of additional decorative stitch possibilities. Stitches can be changed quickly and easily on some machines as the pattern discs are built into the machine. Others have interchangeable pattern discs. Free embroidery is possible.

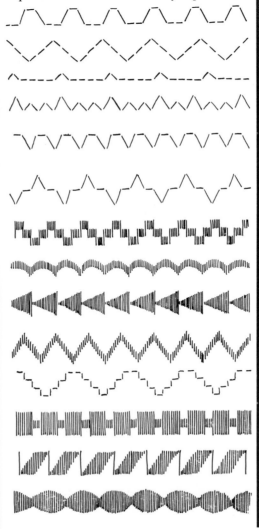

Super-Automatic —
These machines are able to carry out all the operations mentioned in previous categories. Additionally, the mechanism of the machine enables the fabric to be carried automatically backwards and forwards by the feed dog at the same time as the needle goes up and down, sewing straight or from left to right. Thus, stitches similar to those sewn on industrial machines may be carried out.
Super-automatic machines aid the sewing of stretch fabrics, for the action of the feed enables extendable stitches to be sewn. (These resemble hand back-stitches.) The most widely used practical stretch stitches are as follows:—
(a) Overlock-type stitch — back stitches the seam and overcasts at the same time.

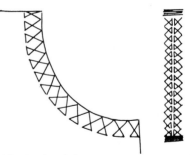

(b) Elastic triple seam — sews two stitches forward and one backwards or a similar sequence. Ideal for jersey or elastic fabrics, underarm seams or, in fact, anywhere on a garment where a great deal of strain is placed on the seam.

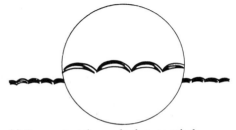

(c) Super-stretch overlock-type stitch — extendable straight stitch with slanting overcast, ideal for loosely knitted fabrics, hand or machine knitting or very stretchy fabrics such as knitted Crimplene or stretch towelling. It enables swimwear to

Equipment for Sewing

be well-constructed and sweaters to be made up in the same manner as employed by manufacturers.

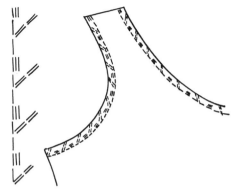

As well as the practical aspects, which of course are the most important as far as actual dressmaking is concerned, the super-automatic type of machine can offer limitless possibilities for decorative work with both the automatic and fully automatic stitches and with the free embroidery aspect.

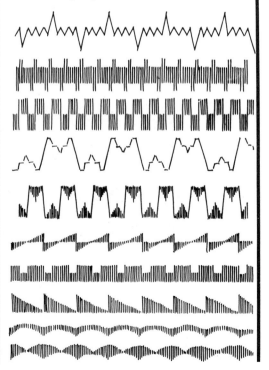

A wide variety of attachments is available for most sewing machines.

Pressing Equipment —
For good results it is essential to press as you sew, so do not economise here.

Iron* —
dry, steam and steam and spray are all available. All should have markings in line with the latest International Textile Care Labelling Scheme. All new irons are now thermostatically controlled. Non-stick "Teflon" coated sole plates are available on some irons. Only buy an iron which is B.E.A.B. approved. Dry irons can be very light in weight and are easy to use on thin fabrics, or with a damp cloth. Steam irons are very useful in home dressmaking and may sometimes be used without a pressing cloth. Steam and spray irons are an advantage in home laundering, but offer little extra to the home dressmaker. A flex holder is an optional extra which fits onto an iron to hold the flex off the fabric.

Ironing board* —
It is possible, but difficult, to use an ironing blanket on a table or bench. Choose a wide board that can be adjusted in height. It should be sturdy enough to stand level, and the top should be well padded. The removable cover should fit snugly without wrinkles; special asbestos covers or silicone treated covers prevent scorching. Extras such as wheels, flex holders and fabric bags are available with some good quality metal boards.

Sleeve board* —
This is like a tiny ironing board, specially designed for pressing small, shaped areas such as sleeves and necklines. It should be well padded, with a snugly fitting cover.

Pressing cloth* —
Use a square of muslin or soft cotton for most fabrics. A woollen cloth used with steam prevents flattening the surface of woollen fabrics. (Special pressing tissues are available.) Pressing with a cloth between iron and fabric prevents the garment surface becoming shiny. Brown paper can be used, especially under folds to prevent the edges of darts and pleats showing through.

Tailor's ham* —
This is a small, tightly-stuffed cushion used under curved areas such as darts during pressing. Make one out of calico stuffed with kapok or sawdust; it should be a rounded oval about 25 cm × 15 cm.

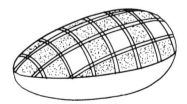

Clothes brush* —
Use the brush to remove fluff from the fabric, and to raise the surface of fabric after pressing. The back of it may be used with steam to bang the edges of hems and tailored clothes as directed in the pattern instructions.

Sponge —
A clean sponge is useful for damping fabrics during pressing.

Mist sprayer —
Also used for damping down fabrics during pressing.

Equipment for Sewing

Coat hangers —
Keep a few in the sewing area for hanging partly made garments, and for allowing skirts to hang before turning up the hem.

Needle board —
This is a piece of strong canvas covered with fine wires, used for pressing pile fabrics such as velvet. The fabric is placed with the pile downwards onto the wires so that it cannot be flattened during pressing.

Seam roll —
A long, firmly-padded roll used to press seams so that ridges do not form on the right side. Buy one, or pad a piece of broom handle and cover it tightly with calico.

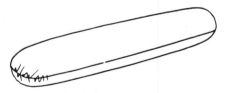

Press mit —
Like a small tailor's ham, made to fit over the hand — use it for hard-to-reach curves.

Mirror* —
A full length mirror is enormously helpful for checking the appearance of garments during fitting. A three-part mirror, hinged so that it folds out, is best but perhaps too expensive for most home dressmakers. (At auctions and in junk shops you will often find old hinged mirrors that can be stripped and modernized to suit the purpose.)

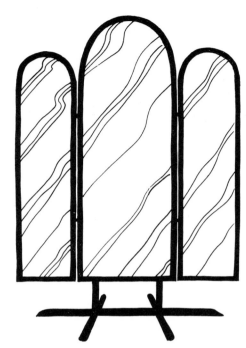

Measuring and Marking Equipment

Tape measure* —
Choose a good quality tape measure that will not stretch with metric and imperial markings.

Transparent ruler* —
Buy at least one ruler. A clear plastic one with plain edges is the most useful.

Metre Stick* —
Used for checking the straight grain when laying out patterns on fabric, and for marking hem lengths — it may be flat or round, wood or metal.

Hem gauge* —
Buy a plastic one, or make one from strong card. Used for measuring the depth of a hem so that it can quickly be turned and pressed.

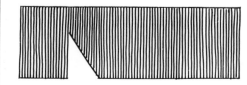

Sewing gauge —
This is a special kind of ruler with a sliding marker, used for measuring buttonholes, pleats, etc. A dressmaker's gauge also has scallopped edges for measuring scallops.

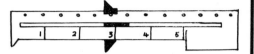

T-square —
Has many uses, including checking the straight grain. A triangle, or tailor's square, may be preferred.

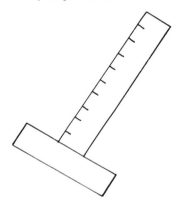

Tailor's chalk or chalk pencil* —
Available in several colours and used for putting pattern markings and alterations onto fabric. (The wax type may be difficult to remove. A small brush will remove the French chalk type). Sharpen chalk occasionally for accuracy in marking; pencils give thin, precise lines. Have at least two colours for different markings.

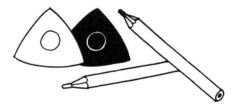

Tracing wheel —
Used with dressmaker's carbon paper to transfer pattern markings onto fabric.

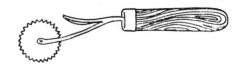

Equipment for Sewing

Dressmaker's carbon paper —
Special carbon paper, available in several colours, for use with a tracing wheel.
Instant tailor-marker —
A relatively new device for speedy tailor tacking. It holds a machine spool of thread.
"Scotch" Magic Tape —
Can be used in place of, or as an aid to, tacking. Relatively expensive but quicker than tacking.
Hem marker —
Powdered chalk is puffed out in a thin line at the required hem length. Some models use pins, or both pins and chalk. A useful aid if there is no one to help pin up a hem.
Pins* —
Choose good quality, stainless steel pins, and keep them in a box lined with special paper to protect them from rust. Never use rusty pins. It is possible to buy a pin dispenser, rather like a salt pot, so that pins pop up ready for use. Lillikins are small, fine pins for delicate fabrics. Glass-headed pins are expensive, but easy to pick up and hard to lose in a garment. Lace pins are made from stainless steel and so will never rust.
Pincushion* —
Attractive pincushions of all types are available, but the most useful ones fit on a band round the wrist.

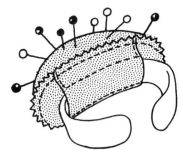

Magnet* —
Very useful for picking up pins and needles from the floor or worktop.

Cutting equipment
Well-designed, sharp scissors are essential for accurate cutting out. Choose hot-drop forged steel blades, bolted or screwed together for long life. Store them in a safe, dry place, oiling the screw occasionally. Make simple leather sheaths to keep blade points in perfect shape. Always use

dressmaking scissors in the shop before buying to be sure they feel right to you. In use, have them sharpened regularly.
Cutting-out shears* —
Buy bent-handled shears so that one blade rests flat on the cutting out surface. (Left-handed shears can be bought in specialist shops). The handles are of two different sizes to fit the thumb and fingers, and the blades are usually 18 – 20 cm long.

Paper cutting scissors* —
an old pair of scissors should be kept for cutting patterns, etc. Do not use dressmaking shears.
Embroidery scissors* —
they have fine, sharp points and are useful for trimming and snipping fine details, cutting buttonholes, etc.
Stitch ripper* —
an inexpensive aid to unpicking seams.
Electric scissors —
very light and easy to use for cutting heavy-weight fabrics.

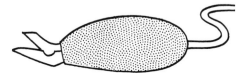

Pinking shears —
the serrated blades are used for trimming the edges of non-fraying fabric so that overcasting is unnecessary. Use them carefully as they are difficult and expensive to sharpen.

Buttonhole scissors —
an adjustable screw can be set so that a cut of the required length only can be made.

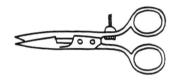

Jersey scissors —
the finely serrated edges give ease in cutting knitted fabrics.

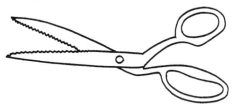

Scissor gauge —
this sliding device fits onto only one blade on the scissors to make it easy to cut long bands of fabric to the required width.
Cutting-out board —
useful for those who only have a small table, this folding board can be laid on top to support the full width of the fabric. Usually marked with a grid and lines to indicate straight and true cross grains.

Needles
(See also chapter on Haberdashery).
Buy a selection of good quality needles and keep them in a needlecase so that they are readily available. Self-threading needles are available. Use needles suited to the fabric and thread used, but personal preference should dictate the final choice.
"Sharp" — long, oval-eyed, all purpose.
"Between" — shorter than sharp. Bevelled edge for fine sewing.
"Calyx-eyed" — quickly threaded because of opening at top.
"Darner" — long needle. Long eye to take wool or thick thread.
"Milliner" — long, round-eyed, thin — use for hand-shirring and basting.
"Crewel" — embroidery. Long eye, takes embroidery thread. Similar to "Sharp's" length. Available in sizes 1 – 12. The greater the number, the finer the needle.
"Ball and Uni-point machine needles" — for elastic fabrics — can be used for knits. With rounded point, they do not pierce and damage fibres, but push the yarns aside.

Equipment for Sewing

"Beading needle" — straight, fine needle with long eye. Can thread both pearls and beads.

"Leather point" — has small curved blade to slit hole in leather — facilitates machine sewing.

Selection of machine needles for all weights of fabric.

Bodkin — thick needle with blunted end. Long eye. Used for threading cords, ribbons, tapes through lacing holes.

Needle threader* —
this device, which costs only a few pence, makes threading hand or machine needles quick and easy.

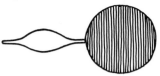

Thimble* —
Few competent needlewomen would consider hand sewing without a thimble. It is well worth the effort of learning to wear one. It should fit snugly on the middle finger of the sewing hand, and may be plastic or metal, plain or fancy.

Adhesive plasters* —
Always have them nearby when sewing because blood from a prick or cut can ruin fabric.

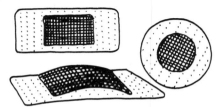

Threads
(Also see the chapter on Stitches and Threads)
Tacking thread* —
Special thread is available and should be used in a colour contrasting with the fabric. It clings to the fabric yet can be broken and pulled out easily when required.

Sewing thread* —
Consider the type, weight and colour of the fabric. First select the type and thickness of thread required, and then the colour. "Sylko" for natural fabrics — cotton, silk, wool, linen. "Star" for man-made fabrics — nylon, polyester, acrylic, etc. Dewhurst "Strong Thread" or "Sylko No. 40" — for button sewing. "Sylko Perlé No. 5 — for hand and machine embroidery. "Sylko No. 40 and 50" — for machine embroidery. Secure the loose end of thread on the reel after use, to prevent tangling.

Miscellaneous
Awl or stiletto —
A tool with a round shaft and sharp, pointed end, mounted on a handle. It is used for making the holes for eyelets, for holes in some types of embroidery, and sometimes for pulling out tacking threads.

Beeswax —
Buy a small piece in a holder and use it to strengthen thread and to reduce the chance of knotting.
Crochet hook —
Can be used in mending woollens, and for other odd jobs such as poking out corners of collars.

Dress form
(or dressmaker's dummy) —
An expensive item only needed by those who intend to do a lot of dressmaking for themselves. Choose one with as many adjustable measurements as possible. It should be on a sturdy base.

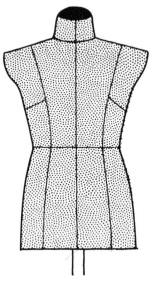

Embroidery hoop or frame —
used for hand and some machine embroidery. Two hoops fit tightly together to hold the fabric taut. Ask for advice at a specialist needlework supplies shop.

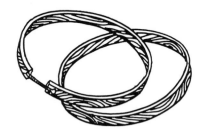

Mushroom —
Useful for darning knitted woollens.

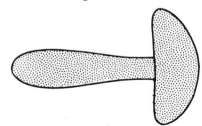

Equipment for Sewing

Orange sticks —
Use an orange stick to push out the corners of collars and cuffs when turning them during construction.

Pattern paper —
large sheets or rolls of flimsy graph paper used for making patterns.

Tissue paper —
sometimes needed for placing under a fabric whilst machining so that it does not catch in the feed teeth.

Tweezers —
pull out tacking threads, and any machine stitches that have been wrongly placed.

4. Using a Sewing Machine

It is human nature to blame equipment when things go wrong. In the majority of cases when things DO go wrong whilst using the sewing machine the user is to blame.

1. In the first instance, refer to the instruction book supplied with the sewing machine. Read it thoroughly to gain a good, basic idea of the stitching techniques possible when using the machine.

2. Sewing machines, like cars, become thirsty from time to time, especially when in constant use; the machine must run quietly and smoothly for maximum efficiency. If this is not the case, and the machine is functioning in a noisy, sluggish manner, something must be wrong. Generally, a noisy machine indicates that cleaning and oiling are necessary.

3. Clean first and oil afterwards — this applies to all sewing machines, no matter what make or type. Most accessory kits include a cleaning or dust brush, and this must be used to remove all dust, lint and fluff before any attempt is made to oil. Use only the highest quality, fine machine oil and always refer to instruction books for the location of the oiling points.

4. Remember — the machine should be oiled before use and not afterwards. Only two small droplets of oil need be applied to each oiling point — following the instructions in the book exactly. Careless oiling results in the machine becoming flooded with oil and therefore spoiling the fabric being sewn.

5. After oiling, wipe the machine over with a clean duster and run it for a minute or so unthreaded, on a spare bit of fabric.

6. Sewing machines in constant use need regular care and attention. If they are well cared for, it will seldom be necessary to call in the services of a mechanic.

Machine stitching at work
There are two separate threads which are operated by the sewing machine:
1. Controlled by the bobbin which runs underneath the cloth.
2. Controlled by the needle which stitches through the cloth from the top. When machining, the threads are passed round each other and tightened to form a stitch. Even running of the threads, and the way they pull against each other, is referred to as the tension. To have perfect sewing the tension must be accurate. Controls can be adjusted to give the correct tension.

Correct tension

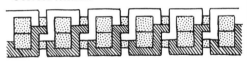

Top tension too tight (or bottom tension too loose).

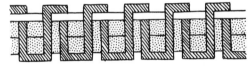

Bottom tension too tight (or top tension too loose).

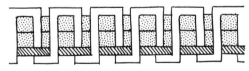

Length of stitch for various weights of fabric
1. Machine basting or tacking, using the longest stitch on the machine, can be carried out. This is generally only temporary stitching.
2. On thick and heavy fabrics, long stitches should be used. Conversely, short stitch lengths must be set for fine and lightweight fabrics.
3. Fullness can be eased in evenly by setting the length to approximately four stitches per centimetre. The index finger should be placed lightly on the fabric behind the sewing foot whilst sewing. This is sometimes referred to as "ease plus".

5. Problems that may arise when using a Sewing Machine

Stitches of uneven length
Causes —
(a) Stitch size indicator incorrectly adjusted. Vibration may cause it to move.
(b) Needle in wrong way round.
(c) Incorrect pressure.
(d) Feed dog badly adjusted.
(e) Feed dog clogged up with fluff or dirt.

Upper thread snaps
Causes —
(a) Upper tension too tight.
(b) Poor or rotten thread.
(c) Incorrect threading.
(d) Needle set too high or low.
(e) Needle bent or blunt.
(f) Needle too fine for thread.
(g) Needle inserted wrong way round.
(h) Needle rubs against presser foot, needle plate or shuttle.
(i) Sharp or rough place on shuttle or needle.

Lower thread snaps
Causes —
(a) Lower tension too tight.
(b) Poor or rotten thread.
(c) Bobbin case incorrectly threaded.
(d) Bobbin wound too loosely or too tightly.
(e) Bobbin wound too full.
(f) Bobbin wound unevenly.
(g) Rough or sharp edges on bobbin.
(h) Rough or sharp edges on lower tension spring.
(i) Burr or rough edge on needle plate.
(j) Dirt or accumulation of thread in race or bobbin case preventing bobbin turning freely.

(Never be tempted to buy cheap unbranded thread in sales or from street markets, as it will generally be very old, faulty and rotten).

Equipment for Sewing

Stitches missed
Causes —

(a) Needle blunt.
(b) Thread too thick for the needle.
(c) Needle threaded incorrectly.
(d) Needle in the wrong way round.
(e) Needle set too low or high.
(f) Wrong type of needle.
(g) Wrong length of stitch.
(h) Needle bent.
(i) Needle too small for thread.
(j) Needle too long or too short.
(k) Oil on needle.
(l) Shuttle hook blunt or worn.

Seams puckered
Causes —

(a) Top and bottom threads different.
(b) One or both tensions too tight.
(c) Wrong sewing foot.
(d) Incorrect thread.
(e) Dull needle causing side puckers.

Stitches looping underneath
Causes —

(a) Tension incorrect — top too loose or bottom too tight, or both.
(b) Fluff or thread caught in tension discs.
(c) Two weights of thread used.
(d) Incorrect threading.
(e) Thread caught under lower tension spring.
(f) Dirt or fluff in race.

Stitches looping on top
Causes —

(a) Incorrect threading.
(b) Different weight of thread used on top and bottom.
(c) Thread or fluff caught in tension discs.
(d) Incorrect tension — bottom tension too loose, top tension too tight, or both.
(e) Bobbin incorrectly threaded.
(f) Thread caught under lower tension spring.

Broken needle
Causes —

(a) Needle too fine for type of fabric used.
(b) Poor quality thread which knots easily.
(c) Needle badly centred and hitting needle plate or sewing foot.
(d) Upper tension too tight.
(e) Fabric pulled when sewn so that the needle bends and hits the foot or needle plate.
(f) Needle bent, of poor quality, badly inserted (either the wrong way round or at the incorrect height).
(g) Presser foot incorrectly attached.
(h) Failure to lift needle before removing material.
(i) Zig-zag setting too wide when using twin needles.

Machine not running properly
Causes —

(a) If machine has two speeds, it could be set at slow speed.
(b) Fluff or thread caught around the race.
(c) Bobbin winding apparatus engaged.
(d) If machine is belt driven, belt may have stretched.
(e) Faulty power plug.
(f) Wrong oil used or the machine may not have been cleaned or oiled for some time.
(g) Thread wound round wheel.
(h) Tight bearings.

Tangled thread at beginning of seam
Causes —

(a) Bobbin thread wound in wrong direction or bobbin wound too full.
(b) Underthread not drawn up.
(c) Both threads not pulled back under presser foot and held for first two or three stitches.
(d) Improper oiling and cleaning of machine.

Machine jammed
Causes —

(a) Threads jamming bobbin case.
(b) Threads wound round upper thread holder.

Staggered Stitches
Causes —

(a) Too little pressure on presser foot.
(b) Take up spring missing, broken or weak.
(c) Take up spring incorrectly adjusted.

Material not feeding through correctly
Causes —

(a) Stitch length regulator turned too far so feed is out of action.
(b) Dirt around feed dog.
(c) Feed dog incorrectly set.
(d) Pressure incorrect.
(e) Bent presser foot or feed dog.

Bobbin winds incorrectly
Causes —

(a) Drive wheel on winder not bearing firmly enough on hand wheel or belt.
(b) Rubber tyre on bobbin winder wheel loose, greasy, worn or rotten.
(c) Thread guide on winder bent, making thread pile up on one side of bobbin.
(d) Wheel that operates thread guide of winder badly set or not turning freely.

Hand wheel hard to turn or set
Causes —

(a) Thread jammed in race.
(b) Thread or dirt in bearings.
(c) Bearings rusted or jammed.
(d) Bearings too tight.

Machine runs noisily
Causes —

(a) Lack of oil.
(b) Accumulation of fluff in moving parts.
(c) Loose bearings.
(d) Loose shuttle in holder.
(e) Loose bobbin case.

Body Measurements

It is not possible to choose patterns and clothes, or to begin making a garment, until an accurate set of body measurements has been taken.
Pattern sizes are generally based on measurements *round* the body, eg. bust, waist or hip sizes. Figure types are based on *height* and on back neck to waist length, eg. misses, women's, junior petite. A suitable amount of "ease" is allowed for in the pattern styles. It is impossible to check *all* one's own measurements, so enlist the help of a friend. If a friend is not available, ask for help from an assistant in a paper pattern or fabric department.
The more measurements taken and the more accurate they are, the better will be the fit of the finished garment.
Notice that it is *not* sufficient to take only bust, waist and hip measurements.
Wear suitable underwear and shoes. Measure snugly but not tightly. Copy out the following chart and record your own measurements. Re-measure at frequent intervals, as your size may vary even if your weight has changed very little. Details of how to take measurements, including measuring for trousers, follow the chart.

1. Measurement Chart

Date:
Height:
Bust:
Waist:
Hips:
Back neck to waist:
Shoulder width:
Back width — armhole to armhole:
Shoulder length — right:
Shoulder length — left:
Front bodice — centre front:
Front bodice — right:
Front bodice — left:
Side bodice — right:
Side bodice — left:
Chest — above bust:
Chest — on bust at front:
Chest — diaphragm:
Upper arm:
Shoulder to elbow:
Sleeve length:
Wrist:
Neck:
Centre neck to hem:
Waist to hem:

2. Taking Women's and Girls' Measurements
General

Height — stand on the floor with bare feet, back to a wall, looking straight ahead. Chalk a tiny mark on the wall level with the top of the head. Measure up to this mark from the floor.
Bust — best taken by your assistant who should stand behind you. Measure over the fullest part of the bust, with the tape very slightly higher at the back.
Waist — tie a piece of string round the natural waist, then measure the string without removing it. (It will also be needed there for other measurements.)
Hips — place tape round fullest part of figure, generally about 23 cm below waist for Misses and Women's, or 18 cm below the waist for Miss Petite, Half-size, Junior Petite, and Young Junior/Teen.
Back neck to waist — find the bone that sticks out at the nape of the neck and measure from this point straight down to the middle of the waistline.

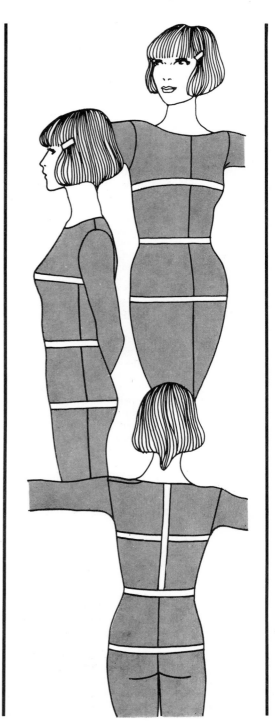

Body Measurements

22

Shoulder width — clasp hands together at the front waistline, with arms slightly forward and raised. Measure across the back from shoulder point to shoulder point.

Back width — measure across the back at shoulder blade level, starting and finishing where the normal armhole seams lie.

Shoulder length — measure from the base of the neck to the point of the shoulder each side. (The two measurements are often slightly different.)

Front bodice — centre front — from neckline straight down to waistline. Then measure from shoulder seam placement to waistline each side over the breast.

Side bodice — stand upright with hand resting on hip. Measure each side from 25 mm/2·5 cm below the armpit straight down to the waistline. (There may be a difference between the two sides.)

Chest — above bust — measure round at underarm level above breasts. On bust at front — measure from underarm seam to underarm seam over the bust. (Where this measurement is 5 cm or more than the back width, the paper pattern may have to be altered to allow more room.)

Diaphragm — take this measurement round the rib cage half-way between the waist and the fullest part of the bust.

Shoulder to elbow — bend the arm and measure from the point of the shoulder to the point of the elbow.

Sleeve length — bend the arm slightly and measure from the point of the shoulder to wrist, over the bend. It is also useful to measure 25 mm/2·5 cm from below underarm seam to the wrist, with the arm straight.

Wrist — for long sleeves measure round the wrist over the wrist bone.

Neck — for garments with closely fitting necklines measure round the fullest part of the neck.

Neck to hem — measure from nape of the neck (at the back) down to the required hem level, holding tape into waist.

Waist to hem — for skirts, measure straight down to the required hem level.

Trousers

Wear suitable undergarments and the shoes that will be worn with the trousers. Take the following measurements:

1. Waist to crotch — a very important measurement — accurately assessing this will make a big difference to the final, overall fit. Sit on a firm flat seat, and take the measurement from the side waist to the seat. On the actual pattern piece the waist to crotch measurement should be equal to your own measurement plus 13 mm – 25 mm for ease. (A little extra is allowed on this measurement to make it possible to sit or crouch and to move around easily.) If the pattern does not conform to this measurement it must be shortened or lengthened accordingly.

2. Waist — use a piece of string tied round the waist to locate exact natural waistline.

3. Upper hip — measurement is taken round top of hip bones, usually 7·5 cm – 10 cm below waistline.

4. Seat — measure around the fullest part of the hips. This may be anything from 20 – 25 cm below waist, depending on the proportions of the figure.

5. Thighs — around the largest part of the upper thigh generally about 5 cm below the crotch.

6. Knees — take two measurements, directly above and below the knee.

7. Calf — around fullest part of the calf.

8. Length — side waist to floor or required length of trousers.

9. Instep — measurement taken around heel and over instep.

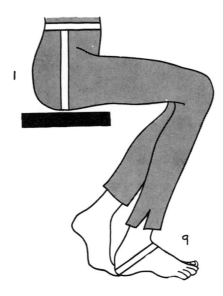

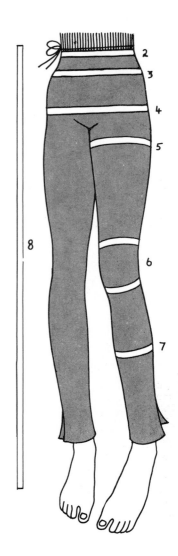

3. Taking Boys' and Men's Measurements
General

A few basic measurements are essential for buying or making clothes for boys and men. When making closely fitted or tailored garments several more detailed measurements should be taken. Shirts are usually made to fit by neck size, although some also state chest size. Jackets and suits are sized by chest measurement. Trousers are fitted to waist and inside leg measurements.

Body Measurements

Basic height — measure without shoes.
Neck — measure round fullest part of the neck and add 13 mm for ease.
Chest — measure round the fullest part of the chest round under the arms.

Waist — tie a string round the natural waistline and measure this length. Note that men may prefer to place trousers higher or lower than the natural waistline.
Seat or hips — place the tape round the fullest part.
Inside leg — this measurement is taken over the clothes being worn. Measure from crotch to the top of the shoes.
Outside leg — (trouser length) — measure from the natural waistline down the side of the leg to the required length.

   Other measurements
Shoulder — from base of neck to the point of the shoulder at the top of the arm.
Centre front — measure from base of neck straight down the front to the waist.
Back width — measure across the shoulder blades from armhole to armhole.
Sleeve length — measure from point of shoulder to elbow and then from elbow to wrist bone, with the arm slightly bent.
Upper arm — measure round the biceps at the fullest part of the upper arm.
Wrist — take measurements over the wrist bone.
Thigh — for closely fitted trousers measure round each thigh at the fullest part.

4. Taking Children's Measurements
As children grow so quickly they should be measured frequently.
Always measure before making or buying clothes for them. No perfect sizing by age system for patterns has yet been devised, so it is advisable to choose by height.
Babies — use weight, age and height to assess the right size pattern. Little alteration is usually needed unless the baby is unusually tall or chubby.
Toddlers — allowance is usually made for the wearing of nappies. Measure height, chest, waist and length from nape of neck to required hem level.
Young Children — as for toddlers, but also take hip measurements and inside leg length for trousers.

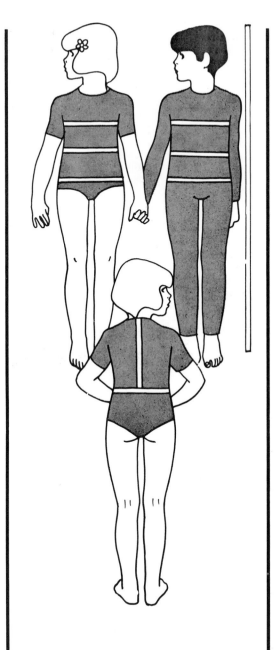

Fashion and You

Fashion is perhaps a less important influence on our way of dressing than it used to be, yet it is still interesting and important to know something about the elements of design. Anyone with an interest in clothes can learn to develop a style of dressing that suits her figure, expresses her personality and fits in with the life she leads. Even those whose desire it is to live in jeans ought to know how to choose the most flattering style and the most suitable fabric, and to be able to wash and mend them when necessary.

Collecting together a set of clothes that is *exactly* right for you and the life you lead is not easy and the fact that it usually has to be done on a limited budget does not help. The advantage of making your own clothes is that the colour, style and fit will all have been chosen and put together with you in mind at far less cost than those bought "off the peg".

1. Planning New Clothes

Take a little time to study pattern books, fashion books, advertisements, shop displays and magazines, checking what is new and making a note or sketch of anything that appeals to you. (Start a scrapbook and add to it from time to time.) Look at the style, colour and fabric and notice the accessories and trimmings. Look through your wardrobe and list all the clothes worth keeping; alter or dispose of those you do not feel happy wearing, clean and repair anything that needs it. Try on those to be kept, see how well they mix and match together. Now make a note of the clothes needed to complete a basic collection that will be suitable for all the occasions in the life you lead. List them in order of importance so that you know which garment to make first. Decide for yourself whether you prefer a few expensive items or lots of cheap and cheerful things that do not last very long. Remember that it is not worth spending a lot of time and effort in making an intricate garment out of poor fabric. A well-made, classic dress or skirt can be worn many times with different accessories, whilst very fashionable ones may be out of date well before they are worn out.

Figure types

It is important to understand that figures vary enormously, and if you know your own figure type and figure faults it is easier to choose suitable and flattering styles. (See the chapter on Choosing and Using a Pattern for details.)

2. Colour

Choose colours that both fit in with other clothes in the wardrobe and suit your personal colouring. Old rules about not wearing blues and greens or reds and pinks together have been proved wrong, but always try out colours and colour combinations, to be sure that you feel happy in them. Highly fashionable colours may date quickly and may do nothing for your colouring or personality. The assorted colours worn by some young people can look exciting, or just a mess! Accessories in matching, toning or contrasting colours can make all the difference to an outfit, drawing attention away from figure faults or brightening a dull colour. Make-up should be related to the colour of the clothes being worn and may need to be altered slightly for each outfit.

Colours can create optical illusions, so that cool and dark colours make you look smaller, while warm and light colours make you look larger. Subtle muted colours can be slimming and are usually expensive looking if worn with carefully chosen accessories. Bright contrasting colours draw attention to the figure and make it look larger. Colours vary so much in shade and tone that hard-and-fast rules about colour schemes are useless. In general:

Redheads should avoid reds, pinks and oranges that clash with their hair colour. Choose natural grey, cream, camel, brown or black and white. Yellows, greens and blues are pretty for a contrast or for accessories.

Blondes should avoid some yellows and oranges but usually look good in pastel shades — blues, greens and browns. Richer colours look good with dark blonde or mousey hair.

Brunettes look good in most bright colours.

Elderly people with white hair look pretty in pastel shades. Sallow skins need warm colours without too much yellow in them. Pale skins need colours strong enough to contrast with the skin. Dark skins look attractive with most colours, although exotic colour combinations can look out of place in the daytime.

There are three main ways of planning a colour scheme for one outfit or for a collection of clothes:

A monochrome colour scheme uses shades of colour, or one colour with black and white.

A contrasting colour scheme uses two or more different colours in varying strengths

A toning colour scheme uses two or more similar colours. Always try out colour schemes by holding the fabric combinations near your face and looking in a mirror to see if they suit your complexion.

3. Line

The style lines of a garment can be used to emphasise or conceal parts of the figure. Most designs include silhouette lines, body lines and feature lines.

Fashion and You

Vertical lines can add height and make the figure look slimmer eg. princess style.

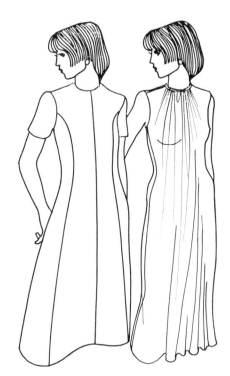

Horizontal lines must be placed at flattering points of the figure as they tend to add to the appearance of width.

Curved seams and draping create soft lines that are usually flattering.
Diagonal lines should appear from left to right when looking at a garment; long diagonals take the eye downwards in a slimming line. Any lines appearing in the fabric weave or pattern should also be taken into account.

Fashion and You

Generally, straight lines are rather severe and give a tailored or classical look, whilst curves and drapes appear graceful and feminine.

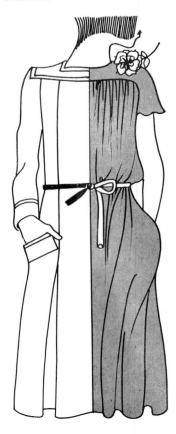

Style lines, or silhouettes, are the ones most obviously affected by changing fashions. In spite of seemingly endless variations there are really four basic silhouettes:

(a) Fitted — the garment fits the natural curves of the body and may show off the figure. Unless well cut and carefully fitted it may crease easily.

(b) Semi-fitted — usually fitted over the bust with a slightly looser cut at waist and hips. It is more flattering to an imperfect figure than a completely fitted garment.

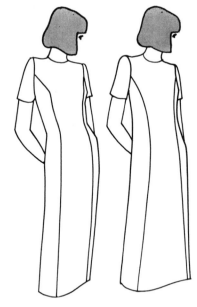

(c) Slightly-fitted — easy to wear because it has quite a lot of room for movement and only barely follows the body outline. May be bias cut.

(d) Loosely fitted — often fitted only on the shoulder, with fullness disguising the body outline from the bust down.

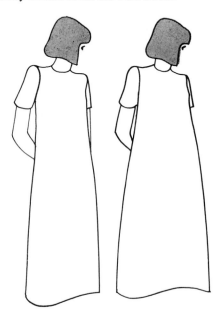

Most paper patterns allow the appropriate amount of wearing ease in the cut, whatever the silhouette. Some very close fitting areas may currently be fashionable, eg. Empire bodices fitted under the bust, shirtwaisters with snug waistlines.

4. Balance and Proportion

A garment looks best when the interesting details are not concentrated in one area alone. Balance can be maintained by keeping an equal amount of eye appeal in two or more garment areas; two halves may be identical so that the garment has a symmetrical look. If one area has special emphasis the whole appearance may be balanced by having another point of interest elsewhere.

Fashion and You

Proportion is also important when relating the areas of the garment to one another and to the figure. The style lines, the design details, the pattern or obvious weave and the figure type should all be taken into account. The scale and size of the fabric and garment must also be suited to the figure type; a full, midi skirt may swamp a tiny slim figure, whilst a skimpy mini will be most unflattering on a tall, plump figure.

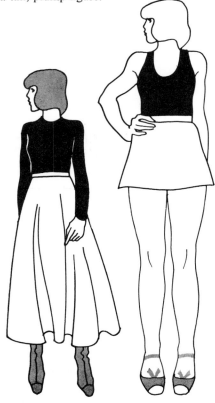

Pleasing proportions are often achieved by planning the garment areas in halves, thirds or quarters, but for any particular figure slightly uneven proportions may be more suitable. It is the overall look that is important; try on a number of ready-made garments to get an idea of what suits you best. Check too, the effect of shiny and dull fabrics, large and small prints, sheer and bulky fabrics and various colour combinations. Additionally when, considering balance and proportion take into account the accessories and trimmings.

5. Fabric and Texture
(See also the chapter on Fibres and Fabrics)
The texture of fabrics also affects the final appearance of a garment. The fibre and construction of fabrics varies enormously, creating stiff or flowing, rough or smooth, shiny or dull, sheer or bulky materials, so that care must be taken in choosing one that is exactly right for the style and figure. Soft, clinging fabrics reveal the figure, whilst a stiff one may conceal figure faults by creating a sleek outline.

Shiny or bulky materials make the figure appear larger so may be useful for anyone who is too thin, but should be avoided by the overweight unless used for trimmings or accessories. Soft, clinging fabric such as fine jerseys, bias cut silk, wool and crêpes make soft, feminine garments.

Fashion and You

Soft, loosely woven fabrics such as heavier woollens, crêpes and jerseys make attractive flared clothes, or those with unpressed pleats.

Lightweight evening fabrics can be draped more closely to the body. Firmly woven worsteds, linens, cottons, silks and heavy cottons or fine tweeds, make tailored clothes with a seamed or sculptured look.

6. Fabric Patterns

Prints and other patterned fabrics add beauty and interest to your wardrobe and are often a high fashion feature that anyone may use. The style and function of the garment should be carefully considered when using a patterned fabric; too many seams and other style details may break up the fabric design so that it is not seen to best effect. Choose a pattern that is suited to the figure in size and colour — small patterns are pretty on tiny figures where larger prints might be too overpowering.

Fashion and You

Vertical strips make a figure look slimmer and taller. Horizontal strips usually appear to add width and reduce height.

Very bright colours or sharp contrasts tend to make a figure appear larger than subtle ones. The main colour should be one that is personally flattering, although combinations of other colours may be used in small areas, eg. a printed pocket on a plain dress. Be sure that eyecatching designs are limited to areas where they will be complimentary and not draw attention to figure faults.

The curves and angles of fabric and garment design should be in harmony, eg. straight, boxy jackets look better in checks than in paisleys. Curved, bodice seams and collars tend to spoil a plaid or striped effect. Consider the direction of the pattern and the body movements so that they are not in conflict.

Today's casual way of dressing means that combinations of patterns and textures formerly unacceptable are now in common use. Make patchwork garments from odd remnants for an economical addition to your wardrobe.

7. Glossary of special words to do with fashions

(f) indicates word of French origin and pronunciation.

A-line — dress or skirt resembling the outline of letter "A".

Accent — a colour or design feature, drawing attention to the finished garment.

Accessories — items of apparel or ornament which are teamed up with clothes to complete an outfit, eg. shoes, hats, scarves, belts, etc.

All-over pattern — a design applied to cloths having no obvious directions (ie. no top or bottom).

Appliqué (f) — a method of applying one piece of fabric to another and stitching down to create a design feature.

Ascot — a broad neckscarf, tied so that one end extends beyond the other.

Asymmetric — unbalanced in design. One side different from the other in shape.

Avant-garde (f) — before its time — ahead of the trend.

Bateau (f) — neckline following the curve of the collar bone.

Bell sleeve — a full sleeve, flaring at the lower edge like a bell.

Fashion and You

Bishop sleeve — a full sleeve, usually gathered in by a band to fit closely at the wrist.

Blouson (*f*) — a bloused effect created by gathering in fullness which is allowed to fall over a seam, as in a bodice over a skirt.

Bodice — that part of a garment above the waist.

Bolero — a jacket of spanish origin, which ends above the waist. Usually close fitting.

Border (*f*) — to finish an edge with trimming or self-fabric.

Boutique (*f*) — a small specialised shop or department within a large store selling fashion garments and/or accessories.

Caftan — a long flowing coat-like garment, often with bell sleeves.

Camisole — a close fitting under bodice, sometimes attached to a skirt, and worn with a jacket.

Cap sleeve — a very short sleeve which only covers the outside of the upper arm, tapering away to nothing on the lower edge of the armhole.

Cape — a bell shaped outer garment, having no sleeves, which hangs from the shoulder. Front opening.

Cardigan — a collarless sweater or jacket with front opening and often with pockets.

Chemise (*f*) — a blouse style cut as for a man's shirt.

Chic (*f*) — an original and stylish way of dressing.

Coat-dress — a front opening dress, having the appearance of a coat. Usually in mid-weight fabrics.

Collection (*f*) — the season's range of fashion garments from a dress designer, as exhibited in spring and autumn shows to buyers.

Couture (*f*) — a garment made mostly by hand by a seamstress.

Couturier (*f*) — a male fashion designer, often with his own dressmaking house.

Couturière (*f*) — a female fashion designer and dressmaker.

Cowl — a soft draped neckline.

Cravat — a wide neckline, tied with the ends tucked inside the front of a garment.

Crew — a round neckline, close fitting to mid-neck.

Culotte (*f*) — a flared leg trouser-like garment, having the appearance of a skirt.

Decolléte (*f*) — bare neck and shoulders, with plunging neckline, as in Empire line dress.

Dicky — a detachable shirt front.

Dirndl — a garment with a full gathered skirt.

Dolman — a sleeve set in a deep armhole, as in a Japanese kimono.

Double-breasted — an overlapped front opening, having two rows of buttons or fastenings.

Edwardian — styled after the fashion of the early 1900's when King Edward VII reigned.

Empire Line — styled after the fashions of the French empire period, decolléte, the waistline close under the bust, and loose straight skirt.

Ensemble (*f*) or Outfit — a complete outfit — usually used to describe a coat and dress combination.

Epaulet — a shoulder decoration of braid or cloth fastened by a button on the shoulder or head of the sleeve.

Epaulet sleeve — a sleeve with a square cut shoulder section extending to the neck in the form of a yoke.

Flap — a loose fabric section, attached by one edge to the garment.

Mare — a widening or spreading of fabric in a garment — bell-like.

Fly — a lap of fabric used to conceal an opening.

Fully fashioned — shaping of flat knitted garment by reducing stitches (unlike the shaping of circular knits, which is by cutting and sewing seams).

Fusset Collar — flared outwards at the top.

Godet — a triangular piece of fabric inset into a garment to give fullness, or as decoration.

Gore — tapered section of a garment. Wider at the bottom edge.

Gusset — triangular or diamond shaped fabric piece inserted underarm to ease sleeve area. Also used in the crotch of trousers and pants.

Halter — a band of fabric extending from one side of the bodice front round the neck and back to the other side of the bodice front enabling the bodice to be backless.

Harem pants (*trousers*) — a garment with softly draped legs, gathered to a band at the ankle.

Haute Couture (*f*) — high fashion, the product of a creative fashion house or group of designers.

Inset (*or insert*) — a piece of shaped fabric inserted for decoration or to aid fitting.

Jabot (*f*) — a ruffle fitted down the front of a bodice.

Jerkin — a short sleeveless pullover or jacket.

Jewel — a simple round neckline, set at the base of the neck.

Jumper — a short simple garment with low cut bodice.

Jumpsuit — bodice and trousers joined in one garment.

Keyhole — round neckline with opening cut in bodice front.

Kick pleat — a pleat to ease a narrow skirt; usually inverted, knife or box pleat.

Kilt — a short pleated skirt.

Kimono — a loose, wide sleeved robe, fastened at the waist by a broad sash.

Lantern sleeve — a bell sleeve with lower part shaped into the wrist, resembling a lantern.

Lapels — a part which turns back, usually describing the front neckline fold.

Line — the style or outline given by the cut and construction of a garment.

Lingerie (*f*) — women's lightweight underclothing.

Lougette (*f*) — a style of garment having a hem below-knee.

Macramé (*f*) — bulky knotted lace in geometrical patterns.

Mandarin — narrow standing collar, close fitting to the neck.

Mannequin (*f*) — a dressmaker's dummy or dress form. Also the model who wears new clothes at fashion shows.

Maxi — hem length falling between mid-calf and ankle.

Micro-skirt — hem length falling to upper thigh.

Middy — slip on blouse typically with a sailor's collar.

Midi — hem length falling to mid-calf.

Mini — hem length falling to mid-thigh.

Motif — a simple design used as decoration.

Negligée — a lightweight decorative dressing gown worn by women, over a nightgown.

Obi — broad sash.

Overblouse — a loose waisted blouse not tucked in at the waist.

Overskirt — decorative skirt worn over another garment.

Peasant sleeve — full sleeve set into a dropped shoulder, and gathered into a waist band.

Peignoir (*f*) — a women's robe that matches a nightdress.

Fashion and You

Peplum — a small flounce around the hips of a garment, usually as an extension of a bodice.

Peter Pan — a flat shaped collar, with rounded edges.

Pinafore — sleeveless overdress, serving the purpose of an apron.

Plunge — a low cut neckline revealing the curve of the breasts.

Prêt à porter (*f*) — fashionable ready to wear garments.

Princess line — a garment fitted with seams instead of darts.

Sash — a fabric band worn around the body as decoration, over a garment.

Scalloped — an edge or border cut with semi-circular shapes.

Scoop — deep "U" shaped neckline.

Semi-fitted — conforming to the general shape of the body, without being closely fitted.

Shawl — a separate piece of fabric, often knitted, worn around the shoulders.

Sheath — a close fitting dress, with a straight skirt.

Shift — a loose fitting casual dress.

Shirtwaister — a dress having a bodice which is buttoned as a shirt.

Silhouette (*f*) — the outline or shape of a garment or figure.

Single-breasted — a centre front closing with sufficient overlap to allow only one row of buttons.

Soutache (*f*) — a narrow braid trim.

Sportswear — informal garments designed for leisure activities.

Stole — a long scarf of uniform width worn around the shoulders.

Tab — a small loop or flap sewn down at one end only — often to keep the pulling and closing of a flap.

Toile (*f*) — a copy of an original garment design, made up in simple cotton fabric, and sold by the designer to firms wishing to make a commercial range. These too may be made for personal use.

Train — an extension of the back of a dress, which trails along the ground, as in a wedding dress.

Trouser suit — a jacket and trouser outfit worn by women.

Tunic — an overdress of simple design worn over another garment.

Turtleneck — a high neck-hugging turnover collar.

V-neck — a simple neckline shaped in the front as a letter "V".

Vent — a faced or lined slash inserted into a garment to allow greater ease of movement.

Vest — a short close fitting garment without sleeves, usually worn over another garment.

Wrap-around — a garment which is wrapped around a person, as in a wrap-around skirt, allowing a good overlap of fabric at the closure.

Yoke — a fitted part of a garment, usually on the shoulders or hips, from which a garment hangs.

Choosing and Using a Pattern

1. Choosing a pattern

Pattern choosing sessions can be great fun. To keep up to date with the latest fashion trends make a special point of visiting local pattern shops and browse through the pattern books from time to time. It is most annoying, after you have chosen a pattern and fabric and started work on it, to find that there is a new fashion idea that you have overlooked — even more annoying if it particularly suits and appeals to you and your friends beat you to it! By studying the designs available from the pattern manufacturers at regular intervals you will find that you automatically know exactly which book to look at when you have a particular garment in mind. You will remember perhaps that one pattern book always seems to offer an interesting selection of blouses or that the skirts in another always seem to appeal to you more.

The pattern companies publish smaller versions of their pattern books at regular intervals with selections of patterns that, as well as being right up to date, are specially suitable for teenagers and people learning to sew. It is well worth paying attention to these when looking for a new idea for your next garment. Make sure that you always have a note book and pencil on these pattern spotting sessions. A few pieces of tracing paper may come in handy too if you wish to remember an idea but are not able to purchase the pattern at the time.

When pattern books are out of date, many shops will sell them to regular customers for a small charge. You and your friends could perhaps club together and purchase one between you, from time to time.

Another idea is to compile your own Personal Pattern book of ideas.

Be self-critical and *honest with yourself* about your figure, and try hard to learn and remember what suits you. If you see a suitable picture of a dress in a magazine or catalogue, cut it out and paste it in the ideas book. Divide the book into sections, ie. blouses, skirts, dresses, coats, jackets, etc. much the same as a real pattern book. If you make it a loose leaf book, styles may be replaced as fashions change. Then, when the time comes to think up an idea for a new garment to make, you have a ready source of ideas at hand which will help you to arrive at a decision more quickly.

Each pattern company caters for a wide variety of tastes although their fashion ideas obviously vary. Intricate or exclusive patterns are generally more expensive than the simple ones.

Figures vary considerably, so patterns for clothes fall into certain categories. Under sixteen, and adult figure types are grouped according to height and proportion. All figure *types* are based on two main measurements — a. height and b. back waist length.

Your dressmaking pattern must be chosen to suit your figure type. Remember to use the charts in the pattern catalogues and learn from them, for they offer very sound guidance. The descriptions Young Junior/Teen, Junior Miss, Women's, Junior Petite and Half-size are usually used now for the grouping of sizes (not ages) and figure types in pattern catalogues.

To find out your figure type stand in front of a mirror in your underwear and compare yourself with the descriptions in the chart. Look at your body proportions and check them against the description, then select the type nearest to your figure. (Few people match exactly.) Now you must choose the correct pattern size. Take your body measurements (see chapter on Body Measurements) and compare them with the appropriate figure type chart.

In general choose a pattern by your bust size. (The manufacturers will already have added extra amounts for ease in wearing, for that particular style). For skirts and trousers choose by waist measurement, unless the hips are large in relation to the waist — in that case choose a pattern by the hip size.

If your measurements fall between two sizes, choose the larger one if you are large boned or like a loose fit, and the smaller one if you have a small frame or like a tight fit. You may find by experience that some patterns allow more ease for movement than others.

When you have determined the correct type and size, choose a pattern from the appropriate figure type section of the pattern book. Look at each sketch that attracts you, to assess how it would suit your figure (which may look different from the glamorous model in the catalogue!).

Note whether it is marked as an easy-to-sew garment, or whether it comes from a couturier section and may be more intricate to make up.

Some ideas for choosing patterns according to your figure:

Choosing and Using a Pattern

Figure	Styles to avoid	Styles to choose
Flat chest.	Fitted bodices, too wide a neckline.	Gathered and draped styles so that bodice has added fullness.

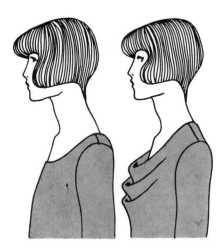

Large bust.	Very high neckline. Frills. Draped and gathered bodices. Full sleeves.	Tailored top bodice. Fitted sleeves. Skirt trimmings. Long revers.

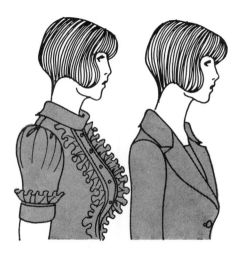

2. Making a Personal Pattern

After you have been dressmaking for a while you will find that you have acquired a collection of patterns. Make sure that you look after these very carefully for you never know when they may come in useful again. You may find that you have some particular patterns that you really like, in which case you will want to use them again and again. Maybe you find a particular sleeve pattern that appeals to you for example. Make a copy of this in woven fabric or better still on unwoven interlining fabric so that it will last. Use this idea for any patterns that you want to use again — it will save you money in the long run.

Inexperienced and experienced dressmakers alike may benefit from using a mock-up pattern known as a fitting shell, standard pattern or toile. A special, basic paper pattern is carefully adjusted to personal measurements, then tacked together in a cheap fabric such as muslin. This muslin garment is carefully and accurately fitted on the figure. All new patterns can then be compared with this "toile" before cutting out and making up so that costly mistakes are avoided. "Confidence" Pattern Kits (for trousers or a simple dress) can now be purchased which contain an inexpensive fabric (not paper) pattern that can be made up into a try-on garment.

Although checking on the fit of each pattern in this way takes a little time it is well worth while. In addition any tricky process or unusual detail can first be made up in muslin before cutting the actual fabric.

To make clothes that fit beautifully and are exactly right for you, it may be a good idea to combine two patterns. Unless you are really knowledgeable, only combine patterns of the same size from the same figure-type range. The structure of the garments should be similar, and if in doubt try out the idea in muslin first.

It is possible, and often desirable, to combine a bodice of one size with a skirt of another, but there will have to be some adjustment at the waistline.

3. Pattern Markings and Symbols

Pattern markings can vary slightly according to the manufacturer, although most markings are very similar. There are

Choosing and Using a Pattern

Figure	Styles to avoid	Styles to choose
Short neck.	Tie neck bands. High polo-necks. Mandarin necklines. Wide shoulder-lines.	Plunging, long, square, or V-shaped necklines, with narrow shoulder-lines.

Plump, short figure.	Wide necks, full sleeves, gathered skirts, frills, horizontal stripes and wide belts.	Fitted sleeves, gored skirts. Princess lines.

a set of standard markings which could be learned by heart.

1. Straight grain of the fabric — these markings are arrowhead symbols instructing the dressmaker to place the pattern on the grain.
2. Place to fold — this is a bracketed grainline. The pattern edge should be placed on the fold of the fabric that is on the grain.
3. Darts — indicated by two broken lines for stitching. For simple darts there is a solid line at the centre, known as the fold line.
4. Notches — showing matching points, they are V-shaped symbols along the cutting line.
5. Seam allowance — broken lines round the pattern area indicate the stitching line. Width of allowance can vary from area to area on the pattern. It is normally 15 mm in width from the cutting line. The hem allowance is usually written against the bottom cutting line.

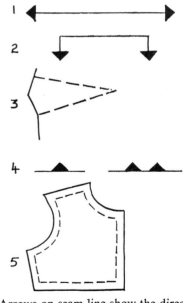

6. Arrows on seam line show the direction in which the seam should be sewn to avoid distortion of fabric.
7. Dots, squares and triangles for matching construction details.
8. Cliplines — usually a small line with arrowhead.
9. Gathering — broken line between two points.

Choosing and Using a Pattern

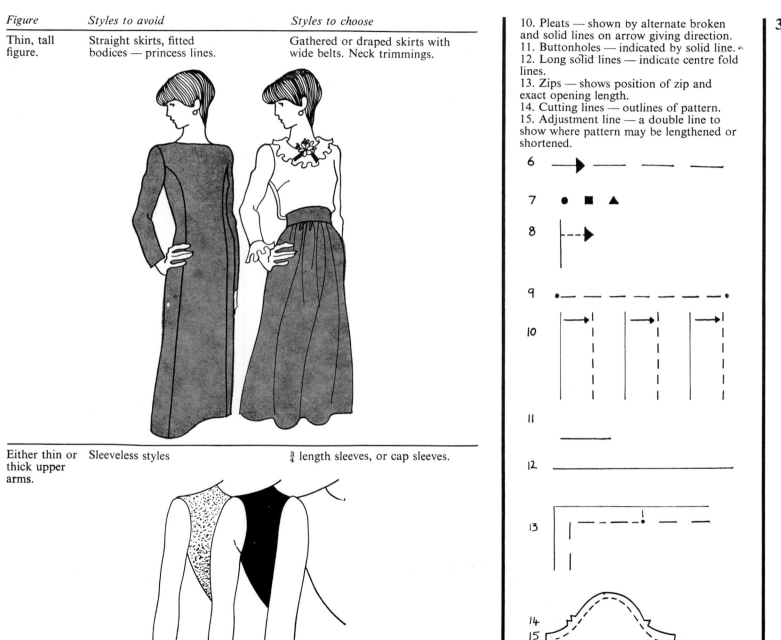

Figure	Styles to avoid	Styles to choose
Thin, tall figure.	Straight skirts, fitted bodices — princess lines.	Gathered or draped skirts with wide belts. Neck trimmings.

| Either thin or thick upper arms. | Sleeveless styles | $\frac{3}{4}$ length sleeves, or cap sleeves. |

10. Pleats — shown by alternate broken and solid lines on arrow giving direction.
11. Buttonholes — indicated by solid line.
12. Long solid lines — indicate centre fold lines.
13. Zips — shows position of zip and exact opening length.
14. Cutting lines — outlines of pattern.
15. Adjustment line — a double line to show where pattern may be lengthened or shortened.

Choosing and Using a Pattern

Figure	Styles to avoid	Styles to choose
Large hips.	Fitted skirts, pockets at hips, too narrow a bodice.	Shaped skirt from waist. Gathers can be used if the waist is small. Use wide neck and shoulder lines to avoid triangular shape.

Neck and shoulders thin.	Wide/boat-shaped necklines.	V-shaped necklines, tie collars, or mandarin standing collars.

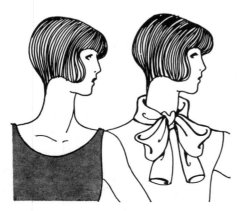

If the pattern you choose has only perforations instead of printed markings, lay the pieces on a dark surface and write the symbols on for yourself. If you are nervous about cutting out, draw round the cutting lines only, with a coloured line and follow this with the scissors.

4. What to Find on the Back of the Pattern Envelope
Standard body measurements; the number of pattern pieces included in envelope; back views; identified pattern pieces; description of the garment; Fabric requirement charts — show fabric widths and pattern sizes. Requirements for interfacing, lining and trimmings (if there are any). Amount of fabric required for different views; sewing notions (haberdashery requirements); recommended fabrics for pattern chosen and those not suitable; measurements for finished garment; information regarding choice of fabrics with pile, nap, stripes, checks or one-way design — pattern pieces should be laid facing in same direction. In the majority of cases extra fabric is required.

5. Information Inside the Pattern Envelope
Cutting, sewing and making-up instructions are given on a sheet; layouts are shown indicating various pattern sizes on different fabric widths. *Circle or mark the particular diagram you will use so that it can be referred to quickly and easily.* Sewing instructions can usually be found on the inside information sheets together with illustrated stages of the garment construction.
Consider the accessories that will be worn with the garment and then buy all the notions (haberdashery items) listed on the pattern. It may be a good idea to match the buttons or top stitching thread to the accessories. Buy an extra button or two in case one is later lost in wear.

6. Preparing the Pattern
1. Select the pattern pieces for view chosen.
2. Put the pieces not required back into the envelope.
3. Check the pattern pieces with the back of the envelope.
4. Cut out the pieces leaving a margin unless working on very fine or very heavy fabrics. (Margins should be cut away and the pattern edge used as a cutting guide on these fabrics).

Choosing and Using a Pattern

Figure	Styles to avoid	Styles to choose
Thick waist.	Cummerbund, wide belts, slim shaped skirts.	Narrow belts. Tapered lines on bodice. Gored skirts.

5. Iron out the creases in the pattern with a warm iron. Do not use steam as it will cause the tissue to shrink.

6. Check your measurements with those shown for your size on the pattern sleeve.

7. Compare the pattern pieces with the adjusted personal basic pattern or unpicked toile already prepared. Transfer any necessary alterations to the new pattern. (If no personal pattern is available see the section on pattern adjustments later in this chapter.) Lay the personal pattern pieces on the new pattern and transfer the fitting adjustments.

7. Adjusting the Pattern

You may be lucky enough to find that your figure measurements correspond exactly with those on the pattern that you have chosen. If they do you will find that only very slight adjustments to the pattern will be needed; often only length will need to be attended to. Whenever adjustments are made to a pattern, either before the garment is cut out or at one of the fitting stages, the aim must be to change the original line and design of the garment *as little as possible*. When a garment needs a little adjustment in an area close to a seam, or by a dart, this can be corrected by making the alteration at the fitting stage. When faults occur where there are *no* seams or darts then a certain section of the pattern may need to be redrawn and the fabric recut to give the right fitting. When a pattern line has been altered, you will usually need to redraw the section altered so that the original shape of the pattern is preserved and that the seams have the same lines or curves as before alteration. On the other hand, if the measurements on the pattern do *not* correspond to yours, certain other adjustments will be needed. Sometimes the bust, waist, or hip measurements will have to be changed. Perhaps your shoulders slope more than usual or maybe you have one hip bone higher than the other. In cases like these, further adjustments will be needed. Altering a pattern piece is very quick and easy once you have learned how to make the various adjustments.

8. Equipment for Pattern Adjustments

Ruler — transparent 30 cm or 45 cm ruler with a variety of measurements for accuracy.

T-square — this is very useful for checking the grainlines, a small transparent one is best, rather than the large wooden variety.

Tissue paper — this is used for insertion between pattern pieces when they are made longer or wider. Use white tissue and iron it smooth and wrinkle free before use.

Thick soft lead pencil — for clearly redrawing pattern lines.

Sticky tape — marking tape that may be written on, to permanently fix the adjustments into position.

Pin cushion — the bracelet type that fits over the wrist is best.

Pins — coloured, glass-headed pins for positioning insertions or additions to width and length — these are clearly seen and not easily lost.

Tape measure — fibre glass is best with centimetres only marked on one face.

Scissors — not the ones that you use for fabric as paper will blunt them very quickly.

9. Special Points to Remember

1. Press pattern pieces and tissue before you start.

2. Always alter adjoining pattern piece when any adjustment is made, otherwise the piece to which it will eventually be joined will differ in length. For example, if the length of the front of the bodice is altered the back of the bodice must be made the same length. Likewise, if a dart is enlarged, the seam on which it is placed must be made from two pieces of fabric equal in length.

3. When redrawing pattern lines always make them clear and bold. Use a thick lead pencil rather than a felt tip pen as the ink may spread into the paper and obscure other pattern markings.

4. Always double check to see that "place to fold" and grainlines are kept absolutely straight using the transparent ruler.

5. When increasing or decreasing the size of pattern round your body (in other words the circumference), you must check that the adjustment is made in exactly the right spot — waist, hip, bust, etc. and not too high or too low.

6. Think of each pattern piece as representing a quarter of your body when making circumference adjustments. A line drawn across your figure at waist

Choosing and Using a Pattern

level and down the centre front of your body will divide it into four sections.

Therefore each skirt or bodice pattern piece will need to be adjusted to one-quarter of the total adjustment needed.

10. To Lengthen

If the pattern is the right size it may be possible just to add a piece on at the hemline to lengthen it. On some paper patterns other places for adjusting the length are also marked. If not, follow the methods below —

Skirts and trousers

1. Make a note of the straight grainline; the adjustment line must be drawn at right angles to it.

2. Draw a line across the pattern about one-third of the distance between hips

and hem levels. (Adjust the crotch length of trousers first).

3. Cut across the pattern on the line marked, separating the two pieces.

4. Cut a piece of plain paper about 15 cm deep and slightly wider than the pattern piece.

5. Lay the pattern pieces on this insert the desired amount apart, and pin or stick them into position.

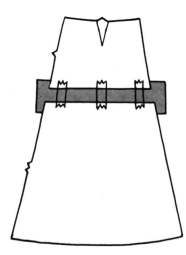

Cut away excess paper.

6. Draw in new seam lines, cutting lines and any dart lines to continue those on the pattern pieces.

7. Repeat on the other skirt or trouser pieces.

Crotch of trousers

1. It is very important that the crotch of trousers should fit well. Measure your crotch length (see chapter on Body Measurements for method) and compare it with the pattern length. The pattern pieces should be measured along the side seam line, from the waist seam line to the bottom of the crotch seam allowance.

2. Insert a piece of paper as described, cutting the pattern pieces about 7·5 cm above the crotch. Straighten the crotch seam from the insertion to the waistline if necessary.

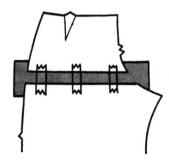

Bodice

1. Insert a strip of paper as described above, cutting across the pattern between the bottom of the armhole and the waist.

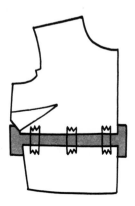

Sleeve

1. Measure your arm length measurement (see chapter on Body Measurements for method) and compare it with the length of the sleeve pattern. Measure the pattern from the seam allowance at the centre head of the sleeve to the hemline.

2. Draw the adjustment line halfway between the top of the sleeve and the elbow. On long sleeves draw another line halfway between elbow and hemline.

3. Cut the pattern, and insert paper to adjust the sleeve to the desired length.

Choosing and Using a Pattern

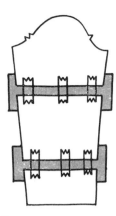

Waistline

A dress without a waist seam may be adjusted for length at the waist if your back neck to waist length is longer that that given on the pattern envelope.
1. Insert a strip of paper at the level of the waist (usually marked on the pattern).
2. Check the total length of the adjustment pattern to make sure that the hemline is still in the right place.

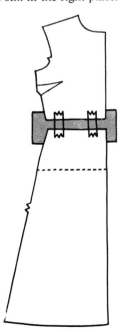

11. To Shorten
1. See the section on lengthening for details regarding *where* to adjust pattern

pieces for the right effect. If there is no adjustment line on the pattern draw it in, then draw another line above that, the exact amount away that the pattern is to be shortened.

2. Fold the pattern so that the lower of the two lines meets the upper one. Crease, or iron, a pleat in the pattern then pin or stick the lines into place.

3. The seam line will have been displaced and must be redrawn. Use a piece of paper as an extension. At the hemline a little of the original seam allowance may have to be trimmed off.

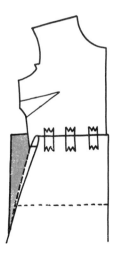

Skirts and trousers

1. Follow the general instructions above. Adjust the crotch length of trousers before shortening.

2. If only a small adjustment is needed to a pattern that is the right size and shape, a little may be cut off at the hemline to shorten the garment, following the shape of the pattern piece.

3. To raise the hipline shorten along a line just above the pattern hipline. If this is not necessary, the adjustment may be made about mid-way between knee and hemline.

4. Pin a paper extension to the side of the pattern and draw in a new seam line.

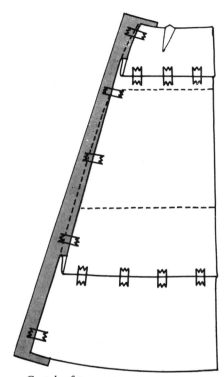

Crotch of trousers

1. Compare body and pattern measurements as described for lengthening above.
2. On the adjustment line make a fold, and then extend the pattern with a paper strip at the sides. Tape the new seam line into the original stitching line. Redraw the cutting line.

Bodice and sleeves

Shorten in the same places as described for lengthening. Follow the general instructions for shortening at the beginning of the section.

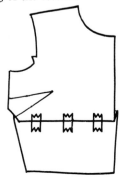

Choosing and Using a Pattern

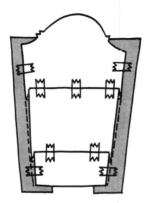

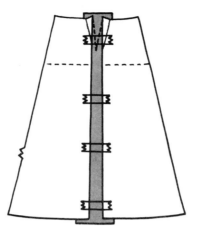

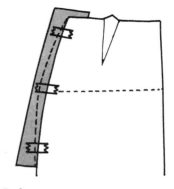

12. To Enlarge

If adjustments are up to 5 cm in width extra paper may be added at the sides of pattern pieces. Where more than 5 cm must be added it is better to insert a whole strip of paper into the pattern piece.

General methods

a. *Up to 5 cm extra*

1. Place the edge of the pattern piece onto a strip of plain paper about 10 cm wide extending along the area to be adjusted.

2. Measure out the required amount from the seam line (remember to measure only one-quarter of the total extra width needed on each side seam, for a normal four piece garment).

3. Draw in a new tapered seam line and a cutting line. Trim off excess paper.

b. *Over 5 cm extra*

1. Draw a line down the pattern pieces, parallel to the straight grainline.
On bodices this new line should be halfway between the neckline and the edge of the shoulder. On skirts, halfway between the side seam and centre line.

2. Cut and insert a strip of paper as described for lengthening a paper piece. Relocate darts as necessary.

Skirts and trousers

Compare your waist and hip measurements with those on the pattern envelope.
If up to 5 cm extra is needed on enlargement throughout, follow the general methods.

Waistline

Add a quarter of the extra width needed at the waistline to each side waist pattern piece and taper the new seam line down to the hipline.

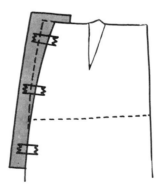

Hipline

Add a quarter of the extra width needed at the hipline, to each side hip pattern piece and taper the new seam line from the waistline to the hipline and back to the seam line in the hem area.

Bodice

Follow the general methods given above if extra width is needed throughout (remember if using a strip of paper that only a quarter or half the total should be inserted). Small adjustments may be made in the bust and waist areas by extensions at the seam line in those areas.

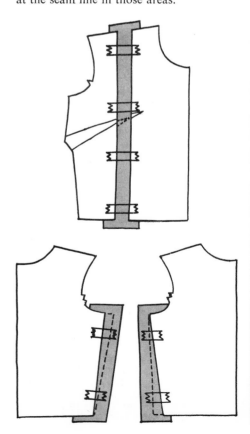

Choosing and Using a Pattern

Sleeves

Follow the general methods given above for inserting a strip of paper. If the sleeve is too small at the wrist a slash can be made (instead of cutting the pattern into two) and a shaped strip inserted.

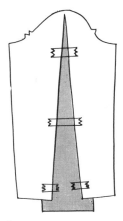

13. To Reduce

To reduce the width of a pattern piece reverse the methods given for enlarging, ie. if up to 5 cm needs to be taken out alter the sides of the pattern pieces, if more than 5 cm draw an adjustment line parallel to the straight grain line and pleat the pattern piece there.

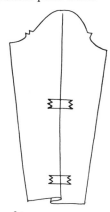

Skirt and trousers

Compare your waist and hip measurements with those on the pattern envelope. If a general reduction in width is needed throughout make a vertical pleat in the pattern as described in the section on shortening.

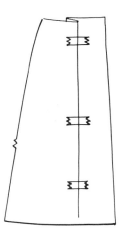

Waistline

1. Measure in from the original side seam line to a new point one-quarter of the amount to be reduced along the waistline.
2. Draw in a new seam line, tapering from the new waistline mark down to the original hipline, following the shape of the pattern piece.

Hipline

Mark a new hipline mark one-quarter of the amount to be reduced in from the original side seam line. Taper the new seam line from that point out to the waistline and the seam line in the hem area.

Bodice

To reduce the bodice throughout fold the pattern along the line previously suggested for enlarging on bodice.

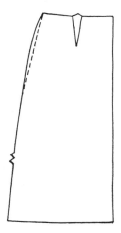

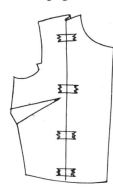

To reduce only the bust or waist areas, mark a new seam line at the top or bottom of the underarm seam and redraw that seamline.

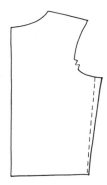

Choosing and Using a Pattern

14. Adjusting the Pattern when pinned together

Unless there is a known figure fault for which a large specific adjustment always has to be made, other minor adjustments are better made on the figure. Pin together the main pattern pieces and try them on (do this carefully or the pattern may tear). Wear the right foundation garments and shoes for that garment and stand naturally in front of a mirror. The pattern will only be half a garment of course. If possible, ask someone else to help you with this pattern fitting as it is difficult to fit oneself properly. (A pattern may also be tried on a personal dress form.) The shoulder, neck, and bust and waist line of a bodice should be carefully checked for a good fit. The waist and hip lines of skirts or trousers should fit well but with enough ease for movement. If adjustments are slight re-pin the pieces accordingly. For larger adjustments make a note of the alterations on the pattern or on a separate piece of paper.

15. Adjusting the Pattern for Specific Figure Faults

Large bust

1. Cut the pattern from the shoulder nearly to the waist, and from the centre of the bustline nearly to the underarm seam.
2. Put the paper under the slashes and pin it in place to add the extra amounts needed.

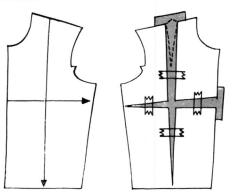

Small bust

The pattern piece will usually have to be made narrower and shorter. Often it is sufficient to shorten it and make a larger bust dart.

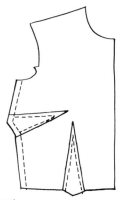

Low bust

If the bust dart is too high the bodice will appear tight and unflattering. Slightly shorten the pattern if necessary then lower the point of the dart.

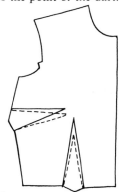

Flat chest

Shorten the pattern across a line above the bust, then scoop out the bottom of the armhole which will have been raised. A slightly smaller bust dart is usually required.

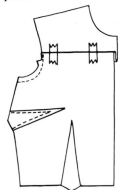

Narrow chest

Pin a wedge-shaped piece out of the centre front from the neckline. It is essential to mark a new straight grain line parallel with the new centre front. Reduce the bust dart a little.

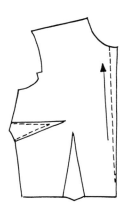

Round shoulders

Split the back bodice across almost to the underarm seam and open up the pattern to the size required.

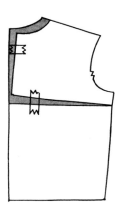

Broad shoulders

Slash the back bodice from the shoulder seam almost to the waist. Insert a shaped strip of paper.

Choosing and Using a Pattern

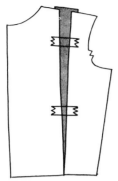

Narrow shoulders
Cut a diagonal line from about halfway along the shoulderline to halfway down the armhole. Overlap the cut edges to reduce the width, then draw a new seam line.

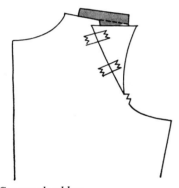

Square shoulders
Extend the top of the armhole seam to raise the outer shoulder line. Raise the bottom of the armhole to match or it will be too loose.

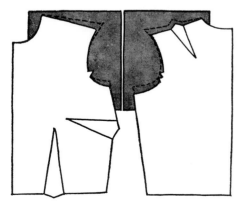

Sloping shoulders
Starting at the neckline, slope the shoulder seam line down to the armhole and lower the bottom of the armhole a little or it will be too tight.

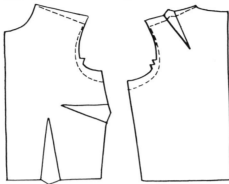

Prominent hip bones (trousers)
Unpin the darts and re-pin them to fit, making them bigger and shorter. If necessary make the waistline wider by extending it at the side seams.

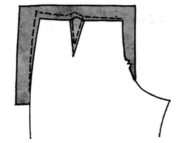

Thick waist (bodice)
Slash from the waistline almost to the armhole. Open out and insert a shaped piece of paper.

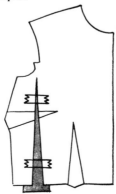

Thick waist (skirt)
Slash from the waist almost to the hem. Insert a shaped piece of paper.

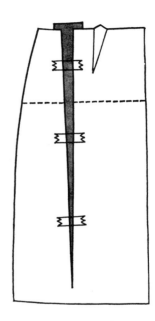

Large seat (skirt)
Slash the skirt as shown and insert paper to increase size. Bodice pieces should be enlarged to match at waist if necessary.

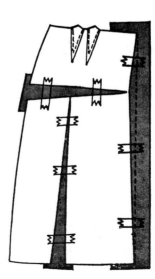

Choosing and Using a Pattern

Large seat (*trousers*)
Unpin the darts and let the back of the
pattern fall into position without creasing
or pulling. Add extra paper to top of the
back inner leg seam. Repin darts, and
add to waist side seams if waistline is
too tight.

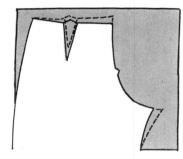

Flat seat (*trousers*)
Make folds across the top of the hips and
down the legs to take out excess, then
repin darts to fit. If waistline is still too
large take out excess at side seams.

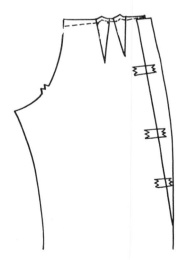

Hollow back (*skirt*)
Pleat across the skirt above the hip line,
with a wide fold at the centre back and
almost nothing at the side seam. Draw a
new centre back line.

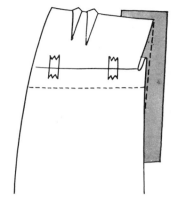

Large stomach (*skirt*)
Make larger darts in the skirt front.

Large stomach (*trousers*)
Unpin the darts and allow the front of
the pattern to drop until the side seams
lie flat. Add a piece of paper to the front
inner leg seam then repin the waist
darts to fit.

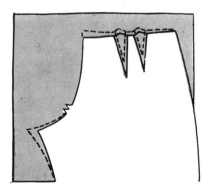

Flat stomach (*skirt*)
Move the darts in the skirt front nearer
to the side seams.

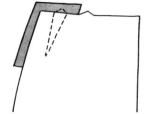

Plump upper arm (*short sleeves*)
Insert a straight strip of paper down the
centre of the sleeve.
Plump upper arm (*long sleeve*)
Slash as shown in diagram. Lay pattern
pieces on a sheet of plain paper, and
pin or stick into place.

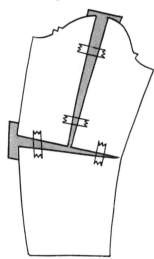

Fabrics and Fibres

Note that a list of names and special words to do with fabrics appears at the end of this chapter.

1. Choice

It is so easy to impulsively buy a length of attractive fabric only to find that it is quite unsuitable for the pattern chosen. Remember that you must be able to handle the fabric easily. Look at the charts that follow and select a suitable fabric type for the garment that you wish to make.

The majority of pattern envelopes give suggestions for choice of fabric and it is advisable to follow those closely, so that the garment will make up successfully. It is unwise, for example, to make up a pattern specially designed for jersey fabrics from a woven fabric. Jersey fabrics have built-in ease and stretch and for this reason patterns that are recommended especially for them often exclude construction details such as darts. Under these circumstances, if a woven fabric were used the results might prove very disappointing.

Points to remember

1. The fabric should be suitable for the wearer. Good and bad figure points should be considered so that good points are emphasised and bad points disguised.
(i) Tall, thin figures should not wear vertical stripes.

(ii) If natural complexion is highly coloured — multi-coloured prints should not be worn.
(iii) Short dumpy figures are not complimented by large designs, horizontal stripes or shiny fabrics.

2. Fabric should be selected so that it will blend from the colour and texture point of view with other items of clothing in wearer's wardrobe, as in the case of mix and match separates. A top, for example, can be patterned with the trousers made in a plain colour, or a skirt can have a checked design whilst the top may be made plain, picking out one of the colours in the skirt. The colour should be suitable for the occasions on which the garment is to be worn.

Fabrics and Fibres

When selecting a fabric for home sewing check the following characteristics:—
(a) Is it soft or stiff? Will it drape?
(b) Will it stretch and recover its shape?
(c) Will it shrink?
(d) Can it be washed or dry-cleaned?
(e) Will it cling in wear?
(f) Is it rough or scratchy?
(g) Is it soil and stain resistant?
(h) Will it be cool or warm in wear?
(i) Is it absorbent?
(j) Is it colourfast?
(k) How does it handle?
(l) Will it need ironing?

4. The fabric should be of an appropriate weave or knit for the item of clothing to be made. Choose closely woven fabrics (especially in woollens) for tight-fitting garments. Full skirts, loose-fitting coats and short jackets can be made in loosely woven fabrics.

5. Fabrics should be easily and readily cleaned and washed, depending on the amount of wear they are to receive. Remember to make enquiries regarding washing, cleaning and sewing at time of purchase so that expensive mistakes may be avoided.

6. Have fun when selecting fabrics to be worn together, but avoid a muddled effect. If you wish to mix fabrics there should be one common factor, such as a colour or design, borne in mind. An infinite variety of plain fabrics may be used together and any patterned fabric that highlights one of the plain colours used can be included. Do not forget texture. Compare fabric and aim to have contrast in texture where possible. If you find it difficult to choose colour schemes with the right balance of design and colour, copy ideas from the colour schemes in shop windows, on television and those shown in magazines. It is always a good idea to try on ready-made garments to see which colours and designs suit you best.

3. Do not choose a fabric with a busy design when making a garment with unusual lines, pin-tucking, or some other definite or unusual stitching detail. The fabric design will detract from the finished effect and many hours of handwork may be unnoticed.

Fabrics and Fibres

FABRICS SUITABLE FOR BEGINNERS

Fabric	Widths	Uses	Advantages	Disadvantages	Laundering Notes
Calico cotton	90 cm	Overalls, household goods, aprons .	Stays in place and does not slip when sewing. Hardwearing, does not fray.	Cannot be used for fine sewing.	Easy to wash in hot water. Can be starched.
Cambric cotton	90 cm	Handkerchiefs, underwear, blouses.	Soft to handle, will not fray. Is slightly glossy. Suitable for gathering, and presses fairly easily.		White cottons should be boiled.
Cotton, mercerized	90 cm	Dresses, shirts, nightwear, children's wear, blouses.	Presses easily. Can be gathered and tucked. Useful for embroidery. Will not fray. Easy to handle. Usually reversible.		Iron either side whilst damp.
Gingham, cotton or polyester	90 cm	Overalls, housecoats, beachwear, children's garments.	Readily pressed, easy to handle. Gathers well: variety of smocking can be used. Patterned on both sides.	Will not pleat well.	Wash in hot water. Can be starched for extra stiffness. Press whilst damp on either side.
Lawn, cotton or polyester	90 cm	Blouses, dresses, underwear.	Will not fray, crisp but easy to work with. Presses easily, suitable for gathering.		Can be pulled into shape whilst wet. Can be starched.
Piqué cotton	90 cm	Skirts, shorts, jackets, dresses, blouses, collars, cuffs.	Will not fray, maintains shape and wears well.	Too springy for gathering: ribs should be matched.	Starch to keep crispness. Iron on wrong side whilst damp.
Poplin cotton	90 cm	Children's wear, shirts, bodices.	Will not fray. Firm to handle. Can be gathered and pressed easily.		Iron either side whilst still damp, with hot iron.
Seersucker, cotton or polyester	90 cm	Dresses, underwear, nightwear; blouses, children's garments.	Will not fray. Easy to handle. Very little pressing needed except for seams; will gather; hangs well.	Cannot be tucked or pleated. If pattern is large, care must be taken in matching the seams.	Press lightly if needed, when dry.
Viyella, Clydella and Dayella	90 cm	Blouses, dresses, nightwear, children's wear.	Will not fray. Easy to handle.		Wash in warm water. Iron when dry.

Fabrics and Fibres

FABRICS SUITABLE FOR SEMI SKILLED NEEDLEWORKERS

Fabric	Widths	Uses	Advantages	Disadvantages	Laundering Notes
Afgalaine	140 cm	Jumper suits, dresses.	Suitable for all types of clothes. Pleats, tucks and gathers well.	Can fray.	Shrinks if washed. Dry clean only.
Bouclé, wool	140 cm 150 cm	Suits, coats, dresses.	Will not crease; lightweight; will drape. Hangs well.	Stitching difficult to keep straight if weave is heavy. Will not pleat easily.	Should be well brushed. Dry clean only.
Chintz	122 cm	Dresses, soft furnishings, housecoats.	Will not fray. Presses easily; hangs well in unpressed pleats.	Cannot be gathered if the glaze is too high. Tough to handle.	Starch when the glaze becomes impaired. Iron on right side when damp. Washes easily.
Cotton, satin	90 cm	Skirts, blouses, dresses, shirts.	Strong, will not fray. Hangs well. Often crease resisting. Presses well. Will tuck and gather easily.		Use hot water when washing. Iron when damp on right side. Glazed surface helps repel dirt.
Crêpe, wool or acrylic	90 cm	Nightwear, dresses, blouses.	Tucks, gathers, drapes, hangs well. Can be embroidered successfully.	Springy.	Press either dry or slightly damp on wrong side with warm iron so that glaze is avoided. Some may only be dry cleaned.
Crêpe de Chine	90 cm	Nightwear, blouses, lingerie.	Easy to handle, will not fray badly. Usually reversible.	Ironed-in creases very difficult to remove.	Irons and washes easily. Iron when damp.
Denim, cotton	90 cm 122 cm	Boiler suits, jeans, shirts, overalls, dresses, dungarees.	Is hardwearing, will pleat well, will not fray; very strong.	Does not gather easily.	May be boiled, iron whilst damp. Normally colour fast.
Flannel, wool	122 cm 140 cm	Suits, dresses, blouses, skirts.	Hangs well; will pleat. Does not fray; suitable for tailored styles.		Wash in warm soapy water. Rinse well. Press on wrong side.
Gabardine, wool	140 cm	Suits, jackets, coats, skirts.	For all tailored styles will pleat well; strong material.		Should be well brushed. Dry clean only.
Linen	90 cm 115 cm	Suits, skirts, dresses.	Pleats and hangs well. Presses readily; suitable for tailored clothes. Keeps shape well.	Creases and frays badly.	Washes and presses well. Iron on wrong side unless surface is glazed.
Marocain	90 cm	Evening wear. Blouses for older women. Dresses.	Drapes, tucks, gathers hang well.	Shiny back, so material slips when cut and sewn.	Wash in warm soapy water. Dry clean. Press on wrong side.
Muslin, cotton	90 cm	Blouses.	Ideal for fine sewing; can be tucked and frilled.	Will fray.	Will shrink when washed.

Fabrics and Fibres

FABRICS SUITABLE FOR SEMI SKILLED NEEDLEWORKERS

Fabric	Widths	Uses	Advantages	Disadvantages	Laundering Notes
Organdie, cotton	90 cm 122 cm	Children's dresses, blouses.	Ideal for fine sewing; can be tucked and rolled. Good for hand or machine embroidery.	Springy, will not gather easily. Frays a little. Transparent.	Irons and washes easily. Iron when damp; can be starched to keep crispness, will shrink.
Sateen, rayon	90 cm 76 cm	Underskirts, linings, for fine dresses of nylon, net or lace.	Other materials can be set over without it clinging.	Will fray. Can slip whilst being cut out or during sewing.	Loses much of its body when washed. Can be stiffened with gum arabic.
Satin (lingerie) polyester, rayon	90 cm	Lingerie, nightwear, blouses.	Can be gathered, embroidered and tucked. Hangs and drapes well.	Frays easily.	Most lingerie satins can be washed with warm soapy water. Iron on right side when damp.
Serge, wool	140 cm 150 cm	Coats, jackets, suits, skirts.	Will hold pleats. Will not crease easily.		Brush well. Dry clean.
Silk	90 cm 122 cm	Suits, dresses, children's clothes, lingerie, blouses, evening clothes.	Pleats and gathers easily. Very strong but soft material. Ideal for fine sewing, keeps shape. Hangs and drapes well.	Frays badly.	Presses easily. Wild Silk should be ironed when bone dry.
Tweed wool polyester	140 cm 150 cm	Skirts, suits, coats, jackets, dresses.	Will hold pleats. Will not crease easily.	Will fray, can be bulky to wear.	Brush well. Dry clean.
Voile, cotton	90 cm 106 cm	Dresses, blouses.	Good for fine sewing, can be tucked or frilled.	Will fray, make sure seams are strong and reinforced.	Irons, washes easily, needs to be stiffened. Iron whilst still damp.
Winceyette, cotton	90 cm	Nightwear.	Will not fray, strong material, will press easily.		Will shrink, wash in warm water, can be ironed dry or wet.
Worsted, wool	140 cm 150 cm	Skirts, coats, dresses, jackets, suits.	Pleats well, strong material, suitable for all tailored styles.	Clumsy to work on, tends to be bulky. Highly inflammable unless treated.	Should be well-brushed. Dry clean.

Fabrics and Fibres

| FABRICS SUITABLE FOR SKILLED NEEDLEWORKERS

Fabric	Widths	Uses	Advantages	Disadvantages	Laundering Notes
Chiffon	90 cm	Blouses, evening wear, neckwear, nightdresses.	Drapes, gathers, and hangs well.	Easily frays. Delicate material which needs skilled handling.	Warm soapy wash. Press with a warm iron.
Georgette, silk, nylon	90 cm	Dresses, blouses, neckwear, lingerie.	Gathers and drapes well. Will not fray easily.	Seams and edges tend to stretch.	Wash in warm soapy water. Press with a warm iron.
Jersey, silk, cotton, wool	102 cm 122 cm 140 cm 150 cm	Blouses, suits, dresses, skirts, coats, trousers.	Drapes and hangs well.	Cut edges tend to stretch. Handle gently so material will not be distorted. Should be sewn with a stretch stitch.	Some need to be dry cleaned. Press along grain so shape will be maintained.
Moiré, taffeta, rayon	90 cm	Evening dresses.	Gathers and flares hang well. Maintains crispness.	Frays badly, water marks. Pattern should be matched at seams.	Dry clean only.
Nylon	90 cm 122 cm	Dresses, children's clothes, lingerie.	Does not need much pressing. Fine but strong.	Frays easily. Transparent.	Washes easily, use warm soapy water. Dries quickly. Do *not* use hot iron.
Taffeta	90 cm	Blouses, petticoats, dresses.		Frays badly.	Dry clean. Press wrong side. Glazed on right side.
Velvet, silk, rayon, nylon, cotton		Jackets, dresses, evening wear.	Hangs and drapes well.	Can only be cut in one direction. Not easy to press. Pins tend to mark the pile, so pin with fine needles.	Some need dry cleaning. Corduroy velvet washes well. Press with iron on the wrong side.

Fabrics and Fibres

3. Fibres

In recent years fabrics have been produced from man-made fibres in addition to natural fibres such as cotton and wool. It is useful to have some knowledge and understanding of fibres, so that it is possible to choose the right fabric for each garment. The ways in which fibres are made into yarns and the yarns made into finished fabrics also affects the choice and use of fabrics. The naming of material may be rather misleading, as the actual name often applies to the construction; the fibre content may be of natural or man-made origin, or a combination of both.

Natural fibres

Cotton (vegetable)

Large quantities of cotton are still used. The fluffy seed-pod (or boll) of the cotton plant contains cotton linters that can be cleaned, combed, carded and processed into thread.

Cotton makes strong, absorbent, easily washed fabrics that are comfortable to wear and range from fine smooth voiles to thick towellings. They are mothproof but may be affected by mildew in damp conditions. If stained by accident most white cottons can be bleached, but unless pre-treated may shrink in washing. A great variety of finishing processes are applied to cottons and they can also be blended with polyesters, wool, etc.

Linen (vegetable)

The fibrous stalks of ripe flax plants are processed and spun into threads. Linen fabrics are even stronger than cottons and are cool and absorbent in wear. Although more expensive than cotton it is very hard-wearing. Bleach may be used on white linens although bacteria or acid may cause rotting. Linen is mothproof. Special finishes have to be applied to prevent shrinking and creasing; blending with man-made fibres also achieves this effect.

Silk (protein)

Silkworms spin filaments for their cocoons and these fibres can be spun into thread. Silk is expensive but makes luxury fabrics that are very strong, warm, absorbent and springy. Unless labelled "washable" silk needs dry-cleaning.

Wool (protein)

The hair and fur of animals is suitable for making into fabrics. In addition to wool from sheep, luxury fibres are obtained from other animals, eg. Alpaca and Cashmere from special goats, Angora from angora rabbits, Mohair from angora goats and Vicuna from South American llamas. Although not a strong fibre, wool makes very elastic, warm and absorbent fabrics in a range of weights from light crêpes to heavy tweeds. Wool is generally crease resistant but is readily attacked by moths and bacteria and is affected by strong bleaches. Except for wools labelled "machine-washable" or "dry-clean only" special care needs to be taken in washing. Hot water will shrink it and too hot an iron will scorch it.

Man-made fibres (listed alphabetically)

Acetate

See also triacetate below. Some trade names — Dicel, Lansil.

Acetate is derived from cellulose obtained from wood pulp or cotton linters which is reacted chemically to form cellulose acetate. This is then dissolved in a solvent to give a viscous liquid which can then be spun.

Acetate is very silk-like so that it drapes well, is absorbent and fairly cool to wear. Satins, taffetas, brocades, surahs, jersey and lining fabrics are commonly made from acetate. They are not particularly hardwearing.

Acrylic

Some trade names — Acrilan, Courtelle, Orlon.

Acrylics are made from acrylonitrile derived from products of the oil industry. These are soft and warm rather like wool, but do not stretch as much. They are hardwearing and mothproof but white acrylics may yellow with age. Much knitwear is made from acrylics.

Elastane (elastomerics)

Some trade names — Lycra, Spanzelle. These are very stretchy polyurethane yarns that are used in hosiery, foundation garments and swimwear. They can be washed gently by hand or machine.

Modacrylic

A trade name — Teklan.
Made from chemicals from oil and coal processing. They are particularly strong and hardwearing so are used for furnishings, overalls, etc. Modacrylics are flame retardant.

Modal

A trade name — Vincel.
Another group of fibres made from cellulose. They are very absorbent and tend to be used in blends for household textiles, workwear, underwear and dresswear.

Nylon

Some trade names — Antron, Bri-nylon, Celon, Enkalon, Perlon, Tendrelle. Nylon is made from products of the oil industry. It can be made in continuous filaments or short lengths made into staple yarn.

Often blended with wool or cotton, it is very strong. If used alone, however, it attracts dirt because of static electricity. Nylons do not stretch, shrink or absorb water so are easily washed, but the low absorbency means that they are clammy in wear. They are moth and rot resistant but white nylon may become grey or yellow with age. Drip dry and minimum iron constructions or finishes are common; nylon is extensively used for hosiery, lingerie and shirts.

There are now anti-static nylon fabrics available for use where static build-up may be a problem — trade names are Celon anti-stat and Counterstat.

Polyester

Some trade names — Crimplene, Dacron, Diolen, Tergal, Terlenka, Terylene and Trevira.

Made from products of the oil industry. Polyesters are very strong and often used to add strength to wool or cotton. The fibres may be "crimped" or "bulked" to make fabrics such as crimplene by ICI. They are generally warm to wear with low absorbency and little stretch. Resistant to moths and rot, they may shrink a little in washing unless specially pre-treated in manufacture. White polyester tends to stay whiter in wear than other man-made fibres. Woven and knitted polyesters are easily washed and can often be drip dried.

Triacetate

Some trade names — Arnel, Tricel. It is made from the same source, but by a slightly different process and is stronger

Fabrics and Fibres

than acetate. They are crease resistant and easy care, and are often blended with nylon.

Viscose

Some trade names — Fibro, Evlan, Sarille, Viloft.

One of the earliest of man-made fibres, viscose is made from natural cellulose in wood pulp. It is very widely used, either alone or in blends. Unless brushed, viscose is fairly cool to wear and soft to the touch. Used widely in linings and dress fabrics.

Yarns

Long strands, or continuous filaments of fibre are simply twisted to make yarn — silk and most man-made fibres are made into continuous filaments.

Shorter fibres are called staple fibres — these include the other natural fibres and some man-made fibres. These are combed, carded, stretched, twisted and spun into bulkier yarns. Yarn count traditionally indicated thickness of yarns "Tex" is now used for this — the lower the tex the finer the yarn.

To make bulky or stretchy textured yarns filaments may be coiled, crimped or looped. Different types, thicknesses and colours of fibres may be combined to make complex yarns with slub, bouclé or other special features.

4. Construction of Fabric

The two most common ways of making yarn into fabric are weaving and knitting.

Weaving

Two groups of yarns are put together at right angles in woven fabrics. "Warp" or lengthwise threads run parallel to the selvedge and are very strong. In the simplest weave the crosswise, or weft threads run alternately over and under the warps.

There are many variations of this plain, or tabby, weave — rib, basket, twill, satin, pile, dobby, jacquard, etc. Look at fabrics under a magnifying glass to see these variations.

Knitting

A continuous yarn can be knitted into interlocking loops forming stretchy and flexible fabric. Recent developments in knitting machines have led to a huge variety of weights and textures of knitted fabrics becoming available.

A wale is a row of loops running lengthwise like warp threads and a course is a crosswise row like wefts. Denier refers to the weight and thickness and gauge is the number of stitches used.

Weft

Yarn can be weft knitted into flat or tubular fabrics as plain, rib, purl, double and patterned constructions. A single continuous thread makes a course of loops which links with the previous and following rows.

Warp

Many yarns are used to produce lengthwise rows of loops which link with the ones on either side. The fabrics, such as raschel and tricot, are relatively cheap and run-proof.

Bonding

Fibres are stuck or bonded together without knitting or weaving so that there is no grain or stretch. They should not be confused with self-lined or laminated fabrics, where two layers of material are fused together.

Felting

Cheap, warm, non-woven fabric is made from wool or fur fibres felted together by heat, moisture, friction and pressure. Made in many thicknesses and colours, felt does not fray, but is seldom durable enough for clothes.

Fabrics are also made by specialised processes such as braiding, crochet, netting, etc.

Finishes

A great many ways of improving the appearance or performance of fabrics have been developed.

Colourfast — these fabrics do not bleed or lose colour during washing.

Crease resistant — some trade names: Bancore, Calpreta, Minicare, Tersilized. Chemicals are used on the yarn or fabric to make it more springy.

Flame-proof — one man-made fibre, Teklan, is actually flame resistant. The law says that night clothes for children and old people must be flame resistant, although many chemical treatments do later wash out. A new process, IWS, is based on Titonium or Zirconium and can be used on wool. It is very effective, easy to apply, inexpensive and permanent.

London shrunk — wool suiting is dampened, then left to dry naturally before tailoring.

Lustre — resins and starches can be applied to cottons to make a crisp, shiny surface such as Everglaze or Chintz.

Machine washable — in addition to the traditional range of fabrics, it is now possible to wash some suede, leather and wools in a washing machine. Look for the special labels and instructions.

Mercerizing — treating cottons under tension makes them very strong and lustrous.

Permanent Press — perhaps better called durable press, this means that fabrics will shed creases and stay in shape without ironing.

Pre-shrunk — some trade names: Rigmel, Sanforized, Tebilized. A process in manufacturing to reduce the amount of shrinkage in home laundering.

Rain proofing — some trade names: Aqua 5, Scotchquard. Silicones can be used on the surface of rainwear to make it water repellent, showerproof or rain resistant. For complete waterproofing (100% resistance to rain) the fabric must be coated with plastic, rubber or wax and have reinforced seams.

Sanforized — see pre-shrunk above.

Size or dressing — glue, clay or wax are added to fabric to add body, but it usually washes out.

5. Colours and Patterns

There are many ways of adding colour and pattern to fabrics.

Dyeing is used in many ways to produce different effects — man-made fibres may have colour added to the filament liquid. Bundles of fibre or yarns may be dipped in dye before processing or pieces of fabric may be "piece-dyed".

Printing is commonly used in various ways to put colour and design onto a piece of fabric. Screen printing is a slow and beautiful way of stencilling complex patterns. In the cheaper, quicker roller (or direct) printing, designs are engraved on rollers. One roller is used for each colour, the rollers dipped in dye and rolled onto the fabric.

Batik dyeing is an unsophisticated method now used commercially for delicate designs. Wax is applied to the fabric in areas not to be dyed, then the whole cloth is dipped in dye before the wax is boiled off.

Tie dyeing is another ancient craft now used commercially. Areas of fabric are

Fabrics and Fibres

gathered into tight bunches, then the whole piece is dipped in dye creating pretty "sunburst" designs.

Machine embroidery decorates the surface of fabrics and even some suedes. It is combined with cutting or punching out to make a lacy effect. On some fabrics certain areas may be dissolved away carefully to make a kind of lace. This is sometimes described as a burned out effect.

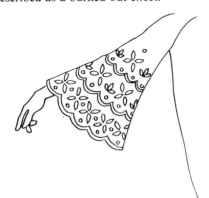

6. Stretch Fabrics

Most fabrics will stretch a little but some yarns are now produced that have built-in stretch. Some of the stretch fabrics available in retail shops are — towelling, velvet and jersey.

Stretchy yarns are made by tight twisting or crimping of the yarn. Special extendible fibres may be used or the fibres may have a fine rubber core.

Knitted fabrics made from these yarns stretch the most and many stretch both ways — use these for sportswear. Warp stretch or weft stretch fabrics stretch only in one direction.

When choosing and using stretch fabrics, paper patterns specially designed for these must be used and the pattern instructions followed carefully. A stretch stitch should be used for sewing when possible — follow the instructions in the sewing machine handbook. If a lining is necessary it should be of a jersey fabric.

7. Self Lined Fabrics

(Once called bonded fabrics)

Some of the original "bonded" fabrics were stiff and far from supple, giving garments rather a blown up appearance. Today, however, this self lining technique has progressed to the point where the fabric can be manufactured for its appearance only, because it can be made easy to handle by the self lining process. Very experienced dressmakers and sewing advisers have tested these "second generation" self lined fabrics and have found that in almost every instance the advantages are tremendous. The following points will be of interest.

1. Time and money can be saved — there being only one cutting operation for fabric and lining. They are purchased for the price of fabric alone.
2. They resist fraying — reducing the need for overcasting — thus making button holing (whether by hand or machine) much simpler.
3. They give better stitch retention.
4. They travel very much more freely over the needleplate of the machine.
5. They are completely stable. Patterns and checks cannot twist out of shape and the fabric retains a soft, fluid drape.
6. Garments made in self lined fabrics keep their shape well, stay smarter and retain their tailored look for longer.
7. Creasing, bagging and seating are resisted through properties built into the fabric by self lining.
8. Above all, they can give great encouragement to the new dressmaker and help her realise that a very professional finish is well within her reach, as they are so very easy to handle.

Many of the self-lined fabrics available drape and handle so easily that one would not guess that they had even been through a self lining process. Many dressmakers, of course, will still use an extra lining to give that expensive, professional finish to the inside of the garment.

8. Swing Tickets

Try to get into the habit of making your own swing ticket for every garment you sew. Unless details are written down it is so easy to forget vital information about the fabric. The swing tickets can then be hung together in a bunch or each are attached to the hanger used for that garment.

Write down all the useful information, such as fibre content, fabric construction, any special finishes, whether it is colourfast, whether trimmings are washable, washing (or dry cleaning) and ironing instructions, etc.

9. Estimating Fabric Quantities

It is sometimes useful to be able to make a quick calculation of the amount of fabric needed for a garment. It depends on the fabric width but measure as follows for 90 cm.

A dress — measure the length from nape of neck to desired hemline. Double this and add 13 cm for turnings and hem. Short sleeves need an extra 45 cm, long sleeves an extra 70 cm. A full skirt will need one extra waist to hem length.

A plain skirt — measure from waist to desired hemline. Double this and add 13 cm for turnings and hem.

A blouse — measure from nape of neck to waist. Double this and add 35 cm for tucking in and add 45 cm for short sleeves — 70 cm for long sleeves.

A nightdress — measure from nape of neck to desired hemline. Double this and add 13 cm for turnings and hem. Add 45 cm for short sleeves, 70 cm for long.

A housecoat — as for nightdress but calculate three times the total length.

Pyjamas — measure from nape of neck to jacket hemline and trouser length. Double

Fabrics and Fibres

the jacket length and add 13 cm. Add this to double the trouser length plus 13 cm and enough for sleeves as above.

Note that extra fabric is needed for stripes, checks, nap, etc. If in doubt do a mock pattern layout, for the exact length required.

10. Glossary of Fabric Names and Terms

Bolt — A length of fabric as delivered by a mill, usually wound onto a board or tube.

Brocade — A colourful Jacquard-weave fabric with the design over a satin ground.

Broderie anglaise — An embroidered cotton fabric with cut-out designs. Often used as trimming.

Calico — A flat-finished mid-weight plain-weave cotton fabric, usually of plain colour.

Chiffon — A soft ultra-light plain-weave fabric, appearing to float in the air when handled.

Circular knits — A method of knitting which produces wide-width knitted fabrics in a continuous tube which is slit from end to end before sale. There is no selvedge.

Colour fast — A coloured fabric guaranteed not to lose colour in wash or wear.

Corduroy — A cut pile fabric, with a ribbed surface, and a strong, plain backing.

Crêpe — A light to medium weight fabric, having an all-over textured look.

Deep pile fabric — See Fur Fabric.

Denim — A very strong mid-weight twill-weave fabric, usually made of cotton and fully washable. Available in pale colours — traditionally blue.

Felt — A non-woven fabric, produced by pressing and heating a mass of loose fibres together to form a sheet. Often quite thick. Usually plain coloured.

Flannel — A woollen fabric of plain or twill weave having a soft, napped surface.

Fur fabric — A fabric resembling fur, made with synthetic fibres — usually acrylic or nylon.

Gabardine — A tightly woven fabric, with an obvious twill weave.

Gingham — A plain weave fabric, usually using yarn dyed threads to make a prominent check pattern on a white ground.

Grosgrain — A fabric having a pronounced rib (often seen in ribbon fabrics).

Interlining — A woven or non-woven fabric used in garment construction. The unwoven ones have great stability, no bias stretch, and are non-fraying. "Lantor" interlinings are available in various weights.

Jacquard — A patterned fabric with the design coming through from the back of the fabric, to appear on a plain ground.

Lace — A fabric made up of a network of threads drawn together to form decorative designs.

Lamé — Metallic threads incorporated in fabrics to give a glittery appearance.

Lawn — A fine, lightweight woven cloth (used frequently for blouses and handkerchiefs).

Macramé — Lace fabric made with heavyweight threads.

Nap (or pile) — A soft, raised surface, often on woollen fabrics.

Net — A mesh fabric (often knitted) of various weights.

Organdie — A plain woven lightweight material with a crisp finish.

Pelt — A natural fur.

Piece — A length of fabric as supplied from the mill, usually of a traditional length.

Piece goods — Cut lengths of fabric as supplied by a retailer.

Piqué — A firmly woven fabric, having horizontal ribs or cords.

Poplin — A light to medium weight plain weave fabric with very fine horizontal ribs.

P.V.C. — A transparent plastic film (of polyvinyl chloride) bonded to woven or knitted fabrics to make them waterproof and hardwearing.

Remnant — An odd length of fabric left at the end of a piece. Usually sold by retailers in their half yearly Sales.

Sailcloth — A very strong, firmly woven cloth, available in mid to heavy weight and usually in plain colours.

Satin — A fabric weave, which produces a smooth shiny surface on the fabric. Usually made with silk, or man-made yarns.

Seersucker — A woven fabric having a prominent overall surface design similar to blistering. These fabrics are easy care and non-iron.

Selvedge — The finished edges of a length of woven material. Often incorporates the manufacturers name and/or the fabric style name.

Sheer — An ultra-lightweight fabric which is transparent.

Slub — A coarseness in a yarn which produces a variation in the evenness of the weave or knit when the slub appears on the fabric surface. Previously a yarn fault, it can now be carefully introduced by yarn manufacturers to achieve a required effect in fabrics — the slubbed effect. (Traditionally seen in Shantung silk fabric.)

Stretch fabrics — Fabrics containing elastane fibres, eg. "Lycra", are the most stretchy and are ideal for ski pants, swim suits, etc. A smaller degree of stretch is achieved by including crimped polyester or nylon yarns. These fabrics need special stitching techniques.

Taffeta — A plain weave fabric with a crisp handle. Often used for lining garments.

Terry towelling — An absorbent towelling fabric with closely woven loops on one or both sides. May be woven or knitted.

Thread count — The number of threads within a square inch of woven fabric, eg. 24 warp, 24 weft.

Tricot — A lightweight single-knit jersey fabric.

Tweed — A traditional woollen woven fabric with a rough surface and distinctive design. Usually rather heavy in weight and always hard-wearing and practical.

Twill — A weave of cloth, which has a diagonal ribbing on the surface. (See Gabardine.)

Velvet — A rich looking fabric with a cut-pile surface; traditionally made of silk or cotton, it is now also made in man-made fibres, and is therefore washable and crease resistant. The pile on velvet is liable to be crushed with careless handling.

Voile — A lightweight plain weave fabric with a very open weave. Often used for blouses and shirts.

Warp — The threads running the length of a fabric.

Warp knits — A wide width knitted fabric of a more stable type than a circular knit.

Weft — The threads running across a fabric.

Sewing Aids and Haberdashery

SEWING AIDS

There is now a wide range of sewing aids available in the shops, and all dressmakers should review them from time to time. Although some are unnecessary, most small pieces of equipment from reputable manufacturers have been carefully designed to make sewing easier, quicker or more efficient. Keep a good selection in your sewing box ready for use and read instructions when included. Always practise several times before using them on important work.

Bodkin – Ballpoint.
A long thick needle with a ballpoint at one end. Used for threading elastic, cord, tape and ribbons without snagging the fabric. It can also be of help when turning collars, belts and rouleau loops.

Bodkin – Ezy-pull®
An open-ended bodkin which grips instead of being threaded like a needle; thick elastic, cord, tape or ribbon can therefore be used.

Beeswax Holder
A block of beeswax in an easily gripped plastic holder, preventing snarling and knotting if the thread is pulled through it.

Bobbin Box
Make your own, or buy a clear plastic box fitted with niches for holding rows of machine bobbins or spools tidily.

Bound Button Hole Maker
An accessory to use with a sewing machine for easy and accurate preparation of bound buttonholes.

Coat Hangers
Available in many shapes and sizes – when dressmaking avoid the free wire hangers used for dry cleaning. Keep half-completed garments hanging to avoid distortion of fabric.

Curved Square or Ezy-Hem® Gauge
A tailors' square with a curved edge for drawing accurate curves and making evenly measured turnings. Can be used without pinning for pockets, waistbands, hems and pattern alterations.

Dressmaker Kit
A device for transferring pattern markings by chalking both sides of the fabric.

Fashion Ruler
Available in transparent plastic with parallel slots for precision markings of any width turnings, buttonholes or bias strips.

Fix-A-Snag
A small latch hook with a plastic handle for pulling snagged threads through to the wrong side of hand or machine knitted fabrics.

Hem Marker
Use it to obtain level hem lines. This is used to mark the required skirt length on the almost completed garment, with a puff of chalk, or by pinning. Some models mark hemline and sewing line simultaneously.

Invisible Zip Key
A small metal key to attach to the sewing machine, used with adhesive tabs to attach any type of 'invisible' zip.

Leather Punch
A scissor type punch, with a rotating head, which can cut holes of various sizes.

Loose Cover Pins
Two kinds are generally available for holding loose covers, mattress covers etc. in place temporarily or permanently. The twisted pins with a button-like top are probably safest and most secure.

Magnetic Seam Guide
A small metal attachment for the sewing machine; held in place by a powerful magnet, it enables it to form a guide for perfectly spaced tucks, pleats, seams, edge stitching and top stitching.

Marking Pencil with Brush End
Used like an ordinary pencil or tailors' chalk to transfer pattern markings, make alterations, mark pleats etc. The convenient brush on the other end is used to remove marks after use. Not suitable on all fabrics.

Needles: Special Types for Hand or Machine
In addition to the wide traditional range of needles, look regularly in the shops for new developments.
— Anti-static, perfect-stitch and ballpoint needles for knits and man made fabrics to aid penetration between threads, preventing snags and missed stitches.
— Self-threading needles are useful for those with poor sight.
— Colour coded machine needles for easy identification.

Needle Threader
A fine wire loop to make needle threading easy, especially for children or those with poor eyesight. One model has a tiny magnifying glass in the handle.

Sewing Aids and Haberdashery

Oil Tube
Most sewing machines must be regularly lubricated and a non-stain all purpose oil is available in special tubes for this purpose.

Pins
Choose good quality hardened and tempered pins for dressmaking as they do not bend in use. Plastic-headed pins are easy and safe to use. Glass headed pins are finer and longer than normal and worth adding to your workbox for extra holding power.

Plastic Pins
Useful when making up loosely-woven soft furnishing fabrics – they do not drop out.

Point Turner
A plastic point turner is perfectly shaped for turning collars. Some also have markings to use as a stitch guide, to ensure that collar points are symmetrical and a gauge for sewing button shanks accurately.

Quick Un-pic
A small metal and plastic device for removing unwanted stitches. Always choose one with a protective ball on one point. A great time-saver if used carefully. Also good for cutting buttonholes after stitching.

Sewing Gauge
A small rule with a sliding marker for measuring hems, seams, tucks, pleats, buttonholes, scallops etc.

Tailor Marker – Chalk-type.
An efficient method of transferring pattern markings onto the fabric, by inserting a pin into a chalk block, leaving chalk marks on both pieces of fabric when the pin is withdrawn.

Tailors' Chalk Holder
Helpful for use with traditional tailors' chalk to prevent it crumbling in the work box. Look for one that incorporates a sharpener.

Tailors' Chalk Pencil
A holder for sticks of tailors' chalk. Very easy to use.

Tailor Tacker Kit
Not unlike a hypodermic, it comprises a reelholder, needleholder, needle threader and special needles. Much quicker than traditional tailor tacking but it does need careful handling.

Thread Clipper
A flexible scissor-like tool, held in the palm of the hand.

Threads Locks
Plastic discs which fit into the top of thread reels to keep the cut end in place. Very useful for tidy storage of partly-used reels of thread, thus avoiding waste.

Tracing Wheel & Tracing Paper
A serrated rotating metal or plastic wheel on a handle; used with dressmakers' carbon paper to transfer pattern markings, embroidery designs etc. to fabric. Be sure to use carbon paper of a suitable colour and one that can be removed by washing and dry-cleaning.

Transparent Bobbins & Spools
Available to fit some sewing machines, enabling the colour and amount of thread to be seen easily.

Zip Puller
Useful for someone who makes and fits her clothes alone. A hook fitted to a cord is used for pulling up zips in the back of garments. Very useful for the disabled.

HABERDASHERY

New items of haberdashery frequently appear in the shops, and dressmakers should make a point of looking out for them. The cabinets of packaged haberdashery make selection easy.

Adhesive Tape
When ironed on to the wrong side fraying is stopped. The tear can then be machine-darned if necessary. Heavy duty adhesive tape is useful for carpet binding and repairs to plastics or heavy fabrics.

Ban Rol
Shaped and strengthened, flexible waistband stiffening which will not soften or roll over. Be sure to get an explanatory leaflet with each length.

Beads, Paillettes, Sequins etc.
Available in a wide range of materials, colour, shapes and sizes. Generally an inexpensive way of decorating a garment if not used too lavishly.

Belt Stiffening
Special belt stiffening is available, often in kit form, for stiffening and backing garment fabric to make a self-belt. Other stiffenings are available for enclosing in fabric to make belts.

Bias Binding
Bias cut fabric strip with folded edges for binding all edges, especially curved ones, to neaten and strengthen. Available prefolded in soft (nainsook) crisp cotton and in nylon, in several widths and a wide range of colours. Match colour to thread shade number type of binding to fabric used.

Blanket Binding
A wide pre-folded binding, often satin, used for edging and repairing blankets. Can also be used for trimming some household linens, eg. pillowcases.

Bra-Back Repair Kit
To replace worn out elastic and fastenings at the back of a still usable bra.

Brace Clips
A practical, fashionable and decorative fastening for dungaree straps. Available in two sizes.

Bra Cups
For insterting into dresses, especially halter necks and sundresses, also bikini tops that need to be pre-shaped so that a bra need not be worn. Available in several sizes.

Braid
For decoration of clothing and soft furnishing. An enormous range of colours, widths and types available; choose very carefully to be sure to use an appropriate one.

Broderie Anglaise
A very attractive open work trimming for cotton fabrics; embroidered white on white, available flat or frilled and usually with a shaped edge.

Buckles
For fastening belts and flaps. Choose the right size and weight, matching or contrasting colour as required. Kits are available for covering buckle shapes with garment fabric, but they must be made up very neatly to be durable. Some shops operate a 'send-away' buckle covering service.

Buttons
Choose washable, dry cleanable buttons where possible, of an appropriate size, weight and colour. Always take a piece of garment fabric when choosing and match it in both artificial and daylight. Buy one or two spare buttons for every garment, label and keep these carefully. It is usually more economical to buy buttons that are not already pre-packed in groups.

Sewing Aids and Haberdashery

Button Kits
Metal moulds in a variety of shapes and sizes for covering with garment fabric. They must be made neatly to be durable. Some shops operate a 'send-away' button and buckle covering service.

Coat Chains
A short lightweight chain specially made for sewing into the neck of a coat or suit; easier and stronger than sewing a loop.

Cord Lacing
For both practical and decorative purposes.

Piping Cord
A soft cotton cord in various thicknesses that must be washed to pre-shrink it before use. Necessary for piping buttonholes, seams etc. in garments and soft furnishings. A special silky finish cord is available for edging cushions etc.

Pyjama Cord
Available as a replacement if one is lost, or for home-made pyjamas.

Cotton Tape
It is used for loops, strengthening seams, stay stitching etc.

Decorative Patches & Motifs
Very fashionable for decorating garments – buy one or make your own. Can also be used to disguise a hole or tear.

Dress Shields
Fabric shapes for tacking into underarms of garments to prevent perspiration stains. Especially useful for garments which cannot be washed.

Dressmakers Paper
(Pattern or squared paper) For drafting or altering patterns.

Dyes – Powder, liquid or paints.
These are useful and effective but manufacturers' advice on type and method to use must be observed (not all fabrics can be dyed successfully). Dye remover may be necessary before some fabrics can be dyed. Liven up old garments and soft furnishing or use decoratively to produce tie-dyed effects. New paint-on dyes can be used creatively, together with embroidery if desired.

Elastic
Many types are available – select the best one for your purpose: e.g. bra-back, braid, cord, flat, millinery, round, shirring, shoulder-strap, skirt/trouser top, suspender, trunk-top, waistband.

Eyelet & Eyelet Punch
It is sometimes necessary to make eyelets for decoration or as part of a fastening. A special eyelet punch is needed to apply the eyelet rings which are available in several sizes.

Fabric Paint
Available in liquid, powder, crayon or pen form, these methods of applying colour to the surface of fabric and garments offer endless creative possibilities especially for children. It is essential to read manufacturers' advice before purchase to ensure that fabric and paint are compatible. Colours can usually be blended to produce an infinite variety of tones, and can be combined with tie and dye, embroidery etc.

Fringe
A wide range of types and colours are available mostly for trimming soft furnishings. Choose carefully so that fabric and trimming are compatible. It is possible to make fringing by hand or machine.

No Sew Snap Fasteners (and punch)
A type of press fastener which is punched onto the garment, not sewn. It is a fast, strong and fashionable method of fastening clothes and soft furnishings (including plastic, PVC etc.) can also be used decoratively. Plain and fancy designs are available in several colours.

Guipure Lace
Heavily textured cotton lace generally suitable for natural fibre garments for special occasions.

Hooks and Eyes (also hooks and bars)
Available in black and silver in many sizes. It is not appropriate to use one size and colour for all your dressmaking. Bars are less obtrusive than eyes. Adjustable hooks and bars are available for waistbands; they can be adjusted by up to 2 or 3 cm whilst the garment is being worn.

Horsehair Braid
Seldom needed except for stiffening hems of special garments.

Hosiery Mending Thread
Small packets of assorted colours are worth buying to prolong the life of tights and stockings, especially expensive ones.

Initials
Metal, adhesive and sew-on types are readily available or stitch your own. Iron-on embroidered initials have recently been developed with a backing that disappears when ironed on. Attractive on blouses, shirts, bags, hats etc.

Jean Patches
Iron-on patches for 'decorating' or repairing denim jeans.

Kilt Pins
Ideal for finishing home made kilts in traditional Scottish manner.

Labels
Iron-on. Use these with a special pen for marking names, sizes etc. especially on childrens' clothes. Also use them for adding wash-care details. Labels woven or printed with personalised captions etc. are now widely available.

Lace
Available for all types of trimming. Make sure that fabric and lace trimming are compatible.

Lead Weights
Small pieces of lead, sometimes button-shaped, or enclosed in fabric as a chain can be used to weight curtain hems, pleats, dresses, wedding dress trains so that they hang correctly.

Mending Tape
Iron-on tape is available in several colours for 'invisible' mending at home. It should be carefully pressed onto the wrong side of the garment.

Paris Binding
A firm binding sometimes used as a decorative finish.

Patches
Leather and Suede (see also Jean Patches). For decoration or for worn areas such as elbows of jackets.

Peta Stretch®
An extremely useful form of non-roll waist banding used particularly where there is no garment waistband. It is stretchy enough to fit well even where there is a big curve from waist to hip and is good for childrens' garments. It is applied slightly stretched as the waistband for skirts and trousers made from knitted fabrics where no zip is used. Its elasticity keeps blouses and sweaters tucked in and it is very comfortable in wear.

Preparing Fabric

Always examine the chosen fabric carefully, both in the shop and at home, before cutting it. If it is flawed do not accept it. Some shops will allow a price reduction or an extra piece of fabric to compensate for the flaw but make sure that you will be able to avoid it when cutting out the garment pieces.

Some fabrics will need to be specially prepared by pressing, shrinking and/or straightening, so that the finished garment will fit and hang well.

1. General Instructions
1. Check for flaws and for right and wrong sides.
2. Check grain and straighten ends of fabric.
3. Test for shrinkage.
4. Shrink, straighten and press fabric.
5. Re-examine fabric to see if there is an up and down motif, one way design, stripe or a nap, that you may not have noticed at time of purchase.

6. Fabric is usually rolled round into a bolt or bale by the mill and wide fabrics may also be folded in half lengthways. The selvedges will be at both sides of the bolt, or both at one side if the fabric is folded. All fabrics except tubular knitted fabrics have these two finished edges called selvedges which are usually rougher and more uneven on the wrong side of the fabric. If it is not immediately obvious which is the right side, looking at the selvedge can be useful. As long as all pattern pieces are cut out on the same side, it does not matter with some fabrics which side is used.

7. Grain — two sets of thread run at right angles to each other in the fabric. The thread running lengthwise is the "warp" and the thread running crosswise is the "weft" — these are also called straight grains. Sometimes following poor storage or handling the warp and weft do not run at right angles to each other, the weft thread curves towards the centre of the fabric.

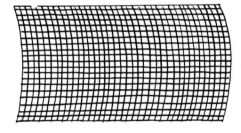

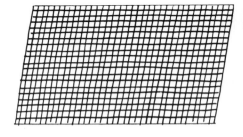

If both weft and warp are slanted, the material is said to be "off grain". It is important that the garment is cut from fabric that has the two "grains" at right angles to one another, as garment cut *ON* the grain maintain their shape and hang well. Those cut from *OFF* grain fabrics may well turn out to be a dismal failure. The "true cross" or "true bias" is a line at a 45° angle from the straight grain.

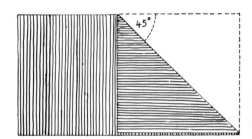

Look at the cut length of fabric to see if it is in any way crooked or the grain not quite straight.

Preparing Fabric

2. Methods of Straightening the Ends of a Length of Woven Fabric
Either:
1. (a) Cut into the selvedge edge with scissors.
(b) Pick up one or more weft threads with a pin.
(c) Take hold of the threads and pull gently, slipping the material along the thread with the other hand.

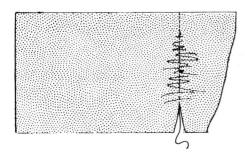

(d) Cut along the line shown by the pulled thread as far as it is visible. Should the thread break, continue cutting along the line it has made until you can again pick up the end.
(e) Continue until the opposite selvedge has been reached.
Or:
2. (a) If the material is ribbed, checked or woven (not printed) with a pattern, use this as a guide for cutting from one selvedge to the other.
Or:
3. Check the material to see if it will tear:
(a) Approximately 25 mm/2·5 cm from the cut end snip into one selvedge with scissors.
(b) Tear sharply to the opposite side then cut the selvedge.
(c) If the material tears easily repeat the tearing process at the other end.
(d) Usually ends of evenly woven cotton, synthetics and silk can be straightened by tearing.
Note that linen fabrics should *not* be torn on the crosswise (weft) threads.
Or:
4. (a) Napped or pile fabrics should be cut on a thread.
(b) Unravel threads on the weft edge until one thread can be pulled off the whole width of the material.

(c) Fringe should be cut off and edge made even.
Fold the fabric in half lengthwise. Ends should be lined up with either a cutting board or a table corner. The weft or crosswise edge should form a right angle with the selvedges proving that the material is on grain. Pre-shrink if necessary before straightening the grain.

3. Methods of Straightening the Ends of a Length of Knitted Fabric
For loosely knitted Jersey pull out one weft thread gradually working across the width of fabric so that the raw edge completely separates from the main length of fabric.
Or:
Run a small tacking thread across the weft carefully picking up the same horizontal thread then cut along tacking.
N.B. It is a good idea on some fabrics to run a line of machine basting along this newly cut edge to prevent stretching.
8. Shrinking — This is an invisible hazard! If you did not receive a satisfactory answer to your enquiries regarding shrinkage, which of course should have been made at the time of purchase, it would be wise to make a *SHRINKAGE TEST*. Some fabrics can shrink as much as 7 cm in a metre. Woollens, inexpensive cottons and rayons are liable to shrink.

4. Tests for Shrinkage
A1. Try a layout of the pattern pieces on the length of cloth to see where a small sample square can be cut for the test — do not just cut a piece off one corner or you may have to buy an extra length to cut out a whole garment piece.
2. Cut an exact square from the fabric exactly 20 cm × 20 cm, keeping a note of exact measurement and soak in hot water for about 15 minutes.

3. Lift from water — remove excess moisture by pressing fabric gently onto a thick towel.
4. Leave to dry naturally.
5. When completely dry measure for shrinkage.
6. If shrinkage has occurred, follow instructions below for pre-shrinking that particular fabric type and pre-shrink the whole length of fabric in question.
Note — this test will also sometimes give an indication of colour fastness if this is in doubt.
B1. Thread-trace a carefully measured square in the piece of fabric. Press with a damp cloth and allow to dry, then measure again.

5. Methods for Pre-shrinking and Pressing Fabrics
(See also the general method for pressing to straighten fabric grain, at the end of this chapter.)
1. *Woollen fabrics*
(Note — never shrink crêpes and georgettes.)
If woollen fabrics need shrinking or straightening or are dry cleanable, use the following method:
(a) Check for crosswise thread or weft ends being perfect.
(b) Material should be left folded in half lengthwise as purchased, with the right sides facing.
(c) Edges of warp ends and selvedge ends should be even. Hand tack ends together.
(d) Use any clean, absorbent cotton fabric (old sheets are ideal) to wrap the woollen material to keep it moist.
(e) There should be a sufficient supply of cloths on hand to equal the length of the fabric. These cloths should be a little wider than the folded fabric being treated.
(f) The cloths should be evenly damp throughout but excess moisture should be removed.
(g) Place the woollen fabric flat on the table. Put damp cloths over it. Fold from one end towards the centre turning the lengths together in wide folds. Press down whilst folding to push the moisture through. The opposite end should be handled in the same manner. A wet cloth should be wrapped around the folded woollen material and then the whole "sandwich" placed in a large plastic bag to enable the moisture to be evenly distributed throughout.

Preparing Fabric

(h) Woollen fabrics should be allowed to remain like this for two to four hours, depending on thickness, to allow the moisture to be thoroughly absorbed.
(i) Unfold the woollen fabric, but do not hang it up otherwise it will stretch and become mis-shapen. Pull and smooth the fabric gently by hand to straighten the grain. When the top layer is almost dry to the touch, rearrange so that the under layer will shrink and dry evenly. Normally pressing is unnecessary. If pressing is needed use steam iron on the lengthwise grain.

2. *Cottons, linens or washable fabrics*
Shrink and straighten as follows:
(a) Check for crosswise thread and weft ends being perfect.
(b) Fabric should be folded in half lengthwise with the right sides facing.
(c) Pin, then tack, selvedges and then crosswise ends together. Put pins a hand span apart, parallel and near to the edges.
(d) The folded length of fabric should be folded into accordian pleats, with folds about the width of a hand apart.
(e) Immerse the fabric in warm water until it is wet throughout. Ensure uniform wetness by checking in between the folds of the fabric.
(f) Lift fabric from water and remove excess water by wrapping it in a turkish towel. DO NOT WRING.
(g) Lay fabric on a flat surface to dry, on a sheet of plastic. Do not hang it up as it will stretch and distort.
(h) Pull and smooth the fabric gently to straighten the grain. Sometimes it will be necessary to pull and smooth it during the drying time to be sure that the grain remains straight.
(i) Press fabric with a steam iron, when completely dry, on the lengthwise (warp) grain.

3. *Man-made fabrics*
Acetate, triacetate, rayon, nylon, polyester, acrylic and other materials.
(a) These fabrics seldom have to be shrunk. Always examine the manufacturer's label to check if the material has been pre-shrunk, or for further information regarding its finish.
(b) Should shrinking not be necessary follow the instructions for straightening the grain as for cottons and linens. If shrinking *is* needed, follow instructions for cotton and linen.

(c) Off-grain materials which are labelled pre-shrunk can be straightened by pressing, unless they have a permanent finish. These are mill-applied durable resins (or stabilising finishes) which lock the material grain in place.
(d) Blended fabrics which have a man made and woollen content should be treated for straightening and shrinking using the method for wool.

4. *Cotton corduroy*
Crushing of pile should be avoided when wet as follows:
(a) Make corduroy thread perfect.
(b) Fold, then soak in water.
(c) Remove from water and gently press with the palms of the hands to rid the cloth of surplus moisture.
(d) DO NOT WRING.
(e) Place the corduroy directly into an automatic dryer, if possible. This will raise the pile and pressing should be unnecessary.
(f) If the corduroy is dry-cleanable only, no preparation need be carried out.

5. *Silk fabrics*
(a) No shrinking is necessary for fine silk fabric and it can be cut directly after purchase.
(b) To straighten off-grain silk fabric, press into shape with a steam iron.

6. *Torn-edged fabrics*
(a) Press raw edges of torn material to restore a smooth grain line. Flatten any rippling edges.
(b) Ends require pressing even though the rest of the material is on grain.
(c) For material torn in both directions press lengthwise and widthwise. (Never deliberately tear a fabric along its length as this can stretch the weft and make the weave distorted.)
(d) To maintain perfect grain, fold the material in half before pressing it.

7. *Jersey fabrics*
The majority of man-made jersey fabrics do not shrink. If in doubt, however, and they are washable, TEST them before attempting to cut out the garment.
Note — if self-lined (bonded) fabrics are found to be off-grain these cannot be straightened, so particular care should be taken to make a very thorough examination at the time of purchase.
(a) If shrinkage has occurred in the test, follow the instructions for shrinking cottons and linens at first stages.

(b) Remove fabric carefully from the water making sure that all the fabric weight is supported. Jersey fabrics tend to hold more water than woven ones so enlist some help — two pairs of hands are better than one. Alternatively, place fabric on a large wire rack, or draining bowl, whilst in the water, lift out the rack or bowl complete with fabric and leave to drain.
(c) On flat surface, very carefully sandwich the fabric between layers of turkish towelling, then with extreme care place the "sandwich" in a spindryer and spin for about 15 seconds.
(d) Remove from spindryer very carefully, and return to flat surface.
(e) Gently rearrange fabric so that it is smooth, straight and flat on a plastic sheet, and leave to dry. Turn layers occasionally to assist the drying process.
(f) Pressing will generally be unnecessary, but if it is needed use a very cool iron, working along length of fabric.

Wool and cotton
Nearly all cotton jersey fabrics are washable and quite a number of washable wool jersey are now appearing on the market. When washing these fabrics some weft shrinkage will *almost always* take place. It is in the very nature of natural jersey fabrics to "elongate" during the washing process.
(a) Shrink wool jerseys as for wool using slightly wetter wrapping cloths.
(b) Shrink cotton jersey as for cotton, and finish as for man-made jersey with a 15-second spin in spindryer.
(c) Both wool and cotton jerseys will need to be lightly pressed into shape and straightened along the length of the fabric. Use a dry pressing cloth and steam iron.

6. General Method for Straightening Grain by Pressing
(a) When fabric has been pre-shrunk and is slightly off grain it can normally be straightened by pressing with a steam iron. (Woollens should not be handled in this way).
(b) Ends of thread must be checked for regularity, and the fabric then folded in half lengthwise with right sides facing. Pull diagonally to straighten ends.
(c) Pin, then tack the selvedge edges together, then the weft or crosswise ends. Remove pins.

Preparing Fabric

(d) If the material is off grain, diagonal wrinkles and puckers will appear when the doubled material is laid flat on a surface.

The wrinkling which will appear will give a good indication of how much the fabric is off grain.

(e) The under layer of the fabric should be dampened with a wet cloth or sponge. When a steam iron is used it will provide enough dampness for the top layer of the fabric.

(f) When pressing the fabric, move the iron along the lengthwise grain.

(g) If the fabric still remains off grain, press the iron along the weft or crosswise grain.

(h) Avoid pressing the centre fold of the material because the crease will be difficult to remove later.

(i) To work out which way to lay out the pattern pieces spread the length of fabric out and check to see if the design has a "right way up" or a nap where the surface of the fabric lies smoothly all one way when brushed with the hand.

Pattern Layout, Cutting and Marking

1. **Printed Layouts**
2. **One Way Fabrics**
3. **Even Checks and Plaids**
4. **Stripes**
5. **Prints**
6. **Border Prints**
7. **Making a Layout**
8. **Cutting Out**
9. **Marking**
   Carbon paper and tracing wheel
   Chalk marks and pins
   Tailor's tacks
   Soft pencil
   Thread tracing

First press the required paper pattern pieces (see Chapter on Choosing and Using a Pattern)

1. Printed Layouts

1. All commercial paper patterns include a suggested pattern layout on the instruction sheet, and the length and width of fabric required. Before purchasing fabric it is useful to practice the layout as it is often possible to buy a little less than the amount quoted. Be sure to follow the layout for the *size* and *style* required, noting that there are usually special layout instructions for one-way designs and pile or napped fabrics.

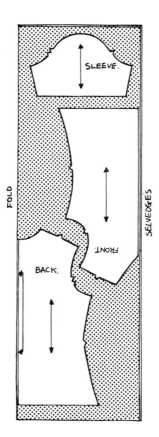

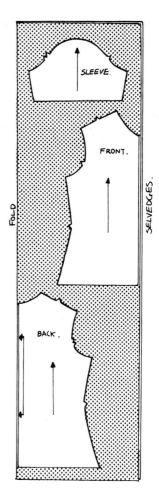

2. Look again at all the pattern pieces to see where the straight grain arrows are placed, which pieces need to be placed next to fold, and whether to place them on single or double fabric. Make sure that pattern adjustments have been completed on all appropriate garment sections and that seam lines and cutting lines have been redrawn where necessary. Use pattern pieces printed side uppermost unless the instructions sheet advises otherwise. If the fabric has a nap, a pile or one-way design see the following section.

Pattern Layout, Cutting and Marking

3. Prepare and pre-shrink the fabric (See Chapter on Preparing Fabrics.) Place it on a large flat surface — if nowhere else use the floor. If the fabric is double thickness pin along the ends, fold and selvedges to keep them in place.

4. Lay the pattern pieces on the fabric according to the layout placing the large, main pieces first.

5. Pin along foldlines and lengthwise grainlines first. The grainlines must be exactly parallel with the fabric grain. Check the grainlines by making sure that the line is parallel to the selvedge of the fabric. Measure the distance from each end of the grainline to the selvedge — the two measurements will be the same if the piece is exactly on the straight grain. Do not try to squeeze in pattern pieces by laying them off the straight grain or the finished garment will not hang well. Do not overlap pieces so that seam allowances are cut off. The pieces should not be placed over the selvedges.

6. Check that the patterns are correctly placed so that, for example, there will not be two left sleeves, or a bodice front on the wrong side of the fabric.

7. Pin down all pieces, with the pins at right angles to the seamline about 6mm from the cutting line. The pins should be about 7cm apart.

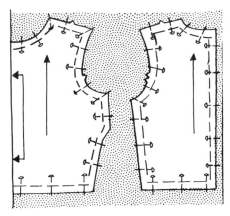

8. If a pattern piece appears on the layout to extend beyond the folded edge of the fabric, leave it in place until all other pieces have been cut out. Unfold the fabric, smooth the pattern piece out, and pin it flat.

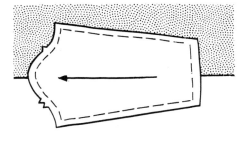

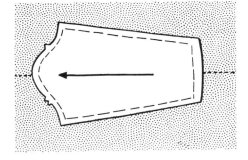

2. One-way Fabrics

If the fabric has a one-way print, an uneven check or plaid, a nap or pile the garment will not look right unless each section is cut in the same direction throughout the garment. In these instances, more fabric is usually needed as the pieces cannot be dovetailed together so easily on the layout.

It is the seam lines and not the cutting lines that will eventually need to match when the garment is being made up. This is important for fabric with a woven or surface design.

The fabric surface must be taken into account in napped and pile fabrics. These feel rough when brushed one way with the hand, and smooth when brushed the other way eg velvet. Some shiny or textured fabrics must also be cut out on one-way layouts as the surface may have a shaded effect in strong light.

3. Even Checks and Plaids

Check to see that the pattern is not marked "unsuitable for plaids". The design chosen should be simple with few pattern pieces. Extra fabric will usually be needed for matching checks and plaids.

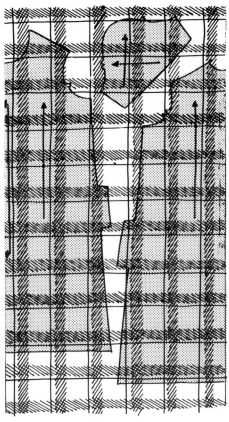

Hold up the length of chosen fabric to see if there are any prominent design lines; these should be carefully placed on the garment for the best effect, and must always be continuous around the garment and from neck to hem. They should also match on bodice and skirt, or jacket and skirt. Uneven plaids should only be used by experienced dressmakers. Follow the "with nap" layout, placing pieces so that notches are matched at the side seams and centre front lines. Start matching from the hem upwards. Diagonal lines, and curves such as sleeve-heads, are not always matched, but shaped seams will stitch into chevrons, if correctly placed. Pay careful attention to details and small symmetrical pieces such as collars. Fashion details such as pockets and cuffs may be cut on the true cross.

Pattern Layout, Cutting and Marking

4. Stripes

Fabrics woven in stripes or wales such as corduroy or printed with stripes should be arranged in a layout as for plaids and checks except that they need matching in one direction only. The stripes should all run the same way in one garment except for special fashion features. Remember that with corduroy the pile or nap must also be considered.

5. Prints

If the fabric has a definite one-way design use the fabric layouts marked "with nap".
If large motifs are a feature of the fabric experiment to see where these should be placed on the figure — not, for example, on the buttocks! Balance the motifs vertically and horizontally and choose simple garments that have few pattern pieces.

6. Border Prints

These are obviously arranged so that the printed border appears along a garment hem. Choose a straight style and match up the print at the side seams as accurately as possible.

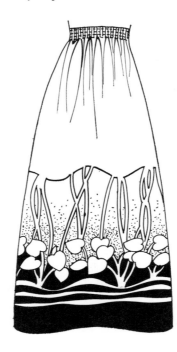

7. Making a Layout

Layouts are simply provided to show the most convenient way of cutting a number of pattern pieces from the minimum amount of fabric. If there is not a printed layout available or if choosing an expensive fabric, make a mock layout to calculate how much fabric is needed. Measure the width of the widest pattern piece — if it is no wider than 45cm the garment can be cut from 90cm fabric. Where some pieces are wider than that it is possible to lay out the pattern on 90cm fabric opened out instead of folded lengthwise, or wider fabric may be necessary.
Use sheets of newspaper, stuck or pinned together, on which to make a mock layout. Look at a commercial paper pattern layout for ideas.

8. Cutting Out

1. Use very sharp cutting-out shears, preferably with bent handles. (See chapter on Choosing Equipment.) Do not use pinking shears — these are for neatening seams.
2. Cut away from yourself to avoid accidents.
3. Keep the fabric as flat as possible placing one hand flat on the fabric piece whilst cutting. Do not lift the fabric up or the shape of the pattern will be distorted.
4. Cut along straight edges with long, smooth strokes using the whole length of the blades. Use shorter snipping movements round curved lines and pattern notches. Notches are often easier to cut using much smaller scissors.
5. Cut along the cutting line *not* the seam line.
6. Cut the pattern notches outwards not inwards, so that they project beyond the edge and can easily be matched up when seaming.
7. Check that each pattern piece is used enough times — some should be cut out more than once.
8. Cut all the main pieces first. Pile them up carefully without folding, but do not remove pins yet.
9. If the fabric will fray badly leave extra seam allowances, and do not cut turnings until they are needed for stitching.
10. When all pieces have been cut out, sort out the fabric that is left! Some large pieces will do for making other small garment or accessories. Put one piece into the pattern envelope for matching or patching later. Throw away any tiny scraps but save other pieces for bound buttonholes, matching, testing, patchwork, etc.

9. Marking

The pattern markings are very important. When pieces have been cut out, transfer all the necessary markings from the pattern to the fabric, before removing the paper pattern where possible.
It is essential that you transfer the construction symbols or marks from the pattern to the wrong side of the garment sections. These markings help give precision to the making-up of a garment. There are basically three methods of marking the garment and transferring

Pattern Layout, Cutting and Marking

the symbols from the pattern to the material.

1. Tracing paper, or carbon paper and the tracing wheel
(a) Put a piece of carbon paper, shiny side downwards, between the pattern and fabric. Pin the pattern back into position.
(b) Place another piece of carbon paper, shiny side upwards, underneath the second layer of material.
(c) Use a transparent ruler for straight lines, run tracing wheel over the pattern marking, applying sufficient pressure to mark both the layers of fabric.

(d) Remove the pattern. When using this particular method, care should be taken to:
(i) Prevent damage to any surface tops.
(ii) Use slightly darker colour or carbon paper to make markings distinguishable on the material.
(iii) Make certain that the shiny sides of the carbon paper are placed to the *wrong* sides of the fabric.
(iv) Mark notches with tailor's tacks in the normal way.
(v) Prevent finger marks on fabric by handling the carbon paper very lightly and carefully.
(vi) When marking has been carried out put carbon paper away so that fabric does not inadvertently become marked in the wrong places.

2. Chalk marks and pins
(a) Lift the pattern edge to mark the position of the notches.
(b) Beginning from the outside of the pattern, put the pins carefully through each of the marked dots on the pattern and fold back the pattern to the pins.
(c) Use a transparent ruler and a sharp

pointed pencil to mark the piece of material held by the pins on the wrong side.

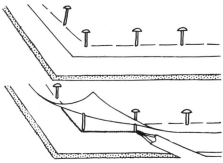

(d) Remove the pattern and work tailor's tacks if desired, as chalk marks easily rub off whilst working.

3. Tailor's tacks
(See the chapter on Stitches and Thread)
(a) Use thread that will contrast with the fabric being tacked. Use one colour for seam lines and another for darts, buttonholes and pleats.
(b) Thread the needle with no more than a metre of cotton, doubled.
(c) Place the tacking stitches at dots and at intervals along the marked lines. Use different colours for different symbols.
(d) Take needle through both the pattern and layers of fabric. Leave a length of cotton 25 mm/2·5 cm.
(e) Take another stitch over the first one, this time leaving a loop. Cut the thread leaving a 25 mm/2·5 cm end.
(f) Continue this method of tailor tacking on the various pattern markings. Do not cut loops on individual tailor's tacks.

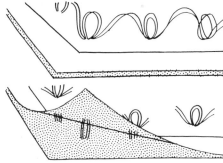

(g) When tailor tacking is complete, remove the pattern gently so that threads will not be pulled out.

(h) Gently separate the fabric layers, then cut the threads between, leaving thread tufts on both layers.

4. Soft pencil
(a) On light colour fabrics some pattern markings can be transferred to the *wrong side* with a 2B pencil.
(b) Push the pencil point through dots, dart lines, etc., or
(c) Cut out the dart from the paper and draw round it. Stick or pin the paper in place again ready for next time.

5. Thread tracing (or trace tacking)
Uneven tacking is used on single layers of fabric to mark the grain lines, centre front and centre back, etc. Use fine thread

Fitting and Alteration

1. Fitting

Figures vary considerably from person to person even though body measurements may be similar. It is therefore essential that accurate fittings of the garment are made during construction. Correct fitting relies a great deal on the accurate placing of the pattern on the grain line of the fabric in the first place, and meticulous detail being paid both to cutting out and to transferring construction marks.

If inaccuracies occur here, fitting is made extremely difficult during the later stages. Additionally the importance of taking correct measurements cannot be stressed too much. Throughout garment construction there is great inter-relation between each stage — the accuracy of each process depending upon attention to detail in previous stages. The final success of the garment depends entirely on this.

If you have been careful to make any adjustments to the pattern that may have been needed, the fitting stage should prove to be relatively simple. For a perfect fit however, some minor adjustments may be needed.

If clothes fit well you will feel comfortable and self-confident wearing them. Garments that hang well and fit where they should, are so much more flattering than those that are lopsided — wrinkled and bulging in the wrong places.

Points to remember at fitting stage
1. Stay stitching should be completed before any assembling takes place. This prevents the stretching of bias edges not yet seamed.
2. Use a dress form, or better still enlist the help of a friend to fit you.
3. Wear the under-clothes and shoes that you intend wearing with the finished garment. These make a surprising difference to the appearance of the fitted garment.

4. Should shoulder pads be needed for the garment have these pinned in place ready for fitting.
5. If the garment is belted, make the belt ready and wear it.
6. Remember to stand in a relaxed manner, not rigid, whilst the garment is being fitted. Move round in it, sit down, bend down, reach up and down; this aspect of fitting seldom has sufficient attention paid to it. A garment must allow enough room for the movements of the body within it so that normal actions are not restricted. At the same time it must fit well.

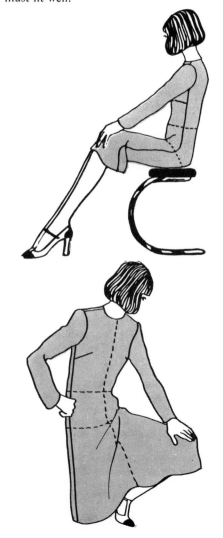

Fitting and Alteration

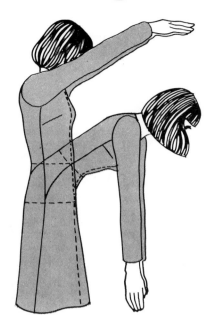

7. Make an effort to look as well groomed whilst your garment is being fitted as you will when you finally wear it. The overall appearance will help you to visualise exactly how attractive your finished efforts will be.

Fitting hints

1. Make sure to trace tack the front and centre back lines on garment pieces, plus the suggested lines for the attachment of pockets, cuffs and other surface details.
2. Tack major parts of the garment together — clip neckline and armholes to stay stitching.
3. Mark the centre front and centre back line of your petticoat with trace tacking. Place centre front and centre back line of garment to these lines and pin. This should help garment to hang straight at fitting stage.

4. Place a 3 cm wide ribbon round the waistline and pin. Pin bodice and skirt to it. It will locate the correct waistline and give added support whilst fitting.

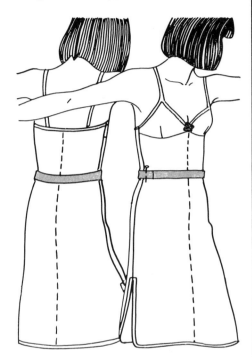

5. Lap centres, seam lines and openings by pinning horizontally. Increase or decrease width by taking in or letting out at *seams* or *darts*, not at closure areas.
6. When wrinkles occur *pat* the fabric into position. Re-locate seams where wrinkles indicate the need. This may mean reducing one seam allowance and increasing another.
7. It may be helpful with some fabrics to lightly press the fitting adjustments before finally sewing. This will give a better idea of the finished effect.
8. Where pockets or flaps occur make sure that they are positioned with the final hemline in mind. It is best to tack up the hemline on a skirt or jacket so that you may check that the proportions are pleasing and flattering to your figure. Pockets may appear too large, too high or too low — they may even give unwanted emphasis to a large bust or broad hips and need to be discarded.

9. Try on the garment in a well-lit room before a full-length mirror — RIGHT SIDE OUT.

10. Check that side seams and centre seams or markings are perpendicular to the floor, and that they are EXACTLY at the side or the centre.
11. Make sure that the waistline seam is located exactly where the pattern indicates and that shoulder seams are straight along the middle line between top of shoulder and base of neck. Clip the neckline to the stay stitching to give a smooth fit. The shoulder seam should end about 15 mm from the base of the neck.
12. Both sides of the garment must look the same. Pay special attention if there are any obvious figure irregularities. Do not rely on fitting only one side of the garment — fit both sides — one side of the body is often larger than the other.

Fitting and Alteration

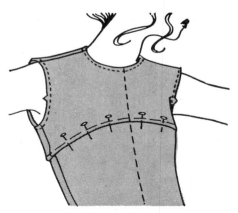

13. Darts at bust line should finish just a little way from the fullest part of the bust; the armhole seam line should be about 25 mm below armpit at lowest point for comfort.

14. Before fitting sleeves, remove the garment and tack any changes to be made on major seams, darts and facings.

15. Try on the garment again with sleeves tacked into armholes. Check fall of sleeves and position of ease or darts at elbow. Make sure that sleeve joins bodice at point of shoulder bone and that cap and body of sleeve are placed as shown in the picture on the pattern envelope.

16. When garments are cut on the cross allow them to hang for at least two days before attempting to mark the hemline. Atmospheric changes as well as the weight of the fabric may cause the fabric to drop, and nothing looks worse than a drooping hemline.

17. If linings are to be used alter these at the same time.

18. Neaten seams step by step at each stage of construction.

19. *Never pull or smooth* fabric into place when fitting as it may distort grain line and stretch fabric. Always *pat* fabric into place.

20. Remember that a certain amount of "ease" is included in all patterns. This extra is to allow for line and movement. The amount will vary from pattern to pattern and seam to seam so do not ignore this when fitting, or the garment may end up looking vastly different from the way the designer intended it to look.

Tacking for fitting

There are two recognised ways of tacking garment pieces together for fitting.

(a) Normal tacking along the seam lines with right sides together. The garment is then tried on **right** side out. (Shown on model in illustration wrong side out, to illustrate stitching.)

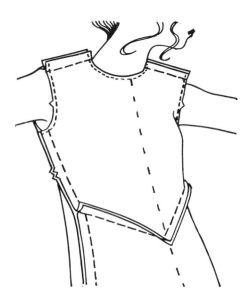

Using a long, thin needle (Milliner's No 8) and a long length of Sylko, sew long even stitches 10–13 mm on straight seams. Slightly shorter stitches are better on curved seams and shoulders. Start with a knot and finish with a few backstitches which can be unpicked later, allowing the thread to be pulled out with the knot. Keep the pieces flat so that the garment does not look creased when fitted. Leave out sleeves and collar for the first fitting.

(b) Surface tacking — where the seams are pinned and tacked flat on the right side to emphasise the design details and to hold the seams flat. Alterations can then be made accurately whilst the garment is on the dress form or figure.

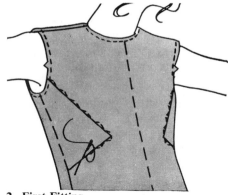

2. First Fitting

Put the garment on, bearing in mind the general points listed earlier. Spend a lot of time just looking at the garment. Note whether it hangs well and whether the grain of each piece is correct. Note the good points that must not be altered by other fitting alterations. Check that the waist and hiplines are horizontal and the centre lines vertical.

Fitting and Alteration

Experiment with the design details to see if moving a pocket, or using a different belt, would improve the general appearance. Now make the necessary fitting alterations, marking with pins on both sides so that when the garment is taken apart it can be tacked on these lines.

1. Check the back shoulder darts if any. If the back is loose or wrinkled, undo the shoulder seams and raise or lower the back *only*.

2. If the wrinkling is below the armhole, lift the whole back piece and re-cut the neck, shoulders and armholes.

3. Check the centre front line, and the grain across the bodice. Alter the bust dart, side seams and waist seam as necessary. If the fabric drags from the bust to the sides of the waist undo the side seams and lift the fabric into the bust darts from below. Re-pin the side seams.

If the bust darts are not pointing to the fullest part of the bust, undo the side seams and darts and raise or lower the points of the darts.

If the fabric bulges under the arm and drags at the armhole, undo the side seams and bust darts. Lower the darts a little at the side seams and let out the side seams above the darts.

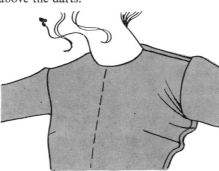

4. Check the neckline. If it gapes, undo the shoulder seams and raise them.

If the neckline is too tight or too high, snip into the seam allowance and mark new seam line with pins.

4. Check the armholes. If they are too tight alter them as for neckline, see above.

5. Partly pin in one sleeve so that the grain hangs straight, make marks on the sleeve and armhole as a guide for tacking in the sleeves for the second fitting.

6. Check the front of the shoulders. If the fabric pulls at the outer end of the seam lines, undo the shoulder seams and let them out.

Fitting and Alteration

If the shoulder seams do not lie flat at the outer edge because of sloping shoulders, undo the seams and put the extra fabric into the seam.

7. Check the darts, grain lines and side seams on the backskirt. If the skirt pulls in below the seat re-pin the side seams to add extra width in the back pieces. Re-pin the waist darts for a smooth fit.

If the skirt pulls across the waist and hips let out the side seams.

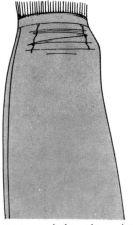

If there are creases below the waistline, hollow out the waist at the back.

If the skirt juts out at the back hem, take in the side seams on the back piece only.

8. Trousers should be fitted very carefully. If the crotch is too low pleat across the

pattern below the waist, re-pin the pattern onto the fabric and reshape the waist area.

If the crotch is too tight release the side seams and lower the curve of the crotch.

If waist or hips are too tight let out the darts and side seams.

If the width of the legs is not right alter the seams equally.

3. Alterations
1. Take the garment off carefully.
2. Trace tack over the pins marking the areas to be altered, then remove the pins. (Use a thread of a contrasting colour.)
3. Remove the threads holding the garment together in the areas to be altered.
4. Transfer these new markings to the paper pattern ready for next time.
5. Make all the required alterations, then tack the garment together again.
6. Tack in the sleeves and collar.

Fitting and Alteration

4. Second Fitting

(a) Look again as for the first fitting, making sure that the alterations have had the desired effect.

(b) If necessary refit the side seams.

(c) Fit the sleeves. The inside seam should be in line with the thumb when the arm hangs naturally. The elbow dart must be at the right level. The grain lines must be vertical and horizontal (except when garment is cut on the cross). If the sleeve is too wide, take in the seam from nothing at the armhole to the required width at the wrist. (Reposition wrist dart, if any.) Reverse this for sleeves that are too tight. If the sleeve cap has loose folds, alter the crown by pinning wider seam allowances. If the sleeve cap is too narrow and causes horizontal creases, let out the seams.

(d) Check that all openings and fastenings will be in the correct place.

(f) If there have been no alterations, provisionally mark the hemline. Make any necessary alterations and put garment together for final fitting.

5. Final Fitting

Look at the whole garment critically and in detail. If it is now fitting perfectly, mark the hemline and proceed to sew the pieces together.

6. Altering Bought Clothes

Even inexpensive clothes will look better if they fit the wearer perfectly. If you like a garment that does not fit well it may be possible to alter it, but decide if the alterations will be worthwhile. It is almost impossible to make a very tight garment fit well, so choose one that is larger rather than smaller than needed. Seams that have been let out often show marks of unpicking. Some fabrics such as poplin, satin and gabardine show alteration marks badly, so avoid altering them. On many fabrics, especially those from man-made fibres, the crease left when a hem has been let down cannot be removed.

Waistlines can be difficult to alter and fastenings such as buttons should not be moved more than about 6 mm or the garment will look unbalanced. In general, follow the fitting instructions given earlier in this chapter.

Belts

It is easier to shorten a belt from the buckle end, leaving the eyelets untouched. Remove the buckle, cut off the required length of belt then replace the buckle.

Waistbands

If the waist is too tight, remove the waistband and replace it with a piece of shaped petersham ribbon. Let out the darts as necessary.

If the waist is too loose, remove the waistband and zip. Take in the darts and side seams to fit, and adjust the length of the waistband. Replace the waistband.

Hipline

Extra width can be gained by unpicking the side seams nearly to the waistband. Machine new side seams with tiny seam allowances.

Creases across skirts

When these form below the waist at the back, pin up the surplus and mark in a new waistline. Remove the waistband and refit the waistline, adjusting the hemline if it is affected by this.

Low crotch on trousers

This is an ugly fault and can be corrected by letting down the leg hems and removing the waistband. Lift the trousers by the waist until the crotch fits snugly. Refit the darts and side seams, mark a new waistline and cut away surplus fabric. Replace the waistband. Apply false leg hems if needed.

Hems on trousers

Straight legs are no problem. Bellbottoms may be taken up but not let down as they usually have faced hems; remove the facing, shorten the legs and put on new facings. Tapered trousers can be let down but are more tricky to take up; undo the side seams, and turn up the legs leaving the side seams unstitched in the hem so that they lie flat.

Necklines

It is difficult to refit a loose neckline. A tight round neck can be eased by removing the facings and unpicking the shoulder seams. Let out the seams, then restitch them. Scoop out the neckline a little if necessary and replace the trimmed facings.

Shoulders

Wide shoulders which slip off the point of the shoulders are unflattering; lift the top of the sleeve further into the armhole.

Armholes

Loose armholes can be put right by unpicking the armhole seam under the arm and taking in the bodice side seams. Adjust the armhole facing to match, then replace it.

Hems

False hems may be created to lengthen a garment to the maximum length. Use a very wide bias binding or crossway strip and apply it as a facing.

To shorten a permanently pleated skirt (it cannot be lengthened) take it up from the waist.

Coats can be lengthend with a false hem, but this requires great care and attention if a good result is to be achieved.

7. Recycling Old Clothes

Clothes in the wardrobe that are in good condition but out of fashion can be "recycled" by turning them into something else. If this is not possible they can generally be cut down for a child.

Fitting and Alteration

Consider using jumble sale bargains for this purpose.

To restyle a garment, use a pattern unless the alteration is simple. Consider making a waistcoat from a jacket, a tunic or smock from a mini-dress, a jacket and skirt from a long dress, a dress into a skirt, etc.
Make sure the garment is clean, then carefully unpick seams where necessary and press them. Unpicking lines may be hidden with top-stitching, worn spots or stains with pockets, darts or trimmings.

Consider changing the trimmings on a garment, adding some decorative stitching, changing the collar or neckline, shortening the sleeves, etc.

First clean the garment thoroughly, unpick it and discard worn or stained areas. Press each piece, and if the wrong side looks brighter and fresher use that instead. Most fabrics are suitable for making into children's clothes (except perhaps evening dresses) but some fabric designs are too large or sophisticated. Pockets and buttons are not usually suitable for re-use in this way and linings should be discarded.
Choose a paper pattern or a style that is fairly simple and has the same number of garment pieces as the old one.
Make coats into jackets, skirts, coats, waistcoats, trousers. Dresses can be made into skirts, dresses, boleros, blouses, trousers, shorts, etc. according to the fabric. Knitwear can be cut or re-knitted into jumpers, tank tops, etc. Any small pieces will make toys.

Trousers - a special case

1. **Points to Remember**

2. **Trouser Style Selection Chart**

3. **Fitting Style and Size**

4. **What to Wear under Trousers**

5. **Making a Standard Pattern**

Trousers — pants, bermudas, jeans, culottes, shorts, gauchos — whatever the style, whatever the name, are now featuring very strongly in dressmaking. At one time trousers of any description were only worn by women and girls for manual work, as part of a uniform or for sporting activities such as skiing or horse riding. They are now very popular and very much accepted as an important part of any wardrobe, both for everyday wear and glamorous evening wear.

1. Points to Remember

A. Whatever the figure type, trousers *can* be worn and will look smart and slimming if the correct style is chosen. Take a long, critical look at yourself from the front the side and then the back, in a full length mirror to help decide upon the most flattering style. Be realistic about figure imperfections and choose trousers that will disguise these. It may mean that those chosen will not be the latest fashion, and however "trendy" you may like to be, wear only those trousers which suit and flatter *you*!

B. Even the slimmest girl will not look her best in badly cut and badly fitting trousers, or in ones that do not suit her particular silhouette. If trousers are too short, for example, they will look skimped, as though there was too little fabric available. If they are generally too big, too wide-legged or too long, they appear to add pounds to the wearer's appearance — just the effect that the majority of people do not want. (Underweight girls take note — a generous cut *can* help you here, but length, waist and hip fitting should be smooth. Bulky fabric helps too.)

C. Take careful note of any real leg faults — thick thighs, large calves, thick ankles or large feet — all these can be disguised by a careful choice of style. For girls with fleshy knees, for example, Bermudas are absolutely taboo — whereas knee length culottes, cut to an "A" line can really flatter and make them look smaller in proportion.

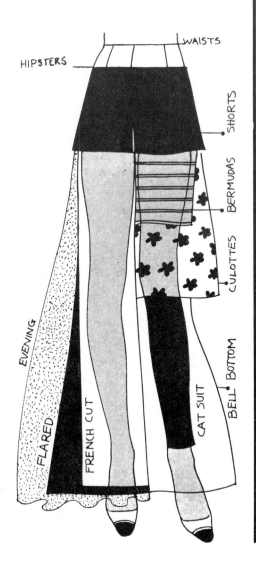

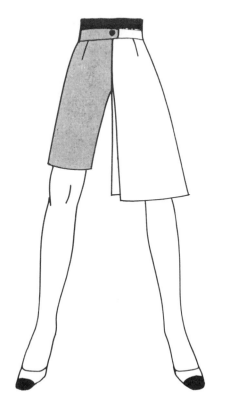

D. Tall, hip-heavy girls will be able to achieve a clean cut, balanced look by wearing a long jerkin or tunic with trousers, thus disguising those few extra pounds and appearing slimmer. Short people, however, need a short, cropped jacket to make the leg line appear as long as possible; long tunics tend to make them look dumpy, rather than emphasising a small and trim figure. Short, plump people, however, can wear a knee length "A" line garment over their trousers in a matching colour to avoid breaking the line. Refer to the following charts to choose the right style.

Trousers - a special case

2. Trouser style selection chart

Figure Fault	Styles to Avoid	Styles to Use
Heavy hips	Hipsters and fitted thighs	The "French Cut" look giving a long straight line from hip to floor as seen from every angle.

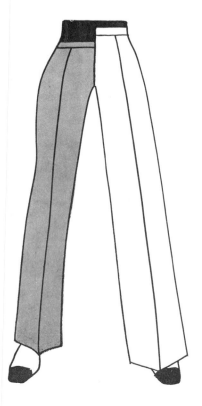

Figure Fault	Styles to Avoid	Styles to Use
Large seat	Hipsters and fitted thighs	Wear shorts with pleats or flare. Long trousers as above.

3. Fitting Style and Size

The principles of trouser-making are very similar to those of skirt-making as far as waist and hip fitting are concerned, and the same rules apply whatever the style of trousers. They may be slim fitting or have full wide legs but as with the skirt, the seams run from the waist down towards the ankle with the warp thread of the fabric running down the centre front and centre back. (Trousers may be cut on the cross if the style is very full and flaring for evening wear, but this is an exception to the general rule.)

Trousers are easy to make, providing very careful attention is paid to the taking of measurements and to fitting. The pattern should be chosen by the waist measurement unless the hip measurement is very much larger than that mentioned on the pattern, in which case choose the pattern by the hip size and adjust the waist to fit. *Choose a pattern that will need as few alterations as possible.*

4. What to Wear under Trousers

Trousers should always be worn with the most flattering underwear. Girdles that are too tight, or pantie girdles that dig into the thighs, change the natural shape of the body and cause unsightly bulges just at the places where they are least wanted. If foundation garments need to be worn, they should be soft and pliable and cause no bulges on the hips or thighs. The best undergarments for trousers are tights with built-in briefs, or very lightweight, long-legged pantie girdles. Girls with fleshy hip/thigh areas who would usually wear firm foundation garments would be well advised to invest in a few pairs of support tights, or even elasticated theatrical tights to give the legs, hips, and thighs overall support and streamlining.

Tight-fitting bikini briefs, under slim-fitting trousers, invariably show through the fabric and spoil the smooth elegant line. It is interesting to note that many European trouser manufacturers make up summer-weight trousers with shaped, interchangeable crotch gussets similar to briefs so that the trousers may be worn without under garments in very hot weather; an idea that could easily be adapted to home dressmaking purposes.

Trousers - a special case

Figure Fault	Styles to Avoid	Styles to Use
Heavy knees	Bermudas — tight mid-thigh shorts (Jamaicas) or fitted shorts. Flares from below knee.	Wear trousers that flare very slightly from just above the knee or from the calf downwards. The straight, French look. Shorts should be pleated or flared.

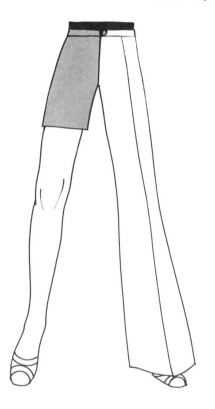

5. Making a Standard Pattern

Once you have found a basic trouser pattern that suits your figure and fits you well you would be wise to make a permanent record of it on some unwoven interfacing. You will then only have to refer to your standard pattern to make the necessary alteration to any other pattern that you may choose — instead of going through the tedious process of taking all those measurements again and again! Remember though — if you gain or lose weight those standard measurements must be revised.

If you happen to have a pair of ready-made pants that really fit well, it would be a good idea to take a pattern from these before they are discarded. Using a stitch ripper and a pair of fine pointed, scissors — carefully unpick the garment until each piece is separate. Press each section carefully and pin out on drafting paper. Be sure that the grain lines of the fabric are placed accurately on the guide lines on the paper and darts and other markings recorded fully. Trousers that have had a lot of wear will generally have spread a little so be prepared for the section of fabric to be perhaps 3 mm larger in the places where strain was taken, and reduce the size accordingly. The pattern can then be transferred to non-woven interfacing for permanence. Always use paper first, it costs less than interfacing if mistakes are made.

Trousers - a special case

Figure Fault	Styles to Avoid	Styles to Use
Thick thighs	Styles that cling at the thigh.	Go for the long straight look, or with slight flare from mid thigh downwards.
Large calves	Tight trousers that cling at the calves.	Wear the long, straight look, or flares from mid thigh or knee.

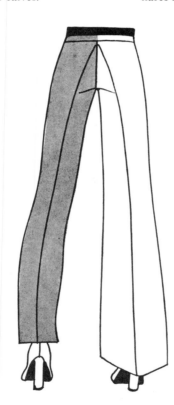

Trousers - a special case

Figure Fault	Styles to Avoid	Styles to Use
Thick ankles	Capris, or trousers that stop short of the ankle — sometimes called ankle flappers.	All the usual styles, but if a shorter look is required Gauchos will flatter — these stop at mid-calf but are wide giving the ankle the illusion of being small.

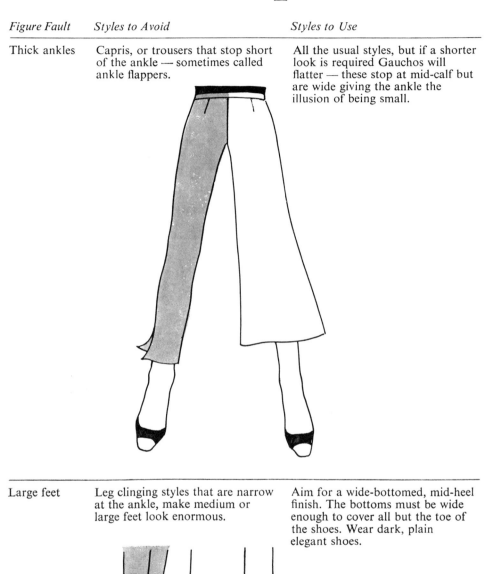

Large feet	Leg clinging styles that are narrow at the ankle, make medium or large feet look enormous.	Aim for a wide-bottomed, mid-heel finish. The bottoms must be wide enough to cover all but the toe of the shoes. Wear dark, plain elegant shoes.

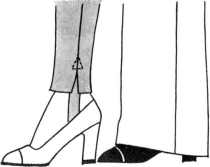

Trousers - a special case

Figure Fault	*Styles to Avoid*	*Styles to Use*
Bandy legged/ Knock kneed	Tubular or tight fitting trousers should not be worn, nor should ankle-flared styles.	Wear the straight look, or styles that flare from just above the knee. Culottes and full-legged styles are also suitable.

Pressing and Ironing

1. The Importance of Pressing

One of the factors that produces a professional finish on any garment is the care and attention given to pressing, right from the preparation stage through to the finished garment. Remember — pressing is *NOT* ironing. In pressing, the iron is lifted, set down, re-lifted and set down, and so on. For many fabrics the hand must bear most of the iron's weight, so that the surface will not be distorted or flattened too much. *AT NO TIME* is the iron moved backwards and forwards across the surface of the fabric as in ironing.

A pressing cloth is needed for success, and the use of steam makes it possible to mould fabrics into shape.

2. Basic Rules for Pressing

PRESS EACH STAGE AS YOU MAKE UP A GARMENT — KEEP THE IRON READY

1. Collect together all the necessary pressing equipment. (See the chapter on Choosing Equipment for details). Clean the iron if needed.

2. Keep some fabric scraps from cutting out to use for pressing tests, they should be large enough for "before and after" pressing comparisons.

3. Always check how the garment fabric stands up to heat, steam and moisture — never use too much of any of these.

4. Use a pressing cloth suitable for the garment fabrics. (For wool — a light, firm woollen cloth. For cotton or cotton blends — a firm cotton cloth). *Never* use a *wet* press cloth. Start with it slightly damp and add more moisture as needed with a sponge. If much more moisture is needed on certain areas use a small brush to wet cloth more liberally.

5. Never press over pins and take out as many tacking threads as possible before pressing.

6. Press on the wrong side of fabrics. Where it is essential to press on the right side, always use a pressing cloth.

7. Try to press with or along the grain of the fabric, or the fabric may stretch.

8. Irons have a range of heat settings for different fabrics — remember to refer to them.

9. NEVER overpress, or the fabric and garment will be spoiled.

10. Use a seam roll under seams, pressing from the wrong side. A tailor's ham, seam roll or end of a sleeveboard should be used for darts.

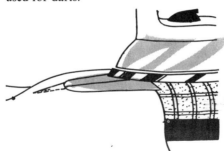

11. Fabrics that are not pre-shrunk, should be shrunk and pressed *before* cutting out.

12. Use brown paper strips under seam allowances, darts or pleats to prevent ridges from appearing on the right side during pressing.

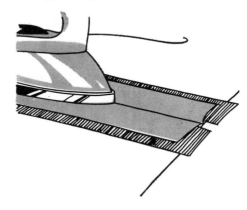

Make sure that the strips are considerably wider than the area to be pressed. For seams in really heavy fabrics dampen them slightly before pressing.

13. Make it a rule to press seams and darts after stitching, or before they are seamed to a further section of the garment. Save time by pressing several seams and darts at the same time.

14. For most fabrics try to keep the weight of the iron in your hand and work with the tip of the iron. Only use a light pressure and do not allow the full weight of the iron to rest on the fabric. Heavier pressure is only needed for firmly woven fabrics or those that tend to be crease resistant.

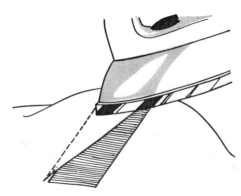

Pressing and Ironing

15. Leave the pressing of creases or sharp edges until you are certain that their position is correct.
16. Generally, press darts, then side seams, then hems. Darts and tacks are pressed along the stitching line, then pressed to one side.
17. If shiny or flattened areas appear on the fabric, hold it over water vapour to revive it.
18. Take care when using a hot iron and steam. Use an iron-holder so that the iron is not left flat on the ironing board.
Switch off and remove the plug from the socket when pressing is finished. It is very helpful to install a socket with a red warning light that lights up when the iron is switched on.

3. Basic Rules for Ironing
1. Have ready all ironing equipment. An iron with a Teflon coated, non-stick sole plate makes the gliding action of ironing easier. Modern aids such as aerosol starch and mist water sprayers also help efficiency.
2. It is most important that fabric is in the right state of dampness for ironing.
3. Iron double parts, eg collars, cuffs, first, starting on the wrong side.
4. Iron on the wrong side for a matt finish, eg for table linen, and on the right side for a glossy finish.
5. Iron with or along the grain of the fabric where possible.

4. Know the Fabric
There are certain points regarding the fabric that should be considered before pressing.
(a) Weight.
(b) Thickness.
(c) Texture.
(d) Fibre content.
Where fabric is made from a blend of fibres always follow instructions for the one that needs the lowest iron temperature.

A. Cotton
Lightweight — use heat setting for silk.
Heavyweight — use heat setting for linen.
Moisture may be used but the fabric must be pressed until dry. Use steam first and then press with steam turned off. Use pressing cloth on the right side when pressing a textured or dull fabric. Chintz and other glossy cottons are pressed dry on the right side to keep the shine. Most cotton is pressed or ironed with a hot iron whilst slightly damp; the fabric must be left completely dry or mildew may occur.

Some drip-dry and minimum-iron cottons are improved by light pressing of seams and edges.

B. Linen
Follow rules for cotton but increase heat and moisture.
Lightweight — use heat setting for cotton.
Heavyweight — use heat setting for linen.

C. Rayon
This needs a low heat — using a steam iron and a light *dry* pressing cloth, press on the wrong side. Always test first.

D. Wool
Woollen fabric should never be subjected to extremes of moisture, heat or pressure. It must never be pressed when very damp or when dry. A moist heat is needed and a wool pressing cloth is preferable.
Lightweight — use heat setting for wool.
Heavyweight — use heat setting between wool and cotton, and preferably a heavier iron.
Should any flattening of the wool pile occur this may be raised with a small, stiff brush immediately after pressing. It is advisable to use two press cloths for wool; a dry one immediately against the surface of the fabric being pressed and then a damp one on top. This will stop press marks or shine appearing.

E. Silk and man-made fabrics
It is seldom necessary to use moisture when pressing these fabrics and when moisture *is* needed only use a minimal amount. Generally a pressing cloth is not needed, but always have a fine cotton one ready to protect fabric just in case. When moisture is needed always test the fabric to see if it water spots. Tissue paper placed between iron and fabric will prevent this. Always use a very low iron temperature as man-made fibres will melt in too great a heat and silk will become brittle.

F. Velvet
Velvet and fabrics with a pile need to be steamed rather than pressed as the surface of the pile needs protection. A velvet board may be used. This has numerous upstanding wires and the fabric is placed pile side down on the board and pressed from the wrong side very lightly, using a slightly damp cloth. If a velvet board is not available use the iron in a vertical position with a dampened cloth placed over the sole plate. The wrong side of the velvet may then be passed to and fro across the surface of the iron plate. The steam passing through the fabric will then

press the velvet without flattening the pile. When pressing velveteen or corduroy, the same methods can be used. Sometimes it will be a good idea, when pressing corduroy on the right side, to use a piece of self fabric (pile side down) as a press cloth. The piles will then interlock and if pressing is kept light no flattening will occur.

G. Lace
Press lace on a bed of several layers of turkish towelling with right side down so that textured surface sinks into the towelling. Use dry pressing cloth and set iron temperature according to fabric type. Always test a spare piece of fabric first. Press very lightly to avoid distortion.

I. PVC and laminated fabrics
Do not use an iron, but hammer with the end of a wooden rolling pin to flatten seams.

J. Elastanes (Lycra, Spanzelle, etc.)
Need no pressing or ironing.

K. Stretch fabrics
Do *not* stretch them whilst pressing. Press seams from the wrong side during making up, and iron very lightly on the wrong side to remove wrinkles.

L. Knitted fabrics
Press in the direction of ribbing using a damp cloth on the wrong side. Avoid stretching during pressing.

M. Fur fabrics
(Do not attempt to press real fur.) To press seams, hems and facings place the fur fabric between two thick, soft towels.

5. Pressing Parts of a Garment
Seams
Press the stitching line to flatten the stitches into the fabric.

Open seams
Push the tip of the iron along to open the turnings. Place a seam roll, or some brown paper, under the seam turnings then press firmly on the wrong side for a flat finish.

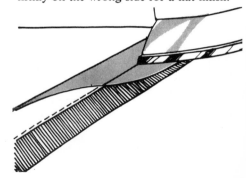

Pressing and Ironing

Enclosed seams
eg. Collar edges — press the stitching line then trim off excess turnings, layering if necessary. Then press the seam open over a seam roll or sleeve board. Turn through and press lightly on the wrong side so that the seam is pushed slightly away from the edge and will not show from the right side.

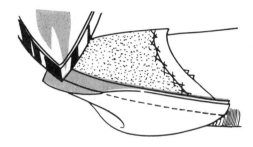

Curved seams
Press the stitching line then clip the seam allowances so that they will lie flat. Press the seam open over a seam roll, tailor's ham or sleeve board.

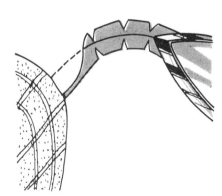

Eased seams
Slightly gathered seams in woollen and some blended fabrics can be pressed to shrink out excess fullness. Use a damp cloth and steam iron with the seam over a curved surface. Steam the fabric by holding the iron *over* the seam not on it. Repeat several times if necessary.

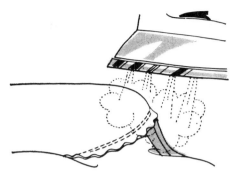

French seams
Press firmly from the wrong side, then lift the seam and push the tip of the iron along to remove any wrinkles in the garment.

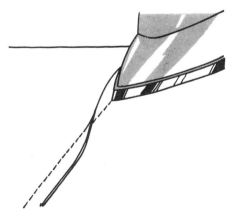

Waist seams
Press them open, or press the turnings up towards the bodice.

Darts
Press them as for a French seam above. If they are cut or trimmed press them as open seams. They should always be pressed over a slightly rounded surface, first pressing the stitching line as for any seam — the iron should not go beyond the point or a crease will appear on the right side.

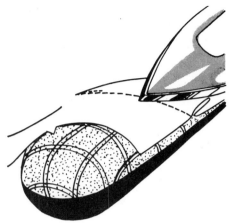

Open the garment out and press the dart lightly from the right side, starting at the wider end. Press underarm and elbow darts downwards. Press waist darts towards the centre front and centre back. Press shoulder darts towards the neckline.

Tucks
Use very little steam or the stitching lines may pucker. Press on the wrong side. Rub the wrong side of pin-tucked fabric over the upturned sole plate of the iron to make the tucks stay upright.

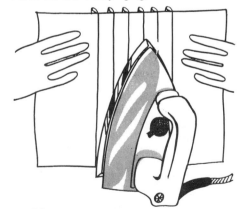

Pleats
Remove all pins but leave tacking threads in place (remember that a fine thread should be used for tacking pleats). With the garment right side down on the ironing board, arrange the pleats carefully into place; use a chair to support any of the garment that hangs off the board. Press lightly over a damp pressing cloth or use a steam iron and dry cloth.

Pressing and Ironing

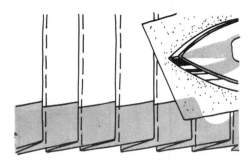

Hold the garment up or try it on, to check that the pleats still hang correctly. Now press heavily to set the sharp creases, first putting strips of brown paper under the folds.

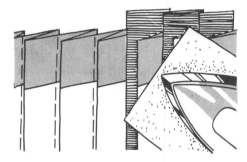

Remove all tacking, and rearrange the pleats with the wrong side down on the ironing board; pin into place if necessary. Press carefully and lightly, then let the fabric remain there until it is completely dry.

Sleeves
With wrong side out, arrange the head over the sleeve board or tailor's ham. Press the seam towards the armhole, moving it round the board as you work.

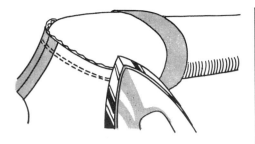

Gathers
Hold the rows of stitching in the left hand, and, from the wrong side, push the point of the iron up into the folds towards the stitches. Take care not to crease the folds.

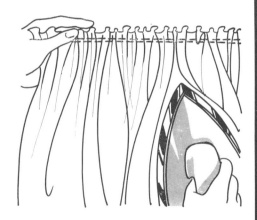

Fastenings
Avoid pressing over press studs, hooks and eyes and buttons or impressions will be made on the garment — press carefully around them, placing the tip of the iron very close.

For zips place the opening right side down onto a thick, soft cloth on the ironing board. Press carefully on the wrong side, using very little moisture or puckers may form. When pressing from the right side place strips of brown paper between zip and placket edges.

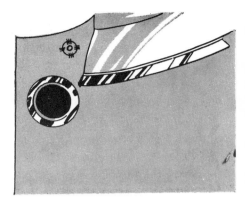

Hems
(See also chapter on Hems.)
Remove all pins and tacking from the finished hem. From the wrong side of the garment press the lower edge firmly using a damp pressing cloth, or steam. Pound the edge with the back of a clothes brush if a really crisp edge is required. Press the top of the hem very lightly or a ridge will form on the right side.

If a soft, lower edge is preferred, steam the hem without letting the weight of the iron rest on the fabrics. Gently pat the edge with the back of a clothes brush to set it into place then let the fabric dry completely.

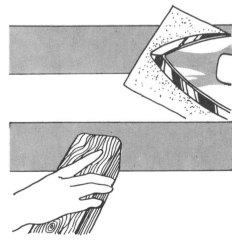

6. Final Pressing of Complete Garment
Although all parts of a garment will have been pressed during the making up process, it is still very important to touch-up the finished article. This will not

Pressing and Ironing

put right careless sewing but will very much improve the final appearance. Where possible do this with the garment on a dress form, but it may be done on a hanger (note that wire clothes hangers are not good for clothes as they mark the shoulder and do not let them hang well). Steam and pull small sections into shape where necessary, putting crumpled soft tissue paper inside to pad out curves until the fabric dries. Let the fabric dry completely before taking the garment from the dress form or hanger. Press in the following order to avoid creasing the areas already touched up:

1. Collars and facings.
2. Sleeves.
3. Bodice and waist seam if any.
4. Skirt.
5. Belts and trimmings.

Trimming and Decoration

1. **A Few Simple Rules to Remember**

2. **Some Suitable Trimmings**
   Hand embroidery
   Saddle stitching
   Decorative tacks
   Machine embroidery
   Topstitching by machine
   Monograms
   Smocking
   Quilting
   Appliqué
   Braids and ribbon
   Bows and ties
   Decorative fastenings
   Fringing, tassels and pom-poms
   Tassels
   Pom-poms
   Fur and feathers
   Lace
   Leather and suede
   Patchwork
   Frills
   Sequins and beads
   Miscellaneous

There are very many ways to make clothes interesting and original by the use of added decoration in some form. A plain, lifeless looking fabric can be made more exciting and acceptable by the addition of braid or ribbon, lace or appliqué. Even a good quality remnant bargain in a colour you would not normally choose can make a useful addition to your wardrobe by using a favourite trimming — take it to the trimmings counter before purchase to see if there is something suitable, but bear in mind that some are now very expensive, so the garment may not be a bargain in the end.

Whatever trimming is used it should always complement the fabric and style of the garment. A heavy, embroidered braid on a richly textured evening dress fabric would lose its impact and look tasteless. On the other hand, imaginative use of trimmings on a plain style can give it an exotic or ethnic look.

Avoid fussy or frilly trimming on casual or tailored day wear, keeping instead to simple braid, ribbon, etc. Evening wear can carry elaborate trimming, beading, feathers, etc. in the traditional manner or in more unusual ways. In general, use simple trims with elaborate fabric and styles, elaborate trims with simple fabrics and styles. Search in upholstery departments too, for trimmings with unusual textures or make your own if you have a modern super automatic sewing machine. Remember that an out-dated garment can be up-dated with a new and stylish trimming.

1. A Few Simple Rules to Remember
1. Do not detract from the line of the garment by adding decorations in odd places — use them to emphasise the line and any unusual features without spoiling the balance of the style.

2. Never add bright decoration at figure fault points. This will only tend to emphasise them.
3. Make sure, before you start a garment, exactly when the decorative effects should be added. Some are added during construction and some are added afterwards.

4. Aim to have trimmings of the same type of fabric as the garment, ie cotton on cotton, and sew them on with the correct thread. Where this is not possible, in the case of cotton braid to be applied to a man-made fabric for example, pre-shrink the braid before use. If you do not pay attention to details like this the garment may take on a puckered look after washing.
5. Test stitching techniques on scraps of the same fabric and trimming before starting on the garment so that if there are any problems these can be overcome without spoiling the garment fabric.

2. Some Suitable Trimmings
Decorative stitches and embroidery (see also chapter on Stitches and Threads)
   (*a*) *Hand embroidery*
This may be applied very easily to most fabrics, taking the form of a stylised design embroidered on collar, cuffs and belt, for example, or used to decorate a complete section of the garment before it is cut out, as with an embroidered yoke or sleeve. If large areas are to be embroidered it is better to do this before the section is cut out or the garment made up; otherwise the garment will be overhandled and look grubby and soiled,

Trimming and Decoration

even before it is worn. Embroidery is, in any case, easier to carry out on a small piece of fabric.

The design should be ironed on from a transfer, thread traced or chalked onto a piece of fabric slightly larger than the garment section. Mark the outline of the garment pattern piece onto the fabric and then work the embroidery inside this outline.

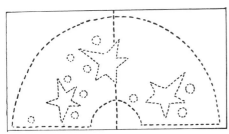

To support the fabric and keep it smooth whilst embroidering (especially if the fabric is flimsy) tack a piece of fine muslin or organdie onto the wrong side of the area. Use a fine non-woven interlining, such as Lantor on medium to heavyweight fabrics (test a scrap of fabric and interlining first).

The backing fabric can, on some occasions, be cut away after the embroidery has been carried out, whilst on others it may be better to leave it and include it in the construction of the garment.

"Vanishing Muslin", available from embroidery specialists, may also be used.

This is a chemical gauze that will pull apart easily by gentle tearing, or may be ironed off with a warm to hot iron after the embroidery is finished. It provides support whilst the work is being carried out and can be dispensed with afterwards. Small motifs may be embroidered after the garment is made up. The same rules apply — if the fabric needs support use a backing. On finished collars and cuffs, though, there will generally be an interfacing as well as two layers of fabric, and this will suffice.

(b) Saddle stitching
This is used on tailored or casual sports wear and is simple to carry out on a completed garment.

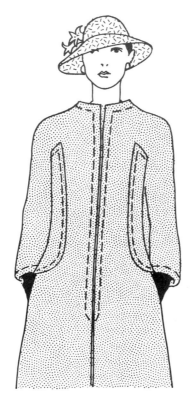

Evenly spaced running stitches, usually 6 mm – 10 mm long, are used to emphasise collar edges, pockets, etc. A contrasting colour is usually used and may be Dewhurst Sylko Perlé, Strong Thread, doubled Sylko or Star.

(c) Decorative tacks — Arrowhead and Crow's Foot
Use these for strength and decoration of pockets and pleats (for method see chapter on Stitches and Thread).

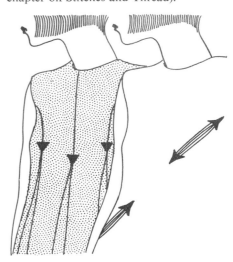

(d) Machine embroidery
Automatic

This may be used in a similar way to hand embroidery and the same rules apply. With machine embroidery it is absolutely *essential* that backing is used in one form or another. The sewing machine, when set to an embroidery stitch, makes a stitch with a very strong pull which tends to pinch the fabric into puckers unless it is well supported. The top tension may be slackened off to eliminate this a little, but this is seldom sufficient.

The following backings may be used:
(a) Non-woven interlining such as Lantor.
(b) Iron-on interlining such as Lantor or Stayflex.
(c) Vanishing muslin.
(d) Organdie or a firm, fine fabric of similar weight.
(e) Architect's tracing paper, or grease-proof paper.
The backing should be evenly tacked or pinned to the wrong side of the fabric to be embroidered. Guide lines for the design should be trace tacked or lightly chalked onto the right side of the fabric. Where an elaborate design is required, this may be drawn on tracing paper first, the paper

Trimming and Decoration

then placed in position on the fabric and machine stitched from the top to transfer the design in line stitching to the fabric. A large variety of suitable threads is available. For a very bold effect, two threads may be threaded through the eye of the needle and used as one. If a heavy needle is selected, Dewhurst Sylko Perlé No 8 may be used through it — this will give the effect of "peasant embroidery", being heavy and textured. Fine cobweb wool may be wound on to a reel and used, as long as the needle is big enough, and Lurex may be effective on evening wear if used carefully. Rows of automatic embroidery stitches may be grouped together to give braided effects that very often look more impressive than the purchased braids themselves.

It is well worth while spending an hour or two every so often experimenting with automatic machine embroidery stitches. Some of the sewing machine companies producing these automatic machines also publish books of ideas, showing many ways in which embroidery stitches may be grouped and mixed to give interesting effects. Always make sure that the thread used is matched in type to the fabric, or, if this is not possible, or the effect not right, pre-shrink the yarn by winding it loosely on a reel by hand and immersing it in soapy water for a minute or two. It should then be rinsed and allowed to dry on the reel and then be rewound more firmly.

Free

If you have an idea for a design of your own you may like to use the free embroidery technique. To do this the feed teeth on the sewing machine will need to be covered or dropped (check with the machine handbook) and the fabric fixed into an embroidery hoop to hold it taut. The sewing foot is removed, and the machine is generally used without a foot of any kind. With many machines there is a darning/embroidery foot that may be used, but this can sometimes block your vision when producing some very detailed stitching. On heavy fabrics it may not be necessary to use an embroidery hoop, but with one, the results are generally better. With this embroidery it is entirely up to the machine operator to use the needle and thread to make the design. This must be done by moving the hoop backwards and forwards — from side to side, or in circles or scrolls. If the work is not moved the machine will just stitch on the spot. Always remember to put the foot take-up lever down before sewing. Without the foot there as a reminder this is easily forgotten and will result in tangled thread. The straight stitch or the zig-zag machine may be used and with practice some lovely designs may be carried out. The hoop should be moved smoothly and slowly and the machine run fairly fast, as a general rule.

(e) Topstitching by machine
This is a popular and simple way of decorating completed garments by emphasising the line or the details. It is also used when making some pockets, collars, pleats, etc., to keep the seams and edges in place. Use double Sylko or Star through the needle in a matching or contrasting colour. Try the stitch length, pressure and tension first on a scrap of the fabric. Test on the same number of layers as for the final garment stitching.

The placing of topstitching is important as it must be evenly spaced from, and parallel to, the edge; use a guide and stitch slowly and carefully. If necessary, chalk or thread trace the line before starting.

Trimming and Decoration

Pivot the work at corners, and sew in the threads at the ends for a neat look. Topstitching may be worked by hand but it is slow and time consuming.

(f) Monograms

A lovely way to personalise a garment of your own or something that you have made for a friend, monograms may be machined or hand embroidered in satin stitch. Initials may be purchased ready to stitch on, or may be embroidered directly onto the garment fabric. As with other embroidery it is wise to back the fabric area, to give it support and to avoid distortion.

Iron-on transfers are available, but you may wish to design your own initials. Do this on tracing paper and transfer the outline to the fabric with thread-traced lines or tailor's chalk. If the monogram is to be machine stitched, use an embroidery hoop to hold the fabric taut, but do not stretch it. Satin stitch or another embroidery stitch may be used. Refer to the sewing machine hand-book.

Monograms may also be made using the appliqué method.

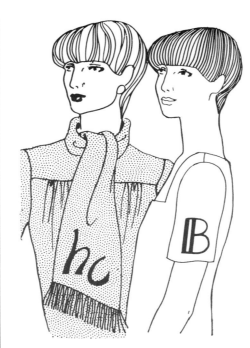

(g) Smocking

This is a beautiful method of controlling and decorating very full areas such as yokes, cuffs, etc.

Extra fabric is needed to create the many close folds or gauging on which the smocking stitches are worked. (See chapter on Gathering and Shirring.) Most smocking is done by hand in a combination of single stitches such as cable or honeycomb. (See chapter on Stitches and Threads.)

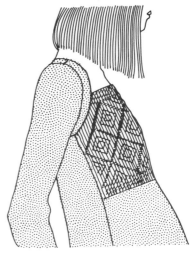

It is possible to simulate hand smocking by using decorative machine-stitching on top of rows of shirring. Prepare the garment area for decoration by shirring as described in the chapter on Gathering and Shirring then work machine embroidery stitches between or over the lines of shirring.

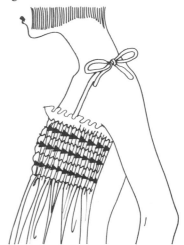

Trimming and Decoration

(h) Quilting

Complete garment sections, or small areas of a garment, may be quilted as a decoration or to add warmth, or both.

There are several methods of quilting two or more layers of fabric, or fabric may be bought already quilted. Complete quilting before cutting out garment pieces. The garment fabric, a padded inner layer such as domette, Courtelle padding, or something similar, plus a backing fabric are sandwiched together and held with stitching.

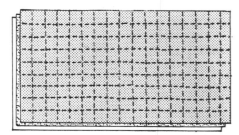

This may be in straight rows, squares or diamonds or may outline the fabric pattern and will produce a raised, padded effect. All layers should be carefully pinned and tacked together before sewing — with slippery fabrics all over tacking at intervals may be needed.

When machine quilting in rows, use the quilting guide that is usually supplied with a sewing machine. This helps to line up each row with the previous one and keeps the lines parallel and equidistant. Trapunto-type quilting leaves the background unpadded so that the design stands out.

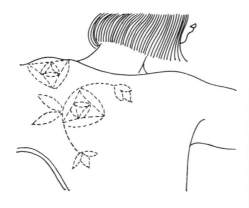

Create your own design or buy a special quilting transfer. The section to be quilted must be backed with a firm but soft fabric tacked in place and then the outline stitched around with small running stitches. The pocket formed then needs padding, by threading thick strands of matching thread through a bodkin and taking them to and fro through the backing fabric until the whole area is padded. Alternatively a slit can be made in the backing, padding pushed through and carefully positioned in the pocket and the slit sewn up. The effects will be very similar. Another way is to place the padding in position with the backing under the area to be quilted — and easing out the padding or clipping it so that there is little bulk on the stitching lines. Choose whichever method seems most suitable.

Appliqué

Separate pieces of fabric are positioned on the top of the fabric and stitched into place by hand or machine.

Attractive, amusing and trendy motifs can be bought, but it is much cheaper to make them. Ideas can be collected from women's magazines, children's drawing books, etc., and made from firm fabric that will not fray. Patches can also be appliquéd on, either simply as a decoration or to strengthen or repair the garment — use contrasting or patterned fabrics (See Chapter on Care and Repair of Clothes for method of attaching patches).

Appliqué by Hand

Draw or trace the design onto a piece of suitable fabric, which can have a piece of lightweight iron-on interlining applied to the wrong side; this prevents fraying and keeps the appliqué in shape. Run a row of fine running stitches all round outline before trimming design to shape. Tack motif into place and blanket stitch into position with contrasting or matching thread.

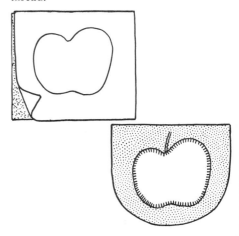

Trimming and Decoration

An alternative way to finish the edges of appliqué is to turn the raw edges to the wrong side along outline and then slipstitch the motif invisibly into position. With this method any backing used should only come as far as the stitching line leaving the turning supple and easy to manipulate.

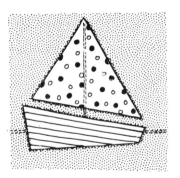

Appliqué by Machine

1. The chosen design should be simplified and then drawn out on tracing paper, with a seam allowance all round.

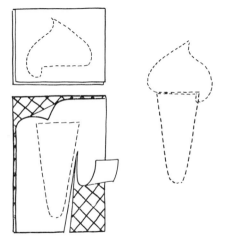

2. The paper should then be pinned to the fabric where required and the outlines machine stitched. The paper may then be pulled away.

3. If the design only requires one layer of applied fabric the procedure is very simple. The fabric should be positioned on the right side and pinned or tacked into place. From the WRONG side, using the machine traced outline, the fabric should then be stitched into place using a STRAIGHT stitch.

4. On the right side the excess fabric should be cut away just outside the stitching line. Then — using a satin stitch or suitable embroidery stitch — the outline should be stitched from the right side to enclose the cut edges.

5. Where more than one layer of fabric is to be applied, remember to apply them in the right order. Smaller details in the design are always added towards the end.

Heat Bonded

It is possible to purchase a sewing aid called Bondaweb, which can be sandwiched between the appliqué and the garment. When ironed according to the maker's instructions, it fuses or bonds the appliqué to the garment. It also helps to eliminate fraying during the cutting and sewing stages.

Braids and ribbon

There is a very wide selection of braids and ribbons available; narrow or wide; flat or textured; plain or fancy. They can generally be grouped as follows:

1. Plain flat ribbon braid and grosgrain Method — these may be stitched into place by hand or straight machining along both sides. Instead of stitching ribbon to a garment in the usual way, try using it to lace up an opening, as a fringe, as a sash round the waist, for basket-weave sleeves, or for crosses or rosebuds on a very feminine outfit.

Leaflets on the uses of ribbon are available from some haberdashery departments. When applying braid be sure to start and finish where the ends will not show. Test sew a practice piece before sewing any onto the garment. Then tack the required length into place. Bands of braid and ribbon may also be inserted between two garment pieces during construction, or used in this way to lengthen a garment that is too short.

A very wide braid or ribbon may need two rows of stitching close to the edges, but narrow ones may be stitched into place with one row of zig-zag or another decorative stitch. Embroidery stitches, in matching or contrasting colours, may also be used. The decorative effect is often improved if more than one row or colour of braid is used. When starting and finishing the sewing, overcast the braid ends and turn them under 6 mm. Sew into place with tiny, hidden slipstitches for a fine finish.

2. Soutache braid. This is a narrow bias-woven braid, often used to outline a rounded design or a style line, or to create a peasant look.

Trimming and Decoration

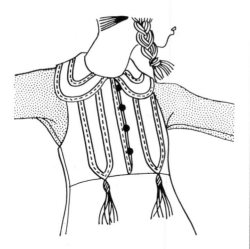

Method — it may be stitched into place with one row of stitching down the middle. The design should be marked in chalk or thread tracing, and the braid tacked into place. Slipstitch or machine into place — when machining use a see-through embroidery foot.

3. Embroidered braids are treated in the same way as plain ribbon — sewn along either side by hand or machine. These should be carefully chosen to complement the basic fabric colour. Be very selective when choosing patterned braid to go on a patterned fabric — if in doubt, don't!

Metallic braids are attractive on evening clothes and tapestry-type braids look good on peasant styles. Amusing braids can be used for children's clothes and many other effects can be created by combining braid with ruffles, bows, machine embroidery, etc.

4. Ric-rac. Available in a vast number of colours and sizes and relatively inexpensive. Many rows may be used together or two pieces may be "wound around" one another to form one braid with an unusual effect. It is available with a matt effect for day wear or in shining metallic form for evening clothes.
To apply it, either stitch straight along the centre or slipstitch it into place along either side — sometimes it may only be necessary to catch down the points. It may be inserted into seams or used under the edges of garment sections so that only the points show. Make sure that the thread matches exactly when only surface stitching is used.

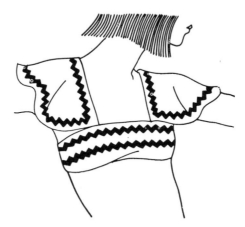

5. Folded braid — or military braid — available in wool, rayon or man-made fibres. Ideal for enclosing raw edges on cuffs, collars, etc. May be pressed into curves for rounded edges — generally only available in plain colours, unpatterned.

Bows and ties
A pretty pussy cat bow or a smart tailored one added to a garment can alter its character completely. Last year's fashions can be updated in this way and with interchangeable bows and belts in different colours, one outfit can be worn on many occasions.

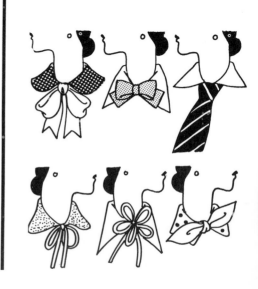

Trimming and Decoration

A drab looking evening dress may be given a new lease of life by adding a beautiful satin sash and bow at waist level, or just below the bust. Bows and ties can be made from all manner of fabrics — knitted, woven, glittery, or plain. Ribbon — satin or grosgrain — can be used for flat bows and many of the fabric cuttings from garments can be utilised in this way. Plain shirts with a bow or a tie at the neckline can be made to look very smart. It is a good idea to attach the bow to a length of elastic for quickness. Kipper ties may also be attached in this way — eliminating the need to have an extra layer of fabric around the neck. Bows may be made from fabric on the straight or bias and there are no specific rules except that all raw edges should be turned in and neatly finished, and the bow should suit the garment with which it is to be worn. There are patterns available for both bows and ties in a variety of styles.

Making a tied bow — if ribbon or braid is to be finished with a bow, or for a sash where the two ends are tied, a neat bow is essential or the whole effect is spoiled. Make a single knot in the usual way, keeping the two ends even in length. Make the first loop with the lower piece, then bring the other end down and round the first loop, making a knot. Now hold the first loop in place, make a second loop and pull it through. Both loops can be pulled tight so that the bow is even in size and the two loose ends are more or less even. Arrange the knot so that it lies flat.

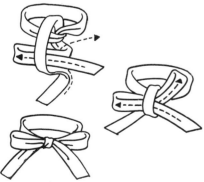

Making a tailored bow — this kind of bow is made up and sewn together, not re-tied each time the garment is worn. Use a finely woven ribbon, or a piece of

the garment fabric made into a flat tube. (See the method for Rouleau in the chapter on Fastenings.) Cut a length of ribbon twice the required width of the finished bow; fold it, and stitch across a little over halfway from the fold. Flatten out the loop that is formed so that the stitching lies on the centre fold. Tack into place then press lightly. Take a shorter piece of ribbon and fold it round the centre of the bow; then stitch it into place at the back.

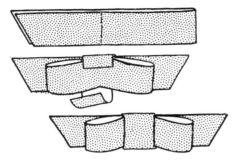

Decorative fastenings

See the chapter on Buttons and Buttonholes, and Fastenings for ideas.

Fringing, tassels and pom-poms

Bought fringing and tassels can be more economical with time and money than hand-made ones, especially if a large quantity is needed. Most lampshade fringing is very reasonably priced and used cleverly will not be recognised for what it is. It may be added to the edge of stoles or ponchos to give them a luxury look for evening wear. Like braid, fringing often looks best in two or more rows. To make fringe — wind any number of yarns round a length of double folded heavy tracing paper the depth of fringe required, inserting a piece of seam binding along one edge. When enough yarn has been wound, sew two or three rows of machining along one edge through yarn, tape and paper.

The perforation made by the needle will allow the paper to be torn away after stitching and the loops that are left may be cut. The yarn must be wound very evenly and quite a number of paper sections will need to be joined to make a long length. This may be an expensive project so make quite sure that the style or colour fringe that you require is not available commercially.

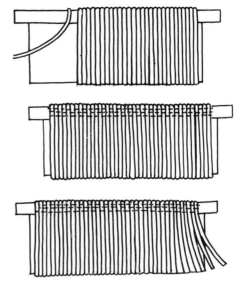

Self fringe — most soft, thick fabrics can have threads pulled out to make a self fringe. Try it on a scrap of the fabric to see if the effect is attractive. Straighten the edge to be fringed by cutting along the grain. Decide how deep the fringe needs to be then pull out a cross thread on this line.

Machine with a narrow zig-zag stitch along this line so that the lengthwise threads are secured in place, then pull out all the crosswise threads below the stitching.

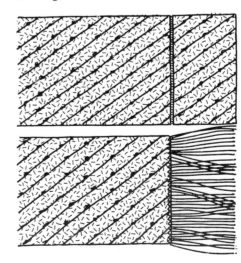

Trimming and Decoration

Fringe made with sewing machine — the rug fork that is available for use with sewing machines may also be used to make fringes. Yarn is wound around the fork and stitched using a zipper foot directly onto seam tape on fabric as each section is wound. After one section has been stitched the fork is slipped out carefully until it is almost out of the loops — exposed part of the fork is rewound and the loops stitched down, and so on, until the required amount has been made. Loops may be left as they are or cut.

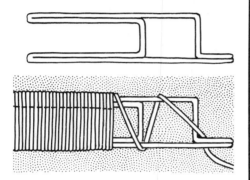

To apply — fringe may be applied under or over an edge, depending on the effect required. If it is to be applied under an edge it must be invisibly slipstitched into place very securely on both edges of the supporting band. If a surface application is required it may be hand or machine stitched using a matching thread.

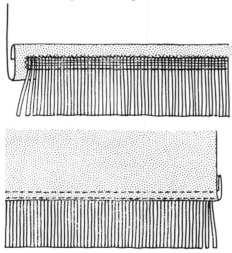

Tassels
They may be bought or made, and applied singly or in rows. To make tassels — cut a piece of cardboard the required width and lay a double strand of the yarn across the top of the card, wind yarn around until there is enough to make a tassel, then tie the double strand round the yarn and remove the card. Tie another double thread round the yarn about 13 mm below the top. Cut the lower loops.

Pom-poms
Make them in the same way as for tassels above, but with much more yarn. Otherwise wind the yarn round two or three fingers, then tie yarn around the middle and cut both ends.

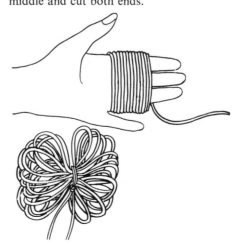

Large, fluffy pom-poms are often made in wool and used to trim knitted scarves and hats. Cut two thick cardboard circles the diameter of the pom-pom needed — use an egg-cup, coffee cup, etc. Cut a smaller circle from the middle, remembering that if this circle is too large a lot of yarn is needed and the pom-pom becomes very heavy. With the two pieces together, wind yarn round and round until the centre hole is nearly closed up, then thread the yarn through a bodkin and keep winding. Cut the strands at the outer edge, and gently push the two pieces of card apart. Take a new piece of doubled yarn or strong thread and tie it tightly round all the threads at the centre, between the two pieces of card. Pull card away.
Leave a long end to this thread with which to sew on the pom-pom. Carefully arrange the cut ends to make a round fluffy ball, trimming off any straggly ends.

CUT 2

Fur and feathers
Fur trimming, real or imitation, can be purchased by the metre in many qualities, wide and narrow. If real fur is to be used

Trimming and Decoration

it is wise to make it detachable as it must not be cleaned by normal dry-cleaning processes. Press studs may be sewn to the lining of the trimming and the garment at the points where it needs securing. Fur collars and cuffs may be purchased ready made and simply slip-stitched neatly into place.

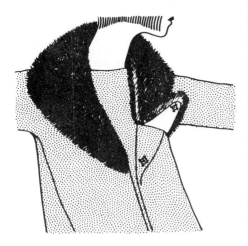

Swan's down and feathers, also purchased by the metre or in strips, are ready to stitch to the garment — they need securing by the stem at intervals, lightly but securely, so that the feathers or down may be eased out to hide the stitches. Feathers are available in every shade imaginable and make a plain garment really exotic.

Lace

This is available in a wide variety of styles — as flat edging or insertion, gathered, re-embroidered, pleated, motifs in cotton or nylon, and in many colours. It can be combined with other trimmings eg. slotted with ribbon for a specially pretty effect.

Fine lace is used on lingerie and baby clothes, whilst thick Guipure types look beautiful on special occasion clothes. Lace edging may be used on collars, cuffs and hems — around pockets and inserted in between seams.

Joined guipure lace motifs may be purchased by the metre and then cut up into individual sections and used according to the desired effect. Cotton lace may easily be dyed to match the fabric that you are using and, providing that care is taken to make sure that the dye is fast, the long term results can be splendid.
Do not risk distorting the lace. Carefully decide whether it should be applied by hand or machine. Most simple lace bands or edgings may be attached to fabric using a narrow machine zig-zag stitch — length $1 - 1\frac{1}{4}$, width $1 - 1\frac{1}{2}$. If there is a transparent embroidery foot with your machine use this to see clearly and exactly where the stitches are falling. (There are other attachable feet that can be used, but in almost every case the transparent embroidery foot is best.)
The cut end of lace edging should be narrowly hemmed or rolled. To join lace use plain seam — trim away turnings to 3 mm and overcast, or use a fine french seam if you are not able to overcast on your machine. The *best* way to join lace however is to lap the edges to be joined, placing them so that there is no break in the design. If there is a pronounced motif in the overlap cut around this and carefully whip stitch it to the underlayer.

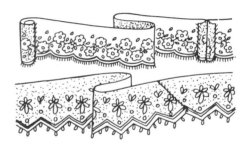

One motif will therefore be double at this point. The excess fabric may be cut away at the back afterwards. On the sewing machine a narrow zig-zag stitch may be used to do this.
As a general rule, if the edges of any lace band are straight it may be applied by machine, but if the edges are curved or scalloped, it is simpler to handstitch it into place. The stitches should be invisible and enclose the edge of the lace. This is called whip stitching.
Insertion of lace in blouses and dresses has become particularly popular recently. The lace is tacked into position and stitched either by hand or machine depending upon whether the edges are straight or curved. If a zig-zag stitch is used, the fabric underneath may be cut away along the edges of the stitches. If a straight stitch is used, the under fabric should be cut along the middle — the edges finished and then pressed back towards the garment fabric, and caught down.

Trimming and Decoration

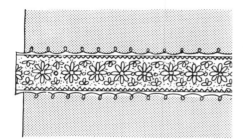

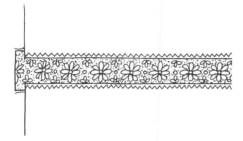

When lace is to be applied to a corner it must either be mitred on the inside edge or gathered so that it will lie flat.

Lace may be bought already gathered or pleated but it can also be done at home. On some lace a thread may be drawn up on one edge. It may be gathered by machine, using the bottom thread to draw up the fullness or with a gathering foot. For pleating, the pleating attachment that is available for some sewing machines will prove very useful. Beware of using too little lace when a gathered effect is required, or the result may look skimpy.

A good guide is to use at least 2½ times the required length.

Leather and Suede

Small pieces of leather, real or imitation, may be used to trim a garment with simple patches, bands, binding, thonging, etc.

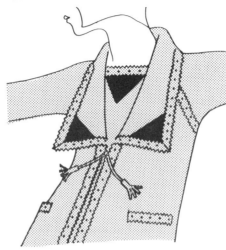

Real leather and suede are now available in beautiful colours including gold and silver, and some of them are washable. They are available in squares and whole skins, but not, of course, by the metre. Choose a simple design for the trim, and appliqué it to the surface of the garment. Buy ready-made thonging or cut very narrow strips, then thread them through eyelets in the garment.

Patchwork

(See the "Learning about Sewing" project wallet on Patchwork for details.) Left over scraps of fabrics can be put together and made into patchwork belts, pockets, etc., to trim a plain garment. Choose an effective combination of colours and shapes for the best effect, experimenting until it looks just right before sewing.

Frills

As with other forms of trimming, there is quite a variety of frilled and pleated trimmings available. Broderie anglaise, for example, is available in many widths, both light and heavily embroidered. The frilling is usually inserted into a band which may be concealed under the edge of the fabric and sewn on by machine, or by hand-slipstitching, according to desired

effect. Almost any fine or medium weight fabric may be frilled or pleated. For frilling, one side of the fabric strip may be gathered and the free edge narrowly hemmed or rolled. A jersey fabric may have a lettuce edge for an extra full effect. (See the chapter on Hems for details.) The fabric strip may be finished on either side and the gathering or pleating carried out along the centre line. In the latter case, the ruffle would be applied by stitching it to the garment along the centre gathering line. Use fabric on the straight or the true bias, the width of frill required plus turnings. Frills may also be made with scalloped edges or edges bound with a contrasting or matching binding. An attractive edge may also be made by using the scallop embroidery stitch that some automatic machines are able to make. The edge of the fabric should be folded under and the stitch worked right on the edge. By using this method the edge is strong and it is not necessary to cut around the scallops.

Sequins and beads

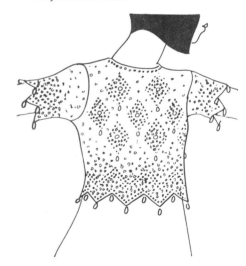

Both may be purchased in four ways — loose, in packets, in strands, as ready-made banding to attach to garment lines or edges, or in motifs. The last two are probably the quickest and easiest to handle. Ropes of sequins or beads can be stitched down in any design required, providing that the design is first chalk marked or trace tacked onto the fabric.

Trimming and Decoration

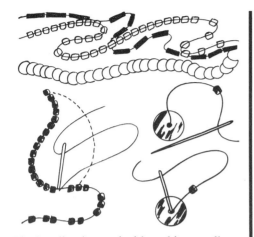

The banding is attached by taking small stitches at intervals over the thread between the beads or sequins. Curves and scroll designs are easy to attach in this way.

Individual sequins and beads may be used to highlight a fabric design, eg a flower centre, and are attached by taking the thread through the fabric, through the hole in the bead or sequin, and back through the fabric. If they are closely spaced, the thread can be carried on from bead to bead after finishing each one securely. If wide apart, each one should be finished individually. For a well-finished look, a sequin may be secured by colour matching a bead to it. Bring the thread up through the sequin, through the bead and back through the sequin to the wrong side. Sequined or beaded motifs may also be slipstitched invisibly into position.

Miscellaneous

Other methods of decorating garments, such as tucks, pleats, binding piping, facings, etc., can be found in the appropriate chapters in Volume Two.

Care and Repair of Clothes

1. **Wardrobe and Workbasket**
2. **Tidiness and Routine**
3. **Minor Problems**
4. **Personal Hygiene**
5. **Washing Clothes**
   Some washing problems
6. **Dry Cleaning**
   Do-it-yourself dry cleaning
   Dry cleaning services
7. **Stain Removal**
   General methods for removing spots and stains
8. **Repairs**
   Buttons and buttonholes
   Collars and cuffs
   Pockets
   Elastic
   Worn edges
   Darning
   Patching

Even in these days of very casual clothes, to be well groomed is still important. Even if clothes and fashions are of little personal interest it is most important to make sure that they are clean and well-cared for; in this way it is possible to get the maximum value out of them. A little time spent on organising a routine for grooming will pay dividends; there will be no last minute panic every morning or on special occasions.

1. Wardrobe and Workbasket

Try to arrange enough storage space for clothes or they will become crushed and soiled in storage. Take out seasonal clothes not currently in use, clean them and put them away. Arrange hanging and drawer space so that all similar items are together eg. all jumpers in one drawer, all heavyweight dresses at one end of the wardrobe, light ones at the other. Some people prefer to store complete outfits in one place each one accompanied by the current accessories, but this is usually unnecessary if a sensible storage system has been thought out. Do allow air to circulate in the storage place or clothes may smell musty. Use the new type of moth-repellent as it has little obvious smell.

Assemble a small workbasket of supplies for repairing and mending clothes and if possible, keep it in a place near to where clothes are stored. If these items are kept elsewhere or scattered around the house there is little incentive to attend promptly to problems.

2. Tidiness and Routine

Set aside a few minutes every evening to care for the clothes and accessories that have been used that day and to prepare those for the next day. Take note of any items needing repair and have regular mending sessions to deal with them. Deal with minor problems as they arise. No one daily system will suit everyone but bear in mind the following:

1. Hang all garments up after wear. (Brush outdoor clothes first.) Close all fastenings, then leave the clothes to air before putting them away. Use good quality hangers.
2. Wipe over greasy collars and necklines on clothes that cannot be washed with a grease-solvent — either a proprietary cleanser or a little carbon tetrachloride on a pad. Air the clothes and the room after doing this.
3. Wash undies and tights every night.
4. Empty, clean and restock handbag.
5. Put out clothes and accessories for the next day; remember that they last longer if not used every day.
6. Deal with any stains or spots immediately without giving them time to become immovable.

3. Minor Problems

Buttons and buttonholes — sew on any lost or loose buttons. Buttonholes on bought clothes unravel easily, so check that there are no loose threads that might pull them undone.
Fluff or pilling — if this is loose remove it by winding sticky tape round the hand (sticky side out) and rubbing it over the fabric surface. Special clothes "brushes" are now available to do this job. On knitwear remove "pilling" with a special gadget which only costs a few pence.
Hems — resew the complete hem on bought garments if they begin to come undone in one place. Make emergency repairs if away from home by using double-sided sticky tape.

Pulled threads — do not cut these but ease them back into place with a pin; if loops are left pull these through to the wrong side where they will not show. (A needle threader is the ideal aid when doing this.)
Tears and holes — darn or patch these as appropriate. An emergency repair can be made to a tear by ironing on a piece of special adhesive mending tape.
Valeting — at regular intervals it is necessary to pay particular attention to some garments, even though they may not yet need dry cleaning.
Work in an area where an iron and ironing board are available. Have ready clean pressing cloths, a sleeve board and a clean strong clothes brush.
Trousers — shake and brush them thoroughly. Press them carefully, paying particular attention to the creases. A hard household soap block may be rubbed along the crease line on the wrong side, to make sharper creases when pressed in the normal way. This also works for pleats in skirts.
If shiny — sponge with a solution of vinegar and water for light colours. (Use about 25 ml to 500 ml water.) Wring out a cloth in clear water and rinse the area. Using a damp cloth under the iron steam lightly on both sides of the fabric.
If baggy — shrink the fabric into shape again by placing a damp cloth over the area and stroking the iron over the top to steam the fibres. Let it dry completely before wear.
Suits, jackets and dresses — brush, sponge and press them thoroughly, attending to shiny and baggy areas as above.
Knitwear — if collars and cuffs have stretched out of shape, wash carefully and dry flat, or have the garment dry cleaned. Sew a few rows of shirring elastic into the wrong side of the rib to give it "stretch" again.

4. Personal Hygiene

A high standard of personal cleanliness will make a lot of difference to the freshness of clothes. Stale perspiration in particular will spoil clothes by making them smell and sometimes by removing the colour in some areas. Wash all over once a day and use good quality

Care and Repair of Clothes

anti-perspirant/deodorant — experiment to find one that really works for you. Soak stained undies in a detergent solution; enzyme detergents are useful but not essential for this.

5. Washing Clothes

(Refer to a book on laundry work for more details, or consult manufacturers of detergents and washing machines — they are real experts.)

Wash garments frequently so that dirt is easily removed. Sort out into piles of whites and coloureds, then according to fibre context. A care labelling scheme covers most washable fabrics and these labels should be available when you purchase a length of fabric; they are normally sewn into bought clothes. When home dressmaking always sew a label securely into the garment for future reference. When fabric is a mixture of two or more fibres choose the washing process for the one needing the mildest treatment.

Detergents — whichever one is chosen it should be used according to the instructions on the packet — try using less rather than more if anything. Dissolve them completely in warm water before putting clothes in to wash.

Bleaching — most protein stains, eg. blood, urine and food can be removed by soaking in detergent, especially enzyme detergent. Follow the instructions on the packet. Otherwise, a mild solution of bleach may be used to remove some stains and whiten some white fabrics — follow the instructions about dilution and soaking.

Hand washing — use plenty of water of the right temperature, so that clothes need not be moved around vigorously. Be sure to rinse thoroughly.

Machine washing — do not overload the machine, and do use the correct washing temperature. Sort the loads carefully beforehand.

Using a launderette — do not attempt to wash huge mixed loads just because the machine has a large capacity. The washing temperature is often very hot so wash only the fabrics that can stand that temperature. Use the recommended amount of detergent.

Rinsing — very thorough rinsing of all fabrics is essential. Most washing machines do this correctly but hand washing is often inadequately rinsed.

Finishing — fabric softeners are very effective when used in the rinsing water for towels, nappies and woollens. Starches may be of natural or plastic (polyvinyl acetate) origin, and are effective in stiffening cottons and linens. Spray-on starch is useful for small areas such as collars and cuffs.

Gum arabic solution is used for stiffening shantung, taffeta silk and lace. Dissolve 100 g gum arabic in 500 ml hot water, then strain it into a screw top jar. Add some to 500 ml water for soaking the fabric, after rinsing.

Some washing problems

Burns and scorchmarks —
for very slight marks use a mild borax solution. (2·5 ml spoons borax to 500 ml hot water.) Wring out a clean cloth in the solution and rub the mark with it. Repeat a few times, then rinse in the same way with a clean damp cloth. Washable fabrics may be soaked immediately in cold milk instead.

Colour "bleeding" —
always test fabrics for colour fastness before washing them with others. If a lot of colour is lost in washing add 25 ml white vinegar to the final rinsing water. If a colour has bled from one area of a garment to another there is no effective remedy.

Iron mould —
these brown rusty looking marks can be removed by pouring salt onto the stain. Soak the salt in lemon juice, and leave to soak into the fabric for about one hour. Rinse well.

Shrinkage —
Wool shrinks easily if washed incorrectly and this cannot be put right later. Some man-made fibres shrink and should be kept slightly stretched during drying. Hang up the garment to drip-dry, first weighting it at the hem.

6. Dry Cleaning

A label on a bought garment will give instructions about the need for dry cleaning. When buying fabric check whether it needs dry cleaning, and then sew a warning label into the finished garment. It is sometimes possible to get away with washing a fabric or garment marked "dry clean only" but this is not advised. Not all fabrics can be successfully dry cleaned. Felt, velvet, laminated fabrics, leather, suede and some other fabrics with special finishes may all present problems. Ask the advice of a reputable dry cleaner if in doubt.

Do-it-yourself dry cleaning machines
These are sited in many laundrettes but the results can sometimes be disappointing although it is relatively cheap. Remember that there is generally no pressing service available so that clothes may come out clean but not in good shape — professional pressing is usually worth paying for on tailored garments.

Dry cleaning services
Remove buckles, belts and buttons before taking a garment to the cleaners. Do all necessary repairs and attach a note of explanation to any known stains. If experience shows that the fabric seems thin and limp after dry cleaning ask for it to be retextured.

7. Stain Removal

The longer a stain is on a fabric the more difficult it will be to remove so always take prompt action. If the garment is sent to the laundry or dry-cleaners, attach a note about the type of stain so that appropriate measures can be taken.

Small stains can usually be dealt with at home, often by the use of cheap chemicals rather than by expensive proprietary cleansers. It is sensible and convenient, however, to stock at least one multi-purpose stain remover in the home. Choose from liquids, powders, aerosols, sachets and impregnated pads and follow the directions carefully for the best effect. A grease-solvent such as carbon tetrachloride is very useful and can be bought at most chemists. It *MUST* be labelled as a poison and kept out of the way of children. It is highly inflammable and the fumes are poisonous, so use it only in a well ventilated room without a fire. Air the garment thoroughly in the open air afterwards.

Care and Repair of Clothes

Other useful cleaning substances are — ammonia, enzyme detergent, hydrogen peroxide, methylated spirit, oxalic acid, sodium hypochlorite bleach, surgical spirit and vinegar.

General methods for removing spots and stains

Test a little of the cleanser on a tiny bit of fabric first.

(a) Hold the stained area taut over a basin and pour the most suitable cleanser several times through the fabric. Rinse well and wash, if necessary, in the normal way.

(b) Spread the stained area over a thick pad. Dampen a clean sponge or wad with the appropriate cleanser and rub it over the stain. Use several applications and always work in from the outer edge of the stain to avoid spreading it further. Smudge the edges to avoid a hard line round the stain.

8. Repairs

Buttons and buttonholes

Worn buttonholes can be made into bound buttonholes, with larger buttons. This is only worth doing on a valuable garment. Stitched buttonholes on bought clothes can be strengthened by stitching over them with buttonhole stitch. If a button has been torn off a garment leaving a weakened area, stitch a piece of fabric or tape over it on the wrong side.

Loops for buttons often break and should be unpicked, then replaced by making a new thread loop. (See chapter on Buttons and Buttonholes.)

Collars and cuffs

Shirt collars usually wear through along the neck fold after much wear. Stiffened collars cannot be unpicked and attached the other way up because of the stiffening slots, but other collars can be turned in this way to prolong the life of the shirt. A collar can be remade by unpicking it and using the underneath facing as a new top collar, or by cutting a piece from the shirt tails to make a new collar.

Cuffs may fray or simply acquire a line of ingrained dirt along the edges. A single cuff can be remade by "shortening" it slightly. A double cuff can have the worn place darned, then be removed and replaced the other way round so that the darned part is hidden in the fold.

Stain	Dry-cleanable, coloured or delicate articles	Washable articles
Beer	Pour cold water through the spot — hold fabric taut. Apply vinegar solution.	Wool and silk — apply vinegar solution. Rinse well. Bleach with hydrogen peroxide. Cotton — wash then use sodium hypochlorite if necessary.
Blood	Pour solution of liquid detergent and water through the spot. Apply vinegar solution and rinse well.	Soak in warm solution of enzyme detergent. Cotton — apply oxalic acid, rinse, then use sodium hypochlorite, if necessary. Wool and silk — apply solution of hydrochloric acid, rinse then apply hydrogen peroxide.
Chewing Gum	Cool garment in a food freezer to make gum brittle. Scrape off gum with back of knife. Treat area with carbon tetrachloride.	Same treatment as dry cleanable articles.
Chocolate	Treat spot with warm water, then apply a borax solution. Rinse. Treat with vinegar solution and rinse well.	Soak in warm solution of enzyme detergent. Wool — treat with hydrogen peroxide. Cotton — treat with sodium hypochlorite.
Coffee	Treat immediately with warm water. Apply vinegar solution and rinse well. If stain persists, dry clean.	Wash immediately in hot water. Soak in solution of enzyme detergent overnight. If the stain persists treat cotton with sodium hypochlorite and wool with hydrogen peroxide.
Fruit juice	Pour cold water through stain. Treat with weak solution of detergent or vinegar. Rinse well.	Wash immediately in normal wash. Treat persistent stains on cotton with sodium hypochlorite and on wool with hydrogen peroxide.
Grass	Treat with surgical spirit or methylated spirit. Dry clean.	Treat with surgical spirits or methylated spirit and launder normally. Treat persistent stains with hydrogen peroxide.
Grease	Apply carbon tetrachloride.	Apply carbon tetrachloride.
Ink (Ball point pen)	Treat with methylated spirits (except on rayon or Tricel). Dry clean.	Treat with methylated spirit or carbon tetrachloride.
Ink (Blue/Black)	Pour water through stain and wash normally. If stain persists, dry clean.	Same treatment as for washable articles.
Lipstick	Treat with carbon tetrachloride.	Treat with carbon tetrachloride. Wash with liquid detergent.
Mildew	Treat with solution of hydrochloric acid. Dry clean.	Treat with hydrogen peroxide or solution of hydrochloric acid. Wash frequently and expose to sunlight.

Care and Repair of Clothes

Otherwise use a patch made from the shirt tail. Another alternative is to add new contrasting cuffs and collar.

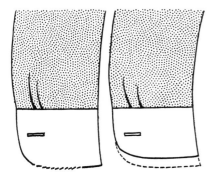

Pockets
It is possible to buy standard size ready made linings for pockets. Otherwise the pocket area can be unpicked and a new strong cotton lining stitched in taking a pattern from the old one. A quick repair can be made to a pocket with a small hole in the bottom, by machining across the lining just above it.

Elastic
Unpick a few stitches of the casing in an inconspicuous place. Pull out the old elastic and cut a new piece the same length. Thread the elastic through a bodkin or attach a small safety pin to one end. Pull the elastic through the casing and oversew the ends firmly together. Neatly restitch the casing.

Worn edges
If the edge of a garment has become frayed it can have a matching or contrasting binding sewn over it. Use leather for heavyweight fabrics and braid or ribbon on others. See chapter on Bindings and Piping for method. With the increasing availability of disposable and limited life clothes darning and patching sometimes seemed unnecessary. As clothes and fabrics have increased so much in cost it has again become a matter of sound economy to repair clothes by darning and patching wherever possible.

Stain	Dry-cleanable, coloured or delicate articles	Washable articles
Nail Polish	Treat with amyl acetate	Treat with amyl acetate.
Perspiration	Treat with vinegar solution. Dry clean.	Soak in solution of enzyme detergent. If stain persists soak in vinegar solution.
Shoe polish	Treat with carbon tetrachloride or turpentine.	Wash normally in warm water with some ammonia added. Rinse and rewash.
Tea	Treat as for coffee.	Treat as for coffee.
Wine	Sponge with cold water immediately treat with detergent solution. If stain dries in, dry clean.	If wet soak in cold water and then soak with solution of enzyme detergent. If dried in soak with detergent in hot water, wash normally. If stain persists, dry clean.

Darning
It is possible to darn a hole in many knitted or woven fabrics, by in fact creating a new piece to fill the hole. Choose a suitable thread which is as near the original in colour, texture and thickness — a darn should be as nearly invisible as possible. Use a long fine darning needle and a darning mushroom if liked (see chapter on Choosing Equipment). If, when making a knitted garment a few extra strands of wool are sewn into a seam they will be exactly right for darning that garment later if needed.

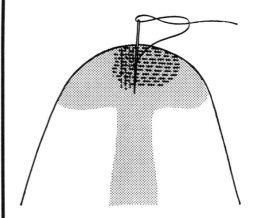

On woven fabrics a few threads may sometimes be pulled out of a hidden seam allowance. If darning by hand is thought too dreary a job, learn to darn with the sewing machine as it is quick and easy. Refer to manufacturer's handbook.

Darning thin places
Working on the wrong side of the fabric chalk round the weakened area. Using small running stitches darn across the weft threads only, spacing the rows closely and evenly. If the thread is likely to shrink leave a small loop at the end of each row. For fabric that is very weak, darn across the other way at right angles to the first rows.

Care and Repair of Clothes

Darning holes in woven fabrics (reweaving)

This is a difficult and tedious job but worth doing on expensive fabrics and garments. Place the damaged area in an embroidery hoop and work from the wrong side. It is useful to study the fabric through a magnifying glass to see exactly how it is woven. Pull some matching threads from a hidden seam allowance in the garment. Using a long fine darning needle, weave a thread across the whole damaged area and over and under the existing threads. Leave a short length at each end of the row on the wrong side and use a new thread for each row. Repeat this across at right angles to the first rows. When completed trim all the thread ends to about 3 mm in length, and press the area carefully on both sides.

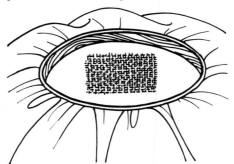

Darning cuts in woven fabrics

First close the edges of the cut or tear by using herringbone stitch. (See chapter on Stitches and Threads.) Then darn as in the previous method above.

Darning a tear (the hedge tear darn)

A large, jagged tear should be patched but if there is a straight or L-shaped tear it can be darned. A tiny tear can be held together by herringbone stitch along (see previous method above). All tears should first have the edges held together with herringbone stitch. Darning is worked over an area of about 10 mm around the tear; outline the area with chalk or trace tacking before darning, as a guide. Darn with small even running stitches along the weft and across the slit. Then darn across at right angles to the first rows.

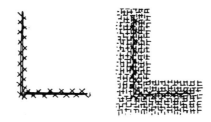

A tear which is on the cross grain should be darned as shown below.

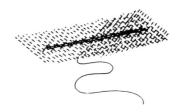

Darning holes (web darning)

New warp and weft threads must be formed across a hole on knitted or woven fabric. Trim the edges of the hole, and place the area over a darning mushroom. Darn over the area (not just the hole) for strength, working on the right side. Sew in new warp threads first, then turn the article and weave new weft threads over and under the warps.

Patching

A large hole or worn patch is difficult to darn, so it is best patched with a piece of fabric. Unless a decorative piece is desired, choose fabric of a similar weight, type and colour with a matching thread. When making a garment save a few fabric scraps for patching purposes; fade it to match the worn garment by washing it in water with a little baking powder in it. A suitable piece may sometimes be obtained from a hem or facing which will then also need to be patched with a scrap of some other fabric. Use wide white cotton tape for patching sheets, tea towels, etc., or save one old article to patch all the other similar ones. The patches must be cut on the same grain as the area to be patched. They are usually square or oblong, and big enough to cover the whole weakened area.

Patching on the right side

Print patch — used for printed and patterned fabrics.

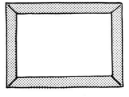

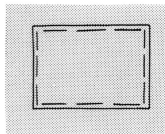

1. Cut a patch, allowing 6 mm turnings all round. Make sure that the pattern is matched exactly to the fabric pattern.
2. Fold and press the turnings to the wrong side, mitring the corners.
3. Pin and tack into place.
4. Fold the fabric level with one edge of the patch and oversew them neatly together. Complete all four sides.

5. Trim away the worn area underneath to about 6 mm from the stitching, and blanket stitch the edges together.

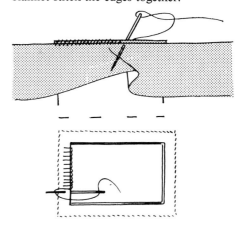

6. The zig-zag stitch and stepstitch on the modern sewing machines are ideal for patching purposes — refer to the machine handbook for instructions.

Cloth patch — used for outer garments such as flannel trousers.

Care and Repair of Clothes

1. Tack round the outline for the patch on the garment.
2. Cut away the worn part to within 6 mm of the tacking. Snip diagonally into the corners.
3. Cut a suitable patch with 6 mm turnings and press in place. The grain and nap must match the garment exactly.
4. Pin and tack the patch into position.
5. Slipstitch the edges of the patch to the garment. Remove the first tacking.
6. From the wrong side back stitch or machine along the slip stitching reinforcing the corners.
7. Press open the turnings and neaten them.

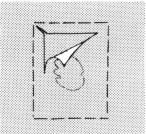

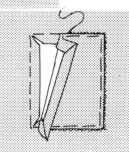

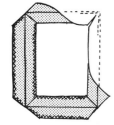

Decorative patch — used on children's clothes, on jeans and on lingerie. Use a contrasting colour or design, a cut out or embroidered motif, etc., as desired. Appliqué the chosen piece over the worn area. Leather or suede patches on jackets, etc., are hemmed or herringboned round the edges with Dewhurst Strong Thread.

Patching machine knitted fabrics — used on lock stitch or stockinette type fabrics.
1. Cut a round or oval patch without turnings.
2. Tack it onto the right side matching the direction of the knitting.
3. Using suitable thread buttonhole stitch the edge of the patch to the garment.
4. On the wrong side cut away the weak part to within 6 mm of the stitching then buttonhole this edge to the patch.
5. For machine patching refer to the sewing machine handbook. There are a variety of stitches that may be used for applying patches to these fabrics.

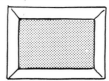

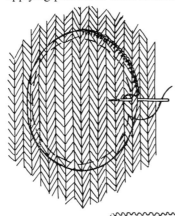

Patching on the wrong side — a strong patch used on aprons, overalls and household linen.
1. Cut a suitable patch allowing 6 mm turnings.
2. Press the turnings to the right side, mitreing the corners.

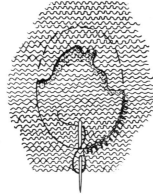

3. Pin and tack the patch into place on the wrong side.
4. Machine all round close to the edge, then cut away the weakened fabric to within 6 mm of the machining.
5. Snip 3 mm into the corners and fold under the raw edges.
6. Pin, tack and machine close to the fold.

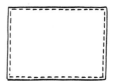

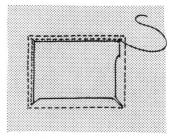

Flannel patch — used for thin woollen fabrics and some knitted fabrics.
1. Cut a matching piece of fabric for the patch, with no turnings.
2. Tack into position on the wrong side.
3. Herringbone stitch it into position.
4. Trim away the worn area underneath and herringbone the edges to the patch on the right side.
Note — on knitted fabrics and on blankets cut the patch a round or oval shape.
Machine darned patch — used on lingerie and household linen. Use fine machine embroidery thread.
1. Cut a suitable patch 13 mm larger than the hole.
2. Tack it onto the wrong side. Tack or chalk round the outline of the hole as a guide.
3. Machine darn all round the patch so that the stitching is 3 mm over the raw edges.

Special Words used in Sewing

Appliqué
A method of decorating a garment by stitching a shaped piece of fabric onto it.

Backing
A term sometimes used to mean mounting a lining onto the wrong side of a garment.

Balance Marks
The points on a pattern where two joining sections of garment must fit together — the marks are transferred to the fabric.

Basting
Another word for tacking.

Bias
(Also called "cross".) An edge or fold of material across the grain.
True Cross or True Bias is at 45 degrees to the straight grain.

Bias Binding
Available as a commercial product, it is cut on the true cross and has the edges folded over. It may be cut as strips from fabric.

Binding
A strip enclosing edge to finish or trim.

Blind Hem
A hem sewn invisibly with hand or machine stitches.

Bodkin
A blunt needle used to pull narrow elastic or ribbon through a casing.

Casing
A tunnel of fabric round a garment enclosing a drawstring or a piece of elastic.

Clip
A cut in fabric (seam allowances) to allow ease on corners and curves.

Construction
The making or sewing together of a garment.

Contrasting
A colour or texture of fabric of a totally different type, ie. not a matching or toning colour or texture.

Cording
Filling a narrow fabric tube with cotton cord, and using it for decorative effects. (See Piping.)

Crossway Strip
See bias binding.

Dart
A pointed, tapered fold of material which takes away fullness in a garment.

Ease (1)
To hold fullness without making pleats or gathers.

Ease (2)
The room allowed on a pattern for body movement.

Edgestitch
Machine stitching placed very close to a folded edge, usually used as a method of neatening open seams.

Enclosed Seams
Those with raw edges concealed during the making of the seam, ie. French or Double Stitched seams.

Eyelet
A round hole in fabric, often to take a cord or thong, finished with stitching or a circle of metal.

Face
The right side of the fabric. Also the application of a fitted piece of fabric to finish an edge.

Fitting Line
(Also called seam line, pattern line or stitching line.)
The line along which two pieces of a garment are sewn together.

Fly
A lap of fabric to conceal an opening.

Gathering
Rows of running stitches pulled up to reduce the width or control the fullness of a garment area.

Grading
See LAYERING.

Grain
The direction in which the thread runs in a fabric.

Grosgrain
A ribbon or fabric having a heavy crosswise ribbing.

Gusset
A fabric piece inserted to ease strain in a garment.

Haberdashery
(Or notions.) All the items, other than fabric and pattern, needed for sewing, eg. pins, needles, binding, fastenings.

Inset
(Or Insert.) A piece of shaped fabric inserted to aid fitting, or as a decoration.

Interfacing/Interlining
Fabric placed between the facing and garment to give shape and support, warmth or bulk.

Kick Pleat
A pleat inserted for ease of movement in a narrow skirt; usually inverted, knife or box pleat.

Lap
An edge extending to cover another edge, eg. a placket.

Lapels
A part which turns back, usually describing the front neckline fold.

Layering
(Or Grading.) To trim two or more seam allowances in steps, to reduce bulk.

Layout
A chart found with bought paper patterns showing ideal placement of paper pattern piece on fabric.

Line
The style, or outline, formed by the cut and construction of a garment.

Lining
An extra layer of fabric attached to the inside of a garment to make it hang better, to neaten it and give it strength.

Marking
The transfer of construction marks from paper pattern to fabric.

Mitre
To make a neat, pointed, triangular or square shape, eg. on the end of a belt, or the inside diagonal seaming of a corner.

Motif
A single design used as decoration.

Mounting
(Or Underlining.) Placing lining fabric on the wrong side of the garment fabric and then sewing them as one piece.

Nap
(Or Pile.) A raised, soft surface with fibres lying in one direction (as in natural fur).

Notch
A symbol on a paper pattern which is transferred to fabric to show matching points. Also the cutting of "V" shapes from seam allowances.

Open Seam
(Also called Flat or Plain.)
Joins two garment pieces with one row of machining, leaving seam allowances to be pressed open flat on the wrong side.

Opening
A part of a garment which can be opened and closed for putting on and taking off.

Pin Basting
Pinning seams before stitching them.

Pinking
The use of a special pair of notched shears to trim raw edges liable to fray.

Piping
A strip of fabric, folded and added into a seam for emphasis and decoration.

Special Words used in Sewing

Pivot
The technique of leaving the machine needle in the work on reaching a corner, and turning the work around the needle, after having lifted the presser foot.

Placket
A garment opening closed by press studs, buttons or zip.

Pre-Fold
To fold and press a binding or garment section before fixing to the garment.

Pre-Shape
To steam fabric into a curved shape before stitching to the garment.

Pre-Shrink
To shrink fabric or bindings by steaming, before making up into a garment.

Puckering
Uneven folds or gathers, usually made by accident when the tension of the stitching is wrong.

Raw Edge
The unfinished edge of a fabric.

Right Side
The finished outside of the garment.

Roll
To produce a soft curved fold (usually on a collar).

Rouleau
A tube of fabric with the raw edges inside; used for fastenings or for decoration. Sometimes used to neaten an edge.

Saddle Stitch
Even, running stitches for decorative effect, often made with thread of a contrasting colour.

Seam Allowance
The width of fabric between the seam line and the raw edge.

Seam Binding
A ribbon or tape used to finish fabric edges.

Secure
To fasten a thread by means of a backstitch or a knot.

Self
Fabric the same as the rest of the garment.

Selvedge
The mill finished edges to a cloth, running in a lengthwise direction.

Semi-Fitted
Conforming to the general shape, without being closely fitted.

Shank
The link between button and fabric; formed either by the threads holding the button to the garment, or by a special piece of the button itself.

Shrink
To subject fabric to steam or water to cause the fabric to contract, either for shaping, or to prevent the garment shape changing during later washing.

Slash
A controlled cut made in fabric in the course of garment construction.

Slit
To cut fabric lengthwise. Also a long narrow opening.

Stay Stitching
A row of machining just outside the seam line on the allowance to maintain the shape of an edge which might stretch in making up.

Stiletto or Awl
A sharp spike for making holes in fabric, usually for eyelets.

Straight Grain
Following the straight threads across or along a piece of fabric, usually with the warp thread parallel to selvedge.

Tack
To join two pieces of fabric by loose temporary stitches.

Tailoring
Special construction techniques using hand shaping, by stitching and steam pressing, to mould fabrics into finished garment, eg. men's suits.

Tailor's Chalk
A special kind of chalk used for marking fabrics during making up.

Tailor's Tack
A special tacking stitch using double thread to transfer pattern markings to the fabric.

Taper
To sew or cut fabric in such a way as to produce a narrowing effect.

Tension
The controlled pull or pressure on thread or fabric during construction. This also applies to correct tightness or otherwise of machine stitches.

Thread Tracing
(Sometimes called Trace tacking.)
Lines of running or tacking stitches used to mark position of centre-front, button-holes, etc. Both ends are left unsecured.

Topstitching
A line of stitching parallel to an edge or seam, sewn from the right side, usually used decoratively.

Trim
To cut away excess fabric.

Trimming
A decorative feature added to a garment.

Turning Allowance
See seam allowance.

Underlining
A term sometimes used for a lining which is mounted on to the back of a garment, before actual garment construction begins. See Mounting.

Vent
Faced or lined slash in a garment.

Welt
A strip of material stitched to an edge or seam, usually on a pocket top.

Wrong Side
The side of a fabric which will be on the inside of a garment.

Yardage
A length of fabric of a given width needed to complete the construction of a garment.

Yoke
A fitted part of a garment, usually on the shoulders or hips, from which the garment hangs.

Zig-Zag
A stitch produced by swing-needle sewing machines — it looks like a row of joined "V"s and is used for neatening, decoration and for sewing "stretch" seams.

Stitches and Threads

Providing that you use the right thread for the fabric — and that your choice of stitch, stitch length, pressure and needle are correct you will be successful with stitching techniques. It is also important to know *why* certain threads are used on some occasions and completely different ones on others. With an understanding of the reasoning behind these recommendations they are much easier to remember.

1. Needles

Whether sewing by hand or by machine you need a needle that is suited to both the fabric and the thread. Fine, delicate fabrics require fine needles — heavy fabrics need thicker needles. With hand sewing it is easy to remember to select the right needle, but with machine sewing this is too often forgotten. There are very many instances where the sewing machine needle is left in the machine until it breaks, and then replaced with the same type. In the days when only natural fibre fabrics were available this did not matter quite so much, although it should surely be common sense to change needles after sewing heavy tweed, before going on to sew silk! These days with so many man-made fabrics available it is a different story. Man-made fabrics blunt needles at a rapid rate, and it is advisable to select a new needle for each new garment or outfit made. If you do not do this you may risk damaging the next garment you sew. A blunt needle can ruin a fine fabric. When man-made jersey fabric is being sewn or even some of the silky woven fabrics that have a little stretch, remember to use a Ball or Uni-Point needle. These are designed to eliminate stitch-missing and reduce the risk of the needles snagging the fabric as they pierce it whilst sewing. Remember that the eye of the needle must be large enough to accommodate the thread that is being used. If it is not, it may bend and the thread will certainly snarl and break. When possible, buy the best quality you can afford.
Those manufactured by Schmetz in Germany are thought to be the best available for machine use even though they are a little higher in cost than others on the market. Poor quality sewing machine needles are uneconomical, for they do not generally last long and give unsatisfactory results.

2. Threads

Why are two threads offered? Why should natural fabrics need to be sewn with natural thread and man-made fabrics with man-made thread? In every case the thread used should have the same characteristics as the fabric being sewn, otherwise the stitching and the fabric will not be compatible in wearing, washing or cleaning. Natural fabrics — wool, cotton, linen and silk, will always shrink, even if only very slightly, in washing. If Sylko — a cotton thread — is used the same will happen and any variation between fabric and thread shrinkage will be virtually unnoticeable. If a man-made thread is used for these fabrics, however, in some cases the results may be disastrous. Cotton and linens, for example, need a high temperature setting for ironing. Although there are thermostatic controls on most irons these days, with use and wear they very often become inaccurate, resulting in the iron temperature range having more variation than it should. If an iron that is too hot is placed on a man-made thread it will melt. The result will be no seams! Conversely, if a natural thread is used to sew a man-made fabric, which seldom shrinks, it may look perfect at the time of sewing, but as soon as it is washed and dried, an unsightly puckered seam will result. This may, of course, be pressed out with lots of care and attention but exactly the same thing will happen once the garment is washed again. This will never happen if a man-made thread like Star is used.
So very many man-made fabrics are also stretch fabrics and as Star thread has a certain amount of "give" it allows the seams to extend even if only sewn with a straight stitch. Better still, use a stretch stitch together with a stretch thread on one of the modern sewing machines that has this facility. Cut threads at an angle (do not break or bite the ends).
The following chart will help with the selection of threads.

Stitches and Threads

Fabrics	Type	Threads	Machine Needle Continental	Machine Needle British	Hand Needle	Stitches per cm
FINE FABRICS such as Net, Organdie, Lace, Lawn, Voile, Chiffon, Tulle, etc.	Natural	Sylko No 50	60–75	7–11	9	5–7
	Man-made	Star	60–75	7–11	9	5–7
LIGHTWEIGHT FABRICS such as Gingham, Muslin, Fine Poplin, Taffeta, Silk, Seersucker, etc.	Natural	Sylko No 50	75–90	11–14	8–9	5–6
	Man-made	Star	75–90	11–14	8–9	5–6
MEDIUMWEIGHT FABRICS such as Poplin, Cotton, Suitings, Corduroy, Linen, Satin, Brocade, Velvet, etc.	Natural	Sylko No 40	75–90	11–14	7–8	5–6
	Man-made	Star	75–90	11–14	7–8	5–6
HEAVYWEIGHT FABRICS such as Sailcloth, Twill, Denim, Coated Fabrics, Canvas, Furnishings, Tweed, etc.	Natural	Sylko No 40	90–110	14–18	6	3–4
	Man-made	Star	90–110	14–18	6	3–4
STRETCH FABRICS Use stretch stitch wherever possible.	Lightweight — Natural	Sylko No 50 + stretch stitch otherwise Star	60–80 Ball or uni point	7–12 Ball or uni point	9	4–6
	Lightweight — Man-made	Star	60–80 Ball or uni point	7–12 Ball or uni point	9	4–6
	Heavyweight — Natural	Sylko No 40 + stretch stitch otherwise Star	80–90 Ball or uni point	12–14 Ball or uni point	9	4–6
	Heavyweight — Man-made	Star	80–90 Ball or uni point	12–14 Ball or uni point	9	4–6
SPECIAL FABRICS	PVC — Man-made	Star	90–100	14–16	9	3–4
	Suede/Leather — Natural	Sylko No 40 or Strong Thread	Spear or 80–110 Leather Point	12–18	9	3–4
BUTTON SEWING	— —	Dewhurst Strong Thread, Sylko No 40	—	—	5–6	—
EMBROIDERY	Machine	Sylko Nos 40 & 50	60–90	7–14	—	—
		Sylko Perlé Nos 5 & 8	100–110	16–18	—	—
	Hand	Sylko Perlé Nos 5 & 8	—	—	Crewel 5–9 or Tapestry 19–23	—

Stitches and Threads

3. Stitching by Hand

Choose the right type of needle and thread. Wear a thimble, especially when sewing firm fabrics; this habit is very soon learned, and makes all hand sewing much easier. Practice stitches until they appear neat and even, working mostly from right to left. (Left handed workers will find it easier to sew from left to right.) Avoid pulling stitches too tight as this causes puckering. Begin and end with one or more backstitches. For tacking you can begin with a knot.

4. Stitching by Machine

(See also chapter on Choosing Equipment). Choose the right type of thread and change the needle if necessary. Prepare the machine. Practice a few rows of stitching on a spare piece of the garment fabric to get the stitch length, pressure and tension exactly right.
(Refer to machine handbook.)

5. Temporary Stitches

Tacking (Also called basting)
Tacking is of prime importance. It can make the difference between a superb finish and a slipshod one. There are times when it is not *essential* to tack, but not very often.
Tacking is used for the following reasons:
(a) To hold the garment together for fitting purposes.
(b) To hold hems, seams and darts in position ready for final stitching.
(c) To mark construction detail on the fabric.
(d) To identify certain parts of garment sections such as centre front lines or hemlines.
(e) To position items to be added to the garment such as zip fasteners, braid, pockets, etc.
(a) Even Tacking
Stitches are equal in length on both sides of the fabric. Work from right to left. Begin with the thread knotted or make a backstitch by pulling the needle through the fabric and going back into the fabric again. Bring the thread back from the start and again push the needle forward to make the backstitch. Then work a regular large running stitch along the area to be eventually sewn. When tacking up a garment for fitting, sew a backstitch evenly every few centimetres for strength, although this will make it

more difficult to pull the thread out later.

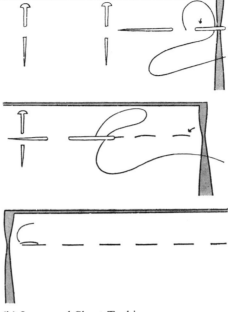

(b) Long and Short Tacking
This quick method produces a long stitch on top and a short stitch underneath. It is used for hems, for joining interfacings and linings to garments, and for marking lines onto fabric.

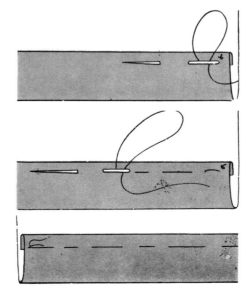

Diagonal tacking
Useful for holding together two or more layers of material to prevent them from slipping out of position until final stitching is completed. The needle is pushed through all layers vertically, drawn out and pushed in again level with the top of the first stitch. The result is a set of diagonal lines running the length of the fabric, with short level stitches on the other side.

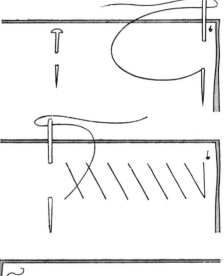

Tailor's tacks
These can transfer pattern markings to two pieces of fabric at the same time. They are only suitable for strong firm cloth because the threads, after cutting, can easily slip from fine, smooth materials. Work single tailor's tacks, or in series from right to left. Work with unknotted double thread. For single tacks take a small stitch through the pattern and fabric layers leaving a thread end of 25 mm/2·5 cm long. Take a second stitch over the first, leaving rather a long loop about 25 mm/2·5 cm then cut the thread.

Stitches and Threads

Do *not* cut through the loop. This avoids the risk of the tailor's tacks pulling out of the fabric at the expense of a small tear being made in the pattern. Remove pattern — pull fabric layers apart and cut threads between. For a series of tailor's tacks take a small stitch through the fabric and pattern layers then take a second stitch over the first, leaving a loop. Repeat this procedure until the seams have been tacked together. Fasten off by cutting thread leaving a 25 mm/2·5 cm end. Cut through the tops of the loops. Remove the pattern very carefully so as not to pull out threads. Separate the material layers, cut the threads between, leaving thread "tufts" on both layers.

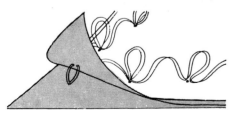

Trace tacking or thread tracing
This is simply carried out by making rows of uneven tacking to mark grainlines, centres of garment sections and positions of pockets and other details. Always use a single thread. This may also be used to mark seam lines instead of tailor's tacks.

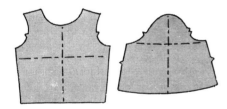

Machine tacking
Some modern automatic machines have a special setting which produces tacking or a chainstitch that can easily be pulled out

again. Otherwise use a very loose top tension and the longest stitch. Only use machine tacking on firm fabrics that will not be marked by the needle.

Slip basting
(Also called slip stitch)
This is the best method to use when matching striped or checked fabrics and for the lapping of curved seams. The seam can be tacked together from the right side so that it is exactly in place before stitching permanently. The edge of a hem can be held down invisibly by slip hemming. Start with the right side of the fabric uppermost, and turn under one seam allowance. Position it over the other, which is kept flat. Place pins at right angles to seam bringing the needle through to right side at fold. Insert needle along fold and bring out about 13 mm to the left. Insert needle below fold under-layer and make a stitch of the same length. Continue in this manner alternating stitches in and below fold.

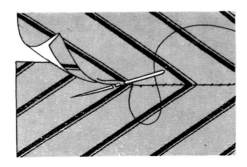

6. Joining Stitches
These can join two or more separate pieces of material together. Make certain that the thread used is compatible with the fabric — Sylko for natural fabrics, Star for man-made fabrics.

Running stitch
A basic straight stitch used where there is not too much strain, and for easing and gathering. For seams make stitches 2 – 3 mm long, and for easing or gathering 3 – 6 mm long. Push the needle tip in and out of the material making small regular stitches evenly spaced in straight or curved lines as required. A long fine needle should be used, pushing it in and out for half-a-dozen stitches before pulling the thread out.

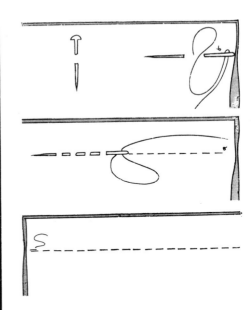

Backstitch
This is a strong handstitch that can be used in place of straight machining, as the stitches look rather like machining on one side yet overlap on the other.
With right sides of the pieces together, fasten on the thread and take one long running stitch. Take a stitch back, then bring the needle out again a little way along the seamline. Repeat. Modern superautomatic sewing machines can also backstitch. The seam resulting from this stitch is elastic and very strong — generally called a triple seam.

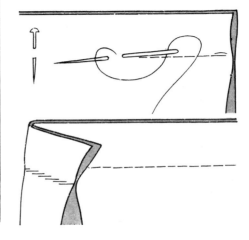

Stitches and Threads

Half backstitch
This can be used for hand-sewn seams and is also useful for under-stitching facings to prevent the edge seams rolling to the right side. The backward stitch is only half the length of the last stitch, otherwise the method is the same as for backstitch.

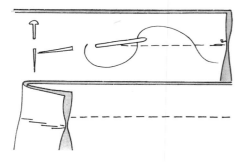

Stab stitch
(Prickstitch or hand picking)
This is similar to half backstitch but the needle is only taken back over 2 or 3 threads each time. It is often used for inserting zips by hand and for fine topstitching of collars, lapels etc.

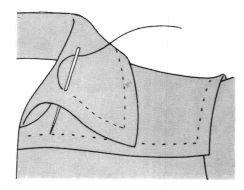

Oversewing
Can be used for joining two finished edges or selvedges together, i.e. ends of deep hems. Move the needle from right to left, over the two edges.
(See also overcasting).
If very tiny stitches are used this may also be called whipstitch. Oversewing may also be sewn with the needle slanting so that tiny *straight* stitches are formed.

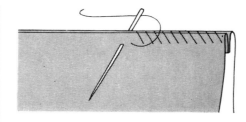

Pad stitch
This is really a tailoring stitch as it is used to attach interfacing to the garment fabric, and to mould it to shape e.g. undercollar, and lapels.
The stitches are similar to diagonal tacks and worked from the wrong side. Point the needle to the left, and take a stitch about 13 mm long through the interfacing to pick up one or two fabric threads. Make another stitch about 13 mm below the first (on medium weight and thick fabrics, these stitches will not even need to go through to the right side). Continue forming slightly curved rows until the interfacing is in place. The stitches on the right side should hardly be seen.

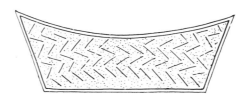

French or swing tacks
are used to hold two layers of fabric loosely together e.g. lining and garment, or the edges of pleats. (Sometimes called bar tacks.)
Work one or two backstitches to secure the thread then make several long stitches of about 25 mm/2·5 cm to join the two pieces of fabric *loosely* together. Sew loop or buttonhole stitch along the length of these threads and finish off securely.

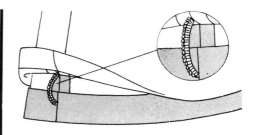

7. Finishing and Decorative Stitches
These prevent raw edges from fraying and/or decorate the garment.
Arrowhead tacks
are sewn at the top of pleats both as a reinforcement and a decoration. They are usually made from embroidery thread in a matching or contrasting colour.
Fasten thread on within the tack area.
Bring needle out at left side angle at base.
Work stitch across opposite angle base.
Sew from right to left parallel to base.
Put the needle through base line to right angle, then bring out on base line within stitch at left angle. Repeat process.
Stitches on base line should touch at centre with the stitches across the point opposite base widening out from angle points. Fasten off on wrong side.

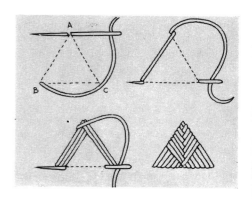

Bar tacks
are used to reinforce pleats, and at the end of buttonholes and slits. They are worked on the surface of fabric, usually on the right side.
Use buttonhole twist. Make several long stitches using two holes only. Sew closely over these threads along the length, using buttonhole stitch.

Stitches and Threads

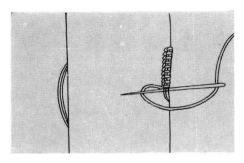

Blanket stitch (or loopstitch)
This stitch is used to neaten raw edges, especially on blankets, and seams, and to strengthen thread loops and bar tacks. It may be used as a simple decorative stitch, and be worked from right to left or left to right.
Fasten on with one or two backstitches.
Push the needle in behind the fabric and through the loop, with the fabric edge towards the worker. Repeat.

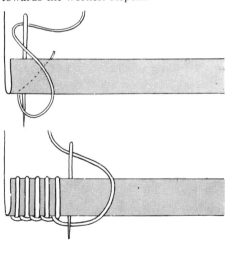

Blind hemming
This is a way of sewing hems and facings into place with stitches that are hardly visible on right or wrong side.
Finish the raw edge of hem or facing, and roll it back about 6 mm. Fasten on securely. Sew a small stitch under one thread of the garment, then pick up one thread of the facing or hem a little further along. Leave the stitches fairly loose. (This may also be carried out on some automatic sewing machines, use the stretch blind hem stitch for jersey fabrics. Refer to your Sewing Machine handbook.)

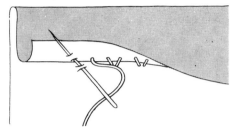

Buttonhole stitch
This is used to neaten and strengthen raw edges, especially on buttonholes. It is worked from left to right.
Fasten with one or two backstitches then loop the thread behind the eye of the needle. With the needle behind the edge push the needle point out over the loop of thread. Pull the needle through, and ease the thread up to form a knot on the edge. The stitches should be close enough to make a continuous row of knots at the edge.

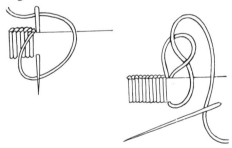

Chainstitch
A decorative hand embroidery stitch. Insert needle into the right side of the material. Hold the thread down with the left thumb. Move needle back to where the thread emerges. Bring out needle and thread a short distance away. Bring the needle out over the loop.

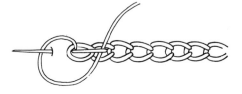

Coral knot stitch
A hand embroidery stitch, with two stitches crossing in the centre. The crossing direction of all the stitches in a design must be the same so that it looks neat and even.
Move the needle from left to right, keeping the needle straight between two lines, making half of the cross. Move from right to left to make the second half of the cross.

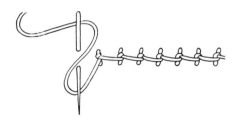

Crow's feet tacks
are similar to arrowhead tacks.
Mark the triangle where the tack is to be sewn, then fasten on the thread by a backstitch in the middle of the triangle. Make a stitch at each angle, inserting the needle through from right to left. Each stitch widens across the angle, quickly filling the area. Stitches must not overlap. Repeat the process until stitches meet each side of the angle. Then fasten off on the wrong side.

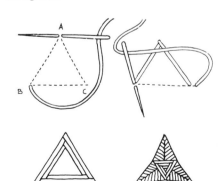

Featherstitch
A hand embroidery stitch. Insert needle to make a blanket stitch, but slant needle to the right. Put the thread to the left under the needle to make a blanket stitch or loopstitch slanted to the left. Repeat the process.

Stitches and Threads

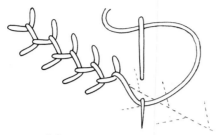

French knots

A hand embroidery stitch often used to make the centres of embroidered flowers. Mark dots where the knots should be. Pick up one or two threads of fabric. Wind the embroidery thread round the needle two or three times. Hold the thread down with thumb and pull needle through, then insert the needle into the material close to the starting point.

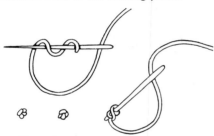

Hemming

Used for garment hems so that the folded edge is held into place.
Move the needle from right to left with the garment held towards the worker and the hem held over the fingers of the left hand. Pick a thread up from the fabric below the folded edge of the hem, then pick a thread up from the folded edge of the hem. Repeat until hem is completed.

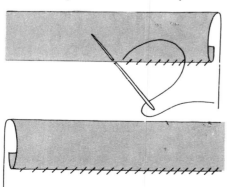

Hemstitching

This is a decorative way of finishing hems on even-weave fabrics used for table linen. A few threads are drawn out at the required depth of the hem. Fold the hem and mitre the corners, tucking in the threads. Tack into place.
Work the hemstitch by bringing the needle and thread to the edge of the drawn threads. Push the needle behind three threads, bring end round and behind the same three threads again. Bring the needle out through the thread loop so that a knot is formed. Repeat. (Various hemstitches can also be carried out on some of the superautomatic sewing machines, ie. Turkish, Venetian, Point de Paris. Refer to Sewing Machine handbook.)

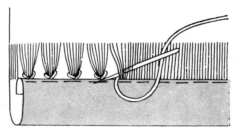

Herringbone stitch

(sometimes called catch stitch).
Used over an edge to hold it flat. Work the needle from left to right over folded or raw edges, forming criss-cross stitches. The edge should be held away from the worker.

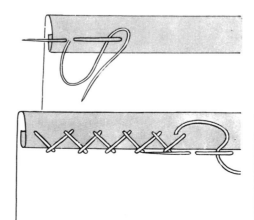

Lazy daisy stitch

This is a variation of chain stitch and is simply a detached chain stitch. Groups of these stitches are usually made together to form flowers in simple embroidery designs.

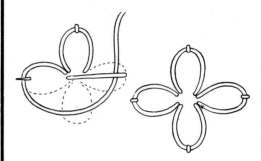

Overcasting

This is a quick method of neatening raw edges by hand, and is often worked on single fabric.
The thread is taken over and over the edge of the cloth, all the way along. Stitches should be small and evenly spaced. (Zig-zag or step stitch may be used instead on swing needle sewing machines, so consult the handbook).

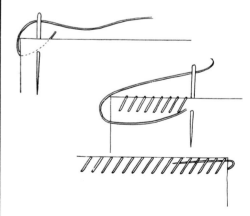

Pin stitch

This is a simple, decorative way of finishing hems on lingerie and fine table linen. It is usually worked from the right side of the fabric, or on a hem that has been tacked and pressed. The stitches are pulled firmly to give a punched hole effect

Stitches and Threads

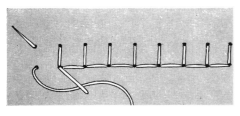

Satin stitch

This is a decorative stitch, used in hand embroidery, appliqué etc. Insert needle at one edge of the design then insert it at the opposite edge. Return to the starting edge by passing the needle underneath the material. Stitches should be close together and parallel. This can fill in a design of flowers, leaves etc. on a garment; it can also be made on a swing needle sewing machine — check with the handbook.

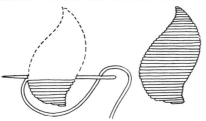

Shell hemming

(see also chapter on Hems)
This is a variation of hemming for use on fine sheer lingerie fabrics. It is worked from right to left on the wrong side. Make a narrow folded hem and press it into place. Fasten on with one or two backstitches. Sew a few ordinary hemming stitches, then take the needle and thread completely over the hem. Pull the loop tight. Repeat, along the hem, making sure that the shells are regular and even in size.

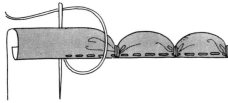

Slip stitch

(Slip hemming).
Used for stitching a hem when stitching needs to be invisible from both sides. Pick up single thread of fabric below fold, push needle through fold for about 6 mm. Repeat.

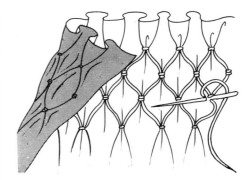

Smocking

This is a way of decorating rows of gathering by placing rows of hand embroidery over the top. (See also chapter on Gathering). The garment fabric needs to be very carefully prepared, and gathered up evenly. There are many stitches used for smocking.

Cable smocking

Work the needle from left to right on a row of dots. Bring the needle out and pick up one dot with the thread above the needle. Gather up. Then pick up the next dot with thread below the needle. Repeat the process until complete.

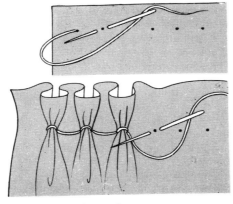

Honeycomb smocking

Work the needle from right to left alternating between two rows of dots. Bring the needle out on the first dot on the left. Use short stitches and pick up the first and second dots and gather material together. Take a second stitch through the same dots. Push the needle out on the third dot in the row below. Pick up the second and third dots and draw together, then take the second stitch through the same dots. Repeat the process until finished.

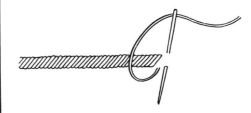

Stem stitch

This is a hand embroidery stitch for outlining designs. The thread must be kept below the needle, and the needle brought out exactly where the previous stitch finished. A row of backstitches shows on the wrong side.

Order of Making a Garment

Follow the instructions given with a paper pattern when possible. Otherwise follow the general order given below for a dress, modifying it for different garments. Remember to fit and press carefully throughout the making-up process. Refer to Volume 1, and the chapters in this volume, for details of each process.

1. Direction of Stitching Seams
Unless the pattern instructions suggest otherwise, go by the following rules:
Side seams — from armhole to waist in bodice; from hem to waist of skirt.
Shoulder seams — from neck to armholes
Darts — stitch from the widest to the narrowest part.
Sleeve — from the shoulder to the wrist.

2. General Order of Making Up
1. Stitch any tucks.
2. Sew all darts and press them.
3. Make and attach pockets if required.
4. Sew seams, neaten and remove tacking and press. Leave centre front and centre back tacking lines in until later.
5. Attach facings to button-through designs.
6. Make buttonholes or buttonloops, or put in zip.
7. Make pleats and gathers.
8. Make up the collar, cuffs and belt.
9. Sew or iron on interfacing to facing. Stitch facings to neck and opening edges. Attach collar.
10. Stitch, press and tack in sleeve. Try on and adjust the fit of sleeves then remove them.
11. Attach cuffs to sleeves or finish sleeve edges.
12. Set in sleeves and neaten armhole seams. Press.
13. Attach bodice to skirt if appropriate.
14. Try on and adjust the fit. Finish fastenings and hem. Press complete garment carefully, removing any tackings and complete neatening.
15. Attach any trimmings. Sew in an HLCC care label. These should be available when fabric is purchased.

Belts and Buckles

A belt, as the finishing touch, can be the making of an otherwise plain outfit; as fashions change, so do waistlines. Belts can be made in such a wide range of shapes and styles that they may completely alter the appearance of a garment; wide or narrow, buckled or tied, above or below the waistline — a belt may emphasise a tiny waist or detract from a plump one. It may be brightly braided or embroidered, or have a really eye-catching buckle and so become the main decorative feature of the outfit with little expense. Some of the old-fashioned buckles that are currently popular can be picked up cheaply at jumble sales or junk shops. Extra interest may also be added by hand or machine embroidery, topstitching, sequins, beads, etc., or just by choosing a beautiful fabric or striking colour. Separates that were not originally intended to be worn together can be teamed up with a belt, and old styles up-dated by a new belt. Many ready-made belts can be purchased but a hand-made accessory is always more exclusive.

1. Taking Measurements

First try out the shape and size of belt required by practising with a piece of paper or fabric. Measure round the body at the point where the belt is to be worn (not always the natural waistline). Use fabric the required width with turnings, but allow about 21 cm for overlapping and fastening. In general the wider the belt the longer the length needed.

2. Basic Belts
Tie

Often used on children's clothes, tie belts may be any width, cut from fabric on the straight grain or bias, or from bought ribbon. Decide on the total length required by experimenting with a piece of cord around the waistline, remembering to include enough for the bow and its two ends.

(a) Cut a piece of fabric twice the required width plus 3 cm for turnings. The ends may be left straight or shaped to form points.

(b) Interfacing is often added, in the waistline area only, to prevent curling. Cut a piece of interfacing 25 mm/2·5 cm shorter than the actual waist measurement, and half the width of the fabric.

(c) Position the interfacing along the waistline area on the wrong side of the fabric inside the seam allowance. Tack or machine baste into position 15 mm from cut edges. Trim interfacing to stitching.

(d) Slip stitch interfacing into position with tiny stitches all round on wrong side.

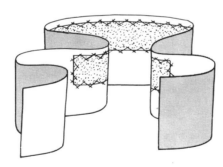

(e) With right sides facing, fold belt in half lengthwise, pin — then tack all round. If the belt is very narrow, lay a piece of strong thread or cord inside and make sure it is secured at one end.

(f) Machine stitch on seam line, leaving a 10 cm opening in the centre of one side for turning. Remove tacking.

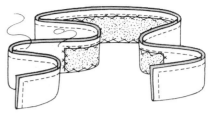

(g) Trim seam allowances and corners, then turn belt to right side. This is easily done with the help of a thick, blunt knitting needle. Use the round point of the needle to push out corners for a neat finish. Pull through a narrow belt with the thread or cord and then remove it.

(h) Roll seamed edges of belt between thumbs and fingers to move seam to edge of belt. Tack all round to hold in position. Slip stitch opening edges together. Top stitch all round if liked.

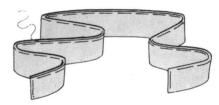

(i) Press very lightly. Remove tacking and dress again.

Ribbon

Use good quality, firmly woven ribbon of the required width; if thick enough it may be used singly, but usually two pieces are lined with interfacing for stiffness.

(a) Cut ribbon to required length.

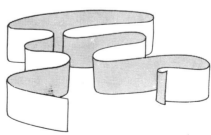

(b) Cut extra piece of ribbon to length of waistline minus 5 cm. This is for facing.

(c) Cut a piece of iron-on interfacing slightly narrower than the piece of ribbon to exact length of extra facing ribbon.

(d) Iron the interfacing onto the facing ribbon and trim ends to a curve.

Belts and Buckles

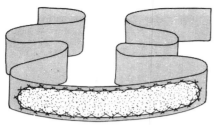

(e) Centre the faced ribbon lining on the waist area of the ribbon. Tack into position, interfacing inside.

(f) Using very short machine stitches carefully sew the stiffened facing ribbon to the ribbon belt just inside the edges. Fasten off the threads securely.

(g) Trim the belt ends to a "V", or a point, to prevent fraying.

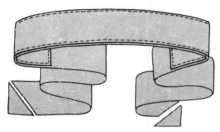

Straight stiffened

This is a very popular way of making a belt from self or contrasting fabric. Petersham (pre-shrunk), organdie, canvas, iron-on interlining or bought belting may be used for stiffening according to the weight of fabric used. Buckles or hooks and eyes are usually used for fastening stiffened belts — see the section on Belt Fastenings. The method below uses bought belting.

(a) The width of belting chosen should be the same as for the finished belt.

(b) Belting should be cut to the size of the waistline plus 21 cm for turnings and overlap.

(c) Cut the belting to a point at one end.

(d) Cut one fabric strip, on the lengthwise grain, twice the width of the belting plus 10 mm and the length of the belting plus 10 mm.

(e) With right sides together fold the strip in half lengthways. Stitch across one end only, trim and press the seam.

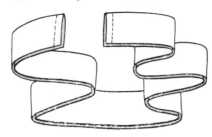

(f) Place the pointed end of belting into this pointed end of the belt; pin one raw edge along the length of the belt. Tack.

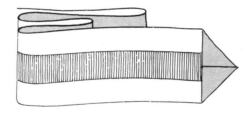

(g) Pin the other edge over the top. If this edge is a selvedge it may be pinned and tacked without turnings.

(h) Slipstitch edges into place as neatly and as invisibly as possible.

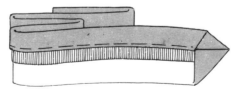

(i) A buckle may now be sewn to the other straight end of the belt, (see the section on belt fastenings) or neaten it and use hooks and eyes as fastening.

Contour

Contour belts are usually stiffened belts cut on a curve so that they fit closely to the body on the line of the garment. Ready-made belting is not usually suitable and an interfacing such as Petersham (pre-shrunk), organdie, canvas, bonded interlining, or buckram is needed; use one or two layers according to the stiffness required.

(a) Cut the paper pattern for the shape desired.

(b) Cut out two pieces of fabric, on the lengthwise grain, using the paper pattern

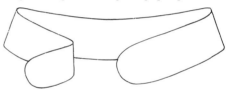

— allow usual seam allowance — 15 mm.

(c) Pin two layers of interfacing together and trace on the outline of the paper pattern.

(d) Within this outline stitch rows of stitching 6 mm apart. Cut along the outline.

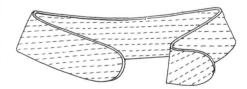

(e) Stitch a piece of bias binding flat along the inner curved edge to prevent stretching.

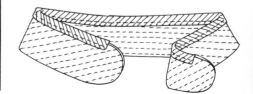

Belts and Buckles

(f) Staystitch around the two pieces of belt fabric to help them keep their shape.

(g) Pin the prepared interfacing to the wrong side of one piece of belt fabric. Fold the seam allowances in, and sew them to the interfacing only with long running stitches.

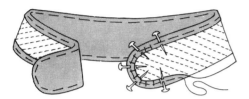

(h) Turn the seam allowances on the other piece of fabric to the wrong side, tack and press. Trim to 10 mm.

(i) Pin this facing carefully to the interfaced belt and slipstitch into place. Remove tacking. Top stitch if required.

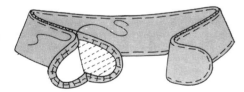

(j) Sew on fastenings as required — see section on Belt Fastenings.

Straight soft

Soft, pliable belts look especially effective on evening wear and day wear with rounded lines. They may be made from many weights of fabric including leather and leather types. Lightweight interfacing is used to prevent too much creasing in use.

(a) Cut fabric to the required length of the belt plus 23 cm for overlap and turnings. Allow 3 cm on the required width for turnings.

(b) Cut the interfacing and belt backing 20 mm narrower than the fabric and exactly the same length. As the backing is narrower it will allow the edges of the belt to roll slightly bringing the seams to the wrong side of the belt instead of on the edge.

(c) Cut all strips to an angle at one end.

(d) Machine baste or tack interfacing to wrong side of backing fabric 15 mm from edges. Trim interfacing close to stitching.

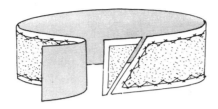

(e) Place the belt and backing together with right sides facing, pin and tack all round. The belt will, of course, be slightly wider than backing so be careful to keep edges together.

(f) Stitch along both sides of the belt 15 mm from edges. Trim allowances and press them towards backing.

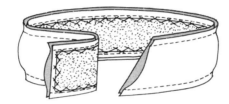

(g) Turn the belt to the right side and press. Turn in slanted edges and slipstitch together.

(h) The buckle used for this type of belt should be narrower than the belt width so that the belt fabric settles into soft folds. See section on Belt Fastenings.

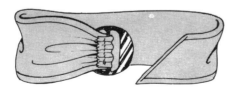

Cummerbund

These are worn by both men and women generally to dress up evening wear and to provide a decorative link between two garments such as trousers and shirt or top and skirt. A cummerbund is a very wide belt that covers the whole midriff, and so that it will shape itself easily to the body is cut on the cross or bias of the fabric.

(a) Cut a length of fabric and lining on the true cross, the length of the measurement round the midriff plus 25 mm/2·5 cm and about 23 cm wide. Treat fabric and lining as one.

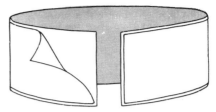

(b) Turn in 6 mm on the two long sides and machine stitch along close to the edge.

(c) Turn in a further 25 mm/2·5 cm and tack lightly into place. Press very lightly.

(d) Make a row of gathers 13 mm inside each end and draw up to the required depth. Fasten ends securely. Make two further rows of gathers at each side of belt about 20 mm apart, to be positioned at side seams.

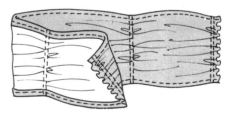

(e) Cut four pieces of boning 13 mm narrower than the belt and make a casing with seam binding.

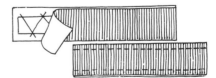

(f) Centre the covered bones over gather lines on wrong side and slipstitch into place.

(g) On right side at either end centre and sew grosgrain 25 mm/2·5 cm wide and 25 mm/2·5 cm longer than width of belt along gathering lines, allowing ends to extend 13 mm at either end of rows of stitching.

Belts and Buckles

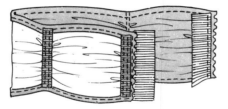

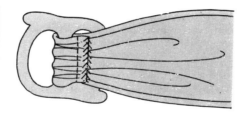

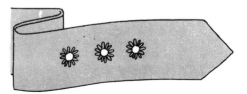

(h) Turn in grosgrain ends and fold grosgrain to wrong side. Slipstitch into place.

(i) Attach hooks to the grosgrain at one end, and eyes to the other so that edges meet exactly and evenly at centre back when fastened.

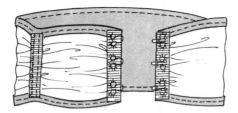

3. Belt Fastenings
Buckles
Buckles are a very secure way of fastening belts and a great many types are available. They may be metal, wood, plastic or fabric-covered and can be designed to catch the eye or be unobtrusive. Kits are available for buckles to be covered with fabric. Buckles may be of the slide, prong and eyelet, or clasp type and each is attached to the belt in a different way. To work out where to place a buckle try on the finished belt and mark the centre front.

Slide —
(usually used for a straight soft belt)
(a) Trim the unfinished end of the belt so that it extends 25 mm/2·5 cm beyond the centre front mark. Stitch 6 mm from the raw edges, then overcast.

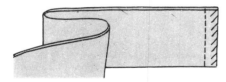

(b) Fit this end round the bar of a buckle narrower than the belt width by forming small pleats, slipstitch securely into place.

(c) Press studs may be attached to keep belt closed on a soft belt like this. Put belt on. Mark positions for press studs with pins on both under and over wrap.
(d) Do not make the fitting too tight or the press studs will frequently pop open.
Prong and Eyelet —
Trim the unfinished end of the belt so that it extends 5 cm beyond the centre front mark. Stitch 6 mm from the raw edges, then overcast.
(b) Make hole for the prong of the buckle at the centre prong mark and overcast the raw edges.

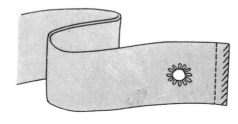

(c) Push prong through the hole, fold down the end of the belt and stitch it firmly in place.

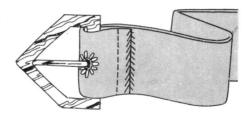

(d) At the other end of the belt make an eyelet at the centre front marking (exact

waist measurements) and one or two others either side, for adjustment.

To make eyelets: an inexpensive kit can be bought to fix metal eyelets into belts or they can be stitched by hand.

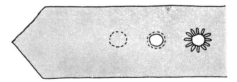

Hand made eyelets —
(a) Mark the position of the holes.
(b) Sew round the marks with rings of tiny running stitches. (Use stab stitches on thick fabrics.)
(c) Pierce holes in the centres with a knitting needle, awl or stiletto.
(d) Satin stitch or buttonhole stitch closely round the edges.

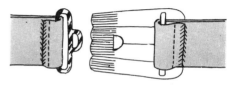

Clasp —
(a) Slip the unfinished belt ends through the buckle and its bar, and fold back the ends.
(b) Try the belt on, and trim the excess away to 2 – 4 cm.
(c) Remove the buckle and stitch across each end 6 mm from the edge. Overcast.
(d) Replace the two buckle pieces, turn back the belt ends and slipstitch securely into place.

Hooks and eyes
Use these for securing closely fitting belts, or together with press studs which will hold the loose end of a belt in place. They may be used with a slide buckle, or on their own to fasten a cummerbund, contour belt or ready-tied ribbon belt.

Belts and Buckles

A belt with an intricate bow or other decoration at the front may be fastened unobtrusively with hooks and eyes at the back.

Sew them securely to the belt, placing them just far enough from the end so that they do not show — see chapter on Fastenings.

Press studs

These cannot take as much strain as other fastenings but are ideal for loose belts, or for holding the loose end neatly in place. First, sew the buckle in place. Try on the belt again, matching the centre fronts. Mark the position for the press studs on both ends of the belt. Sew them securely — see chapter on Fastenings.

Touch and close tape

"Velcro" is a commercially made nylon tape which fastens at a touch by means of "burrs" on two separate strips. It is useful on easy-to-remove loose belts for children and the infirm, or to hold a loose belt end in place. Follow the manufacturer's instructions for use.

4. Belt Carriers

Belt carriers (or belt loops) are needed to keep the belt at the garment waist or hip line during wear. Carriers should be long enough for the belt to slide through easily — usually 6 – 13 mm wider than the belt, according to the thickness of the fabric. Mark the position of the carriers on the garment, and note the width of the finished belt. On children's clothes, belts may actually be fixed to the waistline in one place.

Thread loops

(a) Use a double strand of Dewhurst cotton perlé or thread — colour and type matched to the fabric.
(b) On the wrong side of garment secure thread to seam allowance half the width of the belt away from waist seam or waist line.
(c) Bring thread through seamline and make at least four large bar tacks, finishing exactly, the same distance away from waistline on the other side. As the tacks will be longer than the width of the belt, they will therefore appear rather slack. Check that the belt will easily pass through carriers. These tacks will form the body of the loops.
(d) Work buttonhole stitches to cover the tacks from end to end. When complete, thread ends through seam and secure on wrong side.

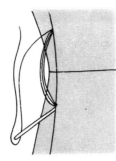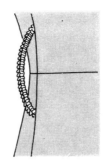

Rouleau carriers
(see chapter on Fastenings for Rouleau method)
Method 1 —
(a) Make rouleau loops 5 cm wider than the belt.
(b) Make an opening either side of the waistline in the side seam of the garment and insert rouleau ends. Position so that the loop is exactly 13 mm wider than the belt. Pin into position.
(c) Slide belt through to check that carriers are big enough.
(d) Restitch the section of seam including rouleau — twice for extra strength.

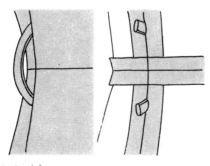

Method 2 —
The belt carriers are used here as a feature of the garment, as on jeans or overalls, and are top stitched into place. The stitching may be done with matching thread or with a bright contrast.
(a) Make lengths of rouleau 4 cm longer than belt width.
(b) Turn under 6 mm each end and press well.
(c) Pin the carriers centrally on the side seams at either side of waistline — use more if desired for effect.
(d) Pass belt through carriers before stitching to ensure that it will pull smoothly through.

(e) Stitch carriers into place securely.

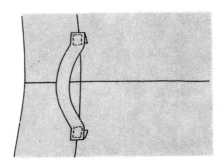

Binding and Piping

1. Cutting bias binding
True bias strip
Continuous bias
2. Joining true bias strips
3. Common bias binding faults
4. Shaping binding before sewing
5. Binding edges
Single binding
Curved edges
Double binding
Corners
Joining
Ending
6. Piping
Without cord (piped edge)
Without cord (lapped seam)
With cord.

Binding is used to neaten and strengthen raw edges on fine or medium weight fabrics. It normally shows on both right and wrong sides, and may be decorative as well as useful, in contrasting or matching colours. Bias binding can be bought in a variety of widths and colours, but it can also be made from the pieces of fabric that remain when the garment has been cut out. If cut on the true cross grain it can be stretched in sewing and fitted neatly round curves. Bias bindings are used for armholes, necklines, waistlines and curved seam edges. For bound openings, see chapter on "Openings". For bound hems, see chapter on "Hems". For bound buttonholes see chapter on "Buttons and Buttonholes". Straight bindings such as ribbon, Paris binding, seam binding and braid can be used without folding on straight edges, e.g., vertical seams in a garment, but will not stretch round curves.

1. Cutting bias binding
True bias strips
(a) Take a square or rectangular piece of fabric. The thread running across the fabric is called the weft and has a little stretch or "give".

(b) Fold one corner of the fabric over. The weft edge should lie along the lengthwise thread.

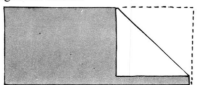

(c) Mark the fold with a line of pins. Press and remove pins. Open out the flap.
(d) Take a ruler and use it as a guide for the width of the bias. Either use pins or tailor's chalk to make lines parallel to the fold line already pressed on the fabric.

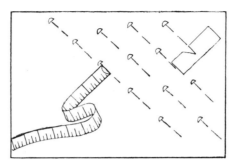

To calculate the required width of strips:
Single — twice to four times the finished width plus two turnings.
Double — four to six times the finished width plus two turnings.
(e) The distance between each length of bias should be measured accurately with a ruler.
(f) Cut along the lines marked.
(g) When all the required strips of bias have been cut they are then ready to be joined.
Continuous bias
When very long strips of bias are required an alternative method is to be recommended.
(a) On the wrong side of a rectangle of fabric prepared on the straight grain, mark a true bias line from an upper corner to the opposite lower side.
(b) Using this line as a guide continue to make parallel lines the width of bias required until length is sufficient.

(c) Mark a 6mm seam allowance on both ends.
(d) Placing right sides together, so that the lines on the lengthwise edges match, pin the edges and stitch. This forms a tube.
(e) Press seam open and cut along line around tube starting at first line (a) until whole strip has been cut.

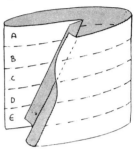

2. Joining true bias strips
(a) Place bias strips flat on the table with right sides up.

(b) Cut short ends parallel with the grain.

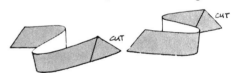

(c) With the right sides facing and the corners overlapping for the depth of the seam, place bias edges together.
(d) Tack on seam line between angles formed by the overlapping corners.
(e) Machine stitch on the seam line. Remove tacking.

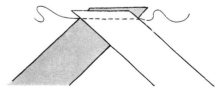

(f) Press the seam allowance flat.
(g) Cut off the protruding ends.
(h) Repeat this process with a number of bias strips until the required length of bias binding has been achieved.

Binding and Piping

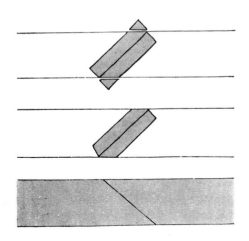

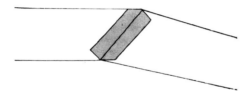

4. Shaping binding before sewing

Strips cut from fabric must have the seam turnings and fold line pressed in. All bindings will fit better if they are stretched and pressed into shape to remove the slack. Bought bias binding has already been shrunk but it can still be shaped.

Folding:

(a) Fold the cut strip in half lengthways, wrong sides together, and press lightly.

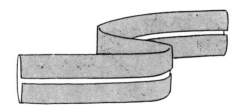

(b) For single binding open it out and fold the cut edges to the centre. Press again.

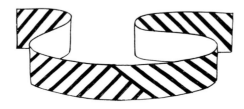

(c) Joins in opposite directions. Caused by failing to cut and place ends of bias strips parallel to each other before sewing together.

3. Common bias binding faults

(a) Joins uneven when the bias has been completed. This is caused by putting edges of fabric together for joining without overlapping the seam allowance.

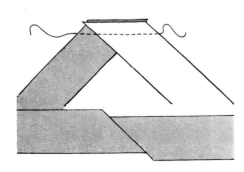

(d) Stripes in opposite directions. Caused by mixing right and wrong sides of woven fabric, or by using fabric from opposite bias.

Shaping:

(a) Pin one end of the strip to the ironing board and stretch the binding into the shape of the edge to be bound.

(b) Press it lightly, using a steam iron. Leave it to cool.

(b) Bias crooked. Caused by the piece of fabric not being exactly at right angles when the join is made.

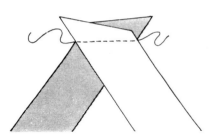

(e) Material grains with irregular weave running in different direction. Caused by confusing the right and wrong sides, or by sewing fabric from opposite bias.

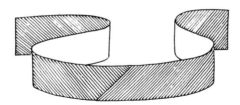

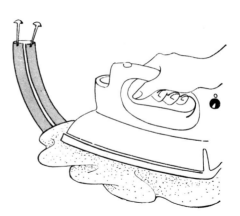

Binding and Piping

5. Binding edges

Before making the raw edges always trim down the seam allowance to 6 mm on stretchy fabrics stay stitch just inside the seam allowance, leaving slightly narrower turnings. Choose a suitable size binding for the garment, i.e., on a small garment use a narrow width. A fabric which frays badly may need a wide binding to enclose all raw edges. The type of binding must match the fabric for ease of washing, e.g., cotton binding on cotton fabric.

If using pieced bias strips the joins in the binding should be placed out of sight where possible as they would look ugly: on the centre front of the neckline for example. About 5 cm of binding should be left at the beginning and end when sewing so that the ends can be finished neatly. When completed, binding should appear of regular depth along its length. It may be applied to the wrong side then folded over to the right side to cover the machining and decoratively stitched down by hand or machine.

Single binding

Straight edges:

(a) With the true bias cut from fabric, press turnings either side of the length to the wrong side. (For bought binding the turnings are already made.)

(b) Fold the bias in half with the wrong sides facing and press.

(c) Unfold the bias binding.

(d) With right sides facing, place bias to edge of garment with the raw edge of bias meeting the raw edge of garment. Leave 5 cm free each end.

(e) Tack just above the crease line of the binding. Then machine stitch in the crease line. Remove tacking.

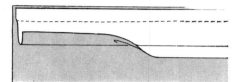

(f) Turn the bias over to the wrong side of the garment with the edge of the strip turned under.

(g) Slip-stitch the bias to the garment over the seamline, picking up machine stitches rather than fabric. Stitches will not then be visible on the right side.

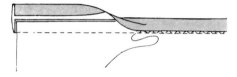

(h) Press the binding.

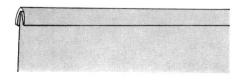

Curved edges

(a) Place binding on the garment as previously instructed for the straight edge.

(b) Stretch or ease the binding around the curve without stretching the garment.

Ease

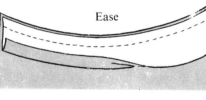

Stretch

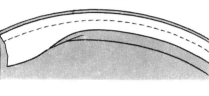

Double binding

Sometimes called French or rouleau binding, this method is used for sheer fabrics.

(a) Trim the seam allowance.

(b) Cut bias strips six times the finished width plus 6 mm to allow for the way binding becomes narrower when stretched.

(c) Fold the strip in half lengthways, wrong sides together. Press the fold, without stretching.

(d) Shape the strip to match the edge of the garment (see section on "Shaping Binding").

(e) Divide the double strip equally into three, lengthways, and press.

(f) Pin, tack and stitch the strip to the edge as for single binding (see previous section).

Quick Method

(An easy method used by professionals) — fold bias in half lengthways with wrong sides facing. Press in crease. Place bias edges to meet garment edge on right side of garment. Tack along seamline and machine stitch. Turn fold of bias to wrong side and slipstitch into place.

Binding may also be tacked into position on the wrong side with fold extending a little beyond stitching line. Binding may then be machine stitched into place from the right side in the line formed by the seam.

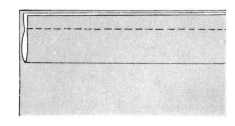

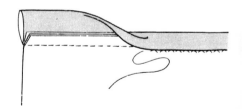

Binding and Piping

Special attachments are available for modern sewing machines so that the binding may be applied and stitched in one action; follow the maker's instructions very carefully.

Another method, nearly as quick, leaves only one row of machining which shows on both right and wrong side, but it depends on careful creasing of the folds. It is used on garments such as cotton aprons which are bound all round, or when there are lots of edges to bind. It works well with bought bias binding and Paris or seam binding.

(a) Prepare bias strip but fold one "half" slightly wider than the other.

(b) Place binding over the raw edges with the narrower "half" on the right side.

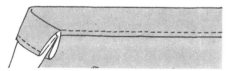

(c) Pin and tack through all thicknesses.

(d) Machine about 3 mm from the inner edge, stitching from the right side so that the slightly wider "half" is definitely caught by the machining all along the length.

(e) Remove tacking. Press from wrong side.

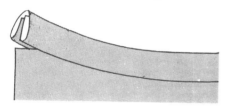

Corners

Outside:

(a) Stitch binding to garment as far as the seam allowance at the corner; backstitch for strength.

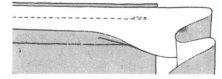

(b) Fold strip diagonally at the corner, pin and tack.

(c) Stitch along the other seamline to the edge of the garment.

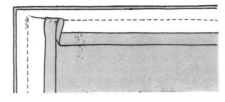

(d) Turn the binding to the inside, forming a mitre at the corner on the right side.

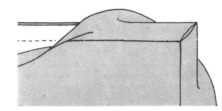

(e) On the wrong side make a second folded mitre in the other direction to avoid excess bulk.

(f) Pin and slipstitch the binding and mitre folds into place.

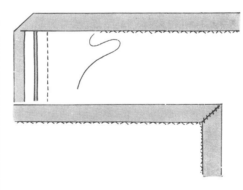

Inside:

(a) Staystitch and clip the garment corner.

(b) Pull out the clipped edges and pin and tack binding to right side as for single binding method. Stitch from the wrong side of the garment.

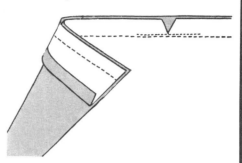

(c) Make mitre on the right side (see previous section). Pull the fold to the wrong side through the clipped edges, and turn the binding over the seam. Make a mitre in the opposite direction.

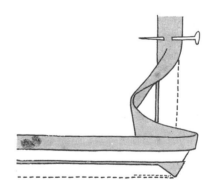

(d) Pin and tack the binding into place. Slipstitch the mitre folds and the binding. Remove tacking. Press.

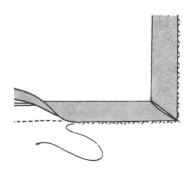

Binding and Piping

Joining

It may be necessary to join binding whilst sewing it to the garment, e.g. on an armhole.
Single or double binding:
(a) Stop machining about 25 mm/2·5 cm before the joining place.
(b) Fold the garment so that the strip ends are at right angles.
(c) Stitch the ends together on the straight grain close to the garment. (Do not catch the garment in the stitching). Trim and press the seam.

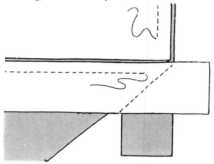

(d) Trim seam allowances at the seam and press it open. Carry on stitching binding to garment.

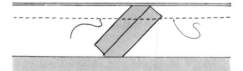

Quick Method
(a) Machine to within about 5 cm of the joining place leaving extra binding on both ends.
(b) Trim one end on the straight grain to 6 mm. Trim the other end in the same way but so that it overlaps by 13 mm; fold under 6 mm on this end, press and pin or tack the folded end over the other end. Carry on machining over the joining area. The ends can be slipstitched for neatness.

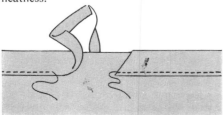

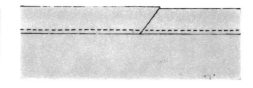

Ending

Where binding finishes at an opening or an edge to be seamed it should be neatened at the ends. The facing or fastening should first be completed.
Single and double binding:
(a) Machine the binding to the garment, extending the stitching beyond the edge of the garment.

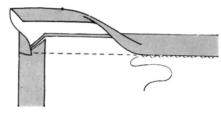

(b) Trim the binding to 6 mm beyond the garment edge and fold it under. Trim off the corner of the garment seam allowance.
(c) Turn the binding over to the wrong side and pin into place. Slipstitch, including the open end.

6. Piping

Piping is used, with or without an inner cord, to outline a style line or collar for decorative effect. It is also often used in soft furnishings such as cushions and loose covers.
A piping is made from a piece of straight or bias fabric, and is held in place by the two pieces of a seam. On the edge of a garment it is stitched between the facing and garment edge.
Without cord
Piped edge:
(a) Mark the seam lines on the garment edge and the facing.

(b) Measure the edge to be piped. Cut a piece of piping fabric slightly longer than this measurement; it should be twice the width of the finished piping plus two turnings. The strip must be bias cut and pre-shaped if the edge is curved (see section on "Bindings").
(c) Fold wrong sides together, along the length. Press and tack 6 mm from folded edge for finished 6 mm piping if fabric is slippery.
(d) Place the strip between the right sides of the seam edges with all the raw edges together.

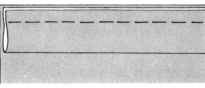

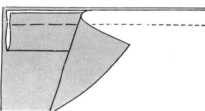

(e) Check that the piping is even in depth when seen from the right side. Machine on the seam line.

(f) Remove tacking. Clip any curves.
(g) Press on wrong side then turn right side out and press again. Complete facing.

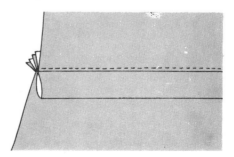

Lapped seam:
(a) Prepare the piping strip as above.
(b) Turn under the seam allowance on the edge that is to be topstitched. Press.
(c) Pin and tack this to the strip 3 mm – 6 mm from the fold.

Binding and Piping

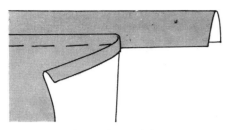

(d) Place the fitting lines of the two pieces of garments together. Pin, tack and topstitch on the fitting line.

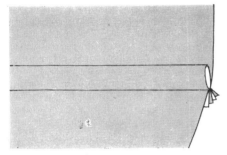

(e) Remove tacking. Press.

With cord

Buy cord suitable for the weight of the fabric and style of the garment. Boil it, to pre-shrink it, before use. Bias strips or braids are suitable for enclosing cord, and the piping or zipper foot on the sewing machine is helpful in stitching close to the cord, especially if it is bulky.

(a) Fold the piping strip in half lengthways but do not press in the fold.

(b) Place the cord in the covering; pin and tack close to the cord.

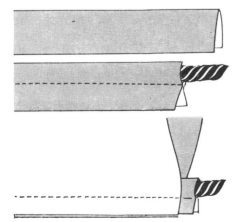

Either (c) Place the covered cord between the seam edges with the cord just above the seam line. Pin and tack. Machine close to the cord using piping or zipper foot.

Or (d) Place covered cord into a lapped seam (see previous section).

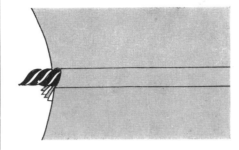

Buttons

The whole appearance of a dress often changes when the buttons are sewn on and, although zips and elastic are common, buttons are still widely used for both practical and decorative purposes. They may be an essential part of the design of the garment or be used to draw attention to a pocket, tab or seamline. A very wide range in plastic, leather, metal and wood is available to complete any look, tailored or casual, with matching or contrasting buttons. Remember to use washable buttons on a washable garment.

1. Choice

(It is important to read the section on Buttonholes before buying buttons.)
On a paper pattern, the number and size of buttons is suggested, but other ideas can make the garment much more individual. Bear in mind the size of the wearer, the fabric used and the design of the garment. Decide how the buttons should be fastened — by buttonholes, loops, braided frogs, etc., and try out several ways of grouping them.

Pin on buttons, or even discs of paper, of various sizes and colours and in different groupings, to see the effect before making the buttonholes. It is often worth spending a little more for good quality buttons, even on an inexpensive garment. Consider, too, having button moulds covered with matching fabric or buy a kit to do it yourself. If alterations have been made to the pattern, the number, size and placement of buttons may also need adjusting. Heavy buttons may drag down a fine fabric, and tiny buttons become lost on thick fabric.

2. Position

Buttons need to be spaced close enough together so that the opening does not gape when closed and they must be exactly opposite the buttonholes. Points of stress, such as a fitted waistline and the fullest parts of the figure, should be secured with a fastening of the same kind. On a belted garment the buttons should be spaced well above and below the belt, and they should never be stitched to a hem.
(a) First make the buttonholes (see section on Buttonholes).
(b) Try on the garment and pin it closed, matching the centre front lines.
(c) Place a pin through the centre of the buttonhole into the underlay.
Horizontal buttonholes — mark through at the end of the buttonhole nearest the opening — the button should later be sewn centrally into this spot on the centre front line.
Vertical buttonholes — mark through a spot 3 mm below the top of the buttonhole, on the centre front line, and later sew on the button there.
(d) Separate the two layers of garment, mark the places for the buttons directly in line and remove the pins.
(e) If the buttons are a particularly important feature sew them on with a few stitches first and try on the garment. Then resew them exactly into position.

3. Thread

Use a strong thread such as Sylko No 40, Star, buttonhole twist or Dewhurst strong thread. A double strand of thread may be used if it is first pulled through beeswax — this makes it easier to work through the buttons and cloth, and it is less likely to form knots. Very thick thread should be used singly for the same reason and the sewing begun each time with two or three backstitches on the right side. Shiny thread is sometimes used for extra decorative effect. Use a length of thread about 46 cm long for sewing on buttons.

4. Sewing on

Buttons without shanks
(a) For sewing on buttons use Dewhurst Strong Thread, Sylko No. 40 or Star,
(b) Buttons should be positioned and sewn approximately half their diameter from the edge of the garment or where indicated on the pattern.
(c) Fasten on thread at the place where the buttons will be attached, by two or three backstitches on the right side.

(d) Centre of button should be placed over the thread fastening.
(e) According to the thickness of the material, determine the length of shank required, remembering that the thicker the material the larger the shank. The shank should be the thickness of the garment edge with the buttonhole, i.e. two layers of fabric and one of interfacing — perhaps about 10 mm thick on a coat. A single matchstick makes a shank about 3 mm long. Place matchstick across the top of the button.
(f) Pass thread across the matchstick and through the second hole of the button to the back of the fabric. Repeat this process until a sufficient number of threads have been sewn for strength.

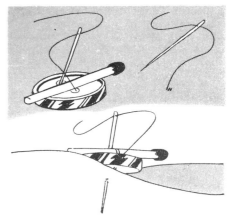

(g) Remove the matchstick and, placing the needle and thread between the button and fabric, ease the button to the end of the shank.
(h) Wind thread three or four times round the stem of the stitches for strength. Take needle to back of fabric and finish off securely.
For very thick or very delicate fabrics see also the section on Reinforced Buttons.

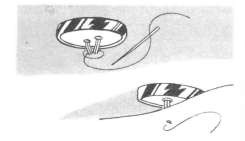

Buttons

Buttons with shanks
Should be at right angles to the buttonholes.
(a) Hand stitch buttons as two-holed buttons.
(b) Push needle sideways through shank holes then down and up through fabric.

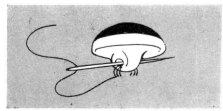

On overalls, buttons with shanks are sometimes made readily detachable for laundering. Eyelets are made, through which the shanks are pushed and toggles secure them on the wrong side. Some buttons are made with studs and caps for the same purpose.

With four holes
(a) These can be sewn as two-holed buttons. Back stitches should lie parallel on wrong side of fabric.

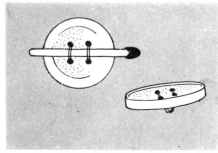

(b) There is a variety of ways in which thread may be stitched through holes. On any one garment make sure that the same method is used for each button.
(c) Crossover stitching is only used on buttons with a sunken centre, e.g. men's trouser buttons. Arrowhead stitching is particularly decorative if stitched with shiny thread.

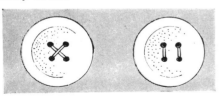

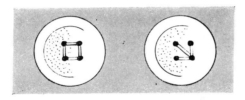

Linen without holes
(a) These buttons are used on household linens and pillow cases.
(b) They should be sewn on as buttons with holes, but no shanks need to be formed.
(c) Stitches should take up one-third of diameter.
(d) Stitches can be strengthened and neatened on both sides by buttonhole stitches being formed over them.

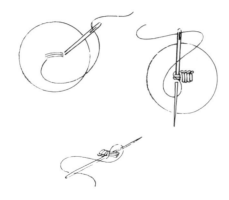

Covered
These are usually made in self-fabric and they may be of any size from tiny satin wedding dress buttons to large ones for a tweed coat. They are made up commercially, or can be prepared at home from a kit, and have either a shank or a padded fabric back which is sewn as for a shank.

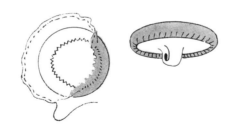

Reinforced
Usually necessary on coats or suits where the button will get a lot of use, or on delicate fabrics which might be dragged down or torn by the continual pull on a button. On thick fabrics — put a small flat button exactly underneath the button on the inside of the garment, and sew through both, making a shank on the right side only. On delicate fabrics — place a small folded square of fine ribbon or seam binding between garment and facing underneath the button. Sew through all layers.

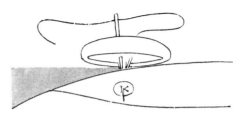

Link
These are used instead of a cuff link, and sometimes to fasten the necks of capes.
(a) Check how long the thread linking needs to be for the cuff or cape to close neatly.
(b) Make two or three loops of thread this length between the two buttons, then buttonhole stitch over them along most of the link. Knot the ends securely.

Jewelled
If the button has sharp edges, or is a rough, irregular shape it can be sewn directly to the buttonhole. Press studs can then be sewn underneath to fasten the opening.

Buttons

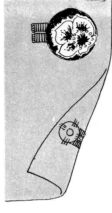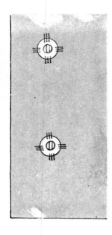

Chinese Ball

These are generally used for decorative purposes only, although they may be used as the buttons in frog fastenings if made from strong, good quality cord and should be sewn on as jewelled buttons if used at an opening. They are made from matching or contrasting cord, braid or rouleau and can be cheaper than bought buttons.

(a) Use cord, or braid or bias strip.

(b) If making a small button cut a piece of cord 20 cm to 25 cm long.

(c) Loop cord.

(d) Loop again putting it under the first loop.

(e) Make a third loop weaving it through the other two loops. Loops should remain open when working them.

(f) Ease the loops together and shape them into a ball.

(g) Ends should be cut, then sewn flat to the underside of the ball.

Buttonholes

The most usual way for buttons to form a closure on a garment is to match them to buttonholes — small slots cut and finished in the fabric just large enough for the button to pass through. Buttonholes must be neatly made to look smart — badly finished ones will really spoil the look of the garment. Generally buttonholes are positioned so that the distance between the end of the buttonhole and the opening edge of the garment is at least half the width of the button. Buttonholes may be positioned vertically, horizontally, or, as a fashion detail, at an angle.

1. Choice

Horizontal — (straight across)
Most popular of all because they take a lot of wear and tear. When sewn by hand they are best made with one square or straight end, and one round end nearest to the opening.

Vertical — (straight up and down)
Are suitable to use when there will be very little strain or pull at the opening or when they are more suited to the style of the garment — on a loose fitting blouse for example. These buttonholes, if worked by hand, may have either round or square ends. Round ended buttonholes are usually used on fine fabrics — delicate underwear, nightwear, evening wear and also on baby garments. The style of the garment and the fabric that is being used will act as a guide to the most appropriate type of buttonhole.

Bound
Give a very professional couture look to coats, suits and dresses, especially when the fabric is of very high quality and the design is distinctive. There are several methods of making them.

Hand worked
Are the best for fine, dainty, summer-weight fabrics, also for underwear and baby garments. They are stronger than bound buttonholes.

Machine stitched
Give a crisp, hardwearing finish for casual or semi-casual wear and tailored garments. The modern domestic sewing machine is capable of producing exceptionally good buttonholes providing the instructions in the handbook are closely followed, the machine is accurately set and the stitching worked slowly and carefully.

2. Points to Remember

1. Buy your buttons *before* you make your buttonholes otherwise you may have to search for a long time to find the right size in the right colour.
Always buy the number that your pattern suggests *plus* one or two more. When buttons are lost it can be very expensive to replace them all.
Look for strength in the buttons that you choose and buy the best quality you can afford. Plastic buttons with shanks very often break and unless they are all moulded in one piece are not worth consideration. Metal ones are ideal — long lasting and durable.
2. Make sure that buttonholes are positioned at the places which take the most stress — at a fitted waistline or at the fullest part of the bust for example — otherwise the opening will tend to gape.
3. If you have to alter the length of the garment make sure that the buttonholes are spaced evenly between the top and bottom button position.
4. If the garment is to be buttoned and belted make sure that the buttonholes are not too near the belt — otherwise the buttons will catch on the belt and pull the opening out of shape.

5. Remember that large buttonholes should be spaced further apart than small ones. Large buttonholes made too close together will look very ugly and unbalanced.
6. If you happen to choose buttons larger than suggested by your pattern — *NEVER* move the buttonhole inwards from the position shown on the pattern. If you do you will alter the centre line on the garment and throw out of balance. *INSTEAD* extend the edges of the fabric to make room for the extra button size, if necessary on both the over and under lap. Make this alteration to the pattern before the garment section is cut out.
7. Always interface buttonholes for support. If you forget to do this they may tear and fray with wear before very long.
8. Test your buttonholes on a scrap of the garment fabric before attempting to sew them on the actual garment. This avoids spoiling the garment if any problems should arise. Take a scrap of the fabric — large enough to handle easily — a scrap of the appropriate interlining and interfacing and sandwich them together in the same order as on the garment. Do not test the fabric *alone* otherwise the thickness will not be the same and the test inaccurate. You may find that you have to use a slightly different method from the one originally intended if the fabric frays, or if the layers are too bulky. It is far better to discover problems at the testing stage than to risk spoiling the garment.
9. Buttonholes should look slim and neat when finished and generally only about 6 mm wide: on fine fabrics they may need to be a little narrower — wider on the bulky ones.

3. Measuring

The size of the button will always determine the size of the buttonhole. The minimum length of the buttonhole must be equal to the diameter of the button PLUS the thickness. About 3 mm must be added to make room for the shank and fabric bulk. To find the correct length of buttonhole a piece of paper about 6 mm wide should be wrapped around the button at its widest point and pinned together where the ends meet. The paper should then be removed — without being unfastened — and flattened, the fold opposite the pin. The measurement from the fold to the pin PLUS 3 mm is the length of buttonhole needed.

Buttonholes

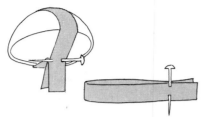

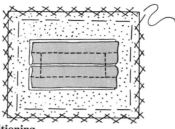

Buttonholes need to be slightly larger than the button for ease of fastening and to prevent too much wear. Thick buttons also need more space in the buttonhole. Allow about:
3 mm for round buttonholes. 10 mm for piped. 3 mm for hand sewn. 6 mm for machine sewn.

4. Interfacing
Choose a suitable interfacing to go with the fabric. A light fabric needs a light interfacing through which the buttonhole may be made for strength and support.

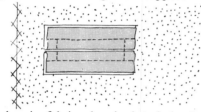

For heavier fabric a heavier interfacing is used and the buttonhole is made through fabric and lining before the interfacing is attached. A slot slightly longer than the buttonhole is cut in the interfacing, and when placed in position the bound buttonhole is pulled through to the wrong side, and the interfacing slipstitched to it all round.

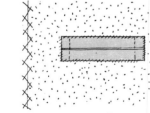

On many garments only a small area around the buttonhole position needs to be supported, about 20 mm wider and larger than the actual buttonhole. A piece of interfacing must be cut and tacked correctly over the buttonhole position on the wrong side of the fabric. The two layers are then treated as one.

5. Positioning
Usually the top buttonhole on a centre closure is placed at least half the width of the button plus 6 mm below the neckline edge. On a dress with front opening the last buttonhole should be from 7·5 cm — 13 cm from the bottom and never on the hem.
1. Mark the position of the buttonholes using machine basting. If the fabric is delicate it is better to tack the lines in by hand, so that the fabric is not marked.
(a) Mark centre front line.
(b) Mark horizontal and vertical lines for the positioning and length of buttonholes.

2. Markings for the position of the buttonholes should be made on the right side of the fabric to make sure that where the garment is cut on the straight grain, the buttonholes follow the grainline exactly.
3. For single breasted centre front openings the centre front line of the underlap is the position for buttons, and the centre front line of the overlap for the buttonholes.
4. For double breasted garments buttons need placing at equal distances either side of the centre front line on the underlap. Make buttonhole markings in corresponding positions from the centre line of the overlap.

5. On most patterns buttonhole positions are shown by a single line with a short line at right angles to one end for horizontal buttonholes, and at both ends for vertical ones.
   Horizontal
These should begin about 3 mm to the side of the button nearest the closure. This allows for the strain or the "pull" the movement of the body causes at the closure point. Use this position for buttonholes where the closure has to take considerable strain.

Buttonholes

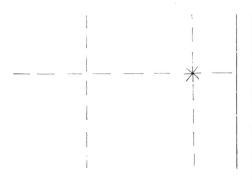

Vertical

These should be started slightly above the point where the button is attached and exactly on the centre line. The strain is taken at the top of the buttonhole. Vertical buttonholes should only be used on openings where there will not be much strain.

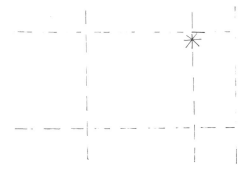

6. Bound

There are several ways of making bound buttonholes, depending on the skill of the worker and the type of fabric used. Bound Buttonholes — One Piece — these should be made before the facing is attached, through the fabric and interfacing only.

(a) Cut strip of fabric either on the straight or bias grain 5 cm wider and 25 mm/2·5 cm longer than the buttonhole. Bias pieces are always preferable as they allow more ease when buttoning and unbuttoning and can make a decorative feature if they are in a checked or striped fabric. As fabric on the bias has "give" it reduces the risk of the fabric pieces pulling away and the buttonhole fraying.

(b) Mark centre of each strip with tailor's chalk and transfer size markings with tacking lines.

(c) Centre strip over buttonhole, position right sides together, and tack all round.

(d) Machine along lines on long sides making sure that each line is kept to exactly the same length — stitch twice for strength and tie thread ends on wrong side.

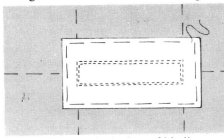

(e) On right side fold edges of binding towards buttonhole centre and press one after the other.

(f) Slash along the centre of the binding between the stitching lines from the wrong side, with small sharp scissors stopping no less than 6 mm from either end. A pin placed 6 mm in from each end will prevent the risk of overcutting. Do likewise on the garment side. If the slash is made too long the triangles left at either end will be too small to handle and the buttonholes will be weak in these places.

(g) From the ends of the slash clip diagonally to each corner being very careful not to cut any of the stitches.

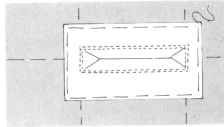

(h) Remove tacking stitches and push binding through the opening. Press away from opening. Make an inverted pleat at both ends with folds meeting exactly in the centre of the slit. Tack folds together.

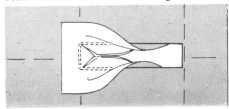

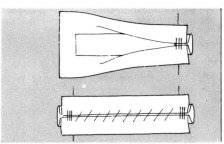

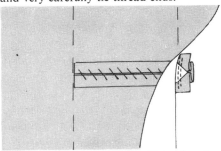

(i) With right side of garment facing you, fold back edge of opening to expose corner triangle. Machine across base of triangle using short stitches — 7–8 per centimetre — stitch each triangle twice and very carefully tie thread ends.

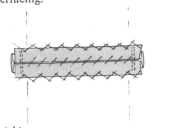

(j) Trim binding and catch stitch edges to the interfacing.

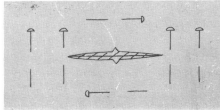

Finishing

(1) Pin and tack facing to the garment through all layers of fabric and interfacing.

(2) Place pins straight across each end of buttonhole to mark size on facing.

(3) Make a slash on facing between pins and clip the centre of each slash.

Buttonholes

(4) Turn in edges and slip stitch facing to buttonhole on the wrong side, making an oval shape.

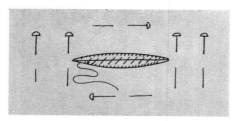

Two piece or piped
These are made before the facing is attached, through the fabric and interfacing only. It is a quick and easy method for firmly woven fabrics.
(a) Cut a piece of fabric 25 mm/2·5 cm wide and twice the length of the buttonhole plus 25 mm/2·5 cm.
(b) Iron-on Lantor interlining to the wrong side.

(c) Fold in half along the length, wrong sides together and tack carefully 3 mm from the folded edge. Trim the edges to 3 mm from the stitching.

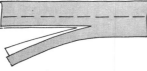

(d) Place two strips on the right side with their cut edges along the centre line of the buttonholes, leaving 6 mm at least each end for turnings. Tack into place.
(e) Machine into place by double rows of stitching over the original tackings on each strip. Start machining in the centre of each strip.

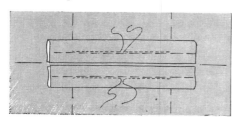

(f) From the wrong side cut the buttonholes between the rows of stitching and cut the corners. Turn strips through and press. Oversew the folded edges together.

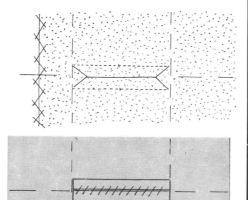

(g) Neaten as for one-piece bound buttonholes (see previous section) or cut a slit in the facing, turn under the edges and hem them into place.
Window method
Probably the easiest method, it is particularly good for bulky or easily frayed fabrics. With this method it may also help to interface afterwards.
(a) Repeat stages (a) – (g) of one-piece method using pieces of organza or similar fabric, instead of self fabric.

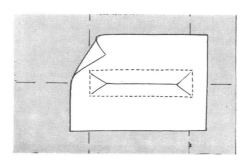

(b) Turn organza binding through to wrong side and press all round to form a window opening. Be careful to ensure that the organza is not visible from the right side.

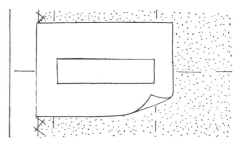

(c) Cut straight strips of the garment fabric about 5 cm wide and 25 mm/ 2·5 cm longer than the buttonholes; these may be on the bias or on the grain.
(d) Place two strips together right sides facing, and machine baste along the exact centre line using longest machine stitch.

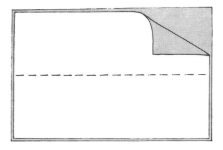

(e) Fold each piece of fabric back, wrong sides together, and press the resulting seam.

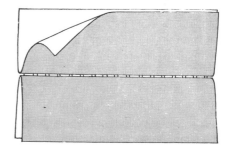

(f) Position the tacked pieces of fabric over the window on the wrong side of the garment with the "seam" exactly centred. Secure with a pin at either end.

Buttonholes

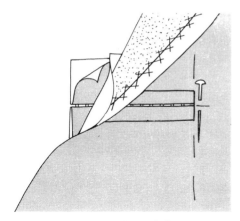

(g) Turn garment fabric back from buttonhole to show seam. Using about eight stitches per centimetre stitch through previous seam and binding on long side of buttonhole, a little beyond seam at each end.

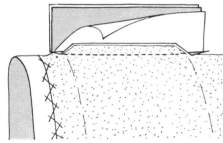

(h) Stitch the triangular ends in the same way — secure thread ends and press.

Finishing window method—
The facing on the window method may be finished in the same manner as the "windows" are constructed. Follow the first three stages of the window method on the facing and slipstitch windows over buttonholes on the wrong side.

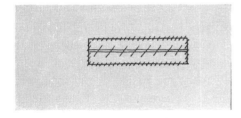

7. Slot
Also called seam buttonholes, these are small openings in a seam near to the garment edge. These slots may also be made in other seams to take belts and tabs for decoration.
(a) Mark position for openings in seam, pin and tack.
(b) Place strips of strong seam tape or ribbon, about 25 mm/2·5 cm longer than slot on marking at seam line and stitch carefully along each edge on both seam allowances.
(c) Stitch seam and back stitch at both ends of each slot.

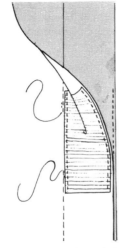

(d) Press seam open and work bar tacks at each end of slot on the wrong side of fabric. Make sure that no stitches show on the right side of the fabric.
(e) Remove tacking stitches from each opening.

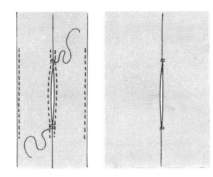

8. Handsewn
Badly sewn buttonholes that are not level or evenly stitched are very noticeable on a garment, and it is always wise to practise first on a scrap of fabric.
Horizontal buttonholes usually have fan-shaped stitches at the end nearest the garment opening, and a bar tack at the other. Vertical buttonholes usually have bar tacks at both ends. See also the section on Tailored Buttonholes. They are sewn after the garment is finished, through all layers of fabric and interfacing.
(a) Mark the buttonhole in the usual manner as described in previous section on Bound Buttonholes.
(b) Place a pin at either end of rectangle and slash along exact centre line. The pins will prevent the slash from going too far. Remove pins.
Note: For extra strength a line of machine stitching can be placed in a rectangle around the slit about 3 mm from the slit.

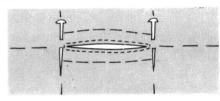

On fabrics that fray badly the edges of the slit may be overcast. Both processes must be done very neatly or this stitching will show on the finished buttonhole, and may make it thick and lumpy.

(d) Starting at the right-hand side, work buttonhole stitches to end of first side. Use a 50 cm length of either Dewhurst Strong Thread or Sylko 40. If a longer thread than this is used it may be very difficult to manipulate, and will tend to cause twisting and knotting.
(e) Insert needle into slash from the right side bringing it out a little outside the stitching line. Bring thread around under point from eye of needle. Draw needle through fabric to form a knot at the edge of the slash.

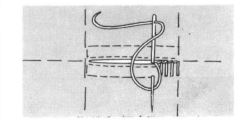

Buttonholes

Continue along the slit to one end then in a fan shape round the end.
Continue in buttonhole stitch along the other side.
(f) Keep the stitches close together to cover cut edge. Keep the stitches very even and do not pull the knots too tight as this will tend to buckle the fabric edge.
(g) Make several stitches across the end just covering the last stitches to form a bar tack. Work buttonhole stitches through fabric and bar tack, and finish neatly and securely. If the straight effect is preferred, both ends may be finished with a bar tack, but generally the fan ends looks daintier.

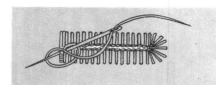

9. Machine Stitched

These are very suitable for casual, washable clothes. Machine stitched buttonholes can be made on modern zig-zag sewing machines and on straight stitch machines with the aid of a buttonhole attachment. The buttonhole attachment is supplied with a set of templates in various sizes. The template of the required length is selected and inserted into the attachment. The buttonholes will therefore all be exactly uniform in length — a good point to remember. Additionally, the templates that are supplied are of both oval and keyhole variety.
The length and placement of the buttonholes should be marked on the fabric in the usual manner and interfacing used as necessary, preferably in a colour as near as possible to the fabric colour. Follow instructions from the machine handbook very closely. This will give the setting for *length* and *width* of stitch required to make a satin stitch. On some modern machines, buttonholes may be worked automatically — this means that after following the setting instructions the machine can be programmed to stitch the buttonhole all round without the operator having to turn the fabric.
As with the other methods of buttonhole making, a test sample should always be made first. As fabrics vary — so will the

machine setting. The same number of fabric layers as for the final buttonhole should be used for the test sample. Where the satin stitch has to be set by the operator it is absolutely essential that the work runs through the machine for the length required without the operator having to push or pull the fabric. If the work does require pulling it means that the stitch has not been set correctly. This will invariably result in the piling up of the stitches, and a lumpy buttonhole. Very strong and neat buttonholes may be worked with Sylko 50 or Star with the stitch not quite as close as satin stitch. A strong buttonhole can be made by running a strand of Sylko Perlé or two strands of Strong Thread under the stitches whilst sewing. Most machines that sew a zig-zag stitch have an extra sewing foot for buttonholing which will allow for this.
(a) First attach the facing and interfacing.
(b) Trace on all buttonhole markings.
(c) Stitch the buttonholes following the machine manufacturer's instructions. For extra strong buttonholes stitch over a second time.

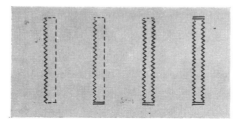

10. Corded

These buttonholes do not stretch but are very strong and wear well. The final appearance is raised and very smart. For bound buttonholes — using the two-piece method — fold the fabric strips around a piece of fine cord or twine. Stitch close to it using a piping or zig-zag foot to hold it in place. Using the one-piece method follow the diagrams below.

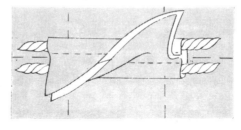

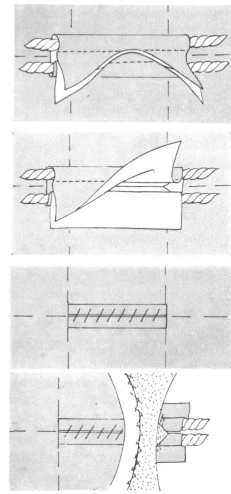

Hand sewn — Pin piece of Sylko Perlé No. 5 twist around the slot, securing it at one end. Work the buttonhole stitch over this and finish with a bar tack at the end with the pin. Cut off the ends of the cord very close.

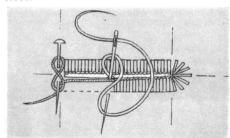

Buttonholes

Machine sewn — Follow the manufacturer's instructions as there may be a special sewing foot to use.

Tailor's

This looks like a keyhole and is sewn in the same manner as a hand-stitched buttonhole. It is used mainly on tailored coats and suits made from thick fabrics, or on casual wear fabrics such as drill, canvas or denim. The hole at the end takes the strain of the thick fabric and a button shank prevents the fabric dragging.

(a) Using an awl (a sharp pointed stiletto), or a sharp leather punch, make a hole at the end of buttonhole marking, nearest to opening edge.

(b) Place a pin across opposite end of marking and slash.

(c) Overcast cut edges all round.

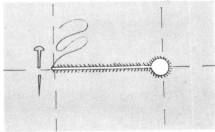

(d) Work buttonhole stitch all round and finish straight end with long stitches to form a bar tack. Work buttonhole stitch through fabric and across bars. Finish securely.

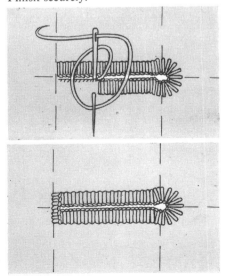

Collars

1. **Making a Collar**
2. **Methods of Attaching Collars**
3. **Types of Collar**
   Flat
   Rolled
   Notched
   Shawl
   Collar with stand
   Standing
   Bias turnover

For other ways of finishing the neck of garments see chapter on Necklines.

Collars are often the focal point of the garment and they are always very much in view, so it is essential to cut, stitch and fit them perfectly. The variety of collars used in dress design is almost endless but they are usually just adaptions of a few basic shapes. Detachable collars can be made for ease of washing.

Many collars rise from the neckline and turn down to create a roll which must be perfectly smooth, without rippling or twisting, and the underside of such a collar should never show. The two ends of a pointed or curved collar need to be identical so that the collar is symmetrical.

Interfacing may be needed to maintain the required shape and body of a collar, and the type used depends on the weight of the fabric and type of collar chosen.

1. Making a Collar

(General instructions only — see sections on types of collars for details.)
(a) Check the size of the collar against the neckline if pattern alterations have been made.
(b) Follow the pattern layout instructions carefully as the direction of the grain on the collar is important. For a collar with a shaped neckline the grain should run parallel with the centre back.

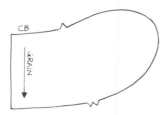

Straight collars are cut either on the straight grain or on the true cross grain.

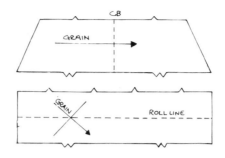

(c) Cut interfacing (if used) exactly the same size and shape as the collar (or to fit exactly inside the stitching line for thick fabrics). This piece is then lightly hand stitched to the fitting line on the wrong side of the collar). Non woven interfacing is excellent as it does not stretch, but woven interfacings must be cut on the same grain as the collar.

(d) Transfer pattern markings onto the two collar pieces (called the collar and under collar) including the centre front, centre back and shoulder lines.
(e) Pin and tack the interfacing to the wrong side of the collar. Trim off the interfacing close to tacking on the neck edge (or use iron-on interfacing, following the manufacturer's instructions). Trim off or mitre corners on interfacing to reduce bulk, just inside seam line.

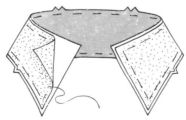

(f) Place the right side of the under collar onto the right side of the collar, matching fitting marks, pin and tack, leaving the neck edge open.

(g) Machine stitch the three layers together, except along the neck edge, in the direction of the straight grain. Start at the collar centre and stitch to one end first. Repeat for the other half but overlap a few stitches to begin with. If the interfacing was hand stitched, machine the collar and under collar together just off the edge of the interfacing. On a pointed

collar sew one stitch across the corner to make it easier to turn through.

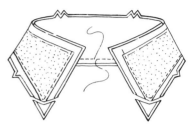

(h) Press the machine stitching.
(i) Trim the interfacing very close to the machine stitching. Trim the under collar seam allowance to 3 mm and the collar seam allowance to 6 mm so that there is no thick ridge at the edge of the finished collar ("layering"). Curved collars — clip all the turnings nearly to the stitching about every 13 mm. Pointed collars — snip off the turnings diagonally across the points, and cut the corners back.

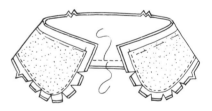

(j) Turn the collar so that the right side of the fabric is outside using a blunt orange stick or knitting needle inside to push points out gently. A fine pin or needle can be used from the outside to pull the corners out fully.
(k) Separate the neck edges and press the seam open from the inside.

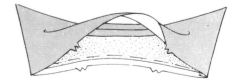

(l) Roll the collar edges, curves and points gently between fingers and thumbs until the stitching is visible at the edge. Then pull the undercollar slightly until the stitching is not visible from the top. Tack and press.

Collars

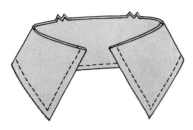

(m) Top stitch if required.

2. Methods of Attaching Collars

A flat, shaped collar is attached with a facing, otherwise the neck seam would show, whereas a standing or roll collar is better stitched directly to the garment without added bulk. Collars on shirts sometimes combine both methods so that the fronts of the neck are faced but the collar is hemmed at the back of the neck. Tailored shirts are usually attached to a band, so that the collar rolls over at the top of the band or stand.

Whichever method of attachment is used the collar must be positioned accurately on the garment. Match notches and balance points exactly and check that the collar is symmetrical at the centre front. Two-piece collars should be butted together and tacked before pinning them to the garment so that a wide gap does not develop at the centre front or centre back. The following pages show some ways of attaching various types of collars — follow the instructions in the pattern envelope for individual variations.

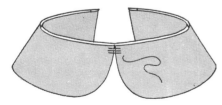

3. Types of Collar
Flat

This collar, often called a Peter Pan, is one of the easiest and most common. It has a curved neck edge and may be varied in width, made in two pieces with a tiny gap at both back and front, or have a curved, pointed or scalloped edge. There is very little roll, as it lies flat on the bodice, and both collar and under collar are cut from the same pattern piece.

Flat collars cut in one piece may be attached without a facing if the neckline is to be worn fastened (otherwise the hemming stitches show), but generally a facing is used.

Attaching without facing:
(a) Separate the neck edges of the collar and under collar (see section on "Making a Collar").
(b) Pin the under collar to the right side of the garment at the neckline, carefully matching pattern markings. Gently ease where necessary. Tack.

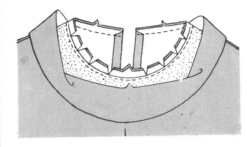

(c) Machine along fitting line. Press well, remove tacking. Trim off the seam allowances (layer to remove bulk), clipping curves where necessary. Press turnings up into the collar.
(d) Rolling the collar over the hand so that the upper collar is slightly stretched, turn under the seam allowance on the neck edge of the upper collar and tack the folded edge down to cover the machining, being careful to match balance points.
(e) Hem neatly into place, picking up original machine stitches.

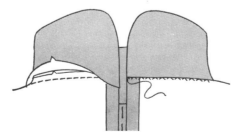

Using a bias strip facing:
(a) Pin and tack the collar carefully into place.
(b) Cut a piece of bias binding, or matching fabric cut on the cross, the

length of the collar. With right sides together, pin and tack it on the neck edge fitting line. Machine through all layers on the fitting line.

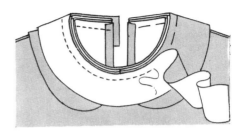

(c) Remove tackings, trim the seam allowances (layering to avoid bulk) and press well with the raw edges and bias strip away from the collar.
(d) Turn the bias strip onto the wrong side, fold under the raw edge if necessary, tack and hem into place.

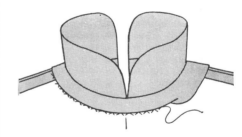

Using a shaped facing:
(a) Prepare the facing by turning the notched edge under and stitching the edge as shown in the pattern instructions.
(b) Pin and tack the facing to the neck edge over the collar right sides together.
(c) Machine stitch on the fitting line, trim and clip the seams.

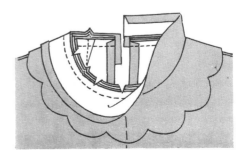

Collars

136

(d) Press the facing to the inside. Hem or slipstitch the facing into place, at shoulder seams only.

Rolled

Garments of light to medium weight fabrics may have collars with a carefully shaped stand so that there is a pronounced roll around the neck. The collar often stands well away from the neck and in this case the collar is cut in one piece on the bias. Rolled collars usually have a two-piece under collar and a slightly bigger upper collar, both cut on the cross. Making up:

(a) Prepare the bodice. Make up the collar (see section on "Making a Collar"), following the paper pattern instructions. The under collar may need stretching to fit, and the upper collar should be pressed so that the seam is not visible at the edge.

(b) The collar must be shaped at this stage to make the roll line. Tack the neck edges together while it is in this position and stitch a thread marking line along the roll line.

Attaching with a self-facing:

(a) Staystitch the garment neck edge and self facing.

(b) Pin and tack the collar to the garment right sides together and make sure that the roll line looks right when worn.

(c) Join the back neck facing to the garment, and finish the notched edge by

turning under the seam allowance and edge-stitching.

(d) Pin and tack the facing over the collar. Machine on the fitting line, facing side uppermost.

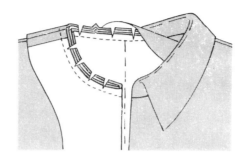

(e) Trim off the seam allowances, layering to avoid bulk. Clip through all the thicknesses nearly to the stitching. Press the facing to the inside and tack down close to the neck seam. Slipstitch the facing into place at shoulder seams. Remove the trace thread from the roll line.

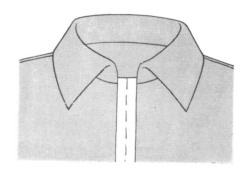

Notched

Sometimes called a convertible collar, this is really a rolled collar with lapels. It always has a front opening and usually one edge laps over. Tailoring techniques may be needed if thick fabric is chosen. For light-weight fabrics make up the collar and attach as for a rolled collar — see last section.

For medium weight fabrics:

(a) Join the two under collar sections together and iron on or sew on the interfacing. Pin, tack and stitch the under collar to the garment neck edge matching notches. Clip curves nearly to the stitching.

Trim off the seam allowances and press the seam open.

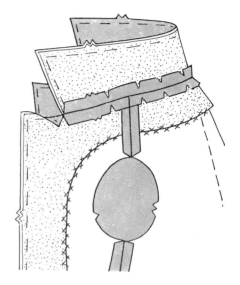

(b) Pin, tack and stitch the upper collar to the neck edge of the facing, clipping edges where necessary. Press seam open. Finish unstitched edge of facing as directed in pattern instructions.

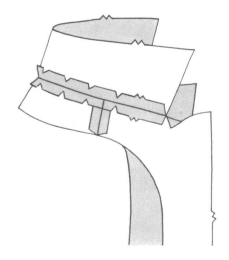

(c) Pin and tack two prepared pieces (i.e. garment and under collar facing and top collar), right sides together, at neck seam only. Try on the garment as it is without joining the other edges.

Collars

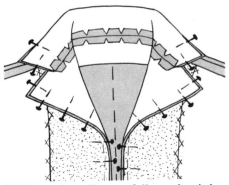

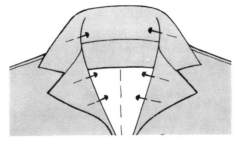

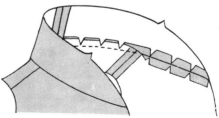

(d) Shape the collar carefully so that it has a smooth roll over and sits well all round — the garment and under collar seam allowances will now show beyond the collar and facing. Pin the edges of the collar together to hold the required position.

(e) Tack and stitch the collar pieces together first, easing and stretching where necessary. Then stitch facing and garment together along the fitting line starting each time at the neck seam. At the corners take one stitch across the point each time, so that when turned through, the notches will be a good shape.

Trim the seam allowances, layering if necessary to avoid bulk. Press the seams open, then in the direction they need to be turned.

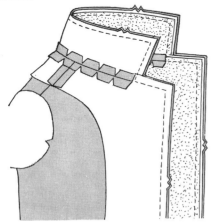

(f) Turn through to the right side and press. Try on to check the way the collar and lapels roll. Pin the roll to hold it in place, and pin again lower down just above the neck seam.

Note that the upper collar should be slightly eased over at the edge to hide the seam and the facing edge on the top of each lapel should be eased over in the same way.

(g) Lift the facing and blindstitch the neck seams loosely together. Anchor the facing down into place at the garment seams. Remove all pins and tacking. Press.

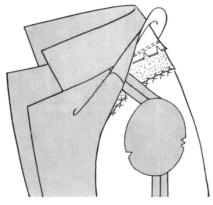

Shawl

This is really another kind of roll collar but the upper collar and lapels are cut in one piece. It is found on dressing gowns and wrap-over coats, and is held with a belt rather than buttons and buttonholes. The edge of the collar may be curved, notched, scalloped, etc.

(a) Join the two pieces of the under collar and press open the seam.

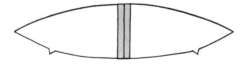

(b) Iron on or catch stitch non-woven interfacing to the wrong side of the under collar and garment along the seam lines.

(c) Pin, tack and stitch the under collar to the garment neck edge, easing if necessary and clipping along curved edges.

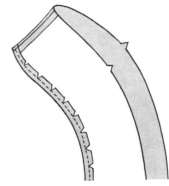

(d) Try on to check the fit.

(e) Join the upper collar and facing at the centre back and press the seam open. Turn under the seam allowance on the unstitched edge of this piece, clipping curves to make it lie flat. Stitch, trim and press.

(f) With right sides together pin and tack facing to under collar and front of garment, matching notches and easing to fit.

(g) Stitch along seam line, clip curves and trim off seam allowance. Press.

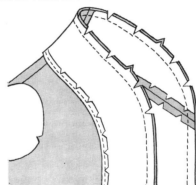

Collars

(h) Turn facing to inside and press. Slip stitch facing over the back neck seam.

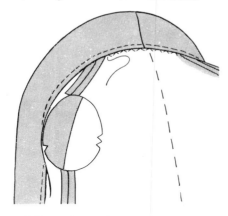

Collar with stand

Shirt and tailored blouse collars are sewn to a band which is attached to the neck edge of the garment. These collars have very little roll and are usually buttoned up to the neck at the front.

(a) Make up the collar — (see section on "Making a Collar"). Top stitch if desired. Measure neck size and adjust pattern piece for band if necessary.

(b) Trim the interfacing for the band and catchstitch or iron it on to one piece of the band within the seam line. Pin and tack it to the under collar, right sides together.

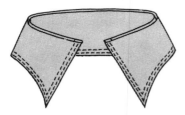

(c) Pin and tack the other band piece to the upper collar, right sides together, clipping the seam allowance as necessary so that it lies flat.

(d) Stitch the ends and upper edges together along the seam line to within 15 mm of the neck edges, leaving neck edges open.

(e) Trim off the seam allowances, layering to reduce bulk, and clip nearly to the stitching where needed so that it lies flat.

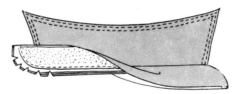

Press band away from collar so that collar is enclosed in band at neck edge.

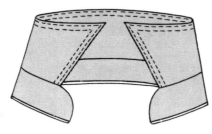

(f) Prepare the garment, including the front opening. Stay stitch the garment neck edge.

(g) With right sides together pin and tack the interfaced band piece to the garment neck edge, clipping if necessary so that it lies flat.

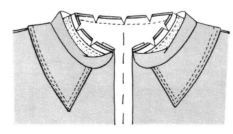

(h) Stitch, trim and layer seam turnings to reduce bulk.

(i) Press seam allowances towards the band on the front edge of the band and trim off seam allowance. Pin folded edge over seam and slipstitch into place.

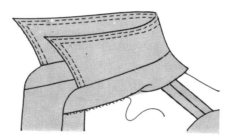

Standing

Standing

This straightforward collar, known as Mandarin, can take on many forms according to the style of the garment. It is often attached so that the collar itself finishes the neck edge, and may be fitted stiff and close to the neck, or take a softer looser shape. It may be cut in one or two sections and have a straight or curved finished edge.

(a) Interface one collar section. Use non-woven interfacing or cut a bias strip of woven interfacing and iron on or catchstitch it within the seam line.

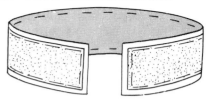

(b) For a one-piece collar fold it in half lengthways right sides together and stitch ends to within 15 mm of the neck edge. If two pieces, seam round three sides, but not the neck edge.

Trim, turn and press ends only, not along the length.

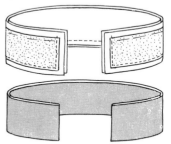

(c) Prepare garment by putting in zip or buttonholes.

(d) Pin, tack and stitch the interfaced side of the collar to the garment neck edge, clipping the seam allowances as necessary. Trim off the seam allowances, layering to remove bulk.

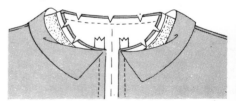

Collars

(e) Press the seam open and then towards the collar.

(f) Trim most of the seam allowance off the remaining collar edge at the neck, turn under on the seam line and tack down over the seam.

(g) Slipstitch into place, picking up machine stitches rather than fabric.

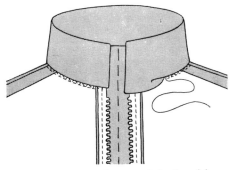

(h) The collar may be topstitched and is usually fastened with hooks or eyes.

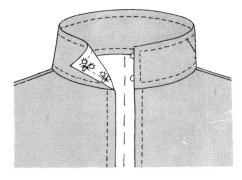

Bias turnover

This is really another type of standing collar, but is often confused with a rolled collar as there is an obvious roll at the neck. It is better known as a turtleneck, or, if cut high and close to the neck, a funnel collar. The collar is in one piece and must be cut on the cross to make a smooth roll.

(a) First staystitch the bodice neck edge. Interface and face the bodice as in the pattern instructions, and make buttonholes or put in the zip.

(b) Attach light-weight interfacing to one half of the collar, extending it over the fold line by 15 mm. Iron on or catchstitch it on within the seam lines.

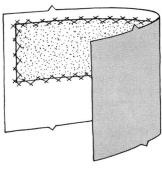

(c) Fold collar right sides together and stitch both ends to within 15 mm of the neck edge.

(d) Trim seam allowances, press and turn to the right side. Press the ends only on the right side, not along the length.

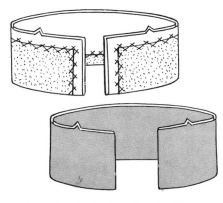

(e) Pin and tack the interfaced collar piece to the neck of the garment, right sides together and notches matching. Clip the seam allowances and ease the collar for a good fit.

(f) Stitch and trim seam allowances, layering to reduce bulk. Press turnings towards the collar.

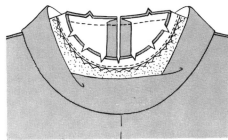

(g) Fold the collar into place and try on to check the fit. Ease the collar over to make a smooth roll line and sew a thread trace line through all the layers.

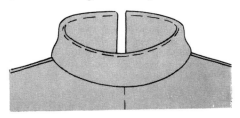

(h) Remove, trim and turn in the raw edge so that it covers the seam, slipstitch into place.

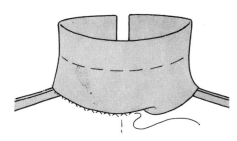

(i) Remove all tacking. Turn collar over and add hooks and eyes as required.

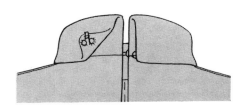

Cuffs

1. **Turned Back Cuffs**
   Straight band
   Shaped
   Shaped with band
   Cut in one with sleeve
2. **Extended Cuffs**
   Band
   Lapped over
   Shirt
   Linked
3. **Detachable Cuffs**
   Inside the sleeve
   Outside the sleeve

For other sleeve finishes see chapter on Sleeves.

The sleeve should always be pinned or tacked into the garment to check first whether the finished length of sleeve plus cuff will be right. Also try out the fit of the cuff round the wrist. Cuffs are then sewn onto the sleeves before the sleeve is finally sewn into place. If there is to be no opening at the bottom of the sleeve the cuff must be large enough for the hand to be pushed through. If the cuffs are to be fastened or lapped over, a facing or placket is used to neaten the opening in the sleeve. Most cuffs are made of two layers of fabric, and one layer of interfacing, cut on the bias. Alternatively, iron-on Lantor interlining may be used. For neat edges the seam turnings should be trimmed, layered and pressed towards the cuff.

For buttoned cuffs either make bound buttonholes before stitching the cuff sections together, or complete the cuffs and then sew buttonholes by hand or machine. Unless other instructions are given in the pattern, prepare sleeves by machining, trimming, neatening and pressing the seams; complete the plackets or faced openings if they are needed. On gathered sleeves, two rows of fine gathering stitches should be sewn round the bottom of the sleeves; sew one on the fitting line and one 6 mm nearer the raw edges.

1. **Turned Back Cuffs**
   Straight band
(a) Place ends of cuff right sides together, pin, tack and machine.
(b) Press the seam open.

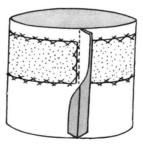

(c) Cuff should be folded in half with the right side outside. (First interface one half if required).
(d) Raw edges should be stitched together.

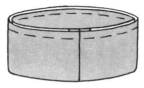

(e) Join cuff on wrong side of sleeve. Seams should meet. Machine both together with two rows of stitching.
(f) Overcast the edges. Press flat and cover with seam binding. Remove tacking.

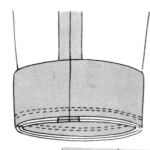

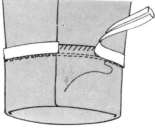

(g) The cuff should then be turned back onto the right side of the sleeve.

Shaped
(a) Sew or iron-on interlining between the top and under-cuffs inside the seam allowance.
(b) The cuff should then be spread open and the seam hidden by rolling the top edge slightly over. Tack the edge and press to hold it in position.

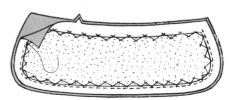

(c) Turn cuff to right side. Press seam on under-cuff. Tack, then machine raw edges together.

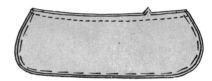

(d) Put right side of cuff to the wrong side of sleeve. Match markings. Tack, then machine stitch the two together. Remove tackings. Press.

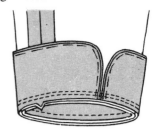

(e) Tack, then machine bias strip on cuff sides of turnings. Remove tacking. Press.
(f) Cuff should be creased away from the sleeve, then the fold of the bias machined on to the right side on the sleeve.

Cuffs

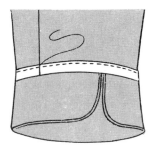

Shaped with band

(a) Sew or iron-on interlining to the band or cuff.

(b) Tack, then machine the top and under-cuffs together. Remove tacking.

(c) Ease the top piece to hide the edge seam then machine short ends.

(d) Cut corners. Turn to right side. Press seams on to under-cuff. Machine stitch raw edges together.

(e) Put the right side of one band to the right side of the cuff and tack, then machine stitch them together.

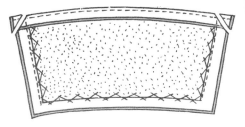

(f) Put right side of other band to under-cuff. Then use first row of stitching as guide to help position it. Machine stitch to the ends and down the sides.

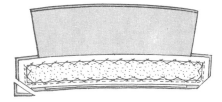

(g) Cut corners. Band should then be turned to the right side.

(h) Place right side of the band to the wrong side of the sleeve. Machine stitch into place.

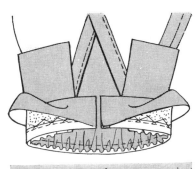

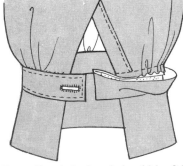

(i) The cuff and the band should be folded away from the sleeve.

(j) Loose edge of band is then turned to hide and cover the stitching. Edge stitch to sleeve.

Cut in one with sleeves

(a) Interface the cuff area before sewing the sleeve seam. Use bias cut or iron-on interfacing equal to the length of the cuff, and twice the depth plus two seam allowances.

(b) Catchstitch interfacing at the fold line and the roll line, or use iron-on interlining.

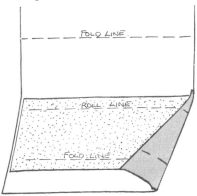

(c) Machine the sleeve seam, noting that the cuff area is usually tapered out towards the bottom edge so that the cuff will turn back easily. Press the seams open.

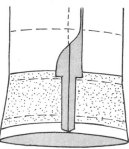

(d) Turn up the bottom edge and topstitch, or neaten it by machine.

(e) Turn the cuff inside along the foldline and tack close to the fold.

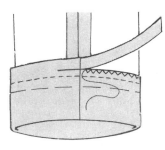

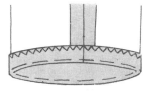

(f) Roll over the folded edge onto the right side of the sleeve forming a cuff. Tack through all the layers to keep the rolled edge in place.

(g) Neatly hem the edge to the inside of the sleeve. Press lightly.

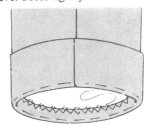

Cuffs

2. Extended Cuffs

Band

(a) Adjust the sleeve edge to fit the wrist, not too closely, and with enough room to push the hand through.

(b) Cut the rectangle of fabric to this length plus two seam turnings, and twice the finished cuff depth plus two turnings.

(c) Sew on or iron-on interfacing to one half of the cuff along length.

(d) With right sides together join the short ends of the band and press the seam open.

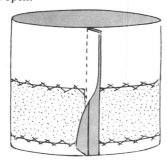

(e) Place the right side of the interfaced half to the right side of the sleeve edge, pin, tack and machine.

(f) Trim and layer the seam.

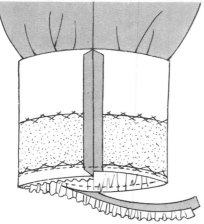

(g) Press the seam allowance into the cuff area, then turn the cuff to the inside along the foldline, wrong sides together.

(h) Tack close to the fold.

(i) Trim the remaining seam allowance, turn under the edge, and hem neatly into place picking up the machine stitching as you sew.

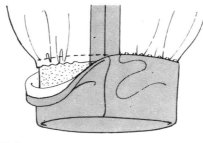

(j) Remove tacking. Press.

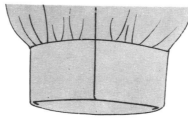

Alternative method — if the sleeve has very full gathers the cuff is attached to the sleeve edge *before* sewing the sleeve or cuff seams. It is easier to machine the gathers into place along a flat surface instead of inside a continuous band. The sleeve and cuff seams are then sewn in one continuous seam.

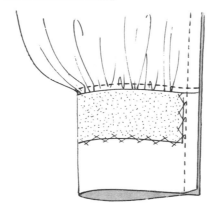

Lapped over

Full length, gathered or pleated sleeves are usually sewn into a cuff that is lapped over and fastened with a button and button-hole. This kind of cuff fits snugly to the wrist, and there must therefore be an opening in the sleeve so that the hand can push through. The sleeve opening is finished with a placket or facing before the cuff is attached. Note that the two sleeves have openings in opposite places.

Continuous Lap Placket —

(a) Stay stitch the slashed area, stitching one stitch across the point. Slash open.

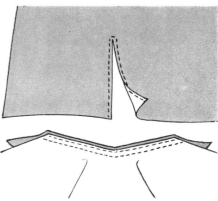

(b) Cut a strip of the garment fabric 3·2 cm wide and twice the length of the slashed opening, along a selvedge if possible.

(c) Stretch out the slash and staystitch 6 mm from edge. Place right side of strip onto right side of sleeve, pin, tack and machine close to the staystitching, with sleeve side uppermost, pivoting at corner.

(d) Press strip and turn it over to enclose the raw edges. Slipstitch selvedge into place to cover machining, or machine through all layers.

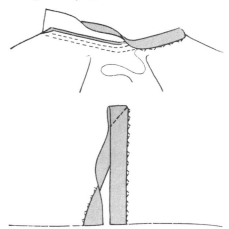

(e) Turn the lap to the inside of the sleeve and stitch diagonally at the top, to reinforce point of slash.

Cuffs

Faced Opening

(a) Cut a strip of the garment fabric 6·5 cm wide and the length of the opening plus two seam allowances.

(b) Turn under and edgestitch two long sides and one short side.

(c) Place the facing centrally over the slash markings right sides together. Machine along stitching lines taking one stitch across the point. Slash open.

(d) Pull facing through to wrong side of sleeve.

(e) Catchstitch the facing to the sleeve without the stitches showing on the right side.

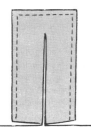

Method for Lapped Cuff

(a) Prepare the opening with a placket or facing as before. Make bound buttonholes if required.

(b) Sew or iron-on interfacing to underside of the cuff.

(c) Fold the cuff in half along its length, right sides together, and machine the ends to within 15 mm of the notch and trim, layer and press seams.

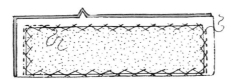

(d) Turn cuff right side out.

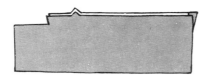

(e) Fold back the front lap of the placket and place the cuff edge level with the fold.

(f) Pin and tack the right side of the upper cuff to the right side of the sleeve, matching notches, and ensuring that the back lap extends beyond the placket as marked in the pattern.

(g) Machine from the gathered side, press, trim and turn the cuff to extend the sleeve. Tack the folded edge of the cuff.

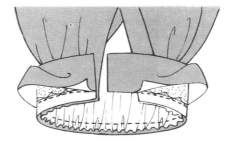

(h) Trim the remaining seam allowance, fold under and slipstitch into place over the machining inside the sleeve.

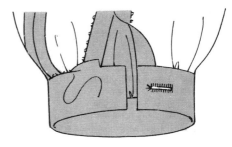

(i) Try the cuff round the wrist to find correct position for button. Sew on button. If bound buttonholes have not been included now sew a buttonhole by hand or machine, or use a press stud under a button for closure.

Shirt

On crisply tailored shirts the sleeve opening is usually finished with a stitched placket and the cuff is topstitched.

Shirt Sleeve Placket

This is a neat, flat, stitched placket that needs great care to make it look smart and uses two pieces of self fabric.

(a) Staystitch the sleeve opening with tiny stitches. Slash along the marked line and out to each corner with sharp pointed scissors.

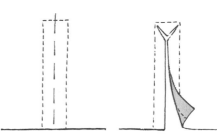

Cuffs

(b) Place the right side of the underlap piece of placket onto the wrong side of the opening edge nearest to the sleeve seam. Tack and machine. Press.

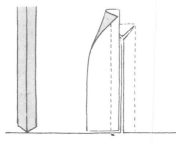

(c) Turn over the binding to enclose the raw edge. Fold under the edge, press it, and topstitch from the right side.
(d) Repeat with the overlap piece of placket on the other edge of the opening, stitching it to the top end of the slash.

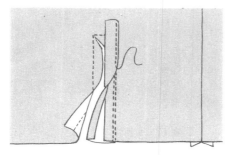

(e) Turn to the right side, fold and press along the fold lines to form a mitre. Pin the overlap over the machining.

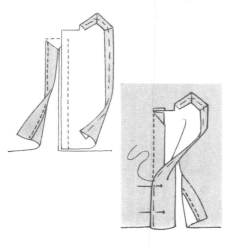

(f) Topstitch the outside fold of the overlap to the top of the opening, tying off threads securely.
(g) Stitch across the placket, including the point of the slash and the top of the underlap.
(h) Leave the needle in at the end of machining, turn the garment and topstitch the remaining edges of the overlap. Tie off the thread ends.

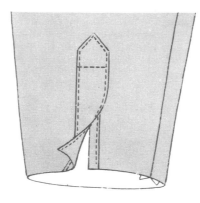

Method for Shirt Cuff
(a) Finish the sleeve opening with a shirt sleeve placket.
(b) Sew or iron-on interfacing to half the cuff, inside seam line. Fold the cuff lengthways, right sides together, tack and machine along the seam line ending 15 mm from the long notched edge.

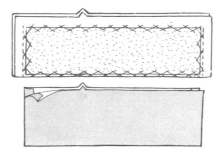

(c) Put the wrong side of the gathered sleeve edge to the non-interfaced half of the cuff. Make sure that the edges of the placket are level with the cuff edges.

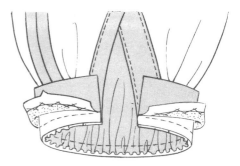

(d) Stitch along seam line, trim and layer the turnings.
(e) Turn the cuff over the sleeve edge, and fold under the turning on the remaining raw edge. Tack carefully into place.
(f) Topstitch all round the cuff close to the edge and, if liked, sew a second row 6 mm further in. Remove tacking, and press.
(g) Sew button and buttonhole.

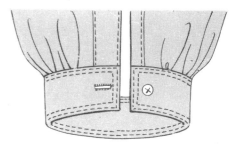

Finished with touch-and-close tape
It is possible to attach a loose band cuff to a long full sleeve, and to make it fit snugly by using touch-and-close tape ("Velcro"). Buttons may be sewn on for extra decorative effect. The cuffs should be interfaced to help them keep their shape. Make and attach the band cuff as above or:
(a) Sew, or iron on interfacing to the wrong side of the cuff piece.
(b) Gather the lower edge of the unseamed sleeve and adjust it to the length of the cuff.
(c) With right sides together pin, tack and machine the cuff to the sleeve edge along the seam line. (Machine from the sleeve side.)
(d) Remove tacking, trim seam allowances and press the turnings towards the cuff.
(e) Fold the sleeve and cuff in half lengthways, matching notches and cuff seam.

Cuffs

(f) Machine along seam line, press the stitching and remove tacking. Trim and neaten the sleeve seam allowances, then press the seam open.

(g) Trim the cuff seam allowance.

(h) Press under the lower edge of the cuff along the seam line and hem it down to the cuff seam, picking up the machine stitches. Press.

(i) Try on the sleeve and make a fold in the cuff so that it fits snugly but not too tightly. This fold should be made on the outside of the wrist and should be overlapped towards the back. Mark the folds.

(j) Cut two 5 cm strips of "Velcro" and hem them into place, using double thread, as the stitching will take the strain when putting on and taking off the garment.

(k) Sew on buttons if liked.

Linked

There are two types — button linked cuff, where a band cuff is extended beyond the edges of the sleeve opening and fastened with linked buttons on cuff through two buttonholes — French cuff, which is a similar cuff but is made much deeper and folded back on itself. Linked buttons or cuff links hold it closed through four buttonholes. It is usual to machine or sew these buttonholes by hand as four bound buttonholes would be too bulky; sometimes the two buttonholes that will show are bound and the two underneath are stitched.

Button Linked Cuff

(a) Sew or iron-on interlining to the cuff.

(b) Put right side of cuff to wrong side of sleeve. Tack, then machine them together.

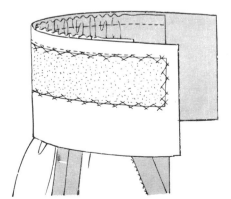

(c) The cuff should be folded with right sides together. Machine the ends. Remove tacking.

(d) Cut corners then turn cuff onto the right side.

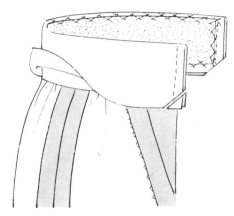

(e) Loose edge of cuff should be turned in to cover the first line or row of machine stitching.

(f) Edge stitch the turning.

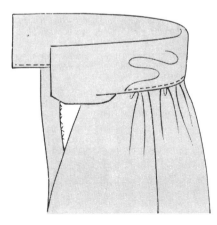

French Cuff

(a) The underneath layer of the cuff will be on the top when folded back so interfacing is sewn or ironed on to the *underneath* cuff piece. Make two bound buttonholes for the top piece of cuff if preferred.

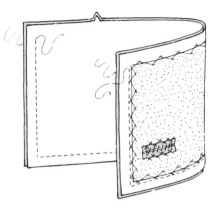

(b) Stitch the cuff sections right sides together ending 15 mm from the notched edges. Trim and layer the seam allowance and turn the cuff right side out. Press.

(c) Finish as for button linked cuff. Fold the cuff back along the roll line.

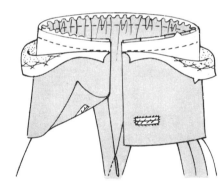

(d) Sew the remaining two buttonholes by hand or machine.

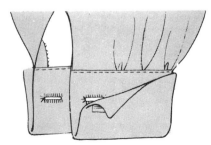

(e) Press the cuff lightly and fasten with cuff links, or with linked buttons (see chapter on Buttons).

Cuffs

3. Detachable Cuffs

These are made either for garments that need dry cleaning or to add a crisp touch of white or colour contrast to an outfit. As they are specially made to be washed frequently it is usual to leave out the interfacing, although modern bonded interfacings are completely washable. Detachable cuffs can be made in a variety of shapes, sizes and styles to turn back over the end of a sleeve or existing cuff, or to extend below a jacket sleeve to look like a shirt cuff. If they are to turn back they need to be tapered so that one edge fits inside the sleeve, and the other fits over the sleeve.

Inside the sleeve

(a) Make up the cuff in the usual way but when it is turned to the right side, press under the seam allowances on the remaining raw edge. Slipstitch this edge.

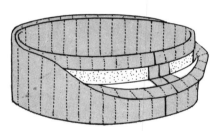

(b) Attach the cuff to the inside of the sleeve with press studs or touch-and-close tape, or slipstitch into place.

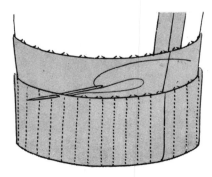

Outside the sleeve

These are aften made with a slit so that they are easier to turn over the sleeve edge.

(a) Stitch each end of the cuff, right sides together. Trim, layer and press. Turn to right side and press again.

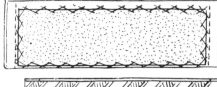
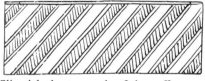

(b) Slipstich the two ends of the cuff together, for about one third of the way, leaving a slit.

(c) Cut a bias strip to fit round the inside of the sleeve. Tack the raw edges together and bind them with the bias strip.

(d) Fold the cuff over the sleeve edge and check that it is the right depth on the outside.

(e) Fasten the cuff to the inside of the sleeve with press studs, touch-and-close tape or slipstitch into place. Roll the cuff over the sleeve edge again and press lightly. A big or heavy cuff may need holding into place on the outside with one or two catch stitches, between the undercuff and outer sleeve.

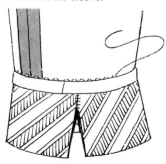

Darts

1. **How to Sew a Straight Dart**
2. **Other Types of Dart**
   Curved
   Shaped bias (*or French*)
   Double pointed (*or concave*)
   Dart tuck
   Dart seam

Darts are tapered folds of fabric stitched on the wrong side of a garment section. They control fullness and turn flat fabric into shapes to fit the human anatomy. Usually the first construction detail in the making of a garment, darts are very important to the finished fit and shape. They must be carefully sewn and pressed for a smooth, rounded effect; the placing and stitching of some types may even provide a certain form of decoration as part of the design. Darts appear on the bodice front to give shaping for the bust and neat fitting for the midriff, on the back shoulders, at the waist of skirts and trousers, at the elbow, and sometimes on the back necklines and bodice front shoulder-line. They taper towards, but do not quite reach, the fullest points of the figure. Adjustments may need to be made to pattern darts to fit individual figures — e.g. tall figures need longer darts. Remember to move skirt darts to match if vertical bodice darts have been altered.

1. **How to Sew a Straight Dart**
(a) Examine the pattern markings carefully to check on position and shape of darts. Transfer pattern markings to fabric with tailor's chalk, or tailor's tacks, making sure to mark in the symbols for matching sides and end of each dart. Left and right sides of a garment normally have darts that match in length and placing.
(b) Fold the fabric so that the dart side markings match, with the point of the dart right on the fold. Put in pins at right angles to the fold. Then tack close to the stitching line. Try on and adjust for fit.

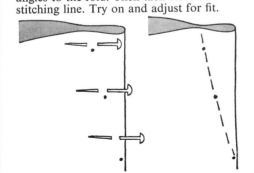

(c) Machine on the stitching line starting at the wide end and tapering to nothing at the point. Run the last two or three stitches along the fold at the point so that no puckering appears on the right side.
(d) Smooth the line of machining between finger and thumb, then sew in ends through stitches on underside at tapered point. Remove tacking.

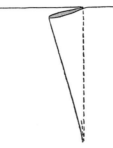

(e) Press on the wrong side along each side of the stitching, then press the dart to one side over a curved surface (to retain shaping and smoothness). Vertical darts are usually pressed towards the centre of the garment, and horizontal darts pressed downwards, but check this with the pattern instructions. Deep darts on thick fabrics are trimmed, opened and pressed flat, then the edges can be overcast.

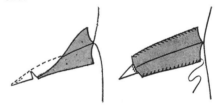

2. **Other Types of Dart**
   Curved
This dart can curve outwards or inwards on the garment — outwards at the waist line of dress bodice front, inwards on trouser and skirt front. It is stitched in a similar way to the straight dart.
(a) Fold centre line of dart and pin.

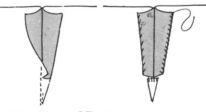

(b) Tack the outer curved lines of the dart (indicated on pattern piece with broken lines).
(c) Machine stitch outer curved lines. Remove tacking. Sew in ends at tapered point.

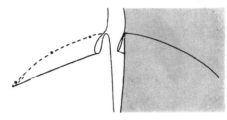

(d) Slash dart through centre of fold.
(e) Press open
(f) Overcast the edges to give neatened appearance and tie threads at the wide end.

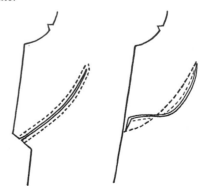

Shaped bias (or French)
This type of dart is slashed first, then pinned, tacked and machine stitched. It occurs on A-line dresses, beginning at hip level and then curving up to give good bust fitting, skimming the waistline. The centre line marking may not be indicated as it is a slash line.
(a) Reinforce the dart by running a line of stay stitching down each side of the dart, just a little inside the outer marking line.

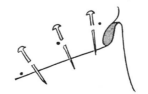

Darts

(b) Slash where indicated.
(c) Turn to the wrong side of the fabric, place the broken outer marking lines together and pin. If ease or stretch are indicated on the pattern (usually between two medium dots) ease and stretch the fabric so that one side matches the other. Pin and tack.
(d) Machine stitch the dart. Remove tacking.
(e) Generally, press down. For heavy fabrics, press open.
(f) Clip when necessary.

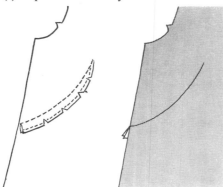

Double pointed (or concave)
This dart is found at the waistline of a fitted dress where the bodice and skirt are cut from one piece, and on close fitting blouses.
(a) Work on the wrong side of the fabric.
(b) Fold along the centre marking lines.
(c) Pin and tack the outer marking lines together — pins at right angles to fold.

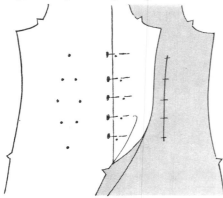

(d) Machine stitch the dart. For a very smooth finish, machine in two stages, starting each time at the centre and stitching to the point and two or three stitches beyond along the fold.
(e) Snip or cut into the fold of the dart at the centre point.
(f) Snip either side of the centre point.
(g) Press the dart towards the centre of the garment. Sew ends into underside stitches at points.

On double-ended darts, to prevent the material dragging on the right side of the garment, snip or cut the widest part of the dart and allow it to "spread". Edges should be overcast.

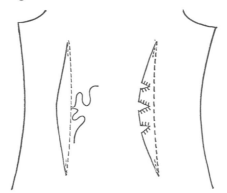

Dart tuck
This dart is a combination of dart and tuck and can "blouse" dresses or shirts, at, or above, the waist edge. In this case, the narrowest part of the dart is at the edge of the fabric and it widens out as it goes inwards to release fullness. Dart tucks may be double ended.
(a) Work on the wrong side of the garment, generally.
(b) Fold the dart on the centre line, pin and tack.

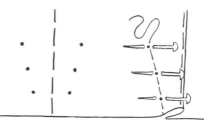

(c) Machine on stitching line from the outside edge of fabric inwards. Backstitch to finish.
(d) Sometimes it may be wise to straight stitch across the end to the foldline for firmness.

(e) Remove tacking and press the dart towards the centre of the garment, but never press the released fullness.

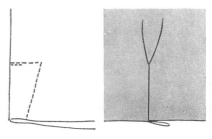

Dart seam
This type of dart is found on the underarm of some dresses.
(a) Cut or slash the solid line indicated.
(b) Stay stitch just inside balance marks.

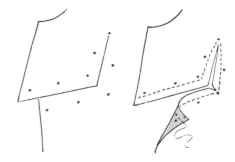

(c) Construction dots should be matched by pinning the broken lines together, working with the fuller side uppermost.
(d) Tack the seam line. Remove the pins.
(e) Machine stitch the seam line, leaving needle in work and pivoting at corners. Remove tacking.
(f) Fasten off the ends by sewing threads into stitches on underside.
(g) Press the dart down towards the centre.

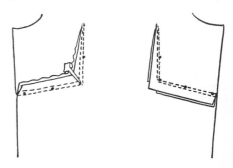

Facings

1. General Instructions
Cutting
Interfacing
Attaching facings
Understitchings
Finishing

2. Straight Facings
Turning corners

3. Bias Facings

4. Shaped Facings
Example — an armhole

5. Facing as Part of a Garment
For faced necklines see chapter on
Necklines.
For faced openings see chapter
on Cuffs.

Facings are used to neaten a garment by
covering the raw edges, to reinforce the
edge and retain its shape. When applied
to the right side of the garment they are
called conspicuous facings and may be a
decorative feature. More commonly
facings are turned to the wrong side and
are inconspicuous from the right side;
in all cases facings show on one side only.
Usually the facing is cut from self fabric
to the same shape as the edge and seamed
with it. Interfacing may also be included to
create a professional, well-tailored look.
Bias binding is sometimes used as a facing
on small areas of delicate fabrics; all other
facings must have one edge neatened as it
shows inside the garment. For added
strength, and to prevent stretching, the
garment edge can be staystitched before
attaching the facing. If alterations have
been made to the pattern or its fitting,
remember to alter the facings too.

1. General Instructions
Cutting
For facing a straight edge a piece of fabric
on the cross grain or the straight grain
can be used. For shaped facings the
grain on the facing should match the
grain on that part of the garment.
The width should always be enough to
give a neat, flat finish.
Interfacing
Choose a suitable weight and type of
interfacing for the fabric and style effect.
If woven interfacing is used it must be
cut on the same grain as the facing
and garment.
Attaching facings
The facing edge and garment edge should

be placed exactly together, matching
notches, centre lines, etc. with right sides
together. Stitch along the fitting line,
trim, layer, snip and press the seam.

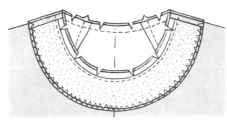

Turn facing to the wrong side, rolling the
seamed edge so that the join is slightly
to the inside of the garment, tack close
to this edge and press.

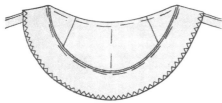

Understitching
This helps to prevent the facing from
rolling to the right side. The seam
allowances on curves are first clipped or
notched, and then layered, or graded.
Press turnings towards the facing. With
the facing lying flat, machine or
backstitch close to the seamline, sewing
through all the layers. Turn the facing
in to the wrong side of the garment
and press the edge.

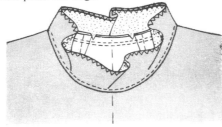

Finishing
The already neatened free edge of the
facing is slipstitched to the lining, or, for
an unlined garment, stitched down only
at the seams.
2. Straight Facings
Used on straight hems or down the front
of cardigan-style jackets and

button-through skirts.
(a) Check that the facing is as long as the
edge, plus turnings, and that it is the
width of the finished facing plus turnings.
It can be cut on the straight or cross
grain.
(b) With right sides together, pin and
tack facing to garment. If facing is to
show on right side put right side of facing
to wrong side of garment.
(c) Machine on fitting line. Remove
tacking. Trim seams. Press.

(d) Understitch (see general instructions).
(e) Turn facing to wrong side, rolling the
seamed edge between thumbs and
fingers to make a "clean" edge. Tack and
press flat.
(f) Stitch facing down on wrong side at
seams to keep it in place.

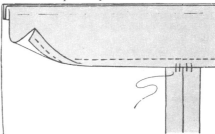

Turning corners
It is necessary to mitre the corners so
that they lie flat — see following
diagrams.
Inside Corner

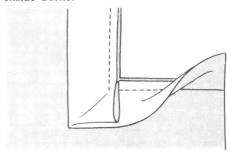

Facings

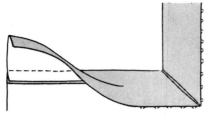

Outside Corner

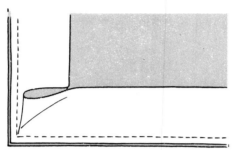

3. Bias Facings

These may be cut from self fabric or lining (see chapter on Bindings and Pipings) or bought bias binding can be used. A thinner fabric is useful to reduce bulk where the garment is thick. Put in the zip before the facing.

(a) Cut a bias strip four times the finished width required, allowing a little extra to allow for the strip to narrow as it is stretched. Double-fold bias tape is suitable if the folds are pressed open.

(b) Fold strip in half lengthways, press lightly and pre-shape to the curve of the garment edge. (See chapter on Bindings and Piping) — complete as for double or French binding but turn the strip completely on to the wrong side of the garment so that it does not show. Slipstitch into place.

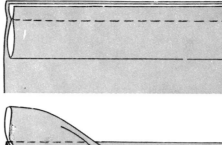

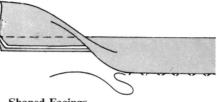

4. Shaped Facings

A separate pattern piece is normally included for the shaped facings which usually neaten armholes and sometimes for necklines, too, if the garment is collarless. The facing matches the shape of the edge to be faced, and is wide enough to lie flat. Neck and armhole facings are usually attached after the garment is made up and the opening completed.

Example — an armhole

(a) Mark fitting lines on garment and facing.

(b) To prepare the facing, stitch, trim and press the underarm seam. Turn under the un-notched edge and edgestitch it, or machine overcast.

(c) Tack bias binding over the seam line on the wrong side of the garment to prevent stretching.

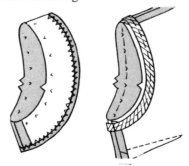

(d) Put the facing onto the garment, right sides together, matching side seams and balance marks. Pin, tack and machine, with facing side up, all round on seam line.

(e) Remove tacking, trim, layer and clip seam. Press.

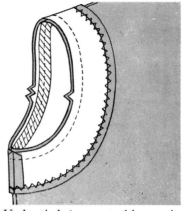

(f) Understitch (see general instructions).

(g) Turn facing to wrong side and press again. A few catch-stitches on the underside of the facing to the seam allowance will hold it flat, and prevent it from rolling to the outside.

(h) Turn the bodice inside out and slipstitch facing to lining, or, if no lining, tack facing to seams.

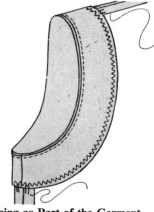

5. Facing as Part of the Garment

Where an opening edge is straight, it can have a fold-back facing which is cut in one with the bodice so that there is no seam at the edge. Faced edges of this type are often overlapped for fastening so the centre and overlap pattern markings must be transferred to the fabric.

(a) Cut and attach interfacing according to the pattern instructions. Stitch the interfacing to the fold line on the wrong side with long running stitches, catchstitch along the other edge of the interfacing to hold it flat.

Facings

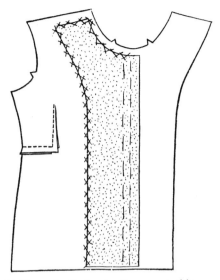

(b) Turn the facing to the wrong side along the fold line. If there are extra pieces of shaped facing to be attached — eg. back neck facing, attach them now.

(c) Seam binding can be added to fold line and neck seam if needed for extra reinforcement.

Neck seam — pin and tack binding centrally over seam line.

Fold line — pin binding to the seam allowance of the interfacing which extends beyond the foldline. Machine into place close to the binding edge.

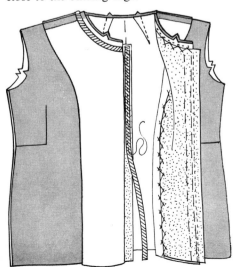

(d) Pin, tack and machine facing to garment at neck edge (do not stitch fold line). Trim, layer and clip the seam allowance. Remove tacking. Press.

(e) Understitch (see general instructions).

(f) Turn facing to the inside and slightly roll the seamed edge between thumbs and fingers so that the seam does not show from the right side of the garment. Press.

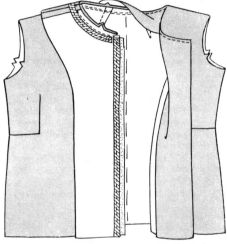

(g) Lift up the facing and catchstitch the facing and seam allowances to hold facing flat.

(h) Finish the raw edge of the facing by turning under and edgestitching, or machine overcast.

i. Catchstitch the facing loosely into place, at shoulder seams, back neck darts, etc.

Fastenings

Almost all garments need openings and fastenings of some description to allow the garment to be put on and taken off.
The fastenings keep the openings in position whilst the garment is being worn.
There are many ways that garments may be fastened and a variety of ways that openings may be finished for durability, decoration and comfort, at the neck, back, front, cuffs, etc. The fastenings may be the main fashion detail, or be completely concealed, but they should always be carefully planned to suit the style and the fabric chosen.

1. Points to Remember When Attaching Fasteners

(a) Always sew fasteners onto material which has been doubled or reinforced, otherwise stitching will show on the right side.
(b) Fastenings should be washable or dry cleanable.
(c) Always use a fastener suited in type and size to garment, fabric and type of opening.
(d) If the fasteners are *not* to be used as a part of the garment decoration they should not be visible.
(e) They should be close enough together and placed exactly, to keep the opening flat when closed.
(f) Sew fastenings after the opening has

been finished and pressed (except loops and bound buttonholes).
(g) The following instructions are for ladies' garments – - remember that men's garments fasten the other way.

2. Button loops
Thread

A thread loop is often used with a small button at the neck edge where it is hidden by the collar. The loop should be as long as the diameter of the button plus its thickness. On underwear and children's wear thread loops may be sewn inside the overlapping part of an opening.
Thread loops may be made a feature of a garment made of fine fabric, where they are worked in groups down the edge of a conspicuous opening.
Use buttonhole twist or double thread in a colour matching the fabric or buttons, finishing the loops with blanket stitch or buttonhole stitch.
(a) Put a thin card behind position of loop. Place pins into position as in diagram.

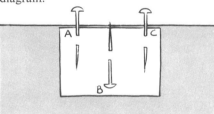

(b) Fasten thread with a double stitch at one pin.
(c) Sew strand back and forth from pin a to pin c, passing the thread round pin b, to finish off at pin c.

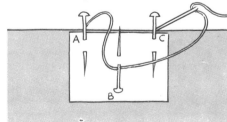

(d) Stranding should continue for required number of strands.
(e) Remove card.
(f) Turn loop round and sew with buttonhole or blanket stitches over the strands. (See chapter on Stitches if in doubt about how to work these stitches.)

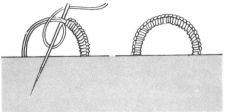

A similar loop can be worked at the waist for a belt carrier, or as a thread eye with a metal hook.
Thread chains can be made instead of loops. These are particularly suitable for lingerie strap holders.
(a) Mark on the garment the place where the chain should begin on the shoulder seam near the armhole. Sew one or two tiny stitches here to secure the thread.

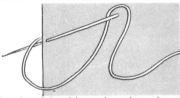

(b) On the right side make a loop by taking another tiny stitch.

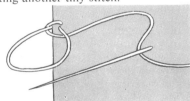

(c) Hold the needle and thread in your right hand and slip the thumb and first two fingers of the left hand through the loop of thread.
(d) Pick up another loop of thread and pull it through the first; repeat several times, tightening as you work.
(e) Make enough loops for a chain of about 3·8 cm.
(f) Push the needle through the last loop and pull it tight to form a knot.

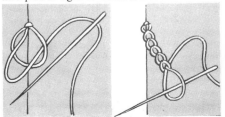

Fastenings

(g) Sew the ball part of the press stud to this end of the chain. Sew the socket part of a press stud to the garment.

Note — strap guards can also be made from narrow ribbon or seam binding.

Rouleau loops

These are very effective when used with covered buttons at an opening where the edges meet with overlapping fabric. The loops are fabric tubes made from bias strips, with either the seam allowances or a length of piping cord to fill the tube.

(a) Cut bias strips of fabric (see chapter on Bindings and Piping). Short lengths will be sufficient for single spaced loops, but often loops are made from one long, continuous strip.

(b) The width of the strip needs to be twice the finished width plus seam allowance. Try out a few loops to get the exact width right for the fabric and garment chosen.

(c) Strips should be folded in half lengthways, right sides facing and tacked.

(d) Machine stitch along length of strip, stretching strip slightly. Remove tacking.

(e) Trim down turning so that it is less than the width of stitched tube, leaving enough fabric to pad out the tube.

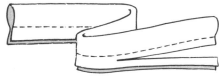

(f) Attach thread to one end of rouleau, and thread through a bodkin.

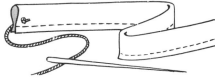

(g) Push bodkin carefully through the tube easing fabric carefully along thread.

(h) Pull length of tube inside out. Remove thread.

Note — the seam thread may break if the rouleau is pulled quickly when turning through. It is possible instead, on a modern sewing machine, to stitch the bias strip with a narrow zig-zag (width 1, length 1) or stretch stitch (without stretching the fabric whilst machining.)

Corded rouleau loops

(a) Cut a bias strip of fabric to fit round the chosen cord plus turnings of 13 mm.

(b) Cut a piece of cord at least twice the length of the bias strip. Mark the centre point.

(c) Place the cord on the right side of the strip and put the two raw edges together.

(d) Move the fabric so that one end of the fabric is just over the centre mark on the cord. Tack fabric in place.

(e) Using a zipper or piping foot machine across the centre mark and along the long edge close to the cord.

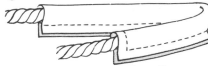

(f) Remove tacking and trim off seam allowance.

(g) Pull the enclosed cord out slowly, so that the free cord is pulled in to fill the tube.

(h) Trim off the stitched end and any excess cord.

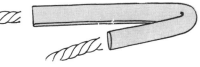

Placing rouleau loops

153

Single loops may be spaced out along the opening, but where a long row of closely spaced loops is needed close together, a continuous piece of tubing is used. Single loops — the loop should extend beyond the edge of the garment about half the diameter of the button plus the thickness of the tubing. The distance between a and c in diagram should be about the diameter of the button plus twice the thickness of the tubing.

(a) Mark the width and depth of loop on the raw edge of the right hand side of the garment opening.

(b) Place loop between pins a b and c with seam of loop uppermost.
Tack along seam line.

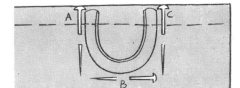

(c) Put facing and garment right sides together with raw edges meeting. Tack, then machine along seam line.

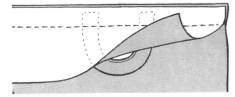

(d) Remove tacking. Facing should be turned to wrong side of garment. Tack, then under stitch turned edge on the inner edge of right side of facing. Remove tacking.

(e) Raw edge of facing should be turned under 6 mm to the wrong side, and edge stitched along the edge to neaten.

Fastenings

Continuous loops — using a long piece of prepared tubing pin a series of loops of the right size into place as above. Machine along the seam line, then trim off the short loops in the seam allowance to avoid extra bulk at the edge of the garment.

Ribbon or braid loops
Ribbon or braid can be used for loops in the same way as rouleau tubes and enclosed in the facing as above. They may also be easily added to the edge after the garment is made up:
(a) Cut a piece of ribbon or braid 1¼ times the diameter of the button plus turnings.
(b) Fold the ribbon across in half and crease, then fold the turnings and crease into place.

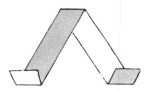

(c) Mark the position if for a single loop. Pin and tack ribbon into place on the wrong side close to the edge.
(d) Either sew each loop into place on the wrong side, or machine on the right side close to the garment edge.

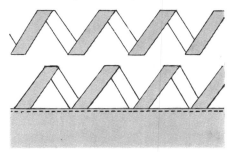

3. Eyelets
These are round openings made in the fabric to take a lace, draw string, buckle, studs, or cufflinks. They can also form the basis for broderie anglaise embroidery. There are special kits available to make and finish the edges of eyelets. These are only suitable for firmly woven, strong material and should not be used on fine or flimsy fabric. Narrow laces can be made from rouleau tubes, ribbon, braid or cord. White shoelaces can be dyed to match the garment.

Hand-sewn
(a) Mark the position for the eyelets carefully on the fabric with tailor's chalk.
(b) Make two long tacking stitches forming a cross on all these marks as the chalk will rub off easily.
(c) Sew a circle of small running stitches around position marked for eyelet — this will reinforce the circle and prevent the fabric stretching.
(d) Punch the right sized hole in the fabric with an awl or stiletto, or cut with scissors.
(e) Using double thread and leaving about 25 mm for finishing, bring needle through fabric from wrong side just outside circle of stitches.
(f) Work right round eyelet with close buttonhole stitches and finish by tying threads securely on wrong side.

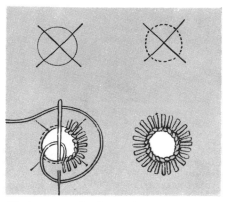

(Eyelets may also be made on some sewing machines. Refer to your sewing machine handbook for instructions.)

4. Frogs
Frogged fastenings are usually used with Chinese ball buttons (see chapter on Buttons and Buttonholes). They are made from fabric rouleau or cord, with one loop long enough to extend beyond the edge of the opening and over the button. It is a good idea to practise first with a piece of string, and then to make up the frog shapes on paper, before sewing to the garment.
(a) Make up the frog loops with the seam of rouleau strip facing the worker; that will be the wrong side of the finished fastening.

(b) Tack each loop as it is made with tiny stitches, then sew to the garment with stitches that do not show on the right side of the garment.

5. Hooks and eyes
These are often used to secure waistbands and neck edges. If the strain will be great, heavy duty hooks should be used.
(a) Hooks are always stitched to the wrong side of overlap. Edge of hook is always in line with the edge of the garment.
(b) Place edge of hook to garment with two stitches under hook.
(c) Secure shaft of hook just above loops with two stitches across it. Pass the needle under the fabric to begin sewing round the loops.

(d) Buttonhole, blanket stitch or overcast round the two loops of the hook.
(e) Three types of eyes can be used with the hook. The metal loop, the metal bar, and the worked bar.

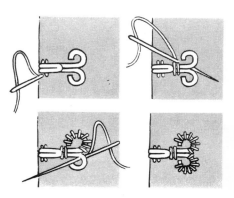

Fastenings

Metal loop
Is used for openings in edges that meet and do not overlap.
(a) Sew to wrong side of edge of garment opposite hook.
(b) Enough of the loop should be placed over the edge for the hook to fasten into it.
(c) Secure ends over the edge of the garment at each side of the loop.
(d) Buttonhole stitch loops into position.

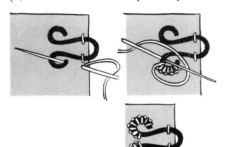

Metal bar
Is used for openings where edges overlap.
(a) Sew bar to right side of underwrap.
(b) Buttonhole stitch round the loops.

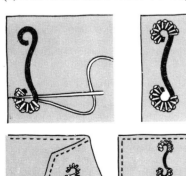

Hand worked bar
May be used instead of metal bar, can also be used for edges that meet.
(a) Strands worked in either Sylko No 40 or Dewhurst Strong Thread.
For overlapped fastenings, bar should lie straight on the material. If bar is used on meeting edges strands should form a loop.
(b) Fasten on thread with a double stitch and then make a straight bar tack across the fabric.
(c) Only a few threads of the fabric are picked up and then the needle is taken back to the other end of the stitch.
(d) Sew required number of bar tacks. Heavy fabric will need more than a fine one.
(e) Work buttonhole stitch across the bars closely from side to side.

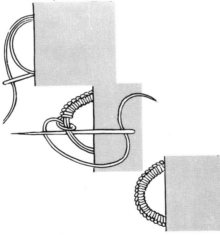

Covered
Cover them with matching thread so that the fastenings are less obvious on important garments.
With double Sylko or Dewhurst Strong Thread sew buttonhole stitches close together until all the metal is hidden.
On heavy duty hooks and eyes use buttonhole twist.

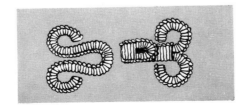

6. Press studs
(Also called snaps, poppers or press fasteners)
These are usually used on overlapping openings where there is little strain.
Where there is no overlap, such as where collars or stand-up neckline edges meet, use a floating or extended press stud.
(a) Press fasteners are made in two parts, one being thick with a hole and the other with a flattened base and a knob in the middle.

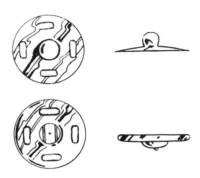

(b) The thick section with a hole (socket) is sewn to right side of underwrap.
(c) The part with knob and flat base (ball) is sewn on wrong side of overwrap. Sew the ball part on first. Rub the knob with tailor's chalk and press it into the other edge of the opening. Sew the socket part exactly on that spot.
(d) Double stitches are used to fasten on and off under the edge of the fastener.
(e) Either oversew or buttonhole stitch fasteners in place.
(f) Use the same number of stitches in each hole.

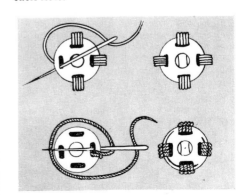

Fastenings

Extended

Sew the ball part on the inside of one edge. Sew the socket part to the other edge through one hole only so that it extends beyond the edge. Where the metal parts would show on an important garment cover them with fabric.

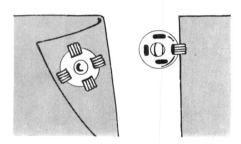

Covered

Cut two circles of matching lining fabric about twice the diameter of the press stud. Sew running stitches around the edge.

Put the two parts of the press stud face down on the wrong side of the circles. Push the knob of the ball part through the fabric, and close the two parts of the press stud together. Gather up the running stitches and fasten them off securely.

7. Tapes and ties

(a) The tape end should be turned over so that the raw edge meets the selvedge edge.
(b) Make a crease across the tape as in diagram, then turn the diagonal fold back.

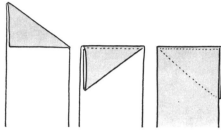

(c) To attach the tape put the edge of the turning to the edge of the garment. Pin in place as in diagram.

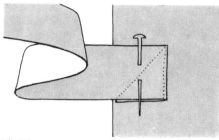

(d) Three of the inner edges should then be hemmed. Do not fasten off the thread but turn the tape back and level it with the edge of the garment as in diagram. Oversew edges.

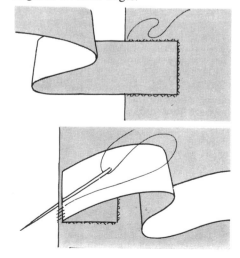

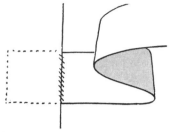

(e) When overlapping the edges with a tie fastening make the tape as instructed above. One tie is stitched to the right side of the underlapping edge and one tie to the wrong side of the overlapping edge. Then place one tape to the wrong side of the overlap, with the raw edge downwards in the place required. Pin in place.

(f) Backstitch or machine round the square as shown in diagram.

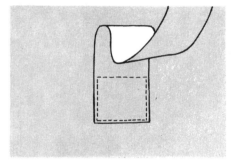

(g) To finish the free end of the tape make a narrow hem on the wrong side.

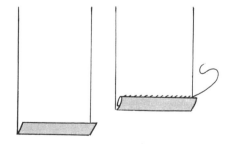

Alternatively small knots or a tiny hand stitched roll may be formed at the end.
(h) A ribbon is attached in the same way as a tape. However, the free end of ribbon is not hemmed.
(j) Cut the ribbon to shape, as shown in diagram.

Fastenings

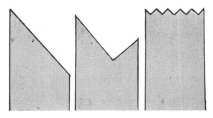

Touch-and-close tape

This is nylon tape made as two strips covered with tiny burrs that act like hooks and eyes; when pressed together the two strips of pile fabric stick together until pulled apart. It is made in a variety of colours and widths (22 mm wide) and can be cut to size as it does not fray. Very useful on loose fitting garments, it should not be used where there is much strain or on thin fabric. Detachable features such as bows, hoods, beading, etc. can easily be put on with touch-and-close tape.

Stitch the tape into place by machining — a small zig-zag stitch can be used. If it is important that the stitching does not show on the right side firmly slipstitch the tape onto the wrong side of the overlap.

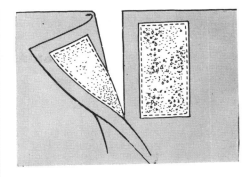

Gatherings and Shirrings

1. **Gathering**
   Hand made
   Machine made
   Gauging
   With elastic
   Gathered ruching
   Shell-gathered ruching
2. **Shirring**
   Hand
   Machine
   Decorative

Gathers are small, soft folds frequently used in the making of lightweight skirts, blouses, sleeves, yokes, frills and children's clothes. The gathers are simply made with running stitches to ease in the material and control fullness. They can be made either by hand or by machine. Usually patterns that have gathers are marked to indicate their position and details are given to show how much material should be taken up in a row of gathering. It is always wise to divide the area that is to be gathered into sections, whether gathering by hand or machine. The gathering threads are left in until the final stitching is completed.
Shirring (also called ruching) is produced with several rows of gathering or gathering and fine elastic. If elastic is used shirring can be used on areas where the size is adjustable, eg. waist, neck, cuffs. It may be decorated with smocking or other embroidery.

1. Gathering

Hand made

(a) Use long double thread of Sylko 50 (overall about 50 cm) or single Sylko 40.
(b) Sew running stitches on the right side along the line to be gathered and another row 6 mm away, leaving thread free at both ends.

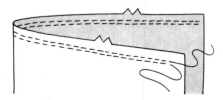

(c) Ease the fabric along the thread gently, from both ends.

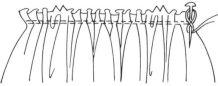

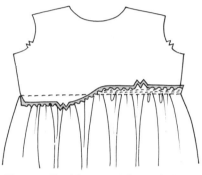

(d) Check that the piece of gathered fabric has been eased up to the correct length before finishing off.

(e) Fasten off with several firm stitches at each end.

Machine made

This produces a very even effect and the gathers are easy to distribute evenly.
On fine fabrics, however, take great care and use a fine needle and thread to avoid fabric damage. Some machines gather automatically with the aid of a gathering foot — refer to the machine handbook for instructions. (Do not use this method where great precision is needed.)
(a) Set machine stitch length to longest stitch and loosen top tension.
(b) Machine two or more rows of evenly-spaced stitching.
(c) Bobbin thread should be drawn up. A heavy thread on the bobbin will prevent the thread breaking.
(d) Ease bobbin thread through fabric and evenly distribute fullness from both ends.
(e) Each end of drawn-up thread should be wound around a pin placed at right angles to the stitching.

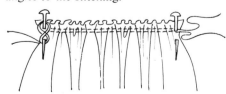

(f) When gathers are even, fasten off with thread ends making several back stitches to secure the gathers.
(g) Gathers may also be carried out on the sewing machine by sewing two rows of zig-zag stitching over cord and then drawing the cords up to required length. This method avoids any strain being placed on the thread. It is very quick, efficient, and simple.

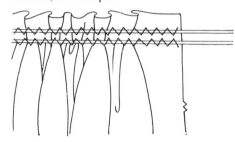

Gauging

This term is sometimes used for many rows of hand gathers holding a large amount of fabric in a small area; it is the method used for smocking. Sew running stitches on the right side, taking a longer stitch under the surface and keeping all the stitches in line.

Gauging is easy to do on dotted or checked fabric, and special iron-on transfers can be bought to mark guide dots on other fabrics.

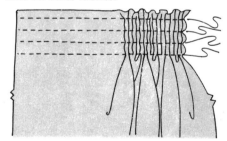

With elastic

This is a simple way of stitching elastic directly to the garment at sleeve edges. Use elastic about 6 mm wide and sew from the wrong side.
(a) Pin the end of the elastic into place.
(b) Machine with a zig-zag stitch over the elastic, stretching it along the fabric whilst stitching. Set the stitch carefully so that the stitches fall between the elastic cords, preventing the elastic from being pierced and later broken.

Gatherings and Shirrings

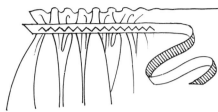

Gathered ruching

This is a form of trimming which is gathered to form frills. It can be used as a decorative edging for children's clothes, and on women's garments where a very feminine effect is needed.

(a) Use either a ribbon or a piece of fabric which has been hemmed along the raw edges.
(b) Make running stitches through the centre of the fabric or ribbon.
(c) Ease fabric on thread as instructed in the section on gathers. Make gathers even.

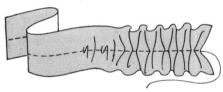

(d) Tack or baste the ruching to garment where required.

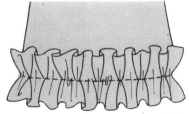

(e) Finally, machine stitch along the line of gathering stitches. Remove tacking.

Shell-gathered ruching

(a) A 5 cm wide bias strip should be cut.
(b) The bias strip must be folded in half lengthwise right sides together and tacked along edges. Machine stitch, then remove tacking.

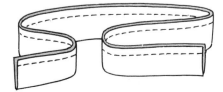

(c) Turn the bias strip inside out, forming a length of tubing 2 cm wide. The seam should be central.

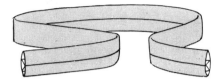

(d) Insert running stitches diagonally from edge to edge on the tubing.
(e) Stitches should not go over the edges of the fabric.
(f) Ease the thread up gently to gather the tubing in, forming shells of equal proportions.

(g) When completed attach the shell-gathered ruching to the garment with slip stitching or machine stitching.

2. Shirring

Hand

(a) Sew several rows of gathers very evenly spaced and pull them up together. Sew off the thread ends, or knot them in pairs.

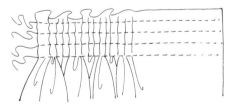

(b) The threads may break in wear so hand shirring is usually backed with a piece of fabric.

(c) Cut a piece of self fabric on the straight, turn in the edges and tack it to the wrong side over the shirred area.
(d) Hem to the gathers.

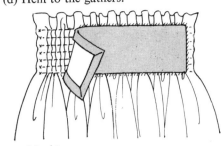

Machine

Method 1
(a) Shirring elastic (fine tubular elastic on a reel) is used on the machine bobbin. Make sure it is wound evenly with very little stretching.
(b) Set the machine to a long straight stitch, and test the top tension on a scrap of the garment fabric as it may need to be tightened. Try two or three rows, holding the fabric flat — it should gather back to half the original length.
(c) Mark the place where the rows of stitching must be sewn.
(d) Machine from the right side with a long straight stitch, holding the fabric taut. The fabric may instead be placed on greaseproof paper to keep it flat whilst stitching. The paper can easily be torn away later.
(e) Machine several evenly-spaced rows keeping the fabric flat each time.

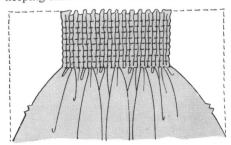

Method 2
On some swing-needle sewing machines shirring elastic may be used in the following way. It needs a buttonhole foot — this usually has two parallel grooves along the underside.
(a) Place the fabric in position ready to sew.

Gatherings and Shirrings

(b) Use a long double strand of shirring elastic. Place one strand in each groove of the foot.

(c) Use a three-step zig-zag stitch to sew the shirring elastic directly to the fabric, pulling the elastic to gather the fabric whilst stitching.

(d) Hold on to the elastic at the back when starting to sew, ensuring that the fabric runs smoothly under the foot. The more the elastic is pulled at the front, the more the fabric will be gathered.

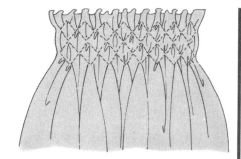

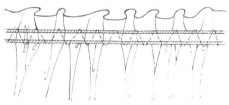

Decorative

(a) Set up the swing-needle sewing machine for shirring, using a three-step zig-zag, serpentine or other similar stitch.

(b) Place greaseproof paper under the fabric to prevent the elastic from gathering up during sewing.

(c) Sew parallel rows of stitching until the required depth of shirring is achieved. Sew in the ends of the elastic.

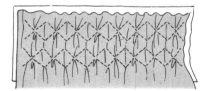

(d) Tear away the paper, removing any tiny pieces with tweezers. Skilled needlewomen may like to match up the pattern on the rows of stitching — join the points of the stitches in one row to the points in the following row, stitching *very* slowly and carefully. The stitching in decorative shirring may be made more obvious by using contrasting colours, or by using double thread through the needle (or a heavy needle and Dewhurst Sylko Perlé).

Godets and Gussets

1. Godets
 Method of insertion in seam or dart
2. Gussets
 *General method for triangular or
 diamond shaped.*

1. Godets
A Godet is a shaped piece of self or
contrasting fabric which is inset into a
garment to add extra width. The most
common type is shaped like a slice of pie,
but godets can also be semi-circular,
oblong or pleated. They make tight
garments easy to wear and are an
interesting and eye-catching style detail.
If the pattern does not include godets
they can be put into seams, darts or slashes
in sleeves or skirts.
 Method of insertion
(a) Cut a pie-shaped (triangular) godet
piece of the required size, making sure
that the straight grain runs down the
centre.

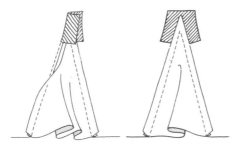

(b) Where the godets are adding extra
weight tack seam binding along the seam
lines of the garment piece.
If the fabric might stretch out of shape,
tack the godet to the garment piece along
the top few centimetres and leave it to
hang for a day or two. Then pin, tack and
stitch the godet into place where it falls,
so that it will always hang well.
(c) Level the godet with the edge of the
garment and finish the hem. For godets
in a seam or dart, end the stitching at the

pattern markings, tying off the threads
securely. Complete as above. For godets
in a slash, staystitch round the slash and
tack a piece of lining over the right side
of the point as reinforcement.

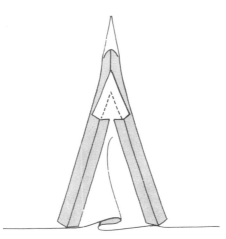

Clip to the stitching at the point and turn
the patch to the wrong side. Pin, tack and
stitch the inset along the slash seam line.
(d) Press the godet stitching:
In a slash — press the seam allowance
away from the godet.
In a dart — slash the fold of the dart and
press the point flat.
Clip the godet seam allowance about
25 mm/2·5 cm below the point, and press
the turnings as shown in the diagram.

(e) Topstitch near the garment edge if
liked.

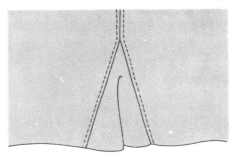

(f) Allow the garment, with the finished
godets, to hang for a day or two, then
finish the hem.

2. Gussets
Gussets are set into a slash or seam of a
garment to allow ease of movement at
underarms or crotch, and may be cut
separately or as an extension of a
garment piece (combination gussets).
They are normally cut as a triangle or
diamond-shaped piece of self fabric, and
must be stitched in carefully so that they
fit well, without being too obvious. It is
vital to try out the fit of gussets, and for
a new pattern it is worth cutting out and
making up the gussets and surrounding
area in a piece of cheap fabric first as a
test. Adjust the height and placing of the
gussets by up to 13 mm if necessary.
 General method
(a) Reinforce the slash points with lengths
of seam binding, or a square of lining
fabric cut on the cross.

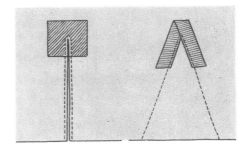

A square of iron-on interlining may be
used instead, pressed onto the wrong side
of the points of the slashes.
(b) Cut the slash to within about 6 mm
of the points and tack the gusset in to try
the fit of both garment and gusset. Make
any alterations, then remove the gusset.
(c) Now slash up to the stitching at the
points.

Godets and Gussets

(d) Triangular gussets — pin and tack the gussets into the slash, with the right sides together. From the garment side machine along the seam line, pivoting carefully at the point. Press the seam allowances away from the gusset, trimming off the edges of the reinforcement squares.

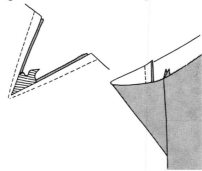

If the triangular gusset is set in at the underarm follow by stitching the underarm bodice seam and sleeve in one long seam. Diamond shaped gussets — stitch all the garment seams, (leaving the gusset area open) and press them open.

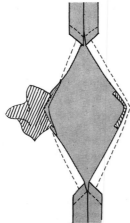

If the gusset contains a dart or seam, stitch and neaten it at this stage. With right sides together, pin and tack the gusset to the garment. Stitch as for triangular gussets, then press seam allowances away from the gusset, clipping as necessary and trimming the reinforcement square.

(e) Gussets may have a lining for reinforcement, and this is either slipstitched into place with edges turned

under, or left flat and neatened with the gusset seam allowances.

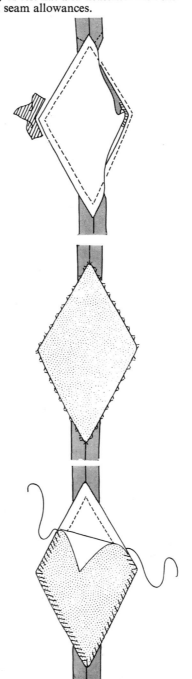

Hems

1. **Points to Note for Perfect Hems**
2. **Depth of Hems**
3. **Making the Hem**
4. **Turning Up the Hem**
5. **Treating Hem Fullness**
6. **Other Ways of Gathering Fullness in Hems**
7. **Corners in Hems**
8. **Finishes for Raw Edges**
9. **Sewing the Hem to the Garment**
   Plain hem
10. **Pressing Hems**
11. **Types of Hem**
    Catch-stitched hem
    Tailor's hem
    Lock-stitched hem
    Slip-stitched hem
    Stitched-edge hem
    Narrow machined hem
    Blouse edges
    Blind stitched by machine
    Stitched and rolled hem
    Quick hand rolled hem
    Taped hem
    Bound hem
    Faced or false hem
    Circular hem – gathered
    Circular hem – taped
    Hems on sheer fabrics
    Shell hems – hand stitched
    Shell hems – machine stitched
    Embroidered hem
    Pin-stitched hem
    Lettuce edged hem
    Hems of lace fabrics
    Stiffened hems

A hem is usually a double fold turned onto the wrong side of a garment edge, to finish the edge neatly and help it to hang well. The length of the hemline and the neatness of the edge are vitally important to the style and appearance of a garment. The placing of the hemline varies according to the type of garment and the current fashion, but above all it should be at a length that is flattering to the wearer. To determine the depth of a hem the fabric and style of garment must be considered. In addition, adjustments may have to be made for striped fabric and pleated edges; in every case the hem must look right. Unless the hem is a decorative feature in itself, it should be as unobtrusive as possible.

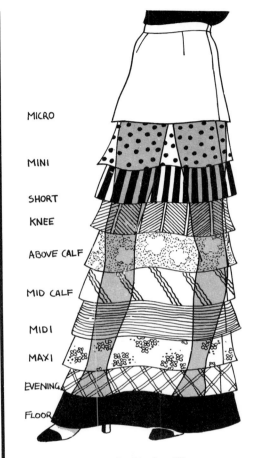

MICRO

MINI

SHORT

KNEE

ABOVE CALF

MID CALF

MIDI

MAXI

EVENING

FLOOR

1. Points to Note for Perfect Hems

1. Match the seam lines when pinning the hem into place then adjust the fullness between the seams.
2. Skirt or dress hems have a more professional look when seam bulk and edge fullness have been eliminated.
3. When taping the hem edge, use bias tape whenever possible.
4. When edge fullness has been adjusted, and if fabric is suitable, steam-shrink with an iron. Put heavy cardboard between the hem and the dress so that only the hem part will shrink.
5. Hemming stitches should only take up one thread of the fabric so that they will not be visible on the right side of the garment.
6. When preparing a hem, check that the garment is of even length all the way round.

7. Insert pins into hem vertically to ensure that all fullness is evenly distributed.
8. Press or press open any seams that run into the hemline before hemming.
9. Enlist the help of a friend to adjust your hems – use a hem marker or a yard rule.

2. Depth of Hems

Straight skirt	5.0–7.5 cm
'A' line skirt	4.0–5.0 cm
Flared hem	13–20 mm
Circular hem sheer	3 mm
Blouse hem	13 mm–3.8 cm
Jacket and Sleeve hem	20 mm–4 cm

Note
When making a hem also refer to the paper pattern instructions, and bear in mind the following points.
1. For a very flared style (heavy, knitted or stretchy fabrics) a fairly narrow hem is needed.
2. For lightweight and flimsy fabrics, straight or floor length garments, the hem needs to be fairly wide.
3. Gauzy fabrics will respond well to fine, rolled finishes, *or* very deep hems. The character of the garment and the position of the hem must be considered before you decide which finish to use.
4. Let your height help determine the hem depth. Tall figures can carry a deeper hem depth than short ones. Deep hems on garments worn by short figures tend to make the whole garment look out of proportion.
5. Narrow 6 mm hems stitched by machine are quick and easy for hardwearing garments, such as children's clothes, nightwear, jeans, aprons, shirts, etc.

3. Marking the Hem

Make any fitting alterations to the garment, then leave it to hang for at least 24 hours before beginning the hem.
(a) Try the garment on with the appropriate underwear, shoes, belts, etc., and fasten all openings.
(b) A second person is needed to mark the hem, and the wearer should stand still on a chair or small table so that the hang of the garment can easily be seen.
(c) Decide on the length of the hemline, and place a line of pins all round the garment at this level, about 5–7 cm apart. If the edge is uneven, measure up from the table using a chalk or pin hem-marker, wooden rule or marked stick.

Hems

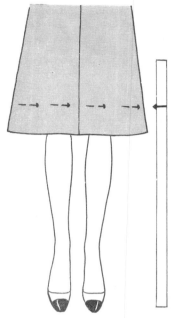

(d) Pin up the hem along this line of pins to get an idea of whether the length is correct. If necessary, experiment to get the length looking right then check that the edge is level all round. Leave the line of pins marking the edge, but remove all others, letting the hem down again. Take off the garment.

4. Turning Up the Hem

(a) Lay the garment on a flat surface. Trim seam allowance on depth of hem.

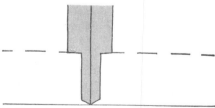

(b) Tack hem up 6mm from final hemline.
(c) Press folded edge only.
(d) Work on the wrong side of the fabric in short sections to prevent the hemline stretching.
(e) Use a tape measure or hem gauge to mark off the hem depth plus turnings from the fold line. Mark this with tailor's chalk or pins and trim off any excess fabric along this line.

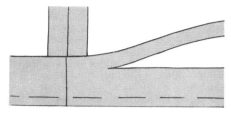

(f) On transparent fabrics, hems are made with two folds the same depth, to hide raw edges.

5. Treating Hem Fullness

Hem fullness can be treated in different ways according to the type of fabric and hem being used.
Method 1 – shrinking (for wools, cottons and linens that are not pre-shrunk).
(a) Use approximately four stitches to the centimetre. Sew a line of ease stitching around the free edge of the hem.
(b) Pull up the ease thread at intervals to adjust fullness evenly.
(c) Put a dry cloth between the hem and the garment. Using a damp cloth over the hem, press well to shrink the excess fabric. Repeat if necessary, then allow to dry and remove ease stitching.

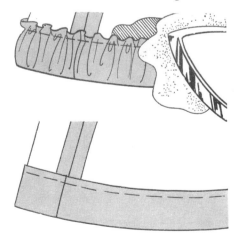

Method 2 – pleats
(a) Make small pleats, tucks or darts all round the hem leaving the tacked edge completely flat. Space these pleats evenly round the hem.
(b) On very thick fabric the surplus material in these pleats can be trimmed away and the edges neatened.

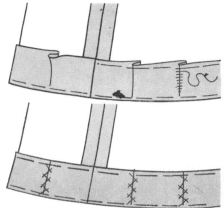

Method 3 – gathers
(a) Machine a row of ease stitching as in Method 1, or a row of gathering stitches by hand.
(b) Pull up the thread at intervals to adjust fullness evenly.
(c) Lift up stitches and gently pull with a pin. Repeat this process in other areas of the hem.

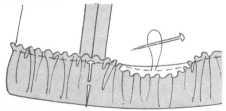

6. Other Ways of Gathering Fullness in Hems

(a) If there is a raw edge, turn under and stitch. Stitching can be used as an ease thread if there are ten stitches to 3cm.

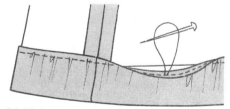

(b) If there is a raw edge to be covered with tape, ease thread can be put in and adjusted before stitching the tape to the hem.
(c) If a skirt or dress does not have too much fullness, one of the seam threads that stitch the tape on the hem can be used as an ease thread.

Hems

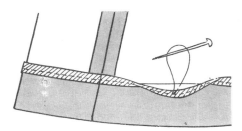

7. Corners in Hems

A hem may join a facing at the corners of a button-through skirt or on the front edges of a jacket. The corners should be mitred to eliminate bulk and make the corners lie flat.

(a) Fold the fabric as shown in the diagram. Press, then open out and trim as shown.

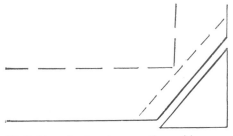

(b) Fold under turnings on three sides. Press.

(c) Turn the hems to the wrong side and oversew at the corner join. Secure the hem.

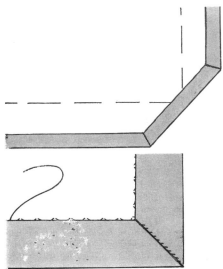

8. Finishes for Raw Edges

Always neaten raw edges before sewing the hem to the garment, making sure that the depth of the hem is very even.

(a) For fine fabrics – turn up the raw edge 6mm, pin and tack, then press into position.

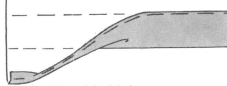

(b) For lightweight fabrics – turn over edges and machine with a straight or zig-zag stitch.

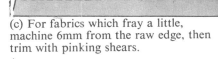

(c) For fabrics which fray a little, machine 6mm from the raw edge, then trim with pinking shears.

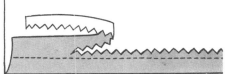

(d) For medium weight fabrics – overcast edges by hand or machine. Make the stitches fairly small and close together. If the material should fray badly, work a row of straight machine stitches, trim closely and overcast into the machining.

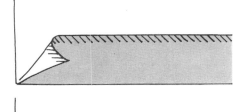

(e) Heavy weight fabric – should be enclosed in a bias strip on the edge of the hem. This can either be made from lining fabric or, if bought bias is used, one fold should be trimmed away to reduce width. Sew in the usual way from the right side, roll the binding to the wrong side but instead of turning it in, let it lie flat. Fix into place by working a slip stitch along the join from the right side, reducing the bulk.

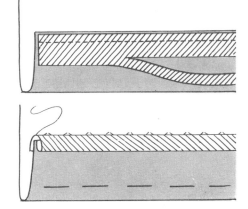

9. Sewing the Hem to the Garment

Plain hem (for other types of hems see the following sections)

(a) Press neatened edge of hem. Deal with any fullness.

(b) Work with the garment flat on a table.

(c) Tack the hem to the garment, near to the tacking line that marks hem edge for sheer fabric, and 13mm away for all other types of fabric.

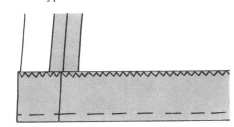

(d) On the hems of fine fabric turn the neatened edge towards you and sew the garment with slip hemming. Take the smallest stitch into the garment picking up one thread of the fabric. Then run the needle through the fold of the turning on the hem for 6mm.

Hems

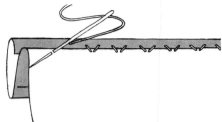

(e) For other fabrics, work with the neatened edge away from you. Roll back the edge with the left hand and work a loose catch-stitch under the edge, taking stitches alternately into the garment then into the hem. Pick only a thread or so of the garment to give invisible stitching on the right side. (If preferred simply hem the edge to the garment). —See chapter on stitches for details of hemming.

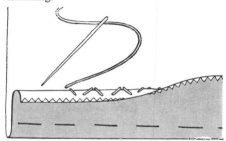

(f) Remove all tacking before pressing.

10. Pressing Hems

For hems on pleated skirts — See chapter on Pleats.

(a) Remove all pins and tacking.

(b) First press hems from the wrong side of the garment. If there is still extra fullness shrink it away as described.

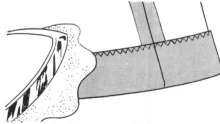

(c) Soft edged hems — hold the steam iron 5–7cm above the hem and steam it well. Pound the hem lightly with a ruler or the back of a clothes brush to shape it. Do not let the iron touch the hem. Let the hem dry.

(d) Sharp edged hems — press the hem from the wrong side to within 6mm of the stitched edge. Pound well if a really sharp edge crease is required. Then, if necessary, press lightly from the right side.

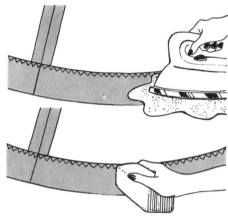

(c) Pleated hems — press seams well before hemming, especially where a seam occurs at a fold.

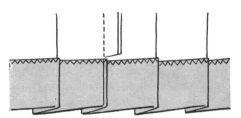

11. Types of Hem

Catch-stitched

This particular hem lies flat without using a tape and is suitable for heavy woollens and other fabrics. It can be used on coats that are lined.

(a) Sew from left to right.

(b) Catch a thread of the fabric in the hem.

(c) Push needle from right to left above hem edge.

(d) Pick up thread in garment below the hem edge. Push the needle from right to left.

(e) Repeat the process until the hem is completed.

(f) Remove all tacking. Be sure that hand stitching of the hem has not been pulled tight. Press.

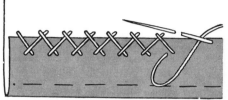

Tailor's hem

This hem is useful for jersey and soft woollen fabrics.

(a) Use approximately three stitches to the cm.

(b) Raw edge of hem should be stitched.

(c) Pink the edge. If fabric frays, either apply seam tape or overcast, rather than pinking the material.

(d) Pull to ease stitching — tack the hem 13mm from pinked edge.

(e) Hem should be folded back against outside of garment.

(f) Slip-stitch the hem. Push needle into the stitched line. Pick one thread in fold of garment material. Take another thread on the stitching line followed by one stitch into the fold. Repeat the process until hem is completed.

(g) Remove tacking.

(h) Press hem.

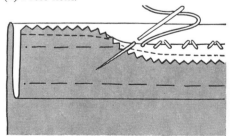

Lock-stitched hem

This is a strong, hard wearing hem.

(a) Sew from left to right.

(b) Fasten on into the edge of hem at the side of the garment.

(c) Take stitch through one thread of the garment fabric.

Hems

(d) 6mm from the starting point, take another stitch through one thread of the garment, followed by another on the hem.
(e) Pass needle over the loop as indicated in the diagram.
(f) Repeat the process until the hem is completed.
(g) Remove all tacking. Press.

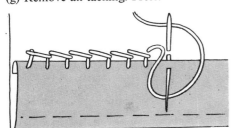

Slip stitched hem
This hem is suitable for firmly woven cottons, lightweight or medium weight fabrics and silk.

(a) Turn under raw edges approximately 6mm and stitch using three stitches per cm.
(b) Pin into position.
(c) Pull thread to ease.
(d) Slip stitch the hem to the garment by picking up a single thread below the fold edge of the hem. Slip the needle in the fold for approximately 6mm. Bring out the needle then pick up another single thread below the fold. Slip the needle into fold edge again, repeat the process until hem is completed.
(e) Remove all tacking. Press.

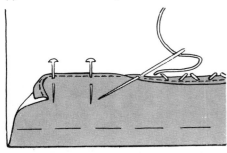

Stitched edge hem
A neat edge for hems that cannot be rolled.
(a) Turn under edge and machine.
(b) Turn the edge again and hem with invisible hemming stitch.

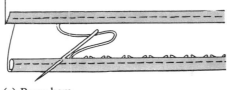

(c) Press hem.
(d) Two other ways to finish this hem —
i. Pink the raw edge. Turn the edge of the hem up and press. Machine as many rows of stitching as required.

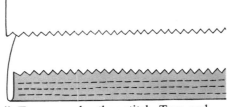

ii. Turn raw edge then stitch. Turn and stitch for the second time. Press.

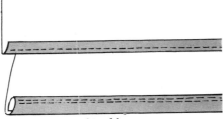

Narrow machined hem
A neat flat edge on fabrics that do not fray.
(a) Use narrow hemmer foot or rolled hemmer foot on the machine. Refer to machine handbook.
(b) When the narrow hemmer foot is used, the material is turned twice and stitched all in one process.

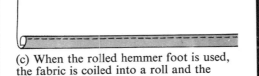

(c) When the rolled hemmer foot is used, the fabric is coiled into a roll and the fabric zig-zagged finally into place.

Blouse edges
Blouse hems should not show a ridge when tucked into a tight fitting skirt. This can be avoided as follows:
(a) Make a line of stitching around the lower edge of the blouse approximately 13mm from the edge. Add another row 6mm away.

(b) Pink the edge.
(c) Should the fabric fray, turn the raw edge under approximately 6mm and stitch around it twice.

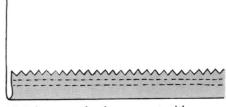

(d) Edge may also be overcast with a narrow zig-zag over a fine cord, and fabric trimmed away.

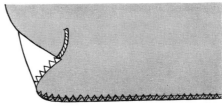

Blind Stitched by Machine
Some machines have a special guide for this stitch — use it on tweeds and other thick fabrics. Follow the machine handbook for details.
(a) Level and tack the hem edge.

Hems

(b) Trim the hem turning to the required depth and overcast the raw edge to neaten it.

(c) Prepare the machine for blind hemming and attach the special foot.

(d) Put the garment, hem downwards, in the machine as shown.

(e) Sew carefully, making sure that only one thread is caught in the fold of the garment or the stitching will show on the right side.

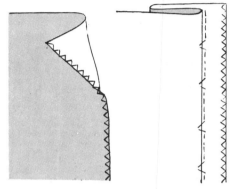

Stitched and rolled hem

Suitable for very lightweight, fine fabrics. It is a useful neat hem for lingerie and the edges of frills.

(a) Stitch 6mm from the edge.

(b) Trim close to the stitching edge.

(c) Between the thumb and forefinger roll the edge along for a few centimetres, making a roll about 3mm deep.

(d) Sew the roll into position by slip-stitching.

(e) If the hem should pucker, snip the machine stitching at intervals.

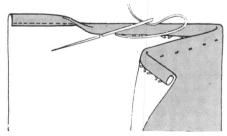

Quick hand-rolled hem

(a) Fold the hem edge under from 3 to 6mm.

(b) Make small stitches on the edge of the fold.

(c) Make a tiny stitch in the fabric a little ahead of the first.

(d) Repeat the stitches – these stitches produce a line of zig-zagging.

(e) Make several stitches like this and then, one hand holding the turned edge at the beginning of the stitches, use the other hand to pull up the thread.

(f) The edge will then form a roll.

Taped hem

(using seam binding or bias binding) Hem suitable for cottons, woollens, fabrics that fray and all heavy-weight synthetics.

(a) Sew three stitches per cm.

(b) Stitch round the hem edge.

(c) Pull thread up to ease fullness so that hem lies flat.

(d) Stitch bias binding or seam tape 6mm from the hem edge.

(e) Press tape gently.

(f) Pin into position and tack.

(g) Hem the tape to the garment.

(h) Remove all tacking. Press.

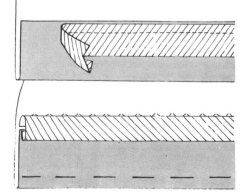

Bound hem (Quick Method)

Use this simple hem where there is no fabric to turn up, or where a bound edge that shows on the right side is acceptable, eg. for aprons, and children's clothes.

(a) Try on the garment, level the hem to the right length and trim off surplus fabric.

(b) Using bought bias binding or crossway strips cut from the garment fabric, bind the cut edge (see chapter on Binding and Piping for detailed method).

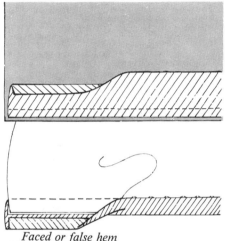

Faced or false hem

This is useful for lengthening a garment by letting down the original folded hem. It can also be applied to the right side as a decorative feature.

(a) Cut facing from bias fabric, or use wide bias binding.

(b) Turn bias under and stitch one raw edge.

(c) Stitch the other raw edge to the skirt edge by placing bias and skirt edge right sides facing and sewing together like a plain open seam.

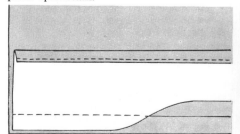

Hems

(d) Press the seam open.
(e) Turn the facing to the inside part of the skirt to the depth of the seam.
(f) Pin and tack.
(g) Slip-stitch facing into position. Remove tacking. Press.

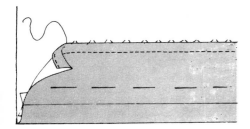

Circular hem – gathered

On a circular skirt the narrower the hem the better the effect as there will be less fullness.

(a) Turn raw edge under, pin, tack and stitch.
(b) Use approximately three stitches to the centimetre.
(c) Pull the bobbin thread from both ends and ease fabric slightly to adjust excess.
(d) Steam-press so that the garment hem will shrink.

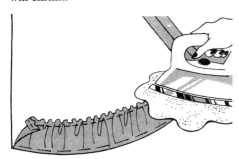

(e) Pin and tack hem.
(f) Stitch hem into place.
(g) Remove tacking. Press.

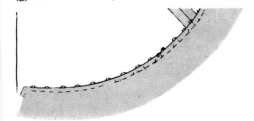

Circular hem – taped

This method is used on circular skirts made from thick fabric.

(a) With about three stitches to the cm stitch around the raw edge.
(b) Pull the two ends of the bobbin thread and gather evenly.
(c) Fullness of hem should be steam-pressed to shrink surplus fabric.
(d) Stitch bias binding or seam tape to the edge.
(e) Pin and tack tape to garment.
(f) Then hem with blind-stitch or hem-stitch. Press.

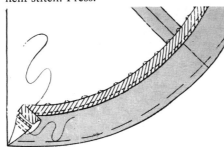

Hems on sheer fabrics

If a plain hem is desired the first and second folds should be almost equal in width so that the raw edge cannot be seen through the fabric from the right side.
A stitched hem may also be used.

(a) Mark the hem line on wrong side.
(b) Fold the excess fabric to the wrong side of the fabric along marked line. Press.
(c) Stitch as close to the edge as possible, using a fine needle and short stitches.
(d) Trim away surplus material close to the stitching.

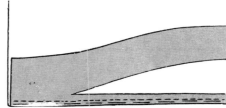

(e) Turn the stitched edge to the wrong side and press.
(f) Stitch close to the edge.
(g) There should now be two rows of stitching on the wrong side, but only one row on the right. Press.

Shell hems – hand stitched

This type of hem gives a decorative finish for cuffs, collars, infant's clothes and lingerie.

(a) Tack a narrow hem.
(b) Sew hem down about 13mm with running stitches. Alternative method so that fewer stitches show on the right side – hem the edge down, taking two stitches every 13mm.
(c) Take two stitches over the edge. Pull thread tight.
(d) The two stitches should be repeated at evenly spaced intervals.

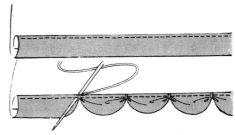

Shell hems – machine stitched

This process can be carried out with a sewing machine using blind hem or stretch blind hem stitch.

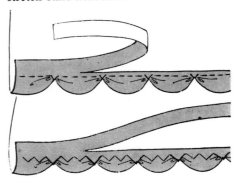

Embroidered hem (for sheer fabrics)

This is a pretty hem for use on baby clothes, fine table linen and evening dresses.

Hems

(a) Mark the exact length for the hem, then turn up the surplus and tack near the folded edge.

(b) Design on paper a simple pattern and then trace it lightly onto the right side.

(c) Using a tiny zig-zag machine stitch (length $\frac{1}{2} - \frac{3}{4}$, width 1) sew all round the design.

(d) On the wrong side, trim away close to the stitching.

(e) If liked, satin stitch over the design on the right side by hand or machine.

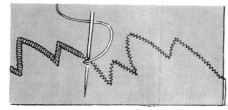

Pin-stitched hem

This stitching gives a punched hole effect as the stitches are pulled fairly tight during sewing. It is used on lingerie, especially on curved edges.

(a) Pin and tack up the hem. Press to get sharp edges.

(b) Work from right to left, and preferably from the right side.

(c) Make a backstitch in fabric below the hem.

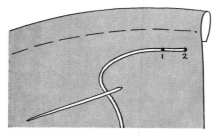

(d) Put the needle back in hole 2 and bring it out above the first hole.

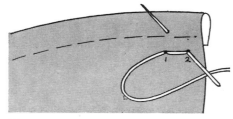

(e) Put the needle into hole 1 again and take a small stitch forward pulling firmly.

(f) Repeat.

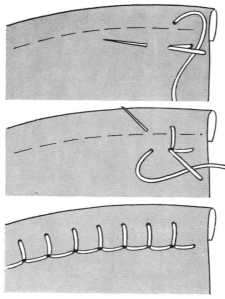

Lettuce edged hem

With many of the very fine, stretchy, jersey fabrics a conventional hem (whether deep or narrow) is often neither desirable nor attractive. For a pretty, flouncy hem finish a "lettuce hem" – so called because it looks so like the crinkly leaves of a lettuce – is the ideal answer.

(a) Tack up a 6mm hem stretching the fabric as you tack so that the tacking is very loose.

(b) Set the sewing machine to a stitch length of $\frac{1}{4} - \frac{3}{4}$ depending on the fabric, and a zig-zag width of about $2\frac{1}{2}$.

(c) Make some test samples first to ensure that the stitching on the garment will be perfect.

(d) With the right side of the garment facing allow the zig-zag stitch to fall first on the fold with the left swing of the stitch, and then off the fold with the right-hand swing. Stretch the fabric during stitching. By making some tests first you will find the stitch length most suitable for the fabric. The idea is to completely enclose the edge, with zig-zag stitches so that when the fabric "relaxes" after sewing it will flute prettily.

(e) When sewn – using very fine embroidery scissors – first remove the tacking and then carefully trim away the excess fabric left on the wrong side after stitching.

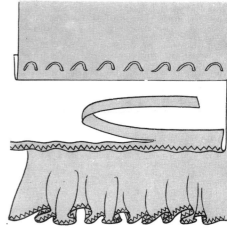

Hems on lace fabrics

(a) Mark length of hem.

(b) Trim away lace approximately 10 mm below the marks.

(c) Horsehair braid should be stitched flat to the edge of the skirt, below the marked length on the right side.

Hems

(d) Turn on the marks and catch the free edge of the horsehair braid to the dress, with long hemming stitches.

Note – Use narrow braid for hems that fall straight. Use wide braid for hems that stand out crisply.

Stiffened hems
Full length evening dresses may need stiffened hems to add stiffness without extra weight. Two methods of making this type of hem are as follows

Method 1
(a) Put horsehair braid on the outside of the skirt 10mm over the lower edge.
(b) Lap the ends, then stitch.

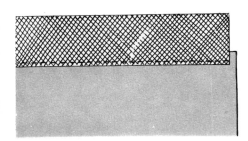

(c) Turn the horsehair braid to the inside, roll the skirt fabric inside for approximately 3mm.
(d) Hem into position. Press.

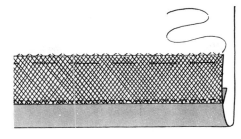

Method 2
(a) In this type of hem the horsehair braid is covered by the hem and is normally 6mm narrower than the hem depth.
(b) Put braid 6mm above the lower edge of the skirt on the wrong side, tack, then stitch along bottom edge of braid. Remove tacking.
(c) Turn the 6mm of skirt material to the inside over the horsehair braid, then tack and stitch. Remove tacking.
(d) Approximately 13mm from the top of the hem, stitch the horsehair to the fabric.

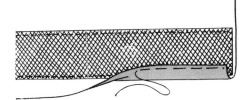

(e) Turn the hem to the inside, pin and tack, then hem into position.
(f) Remove tacking. Press.

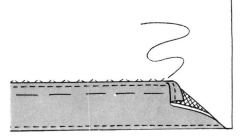

Interfacing and Lining

1. Interfacing (also called Interlining)
In most garments an extra layer of fabric is needed in areas such as openings, belts, collars, cuffs and pocket flaps, to add strength and crispness or body. Special woven and non-woven fabrics are used for interfacing, which is normally placed between two layers of fabric, or between fabric and lining. It is sewn or bonded to the garment, not the facing, in fairly small sections although occasionally a whole garment may need its support. Soft interfacing will help the gentle roll of a collar, while firmer interfacing prevents edges from stretching, but always use one lighter in weight than the fabric. The finished appearance of a garment is much improved by the correct use of interfacing, and it often helps to make the sewing processes easier to handle.

Non-woven interfacing
This is made by fusing fibres without weaving. There is no grain so it does not fray, is easy to cut and sew, and it can be cut out economically. Interlining such as Lantor is washable, drip-dry, crease resistant and it does not shrink, so it is perfect for fabrics made from man-made or natural fibres. It is unaffected by dry-cleaning. Available in many weights it can be used with every type of fabric — it is even possible to make it up alone as a foundation petticoat.
Choose interfacing only slightly stiffer than the fabric — take a piece of fabric to the shop and try them together. Some of the interlining weights available are as follows:
1. Lightweight — can be used on cotton, linen, wool, rayon, satin, and minimum-iron fabrics. Suitable for jackets, coat revers, dresses and skirts.

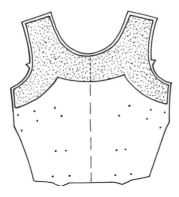

2. Extra Lightweight — can be used on silk, lawn, chiffon, voile and similar fabrics. Suitable for white and all coloured fabrics where the interlining is visible or will show through, as it is fluorescent white and non-yellowing.

3. Medium weight — contains nylon and can be used on white and coloured drip-dry fabrics, Terylene/worsted mixtures, flannel and suitings, satins and brocades. Suitable for bridal wear, waist-coats, tailored dresses, suits and lapels.

4. Heavyweight — can be used on tweeds, heavy wools, velvets, upholstery, heavier satins, and corduroy. Suitable for evening gowns, coats and bridal wear.
5. Super soft — can be used on silks, man made jersey fabrics, and soft wool. Suitable for dresses, thin jackets, evening gowns, dresses and skirts.

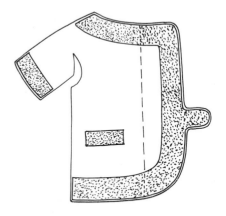

6. Iron-on — can be used on most types of fabrics. Suitable for small areas like cuffs, collars, pockets and waistbands. Iron-on Lantor is simply cut from a pattern, and pressed for 5 seconds onto the wrong side of the fabric with a hot iron over thin paper. It then sticks permanently to the fabric. Check to make sure that the adhesive does not show through the fabric onto the right side — if it does, iron the interfacing onto the facing instead.

Interfacing and Lining

Woven interfacings

Many fabrics are suitable, some of them specially made for use as interfacing. Some of the canvas type are suitable only for tailored garments where they are put on the wrong side of the garment fabric inside the seam line.

Most woven interfacings need pre-shrinking and the grain straightening before pieces are cut out. It is vital that the grain on the garment and the interfacing are the same, otherwise the interfacing may pull the garment out of shape.

Follow the instructions given with the paper pattern regarding the type to buy, and also feel the fabric and interfacing together in the shop before you buy.

Lightweight — use fine lawn or organdie on jersey, tricel, soft brocade, poplin and fine wool.

Very lightweight — use silk organza, net, soft organdie or fine lawn on pure silk, voile and see-through fabrics.

Mediumweight — use calico (tailored garments need soft canvas, wool canvas or holland) on mediumweight wool, rayon blends, gabardine, corduroy, etc.

Heavyweight — use calico on suit-weight cotton, linen or wool (a tailor would use canvas).

Using interfacings

Cut the interfacing from the pattern pieces as described in the pattern instructions. As interfacing does not show when the garment is worn, joins may be made in interfacing to avoid buying large quantities. Overlap the iron-on type so that the pieces match on the fitting lines and press them together. Woven and non-woven pieces should otherwise be machined together and trimmed so that the final piece is exactly the right size. Interfacing is usually slip-basted or bonded into place before the garment pieces are joined, and it may or may not be stitched in with the seams. Heavyweight interfacing may have the seam allowance trimmed away so that it lies just inside the seam lines. Where the facing of an opening is cut in one with the garment, the interfacing is cut beyond the fold line so that an extra strong edge results when the facing is folded back.

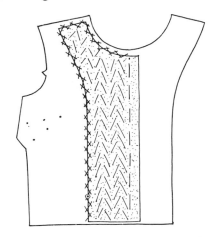

Place the fabric to be interfaced on a flat surface wrong side up, pin and slip-baste into position. If the garment piece is shaped, eg. with darts, lay it over a shaped area such as your knee before fixing the interfacing. (Slip basting stitches are removed later.) Catch stitch loosely along any folds that will not later be stitched. Follow maker's instructions when using iron-on interfacing.

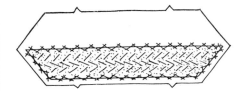

2. Lining

Lining is used on the inside of garments to give them body, help them to hang well and to keep their shape. Because the garment does not come into contact with the body it lasts longer, and special anti-static lining fabric may be used to stop "clinging". On very sheer fabrics a lining may be added for modesty, and linings generally tidy up the inside of garments.

Although a lining does help to prevent creasing, an additional layer is added where wrinkling will be a problem or to stabilize a garment section — the addition of this layer is called mounting (and sometimes underlaying or underlining — not to be confused with interfacing). This extra layer may also add warmth, and since mounting does not hide raw edges a separate lining is also used. Jackets, coats, and skirts, for example could be made from outer fabric, interfacing in small areas, a mounting or underlining and separate lining, with different materials for each. The order of making up is first to mount underlining onto fabric, interface some areas, make up garment, make up lining, then join lining to garment.

Whichever method is chosen the lining fabric should be durable enough to last for the life of the garment, and should be suitable for washing or dry cleaning with the garment.

Mounted linings

(Also known as underlining, underlaying and backing.)

This is an easy way to line garments because the lining and garment fabric are made up as one layer. Many fabrics are improved by mounting, especially if they are loosely woven, but good quality woollens self-lined or bonded fabrics do not need it.

It is vital that the fabric used for mounting is entirely suitable for use with the garment fabric; normally it is lighter and softer, but if it is too thin the garment will be droopy with a poor silhouette. (Ordinary lining fabrics are not always suitable.)

The pure silk used by professional dressmakers makes a garment very expensive but the following can be used:

Lantor interlining in many weights. (See maker's leaflet.)

Chiffon — for embroidered chiffon evening dresses.

Net — for lace.

Organza — for sheer fabrics, silk, lightweight cotton, fine woollens.

Interfacing and Lining

Mull, Lawn, Jap silk — for lightweight dresses and blouses.
Rayon or Tricel taffeta — for medium and heavyweight dresses and suits.
Fine calico — for thick woollens and tweeds.
Fine jersey — for fabrics that are stretchy.

Method
(a) Pin pattern, then cut out the garment fabric pieces.
(b) Remove pins, and put the pattern and the fabric pieces on the lining material and re-pin. Cut these out.
(c) Markings should then be transferred to the mounting fabric.
(d) Remove the pattern, place lining and fabric wrong sides together and tack down the centre of the fabric and lining to hold it together, or press on if using iron-on interlining.
(e) When placing the two layers of dart sections together machine down the centre of the dart to the point. This helps to assemble the dart.
(f) Place extra rows of tacking at equal intervals to hold the lining and fabric together.

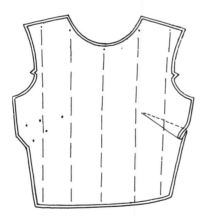

(g) Tack 13 mm from the edge all the way round.
(h) When machining on seam lines remember there will be four layers of fabric so use 3/5 stitches per cm.
(i) Trim and then neaten the seam edges by oversewing (machine neatening can make thick edges which will show through).

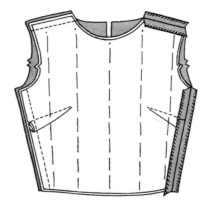

(j) Understitch facings loosely to seam allowances only.
(k) Before turning up the hem prick-stitch lining and fabric together just below the fold line.

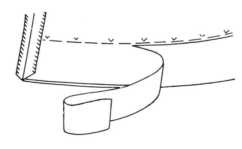

1. Sew the finished hem to the lining only, so that stitching does not show on the right side.

Separate linings
Adding a separate lining improves the whole appearance of a garment, and makes rough fabrics more comfortable to wear. If the garment will be worn unfastened a

luxury matching, contrasting or patterned lining can make a coat or jacket more attractive. When the lining has been made up it may be temporarily hand-stitched into place at neck and armholes or permanently fixed by machining. Professional dressmakers make up sections of the lining, and hand sew each one into place to avoid extra bulk and make the lining wear better. Whichever method is chosen the lining should in no way restrict movement in the garment.

If additional warmth is needed in coats "Milium" a satin lining coated on one side with tiny particles of metal, may be used.

If the garment is to be dry-cleaned then use a lining which will withstand dry cleaning. If the garment is made from jersey fabric then a jersey lining should be chosen.

Choose an anti-static lining for man-made fabrics.

3 The Choice of Fabric and Lining

Garment fabric	Lining fabric
Silk	Jap silk
Cotton	Cotton lawn
Batiste	Cotton lawn
Silk Chiffon	Jap silk
Brocade	Rayon satin for jackets and coats. Tricel for dresses.
Crepe	Jap silk
Wool – lightweight	Jap silk
Wool – heavyweight	Satin
Corduroy	Satin
Cashmere	Jap silk
Lace	Lightweight satin Jap silk. Tricel
Thick coating	Special coatweight satin, or fur fabric
Terylene Lawn	Tricel, Dicel. For a solid look use taffeta
Face cloth (fine)	Tricel or Dicel
Face cloth (thick)	Satin
Denim (cotton)	Cotton lawn
Gabardine wool	Coatweight lining
Fur fabric	Coatweight lining
Suede/Leather	Coatweight lining

Interfacing and Lining

4. Methods

General

Bodice and jacket, coat or skirt — make up in the normal way and interface small areas as usual.

(a) Cut out lining with aid of the pattern and transfer the markings. Make the lining in a similar way to the garment, but without interfacings.

(b) Front shoulder dart must be stitched from shoulder to second dot or approximately 10 cm down from the shoulder. Press darts towards the armholes.

(c) When garment is fitted and darts are placed at the waistline it should be clipped at the waistline *after* machine stitching and *before* pressing.

(d) Sew the lining together as you would the garment, sewing darts and joining seams.

(e) Either machine or handsew the lining to the garment:

(i) Press under 13 mm at lower edge of lining and sleeves lining. Front and back neckline edges should be pressed to the wrong side on the seam line, snipping curved edges to within 3 mm of seam line, to allow curved, turned seam allowance to lay flat.

(ii) The front part of the lining must be turned back so that the lining side seams and garment side seams can be sewn together with running stitches. Begin 5 cm below the armhole and sew to approximately 7.5 cm above the hem. Remove pins.

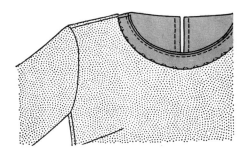

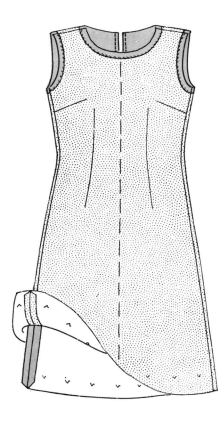

(iii) Sleeve lining should be slipped over the garment sleeves. Match the shoulder seams. Pin back neckline and front edges of lining over garment facings. Hem the lining to the facings.

(iv) Try on the garment, then a few centimetres above the hem, tack the lining to the garment. The edge of a skirt or dress lining may either be slipstitched into place over the garment hem, or attached only at the seams so that the bottom edge of the lining hangs free.

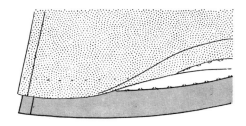

(v) To finish hems and corners on jackets and button-through skirts — see chapter on Hems.

Couture (for experienced dressmakers)
The couture method for jackets, coats, and dresses is:

(a) Pin, tack and machine darts and seams in the sleeves and sleeve linings.

(b) Turn the hem allowance on the sleeve lining to the wrong side and press.

(c) Pin and tack the lining and sleeve together at the hem. Slipstitch. Remove tacking.

(d) Tack the lining and sleeve together at the armhole end, without turnings.

Interfacing and Lining

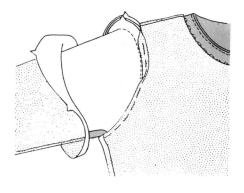

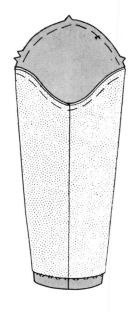

(e) Where gathering is necessary sew gathering thread through both thicknesses.
(f) Make up the garment bodice and sew in the sleeve in the normal way.

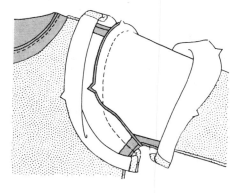

(g) Attach the lining to the bodice as above, but turn the lining seam allowance under at the armholes and tack it over the armhole seam to hide the raw edges.

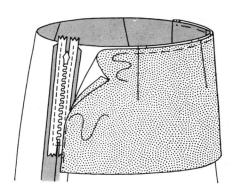

(h) Try on, to make sure it is comfortable to wear. Slipstitch sleeve lining to bodice lining. Remove tacking. Press.

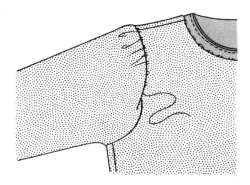

Skirts

Skirts may be completely lined with a separate lining, or a half lining can be used. Finishing just below hip level to prevent "seating" and bagginess, a half lining may be used for the back of the skirt, or for both back and front. For skirts with pleats or slit openings a slit may be left in the lining or the lining may be cut away in that area.

Use strong, good quality lining for skirts
(a) Make up the skirt and complete the zip or placket making any fitting alterations necessary. Transfer the alterations to the lining pattern.

(b) Make up and fit the lining. Press it well, and try it inside the finished skirt for length. Finish the lining hem.
(c) Place skirt and lining wrong sides together, and pin and tack the waist edge.
(d) Fold the lining under round the opening and slipstitch to the skirt.

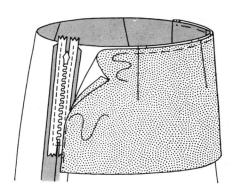

(e) Machine the skirt and lining together on the fitting line around the waist.
(f) Complete the waistband.

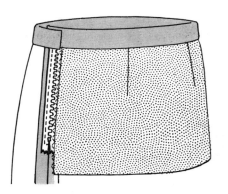

(g) Attach the lining hem to the side seams of the skirt with bar tacks.

Necklines

1. Shaped Facing
General method
2. Slashed or V Shaped
3. Collarless Jacket
4. Bound, Piped or Corded
5. Unfaced Boat Shaped
6. Cowl
7. One Piece Neckline and Armhole
Facing
For shoulders wider than 5 cm.
For shoulders narrower than 5 cm.

The neckline is an important part of a
garment that must be hard-wearing therefore
time and care should be spent on it. When
the garment has no collar it is possible to
finish the neckline neatly and simply with
a facing or binding, but this must be sewn
very accurately for an elegant appearance.
Normally a facing pattern is shaped to fit
a neckline and is included in the pattern.
If a facing pattern is not included then the
facing strip should be cut on the bias.
When the inside curve of a neckline is
bound, stretch the bias into a curve then
press before attaching it. All necklines
should be stay-stitched before making up,
and most necklines keep their shape better
if they are interfaced.

1. Shaped Facings For Necklines
Here the neck edge is finished by
reinforcing it with a hidden facing.
Whatever the shape of the finished
neckline — square, front "V", bateau
(boat-shaped) round or standing — the
method of fitting the facing is similar to
the one given below. The facing may be
fitted onto the right side of the garment
as part of the design, and may be of
contrasting fabric, or stitched with
contrasting thread, as a decoration.
General method
(a) Staystitch the neck edge by machining
each piece next to the seam line, just
inside the seam allowance. This prevents
stretching during making up. Interface
the facing (See chapter on Interfacing and
Lining for details).
(b) Pin and tack the bodice pieces
together, matching balance markings.
Try on and adjust for fit.
(c) Stitch and press any darts, then
machine the bodice pieces together on the
seam line. Press.
(d) Then insert a zip if required.

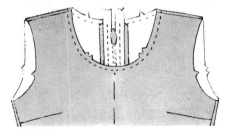

(e) Prepare the facing by pinning the
pieces together, right sides together,
matching the pattern notches. Tack and
machine on the seam line. Trim these
seam allowances to 10 mm and press the
seam open.

(f) Neaten the outer edges of the facing.
(See chapter on Seams and Seam
Neatening for details of neatening).
(g) With the bodice right side out, pin the
facing (wrong side out) to the neck edge.
Check that the pattern notches and the
shoulder seams match exactly. Tack into
place.

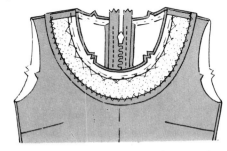

(h) Machine along the seam line round
the neck edge, pivoting at any corners and
making straight lines or smooth curves
according to the style.
(i) Clip curves or corners in the seam
allowance.
(j) Trim away the facing seam allowance
to 3 mm and the bodice seam allowance
to 6 mm. Press the seam stitching.

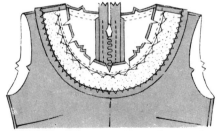

(k) Turn to the wrong side and press the
seam allowance up onto the wrong side
of the facing.
(l) Machine along the facing close to the
neck seam, through all layers. This
understitching will prevent the facing
rolling over to the right side.

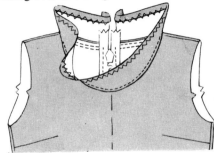

(m) Fold the facing onto the wrong side
of the bodice, rolling the edge so that
the seamed edge falls just inside and
does not show from the right side. Tack
round neck edge through all layers.
Press the facing.
(n) Hem the free edge of the facing to
the seam allowances of the shoulder
seams, not to the bodice.

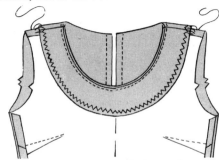

(o) Fold the ends of the facing under and
slipstitch to the zip tape, at least 3 mm
from the teeth. Press. Sew a hook and eye
on the facing ends above the zip.

Necklines

2. The Slashed or "V" Shaped

(a) Usually the pattern is marked indicating the slashed opening of the garment.

(b) The facing should be attached to the garment before slashing.

(c) Place right sides together. Pin and tack facing to the garment. The facing should cover the marked slash area.

(d) Tack a short length of fabric or seam binding over the facing at the point of the "V", as reinforcement.

3. The Collarless Cardigan or Jacket

This type of garment usually has fold back facings and a front opening. The neck and front edges should be taped to prevent them stretching during making up or in wear.

(a) Staystitch the neck edges. Mark the centre front and front fold lines.

(b) Attach the interfacing. (See chapter on Interfacing and lining for details).

(c) Pin, tack and machine the bodice shoulder seam, easing where marked. Trim the shoulder seam allowances to 13 mm and press open.

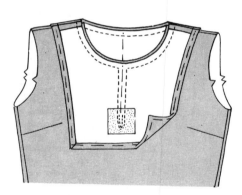

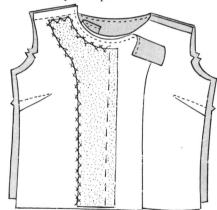

(e) Machine the facing to the neckline edge. Continue the machining down the front 6 mm from the centre then taper the machining to a point at the lower end of the opening. Make one stitch across the point before starting along the second side.

(f) Machine stitch a second time round the point, using a fine stitch.

(g) Cut or slash between machined lines down to the point.

(h) Remove the tacking and then turn the facing to the inside part of the garment.

(i) Understitch the facing and catchstitch the facing down at the seams, (see chapter on Facings for details).

(j) Press the facing to the wrong side of the garment then tack or slip-stitch facing invisibly to the garment.

(d) Pin, tack and machine the back neck facing to the front facings at the shoulders. Press the seams open and trim the seam allowances.

(e) Neaten the free edge of the facing.

(f) With the bodice right side out, fold back the facings along the front fold lines — the facing will be wrong side uppermost. Make sure that the back neck facing is also in place, with wrong side out.

(g) Pin and tack along the seam line round the neck edge. Tack a strip of fabric, or a piece of seam binding, over the seam lines from the shoulder to the bottom of the front opening. Catch stitch the tape into place down the fronts, then machine round the neck edge on the seam line.

(h) Complete as for shaped facing.

4. Bound, Piped or Corded Neckline

(See chapter on Bindings and Piping for details).

Binding of any width can be used to finish all types of necklines, particularly curved shapes where the bias binding will stretch to fit. A crossway strip can be cut from the garment fabric, or bought bias binding in matching or contrasting colours may be used. By filling the binding with cord, a piped or corded edge may be produced making a firm and attractive edge.

5. Unfaced Bateau (or Boat Shaped) Neckline

This very simple finish is used on loosely fitted dresses and jerkins which have no neck fastening.

(a) Staystitch the bodice neck edges just outside the seam line.

(b) Stitch and press the bodice darts, then tack the bodice together for fitting. Make any necessary alterations so that the neckline is exactly the right size, and that it lies flat.

(c) Machine, and press the shoulder and side seams.

(d) Press under 3 mm of the seam allowance of the neckline and shoulder seam.

(e) Fold the neck edges to the wrong side along the seam line, pressing the shoulder seams flat.

(f) Slipstitch the edge of the hem to the bodice, picking up one thread each time so that the stitches do not show on the right side.

(g) Remove tacking. Turn right side out. Press.

Necklines

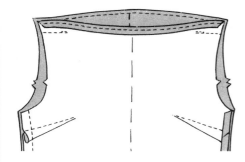

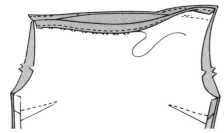

6. Cowl Neckline

The soft drape of a cowl neckline is formed by setting in a yoke cut on the cross. This yoke is usually mounted to give it body so that it drapes well. A piece of fabric cut on the straight grain is also added so that the neck area is supported and does not fall out of shape.

(a) Mount the lining onto the yoke sections. (See chapter on Interfacing and Lining for details of method).

(b) Pin, tack and machine and the mounted yoke sections at the shoulders. Press, clip and trim the seams.

(c) Tack seam binding over the back opening seam lines as marked on the pattern.

(d) Attach a prepared facing to the neck edge and roll it to the inside. Press it very lightly.

(e) Stitch the darts in the back of the stay piece and press them to the centre back.

(f) Join the shoulder seams of the stay pieces. Bind the top edge of the stay with bias binding.

(g) Tack the stay piece to the yoke, wrong sides together.

(h) Tack and stitch the yoke to the garment, finishing the corners carefully.

(i) Pin in the back neck zip and blindstitch the facing to the lining fabric. Some fabrics need a weight attaching to pull the cowl down into soft drapes. Experiment to find the right size and place for the weight.

7. One Piece Neckline and Armhole Facing (Also called a combination facing)

In this method one piece of facing neatens both neckline and armholes. For garments made from thick fabrics the facing may be cut from lining fabric. The method differs slightly according to the width of the shoulder.

For shoulders wider than 5 cm

(a) Prepare the neck and armhole edges by staystitching.

(b) Attach interfacing if required.

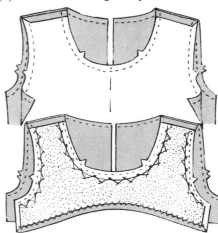

(c) Pin, tack and machine garment and facing shoulder seams separately, press open and trim.

(d) Neaten long un-notched facing edges as these will not be stitched to the garment.

(e) With right sides together pin and tack the facing to the garment. Carefully match the balance marks on the neck and armhole edges. Machine on the seam lines. Trim and layer or grade the seam allowances, clipping the curves.

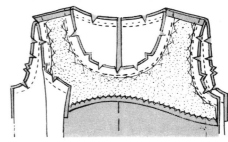

(f) Press the seams, then turn right sides out by pushing hand between facing and

Necklines

garment and pulling the back sections through.

(g) Understitch the facing to the seam allowances on neck and armhole edges as far along as possible.

(h) Pin and tack side seams, then machine on seam line right up to and including the facing. Press seams open.

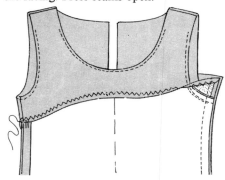

(i) Tack the facing into place, press carefully and catchstitch facing (to the seam allowance only) at the side seams.

For shoulders narrower than 5 cm
In this method the shoulder seams are finished as the final stage, because it would be impossible to pull the facing through the narrow openings on the shoulders.

(a) Staystitch and interface the neck and armholes as before.

(b) Prepare the bodice and facing as before but do *not* stitch the shoulder seams.

(c) Make a tiny, temporary tuck in the garment at shoulders so that the facing will be slightly smaller, and therefore hidden, later.

(d) With right sides together, pin, tack and machine facing to garment along the

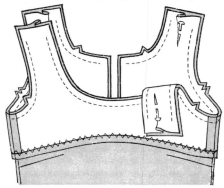

neck and armhole seamlines. Trim and layer or grade, the seam allowances. Clip the curves and trim any corners.

(e) Remove the pins in the temporary tucks then understitch the facing to the seam allowances, as far along as possible.

(f) Fold the facing back and stitch the bodice shoulder seams. Sew in the machine threads securely at both ends. Press the seam flat.

(g) Trim the seam allowances on the facing to 6 mm and press them under on the seam line.

(h) Sew the folded edges together with tiny stitches. Press.

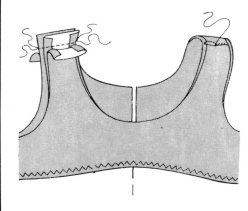

Openings

1. **Continuous Wrap**
2. **Alternative Wrap**
3. **Faced Slit**
4. **Decorative Faced**
   Conspicuous slit
   Bound

Openings are needed for ease in putting on and taking off fitted clothes. There are several ways of finishing openings, and the choice depends on the type of fabric and the placing of the opening (or placket) in the garment. Make openings as neat and invisible as possible, unless the opening is a focal point of the style. Some openings are made so that the two edges overlap — this is called a wrap.

1. Continuous Wrap (Also called Continuous Strip Opening)
This can be used on very fine, thin materials. Adapted for side openings on pyjamas, shorts, shirts and wrist openings on long sleeves. Fastened with hooks and bars, buttons and buttonholes or press studs. This opening can be made in a slash or a seam.
(a) Cut out a piece of fabric twice the length of the opening and 5 — 8 cm wide. Match grain with that of the edge to be bound.
(b) Pull the edges of the opening of the garment apart so that they lie in a straight line.
(c) Put right sides of binding to the right sides of the opening, raw edges placed together.
(d) Tack 10 mm from the raw edges and machine stitch, with the garment side uppermost, pivoting at point of slash and passing fullness behind needle.

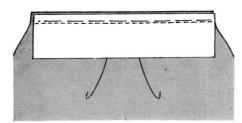

(e) Turn 6 mm on free edge of binding. Fold over raw edges of opening. Tack folded edge above first stitching. Hem into position picking up every machine stitch across middle section of strip.

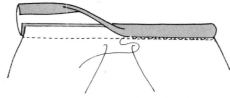

(f) Fold the front part of opening back along stitching line aligned over the back portion. Press.

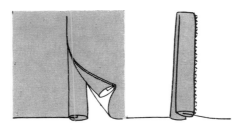

(g) Remove all tacking.
(h) Sew on the fastenings.
2. Alternative Wrap Opening
(a) Stitch wrap until the folded edge has been tacked above the first set of stitching.
(b) Hem from (A) to (B) of the back portion only.

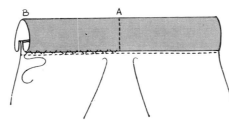

(c) Cut away the back of the unhemmed portion of the wrap.

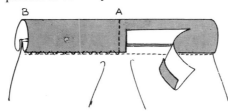

(d) Turn back the front part of the wrap as if finished. Tack the outer edge from the right side.
(e) Tack inner edge from wrong side of garment.

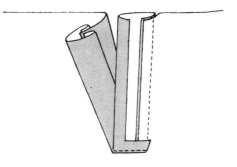

(f) Machine stitch rectangle.

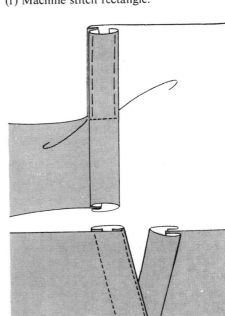

Openings without a wrap are usually faced or bound, and these are not quite as strong as those with a wrap.
3. Faced Slit Opening
The faced opening can be for front or back neck openings, wrist openings on long sleeves set into a band or for zip fasteners where there are no seams. It may also be decorative. Fastenings normally used on this opening are loop and button, hook and eye, zip fastener and link buttons.

Openings

(a) Mark position of opening on the garment, with tacking stitches.

(b) Facing section should be cut the length of the opening plus an extra 5 cm and an extra 5 cm in the width.

(c) Mark the opening on the facing with a line of tacking.

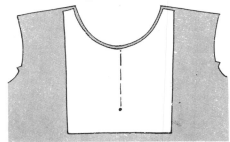

(d) Pin the edges of the facing under to wrong side. Tack then edge stitch to finish.

(e) Put right sides of facing and garment together. Tacking lines should lie over one another.

(f) Add a small square of lining material at the point for reinforcement.

(g) Put pins through tacking lines to find the correct position. Tack both thicknesses of fabric together along the tacking line.

(h) Either machine stitch or backstitch 6 mm from the top of the marked opening to form a point. Slope stitches inwards. In this way a "V" shape will be formed.

(i) Sew a second row of stitching at the point for extra strength.

(j) Snip into line of tacking between the stitches. Clip to point.

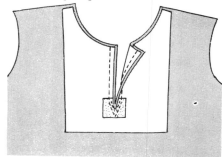

(k) Turn the facing to the wrong side. Pin and tack around opening. Press. Topstitch around the edges of opening on the right side.

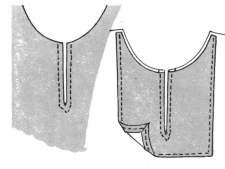

4. Some Decorative Faced Openings

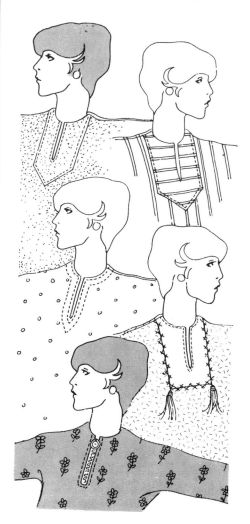

Conspicuous slit opening

This is a similar method of finishing as a slit opening. The facing may have a shaped outer edge and be turned onto the right side of the garment.

(a) Turn under the outer edge of the facing, tack and press into place.

(b) With the right side of the facing to the wrong side of the garment, pin, tack and machine round the slit and garment edge on the seam line.

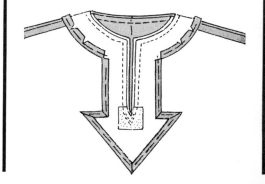

Openings

(c) Turn to the right side of the garment (see Chapter on Facings for details).

(d) Machine round the outer edge to hold it in position. Use a straight or decorative stitch. Press.

The Bound opening:

This is used for front and back neck openings and can be fastened with loops, hooks and eyes and link buttons. A fancy binding strip can be attached to make the opening attractive.

(a) The opening should be cut to required length. It must be cut straight to a thread on straight fabric, and very carefully in the case of an opening cut on the bias.

(b) A piece of material should be cut on the cross twice the length of the opening and approximately 25 mm/2.5 cm wide.

(c) With right sides together place binding to opening — raw edges together.

(d) Pin, then tack to within 25 mm/2.5 cm of the end of the opening on the first side. Fasten off. Pin and tack second side to the same point. Machine stitch, finishing securely. End of opening should have 5 cm unstitched.

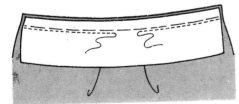

(e) Finish the end by hand using small backstitches and tapering the turning towards the end.

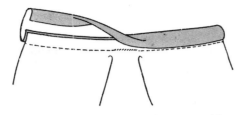

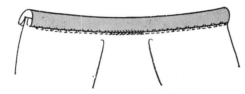

(f) Make 6 mm turning to the wrong side on the free edge of the binding fabric. Turn binding fabric to the wrong side of the garment and tack the folded edge just above the first stitching.

(g) Turning should be made slightly deeper than 6 mm towards the end of the opening so that the bend of the binding will lie flat.

(h) Finally, slip stitch the binding into place on wrong side of fabric.

(i) Remove all tacking. Press. Sew on fastenings.

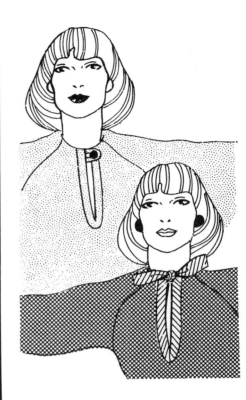

Pleats

1. **General Method**
   Preparation
   Fitting
   Finishing edges
2. **The Hem of a Pleated Skirt**
3. **Pleats with a Seam**
4. **Binding Upper Pleat**
5. **Lining Upper Pleat**
6. **Pleat Styles**
   Knife
   Box
   Inverted
   Kick
   Sunray and accordion
   Dior
   Double and fan

Pleats in skirts, dresses, blouses, jackets and trousers are decorative folds in the fabric which control fullness and give extra width to the garment. They are usually made from three layers of material that can either be left to hang freely from a supporting band, or can be stitched for part of their length to give a tailored fit and finish. A pleat can be made wider at the bottom than at the top to give better shape and hang, improving the appearance of the garment generally. Frequently, pleats are top stitched from the waistband downwards to prevent the strain that results on the release point when the garment is worn. Soft pleats are left unpressed but for a crisp look the folds are firmly pressed.

If pleats are included in a garment section such as the back pleat in a blouse, the pleat is made before the sections are joined together. All skirt pleats are made after the side seams have been sewn and neatened and the seams are hidden under a pleat where possible. It is usually easier to complete the garment hem before pleats are made.

There are a few basic kinds of pleats with many variations. Whatever method is chosen the fabric used should be firm and closely woven.

The directions below are for pleats in skirts as these are the most common. For other uses follow the instructions with your paper pattern.

1. General Method

Preparation

(a) Spread the fabric on a large flat surface where all the pleats can lie flat. Complete accuracy is vital for perfect pleats so be prepared to spend time in preparing them.

(b) Clearly mark all the fold lines. Pleats on patterns are marked with a solid line for folds and creases. Pleat folds are lapped to a line usually indicated by a broken line on the pattern, with arrows to the direction in which pleats are to lap.

(c) Marked lines of the pattern should be transferred to the wrong side of the fabric and the fold lap lines tacked in different coloured threads to prevent confusion.

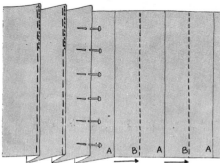

(d) Fabric should be turned to the right side and the fold lines lapped to the broken lines, making certain that the upper edges remain even so that the pleats will hang correctly.

(e) Folds must then be pinned and tacked, then gently pressed. Use only fine strong thread for tacking so that it can be left in until the pleats have been pressed. Then fit the skirt — see next section.

(f) Pleats should be stitched as instructed on the pattern, first completing the hem if possible (see below).

(g) Press the pleats carefully under a damp cloth. Remove tacking.

(h) It is better for pleats to be stitched from the bottom upwards as stitching

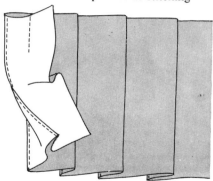

downwards may cause the material to stretch and distort the pleat.

(i) If the fabric tends to be crease-resistant, edge-stitch the underfold of each pleat.

Fitting

It is essential to try on the skirt before stitching the pleats as it is not always possible to get the size right at the first attempt.

(a) Tack the pleats firmly and then tack a piece of tape along the waistline so that the skirt will hang properly during fitting.

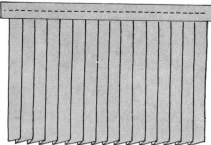

(b) If the waistline is too large or too small remove tape and make tiny adjustments to each pleat.

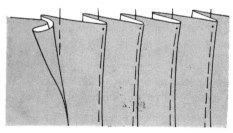

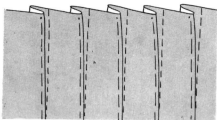

(c) For straight pleats it is important that the edge of the pleats remain on the straight grain of the fabric.

(d) Complete the pleats, zip and hem, then again tack a piece of tape round the waistline.

(e) Try on the skirt before stitching it to the waistband or bodice. Slightly raise or

Pleats

lower the skirt at the waist until the pleats hang exactly right, adjusting the seamline for the waist as necessary. Complete the garment.

Finishing the edges — unpressed pleats
The skirt can be made up before the hem is completed. At this stage remove the tacking so that the pleats hang in soft folds.

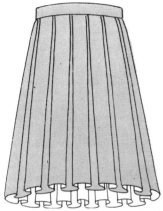

Finishing the edges — pressed pleats
Press the pleats on both right and wrong sides then make up the garment. Remove enough of the tacking so that the bottom edge can lie flat for hemming, but leave in all the placement lines. Complete the hem, press pleats carefully then remove all tacking.

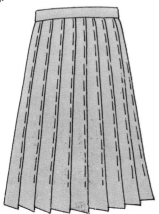

Finishing the edges — Top-stitched pleats
When fitting is completed, press the pleats carefully on both sides. Machine round the waistline 3 mm above the seamline to hold the top of the pleats securely in place.

Topstitch on the right side, 3 mm from the edge of each pleat, down to the pattern marking or to the level most flattering to your figure. Check carefully that the end points of the machining are in a line across the skirt. For extra strength the fabric can be pivoted and one or two stitches sewn across each pleat at the end of the stitching.

Complete the hem, press, then remove tacking.
Note — on springy materials for a far more durable creasing, topstitching may be continued for the full length of pleats but *without* stitching the pleat edge to the garment. The inside folds may also be stitched in this way.

2. The Hem of a Pleated Skirt

A fairly narrow hem, not more than 3·8 cm is used. (On a straight skirt the hem can be folded up and tacked before pleating.)
(a) Tailor tack through all layers of fabric to mark the arrangement of the pleat.

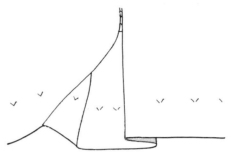

(b) Undo some of the pleat stitching.
(c) Trim away seam allowances to the depth of the completed hem. Press open turnings below this point and cut to 6 mm.

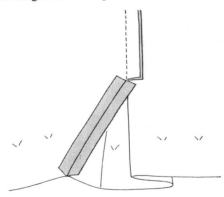

Turn up hem and finish off.
(d) Refold pleats and tack into place.

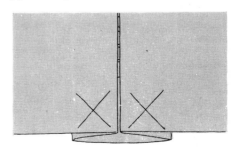

(e) Press — then either stitch the fold of a pleat on the hem section only, if it is a

Pleats

seamed pleat or stitch all the way along the fold. This keeps the pleat hanging in place when wearing the garment.

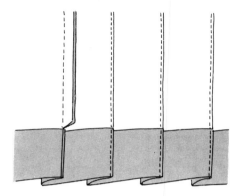

(f) Remove tacking.
(g) Press the skirt gently.

3. Pleats with a Seam
(a) Place fabric right sides together. Fold to fold.
(b) Tack along the length of the pleat.

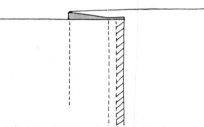

(c) Stitch to the length of the fitted portion of pleat.

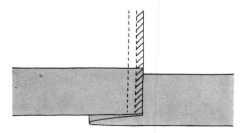

(d) Place fabric right side downwards with the fold of the pleat lying over the stitched area. Pin, then tack pleat into position.

(e) Press the pleat using a piece of thick paper between the pleat and garment to prevent the pleat line from the wrong side marking the right side.

4. Binding Upper Pleat
This method of binding is used to reduce bulk in heavy materials and to give a good fit to the garment.
(a) Snip away area 13 mm either side of the stitched line, and 13 mm above the end of stitching.

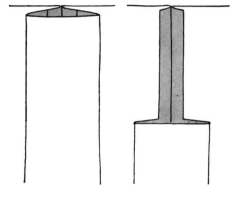

(b) Make the raw edges tidy. (Overcast or Bind). Stitch a length of binding over the raw edges of the top of the pleat.
(c) To give added support to pleat, place straight binding to each end of upper pleat and attach other ends to waist of skirt.

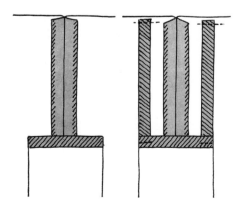

5. Lining Upper Pleat
(a) Cut away top area indicated — this is the upper part of the pleat.
(b) Neaten the raw edges.

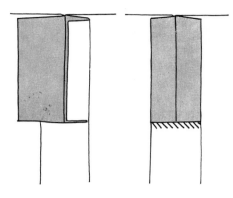

(c) Make a rectangle out of lining approximately 25 mm wider and 13 mm longer than the section already cut away. Fold and tack 13 mm turning to wrong side.
(d) Put wrong side of lining to the inside of the pleat. Tack into position. Oversew lining to cut edge of the pleat turnings. Hem lower edge to inner thickness of pleat.

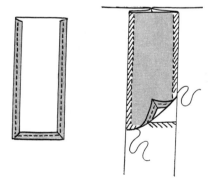

6. Pleat Styles
Pleats are made in many sizes either from folds in a single piece of fabric or with the addition of an extra piece of fabric stitched underneath. Most pleats can be straight or shaped, and used singly or in groups.

Pleats

Knife

These are folds turned in one direction.
(a) Mark fold and placement line either with pins or tailor's chalk. Use a ruler to make certain pleats are evenly placed and spaced.
(b) Create fold line of pleat, press down to placement or lap line.

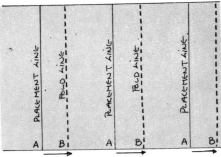

(c) Pin pleat at placement line.

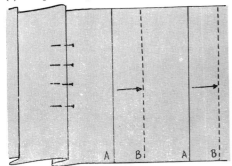

(d) Tack pleat into position.

(e) Stitch through all layers of material, to hip line, or depth required.

(f) Tack across pleats at waistline.

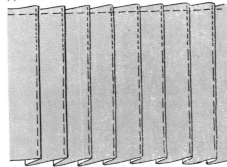

(g) Press.
(h) Remove all tacking except at waistline.

Box

These are made with two folds in opposite directions — the underfolds meet at the centre of the pleat.
(a) Mark fold and placement line with pins or tailor's chalk. Use ruler so that pleats will be evenly spaced.

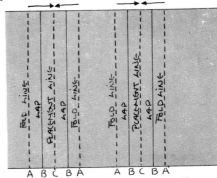

(b) Crease fold lines to placement lines.
(c) Pin pleat.
(d) Tack pleat into position.

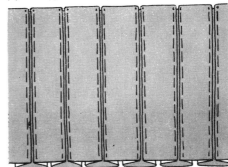

Pleats

(e) Stitch through all fabric layers.
(f) Tack across pleats at waistline.

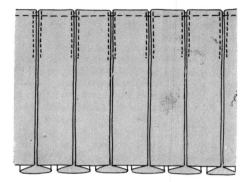

(g) Press.
(h) Remove all tacking except at waistline.

Inverted (box pleats in reverse)

Usually two of these pleats appear on the back and front of a skirt. Two pleats are turned in towards each other.
(a) Mark fold line, centre line and placement line with pins or tailor's chalk.

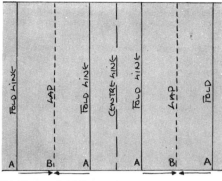

(b) Create fold lines of pleat, press down to the placement line.

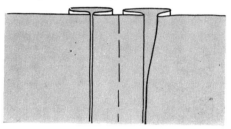

(c) Pin pleats at placement line.
(d) Tack pleat into position.
(e) Stitch through all layers of material
(f) Top stitch upper part of pleats.

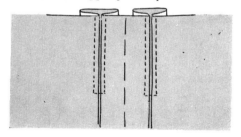

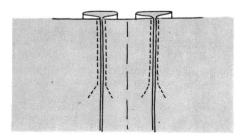

(g) Press and remove tacking.
(h) Press again for a crisp finish.

Kick

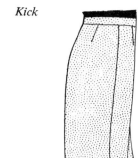

There are several ways of making a pleat in the centre back seam of a skirt. Some patterns are cut with an extension in the seam allowance for a simple, folded pleat.

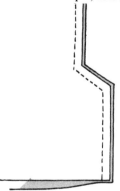

(a) Mark original seam line of pattern on the material. This will be the pleat line.
(b) Mark top length of pleat on original seamline.

Pleats

(c) Place skirt sections right sides together.
(d) Tack pleat line to top mark where pleat ends, continuing up original seam line to waist.
(e) Machine stitch from bottom to top 15 mm seam along the raw edge of pleat extension, continuing up to waistline along original seam line, or pleat extension may be carried up to waistline, as in diagrams below.

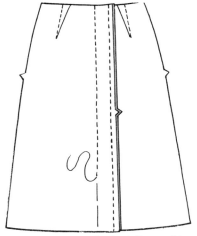

(f) Press seam towards the left, machine stitch to waistline.
(g) Remove tacking from pleat on original seamline.

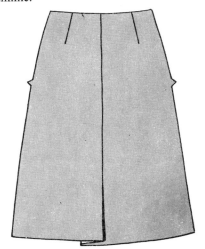

Sunray and accordion
Sunray pleats taper into the waist. Accordion pleats are the same width at both top and bottom. These pleats have folds which stand up instead of lying flat, and it is almost impossible to do this at home. The fabric must be taken to a shop that can arrange for the pleating to be done commercially.

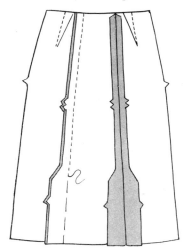

Dior
This is a type of kick pleat, sometimes called a false pleat as extra flaps of fabric are stitched in to provide fullness for ease when walking.
(a) Cut and shape seam allowance of skirt sections.

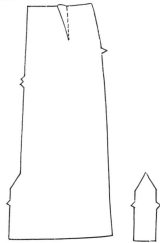

(b) Mark the seam line on the skirt sections.

(c) Mark the length of the pleat on the seamline.
(d) Tack the length of the pleat on the original seamline.
(e) Machine stitch the rest of the seamline towards the waistline.
(f) Press seam allowances open.

(g) Cut underlay of pleat.
(h) Pin, tack and machine the underlay to seam allowance.

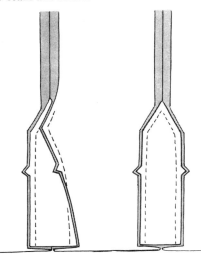

(i) Tack upper end of pleat flat to the skirt. Either catchstitch edges at the top of pleat to skirt on the inside or turn skirt to right side and topstitch through all thicknesses.

Pleats

(j) Remove the tacking from the length of pleat on the seamline.

(k) Press.

(l) When turning up the hem ensure that the underlay is very slightly shorter than the top of the pleat.

Double and fan

Double pleats are set in straight skirts to provide even more fullness but as a wide piece of fabric must be inserted the pleats should be kept short in length or they will be bulky. One pleat is set over the other.

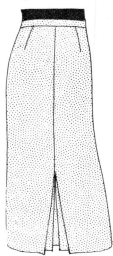

Fan pleats are created by setting two or more pleats on top of each other, grading the width of each pleat to avoid too much bulk. When the pleats are pushed out during walking they spring open, creating a fan effect. Fan pleating is very pretty in evening dresses made of light, firm fabrics where the pleats can start just below the knee.

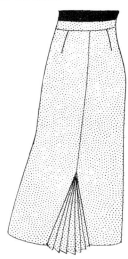

Pockets

1. Points to Remember
2. Types
In a seam
Hidden inside bodice
Included in a style line
Welt
Flap
Bound
Corded
Patch

Look at any range of clothes and it is immediately obvious that there is an enormous variety of pockets, both decorative and practical. Some are simply bags of lining material hidden inside the garment, but many are sewn on the outside as a feature of the design.

Pockets can be plainly or decoratively stitched, in self fabric or contrasting colours, textures, and patterns. Where they are used as an eye-catching detail they must be placed in exactly the right position and carefully finished or the whole appearance of the garment may be spoilt.

Add a pocket to children's clothes, even when the pattern does not include one, and consider using pockets to hide cigarette burns, stains, joins and flaws on ready-made articles. Outside pockets with large openings may need a fastening for security.

Consider the type of fabric and the figure of the wearer when choosing pockets. Thick, tailored styles may look better with hidden pockets and plump figures need pockets placed so that large hips are not emphasised.

1. Some Points to Remember
1. If fitting alterations are made, the pocket position may need moving.
2. Pockets below the waist must be placed where a hand can slip in easily and comfortably.
3. Pockets that are meant only as a decoration should be placed in the most flattering places.
4. If the wearer will be sitting down most of the time, skirt pockets must be placed lower down.
5. As figures vary so much in proportions, the number and size of pockets may need changing to enhance the final appearance.
6. If in doubt, cut out pockets in paper first and experiment with them on the garment pieces or tacked garment, adjusting size and shape if necessary. If trying them on a whole garment tack up the hem.
7. It is usually easier to attach pockets to flat pieces of fabric so that they may be added at an early stage of making up the garment.
8. Accurately mark the final position of pockets by thread tracing. For symmetrical placing, transfer the markings from one half of the garment to the other by pinning the two halves together with the pattern notches matching.
9. Cut pockets on the true straight or cross grain and keep all corners true.
10. Pockets or pocket flaps may need interfacing with interlining to help them keep their shape.
11. For welt flap, patch and saddlebag pockets, match the material grain with the garment grain. When a design of stripes, plaids or checks appears in the fabric the design should match that of the garment exactly, in both crosswise and lengthwise grain. Alternatively the pockets may be cut on the cross for an interesting feature.
12. Two rows of machining may be sewn round pocket bags for extra strength.

2. Types of Pockets
In a seam
This type of pocket is either set invisibly into a construction seam, or it may have a welt on the outside. One section of the bag is usually of garment fabric and one of lining. (Pocket can be made by using a narrow strip of garment fabric and stitching it across the upper pocket lining bag instead of making the section entirely of garment fabric.) The pocket pieces may be cut in one with the garment, as extensions of the seam allowance.
(a) Two shaped pocket bags should be cut approximately 20 cm by 10 cm wide, or from the pattern pieces.
(b) Tack and machine the lining bag section to front seam a little back from construction seam at pocket opening, matching notches and leaving seam allowance at top and bottom edges unstitched.
(c) Tack and machine the fabric bag section to back seam edge a little behind construction seam edge, matching notches.
(d) Tack and machine the lining and fabric bag section together. Press towards the centre front. Remove tacking.

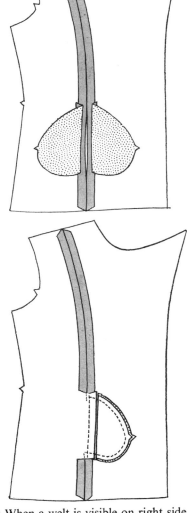

(e) When a welt is visible on right side of garment both pocket bag pieces can be made from lining. Make welt and put it in between lining and garment. Machine stitch along garment stitching line. (See the section on Welt pockets for details.)
(f) Welt on right side of garment must be firmly sewn to garment at top and bottom.

Pockets

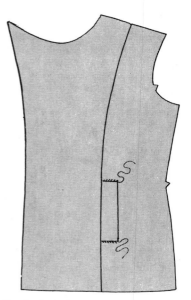

(g) Catchstitch the pocket and seam allowance together to hold pocket into place inside.

Pocket hidden inside bodice
(Sewn between lining and garment facing.) Where no pocket should be visible on the outside part of the garment, one may be inserted at the facing edge between the garment and the lining. This can be placed above the waistline in the buttonhole side of the garment.
(a) Cut two pocket pieces from lining fabric either from the pattern piece, or about 17 – 20 cm by 10 cm including seam allowances.
(b) Turn the straight edges to the wrong side and tack into place.
(c) Place the two pieces right sides together. Tack and machine.

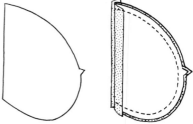

(d) When the garment is being lined place the pocket between lining and garment above the waistline. One edge of

the pocket should be tacked to the facing edge of the garment and the other edge tacked to the matching facing edge of the lining. Slipstitch the two edges.
(e) At ends of pocket catchstitch the facing edge at right angles. This will hold the pocket firmly in position.

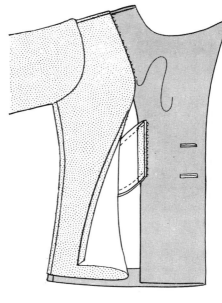

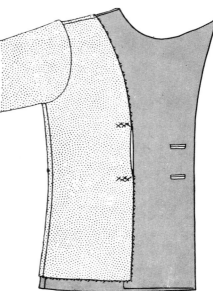

Pocket included in style line
Pockets appearing in the design line of a garment should be made before the garment is tacked together. A pocket may be made in one with the garment bodice, or cut as part of skirts and trousers.

Method 1

(a) Mark the position of the edge of the pocket on the underlay piece with tailor's chalk or tacking.
(b) Put the facing and garment right sides together. Tack and machine on seam line. Snip and trim the turnings. Press.
(c) Turn facing onto wrong side, rolling the edge to bring the seam slightly to the wrong side. Tack into place. Press.

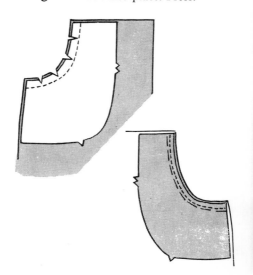

Pockets

(d) Place the wrong side of the faced piece onto the right side of the underlay, matching the edge to the tacked line. Pin and tack into place.

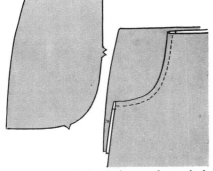

(e) Pin and tack the facing to the underlay to make the pocket bag. Machine pocket bag on the seam line.
(f) Trim the turnings and neaten securely.

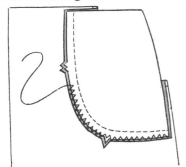

Method 2

(a) Cut pocket sections from self fabric. Some patterns include pocket piece as extension of seam allowance.

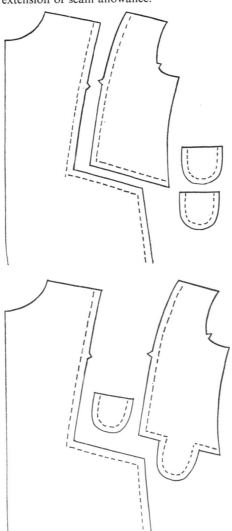

(b) Tack along outer seam line of front part of garment.
(c) Pocket ends should be indicated by crosstacking on tacking line.
(d) Tack inner seam line of side front section of garment.
(e) Tack pocket section in position. Stitch 6 mm below garment seam line. In doing this the pocket seam edge is not visible when the pocket is completed.

(f) Seam binding should be positioned on wrong side of garment as a stay, for strength. One edge should touch the seam line with the tape towards the raw edge. Hem the edges of the tape to the seam.

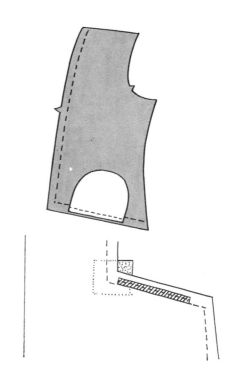

(g) The inner corner should be reinforced.
(i) Tack along the seam line.
(ii) Tack a piece of lightweight fabric, about 5 cm square, over the corner right sides together. The grain must be the same as the fabric grain.
(iii) Machine a "V" from the edges to the point of the corner, taking one stitch across the corner but not through the tacking.
(iv) Turn the seam allowance to the wrong side along the tacked line, pulling the extra square over so that it forms folds.
(v) Cut away the extra square level with the raw edge of the garment piece.

Pockets

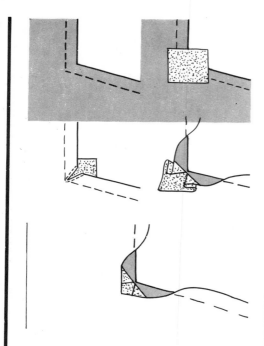

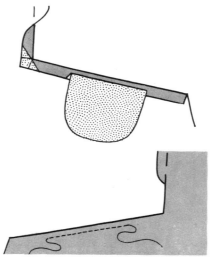

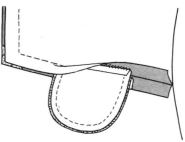

(h) When the corner is reinforced tack the pocket bag section in place, right sides facing and machine approximately 6 mm out on the seam allowance from the seam fold. When the pocket edge is complete the bag edge is not visible.

Turn and tack seam allowance from the shoulder to the turn, then along to the underarm seam. Position sections as in diagram. Match stitching edges. Pin then tack them into position for fitting.
(k) When bodice has been fitted, machine stitch the seam from the shoulder to the front pocket end. Leave long threads to be pulled to the wrong side and fastened off.

(m) Complete top stitching from side of pocket end to underarm seam.

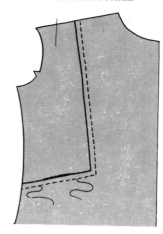

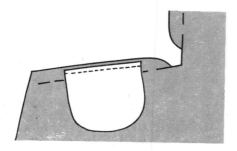

(i) Seam edge should be turned along the tacking at seam line. Tack then steam. Remove tacking then steam again to remove any tacking marks.
(j) Topstitch exact pocket opening across the top.

(l) Pin together the two bag pocket sections, tack then machine stitch. Begin and end machine stitching at the ends of the pocket opening. Remove all tacking.

Welt pockets
These are pockets inserted into a garment, with just a flap or welt showing. They are commonly used on men's jackets, and on coats and skirts. Welts are usually left upstanding with the ends secured to the garment. They may be above or below the pocket opening line. Flaps are normally attached at the top so that they hang down freely. The method given below is for a welt. Directions for flaps will be found with the chosen paper pattern. Welts are sometimes used as mock pockets purely for decoration. The grain of the welt must match the grain of the garment. Two thicknesses of fabric are usual with interfacing. Welts may be cut from one piece of self fabric with the top folded over or two pieces with a seam along the top. They are made rather like collars. (See chapter on Collars.)
(a) Cut the welt piece according to the paper pattern or cut them the same length as the pocket opening plus 12 mm plus

Pockets

seam allowances and the depth of the finished welt plus seam allowances.

(b) Tack or iron on interfacing to the wrong side of the welt. Trim away interfacing seam allowances.

(c) Place two welt pieces wrong sides together, pin, tack and machine on seam line. Trim and layer seam allowances.

(d) Turn right side out, rolling the edge between fingers and thumbs so that the seam is not visible from the right side. Tack near the edge and press. Topstitch, if liked, as a decoration.

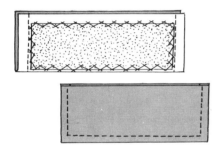

(e) Mark the pocket position on the garment.

(f) Pin and tack the welt below the pocket mark with the cut edges along the pocket line.

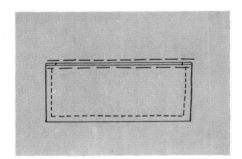

(g) Two pocket bags should be cut out. Lower section in lining should be placed over welt with stitching lines matching. Tack. Upper section should be of fabric and put in with cut edge touching cut edges of welt and bag.

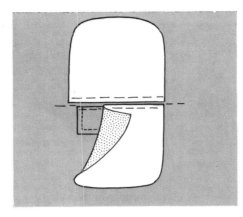

(h) Tack, then machine lower section of welt bag. Stitch back over four stitches on stitching line to reinforce.

(i) Stitch upper bag with stitches ending three stitches short at each end.

(j) Cut pocket opening between raw edges of bag sections to within 6 mm of stitching ends, then out to stitching ends diagonally.

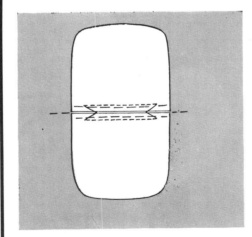

Pull bag sections through to wrong side. Fold welt into the position into which it will fall when completed. Place pins at welt ends, through stitching ends of upper bag.

(k) Tack pocket bag sections together. Garment should be folded away at one end of pocket. Adjust triangle at end of pocket opening into place, then stitch close against pocket across the triangle. Do the same for other side of pocket.

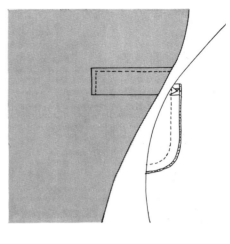

Flap pocket

The flap conceals the pocket opening. The pocket bag pieces are made from lining, with a strip of garment fabric stitched onto one section, where it is seen when the flap is moved. The flaps can be made any shape to suit the garment. Use interlining to give them extra body.

(a) Cut out two pieces of self fabric for the flap. Interface and make up as for a welt. (See section on Welts.)

Pockets

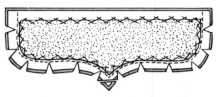

(b) Mark the pocket line on the garment with thread tracing.
(c) Place the flap on the garment, right sides together, with the cut edges along the pocket line.
(d) Tack into position 6 mm away from the pocket line.

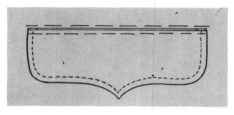

(e) Cut two pocket bag pieces from lining, plus a strip of self fabric 5 cm wide.
(f) Tack this strip to the lining, machine top and bottom edges then catchstitch the bottom edge to the lining.

(g) A 5 cm strip of lining should be cut and used to bind lower edge of pocket opening directly opposite the flap edge.
(h) (i) Put bag section over flap with self fabric strip facing flap. Tack in place — bag edge should match flap edge.

Machine 6 mm from cut edge. Bag and flap should be stitched into position.
(ii) Put cut edge of binding to lower edge of tacking. It should touch cut edges of bag and flap. Tack in place. Machine stitch binding, making seam line two or three stitches shorter than seam above. Remove tacking. Cut garment between edges of bag section and facing to within 6 mm of stitching ends, then cut diagonally out to stitching ends.

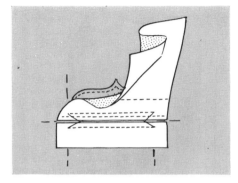

(i) Pull bag and binding sections through opening to wrong side of garment. Flap should remain on right side. Lower edge of opening should be bound by folding narrow section around seam and tacking into place. On right side machine along binding. Catchstitch raw edge to garment.

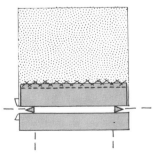

(j) Bag should be folded down over bound edge. Fold the garment away from open end of pocket. Stitch triangle into place in arc. For decorative effect — tack bag to garment and machine stitch on right side of garment in matching or contrasting thread. Stitch down from flap ends.

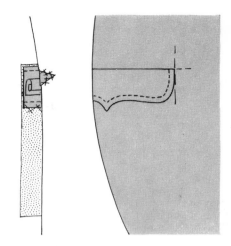

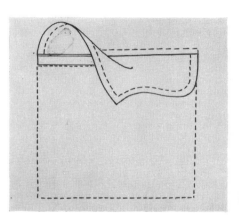

Bound pockets
One piece of fabric can be used to make a binding for pockets in thin and medium weight fabrics. Piped or corded pockets are used for heavy and thick fabrics. Bound pockets are used on lined, tailored garments, and are made in a similar way to bound buttonholes.
(a) Mark the *exact* position of the pocket on the garment with a straight line of thread tracing.
(b) Cut a piece of self fabric on the straight grain, about 8 cm deeper than the depth of the finished pocket, and about 5 cm wider than the pocket.
(c) With right sides together, place this piece centrally over the pocket line and tack along the line.

Pockets

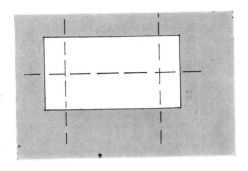

(d) Machine an oblong 6 mm from the pocket line on both sides — it is easier to do this from the garment side.

(e) Cut along the pocket line and out to the corners without cutting the machining.

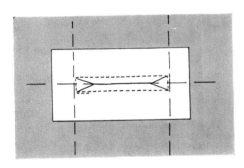

(f) Pull the binding piece through the slit leaving a neat shape on the right side.

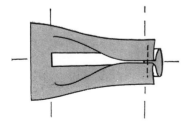

(g) Fold the binding neatly on the wrong side, oversew the folds and press.

(h) Attach to the pocket — place one pocket piece to the wrong side of the garment, and tack into place.

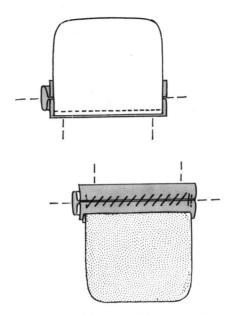

(i) From the right side of the garment machine through all thicknesses just outside the binding.

(j) Press the pocket piece downwards.

(k) Put the other pocket piece over the first, right sides together. Tack. From the right side of the garment complete an oblong of stitching round the bound opening.

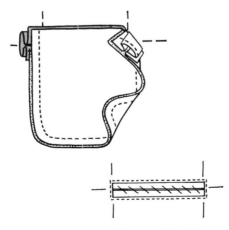

(l) Pin, tack and machine together the two pocket pieces on the seam line — do *not* stitch the pocket edges to the garment.

(m) In an unlined garment the raw edges can be bound for neatness.

Corded pockets

Bound openings can be made from two pieces of extra material, as for a piped buttonhole, with cord inserted for extra interest. They are sometimes used on a curved pocket and may be finished at the end with decorative tacks. The self fabric strips are normally cut on the true bias and a fine piping cord is used. (See also the chapter on Binding and Piping.)

(a) Cut two strips of true bias for each pocket.

(b) Fold bias around cord. Sew small running stitches along the bias, enclosing the cord. Cut away turnings to within 6 mm.

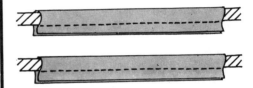

(c) Mark the pocket position on the garment with thread tracing, when hem of garment has been completed.

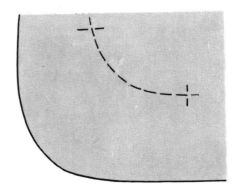

(d) Place two prepared cord strips along pocket position, with cut edges touching. Tack in place. Tack pocket ends at right angles to pocket opening.

197

Pockets

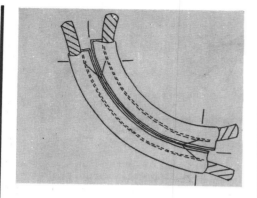

(e) For curved pockets, ease the cord a little on the inner concave edge and place the cord exactly, without stretching to the outer convex edge.
(f) Stitch near cord, forming two parallel rows. Backstitch ends to prevent tearing.
(g) Cut along pocket line to within 6 mm of end of stitching. Cut diagonally out to stitching at ends. Seams should then be turned through opening to wrong side.
(h) Tack two cord edges together on the right side, along the length of the pocket. Press.

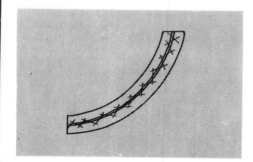

(i) Attach pocket bag as for bound pocket.
(j) Stitch decorative tacks (usually arrowheads) at each end, if liked.
(See chapter on Stitches.)

Patch pockets
These can be many shapes and sizes, but they are generally made from a piece of fabric turned under and stitched to the garment. They may sometimes be made from an oblong of fabric folded in half to form a self lining. (Stitched with wrong sides together and then turned to enclose raw edges.) One edge is neatened and left open. They may be lined or unlined, plain or decorative. Some have a box pleat down the centre, gathers and/or a flap to cover the top edge. The pocket may be stitched down all the way round and have a zip inserted at the opening.

Unlined
(a) Cut out the pocket piece.
(b) In a patch pocket, the top edge should be reinforced and strengthened with interfacing on the wrong side of the material.

(c) For a curved pocket — sew a row of gathering stitches first. Cut a cardboard template the exact size and shape of the finished pocket, then gather the seam allowance over this. Press carefully, then remove cardboard and tack edges in place.
On a square pocket mitre the corners, to lessen bulk where seam or hem appears along two converging edges. Mitre as follows.
Tack seam allowances. Fold over corner of material so that the fold touches the intersection of the two merging tackings. (Grain of top fabric should fall along the grain underneath.) Tack along fold and press. Cut excess material away to within 3 mm of fold. Turn under remaining seam allowance on three sides, butt folded edges of mitred corners together.

(c) Turn down the top edge of the pocket and hem into place. Press.

Pockets

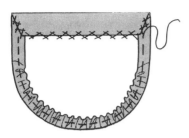

(d) Mark the position of the pocket on the garment with thread tracing.
(e) Pin the pocket into place, try on the garment, and readjust the position if necessary. Tack into place.

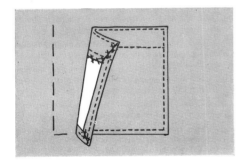

(f) Either:
(i) Backstitch the pocket to the garment from the wrong side, so that the stitches are not visible on the right side of the pocket. If a topstitched finish is preferred, do this *before* attaching the pocket to the garment. A decorative machine stitch can be used.

Or:
(ii) Top stitch the pocket from the right side by hand or machine. It can be difficult to obtain a good finish when stitching through several layers, so pay attention to stitch length, pressure and needle size.

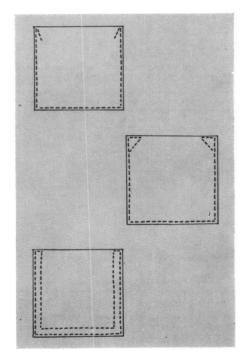

Lined
Pockets in rough fabric need a lining for comfort and convenience.
(a) Cut out the pocket piece from self fabric and from the same pattern, a piece of lining. Trim away lining above the pocket fold line.
(b) Press under the seam allowance to the upper edge of the lining.

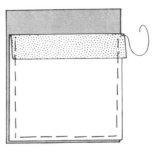

(c) With the right sides together, tack the lining to the pocket.
(d) Fold the top edges of the pocket along fold line over the lining.
(e) Beginning at the top of the hem facing, stitch down one side, across the bottom and up the other side.
(f) Trim the seam allowances and turn right side out.
(g) Close pocket by hemming lining to fabric. Press.

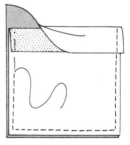

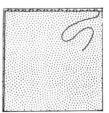

Seams and Seam Neatening

1. Rules for Success

All seams should be smooth when finished so that they hold sections of a garment in place, giving shape and emphasis to the style. Some are decorative as well as functional so if they are puckered, stretched or crooked they should be undone with a stitch ripper and then resewn.

1. Always test a double layer of the actual fabric to be sewn for tension pressure, and stitch length before starting to sew the garment seams.
2. Check whether the fabric is natural or man-made and select correct thread and needle. Sylko for natural fabrics, Star for synthetic.
3. When sewing jersey or knitted fabric, make sure to consult the sewing machine handbook for the right type of stretch stitch to use.
(a) If using a straight stitch machine stretch the fabric very slightly whilst sewing. This helps prevent the seam from breaking during wear. Do not impede the action of the feed.
(b) On a simple zig-zag machine, a stitch length of between 1 and 1½ and a stitch width of 1, with the needle in the left-or right-hand position, will be the ideal setting. The stitch length will depend on the thickness of the fabric. (With the needle moved to the left or right the fabric will receive greater support from the needle plate at the point where the needle penetrates the fabric.)
(c) When using an automatic or super automatic machine there is a considerable number of stitches to choose from, depending on fabric type and sewing operation. Consult the sewing machine handbook.
(d) On jersey fabrics a roller foot assists the feeding of the fabric — these are available for most modern machines.
(e) Always have a Ballpoint needle ready for use when sewing knitted fabrics, they prevent fibre damage.
4. Modern, man made fabrics blunt needles very rapidly — use a new one for each garment to avoid damaged seams and drawn threads.

Hand finishes
(a) Be careful to choose the right stitch technique.
(b) Use the right size needle and thread for the fabric.
(c) Always fasten on and off securely.
(d) Do not fasten on with knots — they come undone, tear delicate fabric and cause lumps in seams and hems when fabric is pressed.
(e) Always wear a thimble on the middle finger of the sewing hand. This will help to make regular sized stitches and prevent finger tips from being punctured by the needle.
(f) Make a point of practising these hand finishes — the finished garment will look so much better for it.

2. General Method
(a) As well as knowing how each fabric should be machine-stitched (size of stitch — type of stitch — type of thread for fabric) a dressmaker needs to know how to carry out a certain selection of hand stitches, such as tacking, joining and finishing, together with some decorative stitches. Practise these before starting.
(b) Seam allowance on turnings — most garments cut from a paper pattern have a 15 mm seam allowance, but some fabrics and seams need slightly bigger turnings. Most modern sewing machines have a seam guide attachment, or seam lines marked on the plate, to make it easier to keep the turnings even during stitching.
(c) Seam width — this is the finished width of seams (such as French), and varies with the type of fabric and type of seam.
(d) Staystitching — this is the first line of stitching on curved or stretchy edges, sewn even before pinning or tacking pieces together. It prevents stretching and can also act as a guide when joining sections together. Machine a row of stitches about 3 mm away from the seamline on the seam turning.

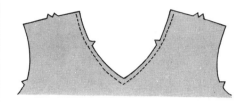

(e) Pinning and tacking — experienced dressmakers sometimes machine seams after pinning them together. Pieces should therefore be pinned together with the pins at right angles to the seamline with the heads lying on the seam allowance. It is then possible to machine along the seamline over the pins, pulling them out by the heads as you go along. It is much safer to tack seams together, particularly where the seam is shaped. Tack close to the seamline with the stitches in the seam allowance. Use tacking thread in a contrasting colour and avoid catching it in the machine stitches.
(f) Finishing seam threads — when beginning and finishing the seam stitching either tie off the top and bottom threads securely, or backstitch about 13 mm at each end so that there is double stitching there for extra strength. When stitching ends in the middle of a seam, pull one of the threads through so that the top and bottom threads are together, then knot them or sew them in.
(g) Pressing — press the line of stitching before trimming, turning or opening the seam. Press again if necessary. It is important to press garment seams well as garment construction progresses.
(h) Trimming — if the fabric is bulky excess seam allowance is trimmed away after stitching and pressing, before neatening. Enclosed seams are usually trimmed to 6 mm.
(i) Layering or Grading — this is a way of trimming two or more seam allowances that are turned together in one direction, eg the edge of a collar. It prevents bulky seams and ridges. Each layer is trimmed to a different width, with the seam

Seams and Seam Neatening

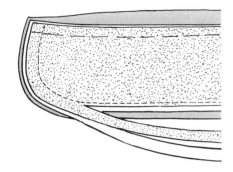

allowance on the most important piece being left the widest.

(j) Notching, clipping or snipping — curved seams must have the seam allowance cut in a special way so that they lie flat. Where the seam curves outwards cut out small notches from the seam allowance but do *not* cut the seam stitching. On inwards curves snip about every 5 mm.

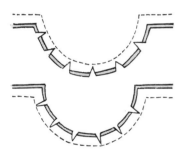

Where there are sharp angles in a seam the seam allowance must be snipped or trimmed off.

Inner corners usually have an extra line of stitching as reinforcement.

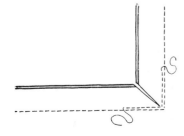

3. Types of Seams

Plain, open seams are the most common and there are several variations of this type.

Plain Open Seam

This is sewn from the wrong side of the fabric, so that little stitching shows on the right side. It is used extensively for side, shoulder and sleeve seams. The seam allowance is either pressed flat or to one side after stitching.

Place the right sides together; pin and tack a little nearer the edge than the seamline. Machine along the seamline. Remove pins and tacking. Press the stitching, then neaten, trim and press again.

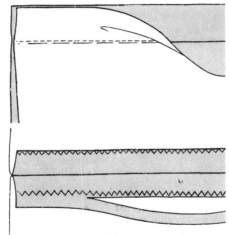

Plain seam eased — there is sometimes a need to ease one edge for it to fit to the other edge when making a seam. First machine close to the seamline on the single layer, within the markings. Pull up the thread until both sets of markings match, and secure the thread ends. Make sure the tiny gathers are evenly spaced and tack carefully to keep them in place. Complete the seam as usual, machining with the eased side uppermost.

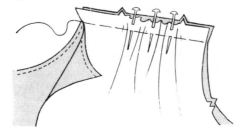

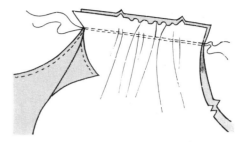

Plain seam, intersecting or crossed — make the two seams in the normal way and press open. With the right sides together pin the two seams, pushing a pin point through to match them exactly at the centre. Pin each side of the seams and machine. Trim off the corners to reduce bulk.

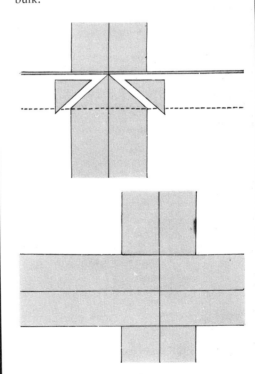

Plain seams on stretchy fabric — on modern sewing machines a stretch stitch may be used, or a narrow zig-zag stitch may be suitable. Otherwise try machining the seam with a piece of tissue paper underneath to prevent the fabric slipping during sewing.

Seams and Seam Neatening

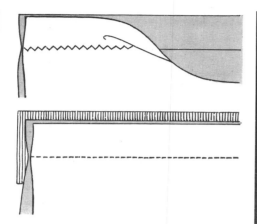

Plain seams with bias cut edge — place the straight edge on a flat surface, then pin and tack the bias edge to it. Stitch from the bias side without stretching.

Plain seam joined at a corner — reinforce the inward corner with a line of machining next to the seamline, and clip in to the point. With right sides together, pin the two garment pieces together with the clipped piece uppermost. Tack and machine on the seamline, pivoting at the corner.

Remove tacking and press the stitching.

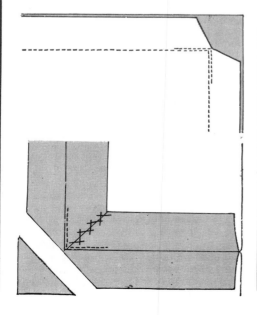

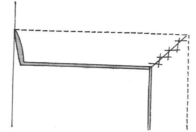

Deal with the seam allowance by:

(a) Pressing the seam open, clipping in from the outer corner, and catchstitching the inner trimmed edges.

(b) Pressing all seam allowances towards the outer edge, trimming the fullness and catchstitching the trimmed edges together.

Plain seam topstitched — this is a way of making a plain open seam visible from the right side. The stitching can be done in matching or contrasting thread and straight or decorative stitch. The simplest way is to press the seam to one side then topstitch from the right side through all layers. One or more rows of stitching may be spaced out as desired.

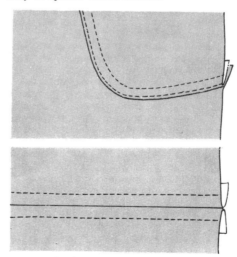

French seam

This is a flat seam that does not show from the right side. It is often used for straight seams on sheer fabrics and those that fray easily. Lightweight clothes, such as blouses and lingerie, that need frequent washing may also be made with French seams. All raw edges are enclosed so no extra neatening process is needed.

Pin and tack the garment pieces, with wrong sides together about 3 – 6 mm nearer the edge than the seam line. The width of French seams varies according to the thickness and fraying quality of the fabric. Machine on this line and trim the seam allowances carefully. Press and remove tacking. Fold the fabric right sides together and roll the seam between fingers and thumbs until the stitching is along the edge. Tack and press into place. Machine along the seam line, keeping the seam very even in width. Remove tacking and press.

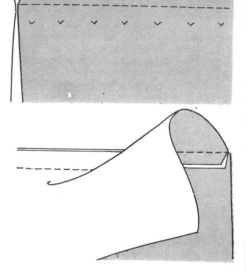

Mock French seam

This is really a way of finishing a plain seam. Prepare and sew a plain, open seam but do not press it open.

Turn in the seam allowances as shown and press into place. Machine along 3 mm from the edge.

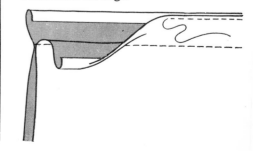

Seams and Seam Neatening

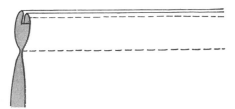

Lapped Seams
(Also called top-stitched and overlaid)
This type of seam is visible on the right side and is very strong. It is suitable for joining shaped sections such as bodice yokes. Extra trimmings may be included in the making of a lapped seam, but it is necessary first to decide which garment piece is to be the overlay and which the underlay. It is usual to lap the yoke onto the bodice or a plain flat section onto a full one.

Mark the fitting lines carefully onto each section. Turn under the seam allowance on the overlay to the wrong side, press and tack into place clipping curves if necessary. Prepare gathers, pleats, darts, etc. in the underlay then place this piece, right side up, on a flat surface. Pin and tack the folded edge of the overlay onto the seam line of the underlay. Check that the balance marks match then machine 3 — 6 mm from the fold through all layers. Trim and neaten the seam allowances on the wrong side.

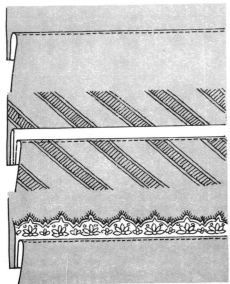

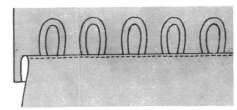

Run and fell seam (Or double stitched)
This is the strongest type of seam. It lies very flat with two rows of stitching on the right side of the garment, so is not suitable for bulky fabrics. All raw edges are enclosed so no extra neatening is required, and there can be no fraying during laundering. The width of the "fell" depends on the type of fabric — it can be as narrow as 3 mm on very fine fabrics. The seam can also be made onto the wrong side and then only one row of stitching shows on the outside.

With wrong sides together (right sides for a fell onto the inside) stitch a plain seam and press it on to one side.

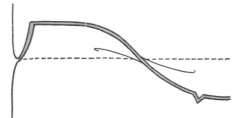

Trim the underneath seam allowance to 3 mm. Trim the upper seam allowance to 10 mm and fold and press it over the lower one. Machine through all layers close to the folded edge. Press.

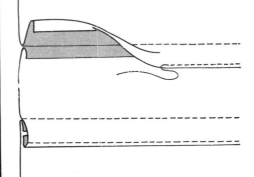

Channel Seam
A third layer of fabric is added to this seam which is used to define or outline important style lines. The extra piece may be in a matching or contrasting colour.
Mark the fitting lines on both sections and trim the seam allowances to 15 mm for a finished channel width of 15 mm. Turn under these seam allowances, press and tack into position. Make a line of tacking down the centre of the length of fabric to be inserted (if no pattern piece is given, cut a strip about 15 mm wider than the seam width). With the strip right side up, overlap the two folded edges (also right sides up) onto it, with the folds along the tacking line. Pin and tack carefully into place. Sew two very straight rows of machining, each 5 mm from the folded edge, through all layers.

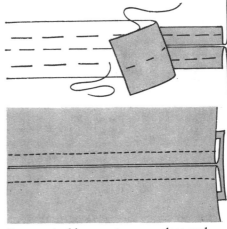

Remove tacking, neaten raw edges and press on the wrong side.

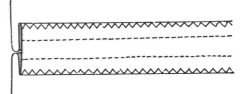

Piped or corded seam (see also the chapter on Binding and Piping)
Piping, or corded piping, may be added to many seams during making up for extra decorative effect. It may be of self fabric, matching or contrasting bias

Seams and Seam Neatening

binding. Prepare piping by folding it in half and tacking along the length. For corded piping fold the binding round the cord and tack it into place.

To pipe or cord an open seam: Tack the prepared piping to the right side of one of the sections along the seam line. Place the right side of the other fabric section over it and stitch through all layers on the seam line.

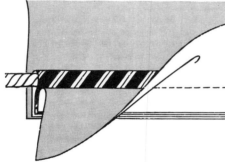

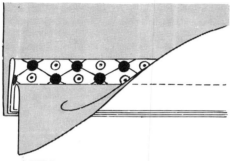

To pipe or cord a lapped seam: Tack the prepared piping along the seam line of the underlay. Place the folded edge of the overlay onto the piping so that the required amount of piping shows on the right side. Tack and machine.

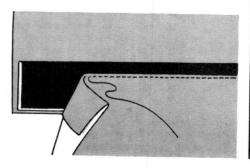

4. Seam Neatening

Edges should be neatened for a smart appearance and for extra strength.

Pinked

Closely woven fabrics which do not fray may simply be trimmed by pinking shears.

Pinked and stitched

This is a little stronger than pinking alone. Machine 6 mm from the edge, then trim off the edge with pinking shears.

Machine overcast

Prepare the machine for a suitable zig-zag or stepstitch and test the stitching on a scrap of the fabric.

(a) Machine about 13 mm from the seam line with a narrow zig-zag and then carefully trim away the surplus.

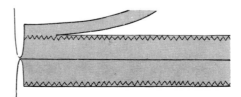

or

(b) Trim off excess seam allowance and machine a full width zig-zag stitch or a stepstitch over the edges.

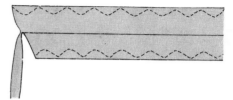

Hand overcast

This is a laborious method but it is suitable for most fabrics, and may be necessary if no sewing machine is available. Use a blanket or overcasting stitch. If the seam is pressed open, trim the seam allowances evenly and sew over both edges separately. If the seam allowances are pressed to the same side, trim them then sew over both edges together. If the fabric might fray, a line of machine stitching may be stitched along edges before overcasting by hand.

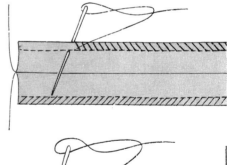

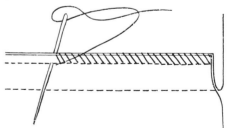

Rolled

This is only suitable on very fine fabrics and is a slow process. Trim off the seam allowance to within 6 mm of the machining. Rolling the edges over between fingers and thumbs as you go, overcast over the top of the roll, catching the overcasting into the machine stitching.

Seams and Seam Neatening

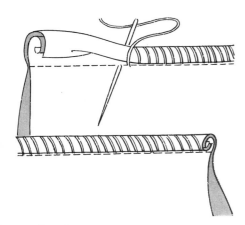

Bound

Use bought binding in a matching colour to bind the edges of heavy, thick, easily-frayed fabrics. Bound seams look neat inside unlined jackets and coats where the seam neatening will frequently be seen. (See chapter on Binding and Piping for the method). Bias binding is necessary for curved seams such as armholes but Paris or seam binding is used for straight seams.

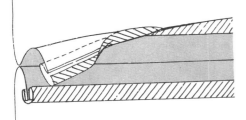

Seam-bound

Here one seam allowance is used to bind over the raw edge of the other. Trim one edge to within 3 – 6 mm of the machining, depending on the thickness of the fabric. Fold and press under the edge of the other seam allowance and slipstitch it over the seam, catching the stitches into the line of machining.

Edge stitched

Use this method for lightweight fabrics. Turn and press under the edges of the seam allowances and machine close to the folds.

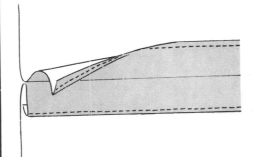

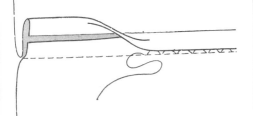

Sleeves

There are many types of sleeves, all of which must be made to fit comfortably and withstand a lot of strain and movement. The fit of the shoulder is also of great importance. The length and style of sleeve is a matter of fashion and will be influenced by the fabric used.

Many sleeves are set into a round opening, but diagonal seams are used in some styles and others have sleeves cut as one with the bodice. Sleeves are always an important part of a garment and care should be taken in making up, fitting and stitching them. They must be cut exactly on the straight grain or true bias in order to hang well.
Before stitching sleeves in, try on the bodice to check that the armhole is the right size for comfort.
In general, sleeves should be completely made, neatened and pressed before they are inserted into the armhole. If the finishing is left until afterwards the weight of the extra fabric will make handling difficult and the sleeves may pull out of shape. Some further pressing may be

needed but usually very little. Always double check that you are setting the right-hand sleeve in to the right armhole and the left-hand sleeve into the left armhole!

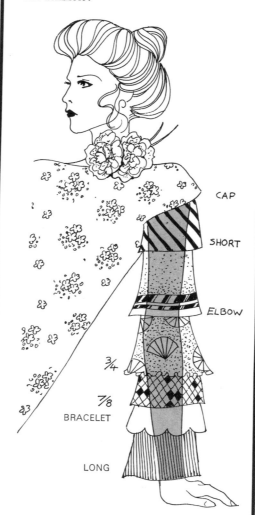

CAP
SHORT
ELBOW
3/4
7/8
BRACELET
LONG

1. Pairing

Note that darts or gathers may be included at the *back* of the elbow on long tight sleeves. When the arm bends it pulls up the back of the sleeve so extra length is allowed for this at the *back*.
The head of the sleeve is made slightly longer for comfort and ease of movement; there is therefore a dip towards the *front*.

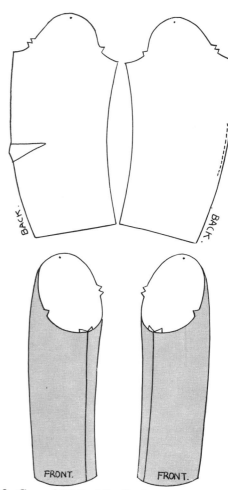

2. General Method for Setting In
(a) Have all construction points clearly marked.

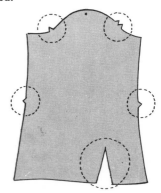

Sleeves

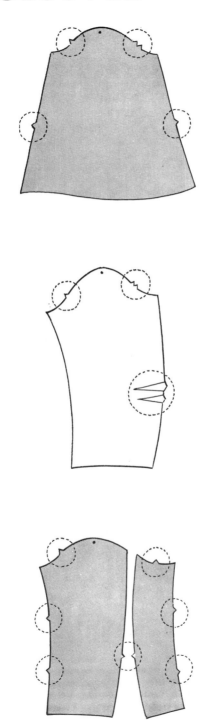

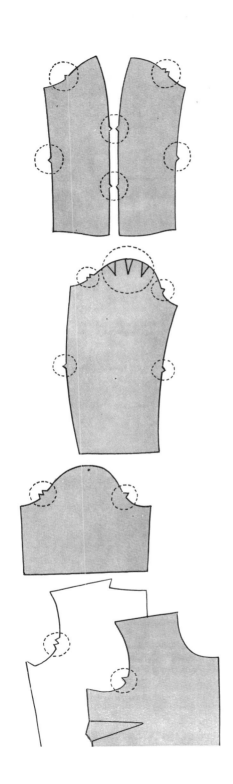

(b) Ease-stitch the head of the sleeve between construction marks. Sew one row of long machine stitches on the fitting line and another row approximately 3 mm nearer to the edge, in the seam allowance. Before sewing, slacken the top tension on the machine and use a strong, smooth thread on the bobbin. Leave long ends of thread at the ends of both rows. (This may also be carried out by hand.)

(c) If any shrinking of the sleeve head is needed it must be eased away at this stage, using a damp pressing cloth and soft pressing pad or roll.

(d) Pin, tack and stitch the underarm seam then press open.

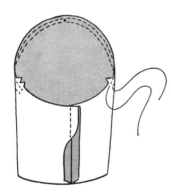

(e) With right sides together, pin sleeves to armhole with sleeve inside bodice.

(f) First pin at balance points, ie. underarm seam and shoulder seam, followed by notches and any other construction points.

(g) Always place pins at right angles to fabric edges, points of pins pointing inwards.

Sleeves

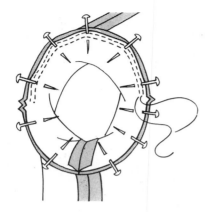

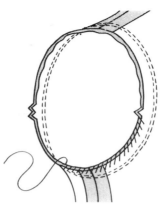

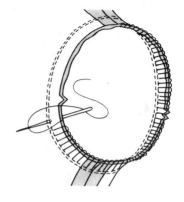

(h) Arrange and ease fullness at sleeve head by pulling on bobbin threads, evenly distributing the fabric. Wind thread ends in figures of eight around pins placed at either end of ease to hold.

(i) From the sleeve side pin and tack sleeve to bodice along the fitting (seam) lines. First tack the smooth underarm section followed by the eased head section. Make sure that no tucks or gathers form whilst tacking. The bias section between the notches at the head of the sleeve should appear "crowded" with the threads of the weave or the loops of a knitted fabric pressing closely together, without any gathers forming.

(j) Try on the sleeve/bodice section and make any adjustments needed.

(k) When the sleeve has been correctly fitted, machine stitch along the fitting line from the sleeve side, starting a little to one side of the matching underarm seams. Sew carefully and slowly, again being careful to avoid tucks or puckers forming. Let the machine carry the fabric through and do not push or pull as this will result in a wavy seamline. Sew right round the armhole continuing beyond the starting point, so that the underarm section is sewn twice.

(l) Remove all tacking.

(m) Lightly press seam allowances only, over the end of a sleeve board, using the tip of the iron. This will help the allowance to turn naturally into the sleeve.

(n) Snip the sleeve allowance at intervals — trim the turnings, and neaten the edges if garment is not being lined.

(o) Turn the garment to the right side and let the sleeve hang downwards holding a closed fist under the shoulder seam. The sleeve should fall smoothly with no puckers and no evidence of fullness in the head.

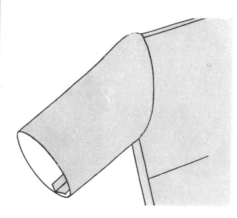

3. Methods of Neatening Armhole Seams
Blanket stitching, or machine overcasting

(a) Set in the sleeve as previously instructed.

(b) Sew a second line of machine stitching 10 mm outside the first row in the seam allowance.

(c) Trim the turnings to just above the second line of machine stitching.

(d) Finally, blanket stitch or machine overcast the raw edges of the turnings.

Binding

(a) Place right side of the crossway binding to the armhole seam allowance on the bodice side, placing the raw edges together.

(b) Tack 6 mm from the edge of the turning to within 3 cm each side of the seam. Leave approximately 4 cm of the crossway strip overlapping.

(c) Stitch under tacking line from the strip side.

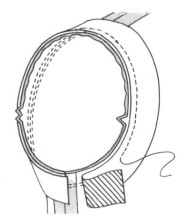

(d) Remove the tacking.

(e) Turn the crossway binding to the sleeve side of the armhole. Turn under the raw edges, pin and tack just above the machine stitching. Slip stitch into position.

Sleeves

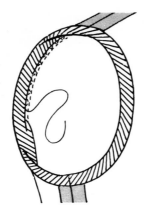

4. French Seamed
This is a useful seam for sleeves in fine material which tend to fray easily and are too transparent for binding. Work the French Seam as instructed in the chapter on Seams and Seam Neatening.

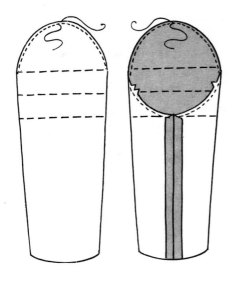

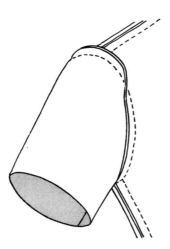

(b) Darts and seams on the sleeve should only be tacked, these can be machined later when the sleeve has been fitted properly.
(c) Always try on the garment with the sleeve. Ease the two threads at the cap head of the sleeve, pull threads up to position the sleeve and tuck seam allowance under.

5. Fitting the Sleeve
(a) The back curve of the sleeve cap should be longer than the front cap curve, when the sleeve is folded lengthwise through the centre, with the stitching lines of the underarm seams meeting. If this is not the case fitting difficulties will occur when placing the sleeve into the armhole.

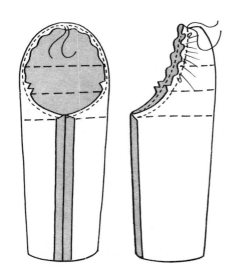

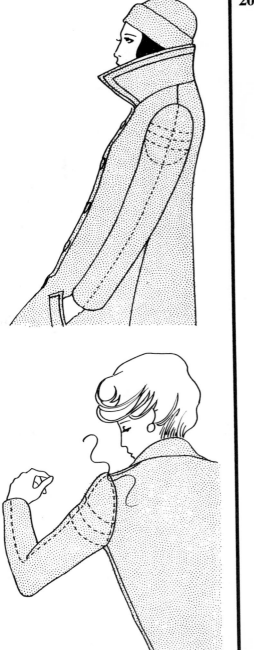

Sleeves

(d) Should the sleeve not fit properly check as follows:

i. Gathers at elbows. These should be distributed evenly above and below the elbow bend.

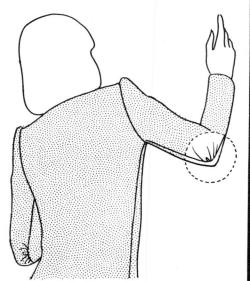

ii. Darts at the elbows. If there is only one dart, it should fall at the elbow bend. If there are two or more darts, they should fall evenly above and below the elbow bend.

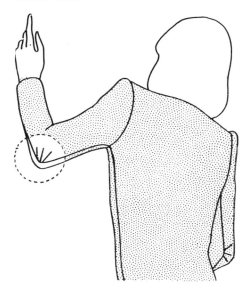

iii. On a two-piece sleeve, back seams of sleeve should be exactly opposite each other across the width of the back.

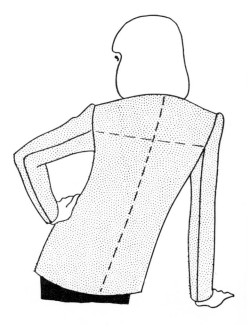

iv. When gathers are used at the head they should finish at exactly the same point on both front and back of garment so that a line drawn between the ending of gathers at back and front would be parallel to the floor.

v. If darts are used at cap of sleeve, the position of the two outside darts should be equi-distant from the shoulder seam.

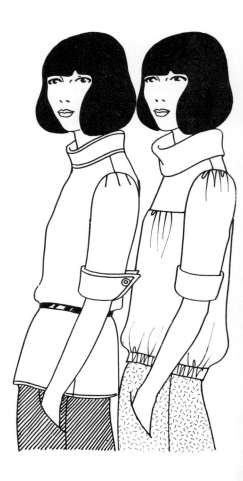

vi. Diagonal wrinkles on the highest part of the sleeve cap result from the sleeve cap being too short.

Sleeves

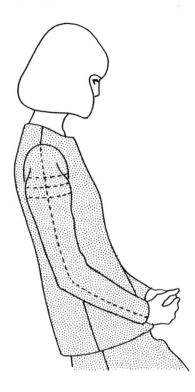

viii. Diagonal wrinkles at the upper front and back arm should be remedied by lifting the sleeve cap up and giving more ease around the armhole of the garment at the front and back.

ix. The underarm of jacket bending outward toward the arm under the armhole means that the bodice is too high at this point. Trim armhole slightly at underarm and re-position sleeve.

211

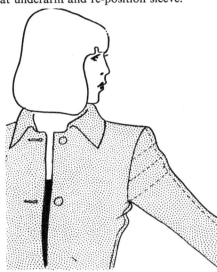

Remedy this by unpinning the cap across the shoulder top and letting out the top part. Repin the sleeve to the garment. If wrinkles are still visible, raise the underarm seam of the sleeve on the armhole of the garment from underarm toward width of chest and back. When the sleeve has been fitted, lower the sleeve stitching line at underarm and trim away extra seam allowance.

vii. When underarm of sleeve bends inwards toward the body underarm, it is because the sleeve is too high at this point. Lower it by snipping the under armhole of the sleeve and re-position at underarms.

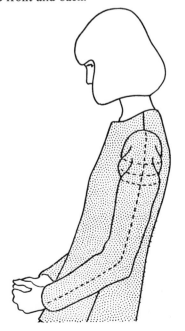

(e) Generally, the length for a long sleeve on a coat or suit should be halfway between the wrist bend and the first thumb knuckle joint. The back edge of the sleeve should reach halfway between the wrist bone and the little finger knuckle. This means that the sleeve is slightly longer at the back edge than at the front. This is to allow for the bend at the elbow.
(f) Close fitting sleeves should be rather long on the wrist but wide sleeves should be shorter.
(g) Many people have one arm longer than the other so make sure to measure the length of each sleeve accurately.

6. Lining
(a) When the garment sleeves have been fitted correctly, the sleeve linings should be tacked and machined to match the garment sleeve size.
(b) The seam at the armhole of the lining should be folded to the wrong side.
(c) Place an ease thread exactly along the fold, beginning and ending at the centre top of the sleeve lining.

Sleeves

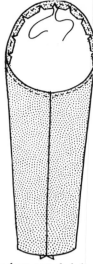

(d) As lining does not shrink, ease the surplus material in the seam allowance on the inside of the sleeve cap and distribute evenly.
(e) Match correct sleeve lining to garment sleeve.
(f) Turn lining and garment sleeve wrong side out.
(g) Match stitching edge of sleeve to stitching edge of garment seam at the underarm. Pin into position.
(h) From armhole to wrist match front sides of the lining and garment at underarm seams. Pin together. Stretch the garment sleeve a little so that the lining will be slack along the seam. Tack seams together to within 8 cm of folded edge at the wrist. Remove pins.

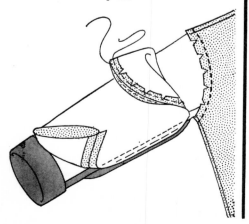

Slip hand through sleeve lining at cap end, take hold of lining and garment at the wrist and turn the lining right side out over the sleeve.
(i) Match armhole seams and darts of lining to garment. Pin together.
(j) Pull ease thread up at sleeve cap of lining and adjust ease around armhole edge.
(k) Pin whole of armhole lining to the armhole of the bodice lining, hiding the stitching line. Pin into place and tack.
(l) Slipstitch cap edge to garment lining.
(m) Remove all tacking. Press.

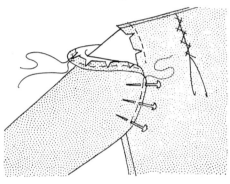

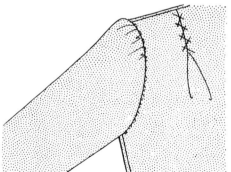

7. Types
There are basically two main types of sleeves:
1. The Set-in sleeve
2. The Raglan sleeve

1. The Set-in sleeve
Finished line will depend on the amount of fullness in the sleeve as a whole and the amount of fabric in the top or cap of the sleeve. The general method given earlier for setting in a sleeve should be followed in detail. The only difference that will occur are the variations in the amount of fullness at the cap of the sleeve. For a full sleeve cap there will be an excess of fabric to distribute along the head of the sleeve — the technique for fitting and setting, however, is the same.
Alternative way to set-in sleeves, used in simple dresses and children's garments.
(a) Pin, tack and stitch front and back of garment at the shoulder seams only. Ease fullness of sleeve at cap as in the general method.
(b) Machine stitch sleeve to armhole. This is carried out with the work completely flat.

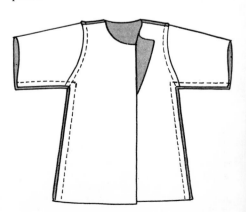

(c) Pin and tack the side seams of the garment and the underarm sleeve.
(d) Tack in one continuous seam, then machine stitch. Remove tacking and press.

Sleeves

2. The Raglan sleeve

This is attached by a diagonal seam from the underarm to the neckline. It gives a smooth, round line and is very comfortable. An ideal style for shoulders that present fitting difficulties. The seam and the dart can fit the curve of the shoulder. The sleeve is often made in two pieces so there is a seam instead of a dart outlining the contour of the shoulder.

(a) Pin and tack seams and darts.
(b) Machine stitch and remove tacking.
(c) Press the seam open.

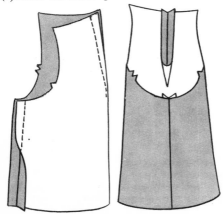

(d) Matching the seams and pattern markings, pin sleeve into armhole.

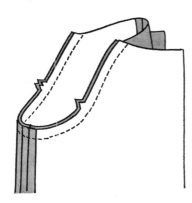

(e) Tack and ease in any fullness.
(f) Machine stitch the sleeve to the garment on seam line.
(g) Press the seam open from the neckline to notches and finish underarm seam between notches, with second row of machining and blanket stitching.

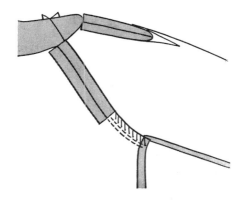

Alternative way to set-in the Raglan sleeve
This time the sleeve can be sewn in flat.

(a) Pin, tack and then machine stitch the sleeve to the bodice seams. Remove tacking.
(b) Press the seams open and clip allowance.

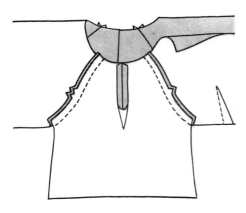

(c) Pin, tack then machine the sides of the dress and underarm sleeve seam making one continuous seam.

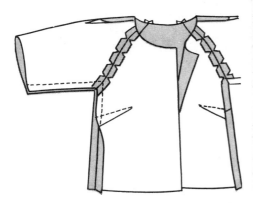

8. Variations
Bell sleeve
This is set in as a standard sleeve although the wrist edge is loose.

Sleeves

Tailored fitted sleeve
This is used for heavier material and is closely fitted to the arm and wrist. It is generally made in two pieces.

Puffed sleeve
A style of sleeve which is gathered at the cap by the shoulder seam to give the appearance of a "puff". It is usually gathered onto a cuff. On some styles only the cuff edge is puffed with the cap smooth.

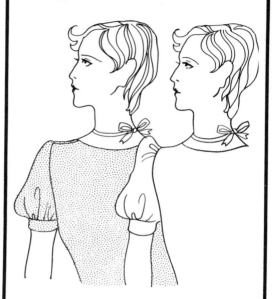

Cap sleeve
A style which is extended from the shoulder and covers the very top part of the upperarm.

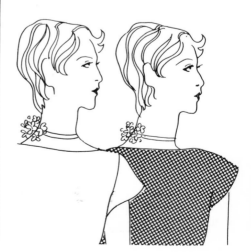

Long gathered
Classic elegant style gathered at cap and cuff. Set in as a standard sleeve.

Magyar sleeve
This is a simple type of sleeve and is just an extension of the garment. The shoulder seam is continued along the curve of the arm and the underarm seam is extended also. Usually the underarm seam is strengthened with seam tape.

Sleeves

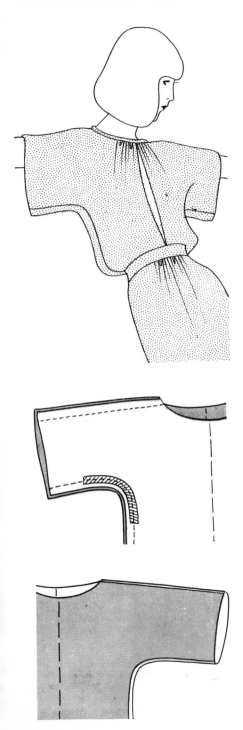

The kimono sleeve
This is not set into a round armhole, but usually fits into a squared-off armhole lower than the usual shoulderline.

A gusset is sometimes set in at the underarm for extra ease of movement.

9. Bottom Edge Finishes
For cuffs, see Chapter on Cuffs.
There is a variety of ways to finish off the edges of sleeves. Ideally, sleeves should be completely finished before sewing them to the garment. All sleeves may be hemmed but other finishes are possible.

(a) Short sleeves
1. Faced
2. Bound
3. Scalloped
  1. Faced
(See also chapter on Facings)

(a) Right sides together, place facing to sleeve, raw edges together, and machine 6 mm from the edge.
(b) Turn the facing up along stitched line. Pin and tack into place on wrong side.

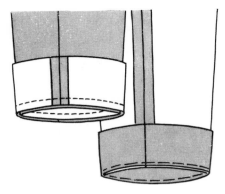

(c) Turn under narrow turning on free edge.
(d) Pin, then tack to sleeve.
(e) Hem or catch-stitch into place, making sure that the stitches do not pull or show on the right side.
(f) Remove all tacking.

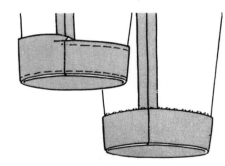

2. Bound
(See also chapter on Binding and Piping)
(a) Cut crosswise strip twice the required finished width, plus twice turning allowance.
(b) Put right side of binding to right side of sleeve. Place raw edges together.
(c) Pin and tack 6 mm from edges, stretching binding a little whilst tacking.
(d) Make narrow turning to wrong side of free edge of binding material.
(e) Fold turned edge over raw edges to wrong side of sleeve. Tack above machining. Hem into position.
(f) Remove all tacking.

Sleeves

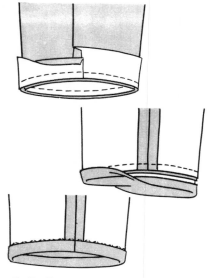

3. Scalloped
(a) Use a coin, or pair of compasses and thin card.
(b) Draw straight horizontal line on a piece of card.
(c) Mark size of scallops by drawing circles.
(d) Draw a line through circles at points of contact.
(e) Cut out card between lower curves.

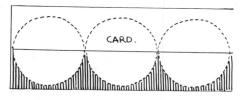

(f) Draw round outline of scallops on wrong side of garment edge; deepest part of curve is the fitting line.

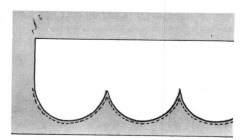

(g) Put right side of facing to right side of sleeve and tack with small stitches along outline of scallops.

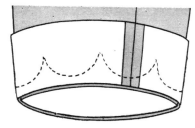

(h) Machine stitch along the shaped outline. Remove all tacking. Cut away turnings to 6 – 10 mm deep.
(i) Clip round the curves and straight into the points between the scallops. Make sure not to cut the stitching.

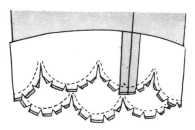

(k) Turn facing to wrong side of sleeve. Use the rounded handle end of a dessert spoon and work round each curve making sure that the seam lies exactly on the edge of each scallop. Whilst doing this, it will help to roll the seam to and fro between first finger and thumb to manipulate it into position. Tack edge to hold in place. Press. Remove tacking.

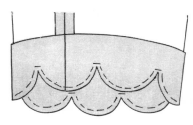

(l) Should the scallops be narrow and the facing wide, slipstitch edge of facing to the sleeve.
(m) Should the scallops be deep and the facing shallow, turn the edge of the facing under and neaten with small running stitches.

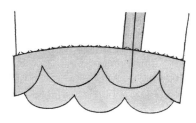

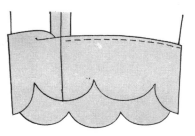

(b) Long sleeves
1. Faced — as for short sleeves.
2. Bound — as for short sleeves.
3. Scalloped — as for short sleeves.
4. Adapted facing.

4. Adapted facing
(a) With right sides together, place facing to sleeve edge, raw edges together. Pin and tack. Stitch on seam line.

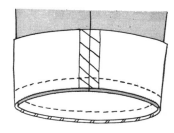

(b) Turn facing to wrong side of sleeve. Leave 3 mm of facing showing on right side. Tack into position.

Sleeves

(c) Edge-stitch right side of facing on seam line just visible.
(d) Turn up or overcast free edge of facing on the inside. Catch facing to seam.
(e) Remove all tacking.

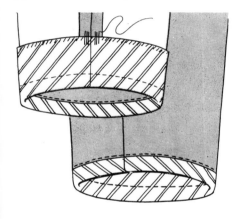

Tucks

Tucks are very like pleats in appearance but they are stitched for all or part of the length so that a fold is formed on the right side of the garment. Where tucks are only partly stitched (dart tucks) they allow the rest of the fabric to fall in soft, unpressed pleats, eg. on a bodice front. Although generally used as a decoration on yokes, cuffs, sleeves and bodice fronts, they may also be sewn in the skirt of a made-up garment to allow the skirt to be lengthened later, eg. on children's clothes, or to hide a join in the fabric.

Tucks look best on simple garments where the tucking runs with the straight grain, although they can be made on the cross. Sewn by hand or machine with matching or toning thread, they help with the fit, control the fullness and also decorate a garment. The width and spacing of tucks may be varied according to the type of fabric and the style of the garment. As the stitching of tucks is clearly seen on the right side it is essential first to practise on scraps of the fabric.

1. Choice of Fabric
Use a fabric with an obvious grain line, and one which is easy to press into sharp creases. It can be difficult to tuck very thick fabrics, and tucking looks most effective on very fine material. Extra decorative effects can be created by tucking on stripes.

2. Widths of Tucks
Very narrow tucks are suitable on fine fabrics or short sections, but long runs or thick fabrics need wider folds. Try out several widths of tucking on a spare piece of the fabric to decide which width looks best – do this before laying out the pattern pieces, so that garment sections to be tucked can be cut out exactly the right size for the required tucking. Note that it is always easier to tuck an area of fabric and *then* cut out the pattern piece. When the width of each tuck has been decided, cut a cardboard template to mark this width exactly.

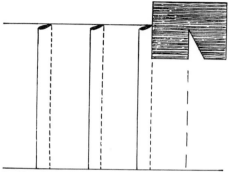

3. Spacing of Tucks
For the best effect use tucks in a series of evenly spaced rows, or in groups of three or more rows. Too few rows look skimped, but a large area may create extra weight which will pull a garment out of shape. Fine tucks probably look best with about 13 mm between the rows. Wide tucks may need a little more space because of the extra bulk of each fold. Practise the spacing when practising the width.

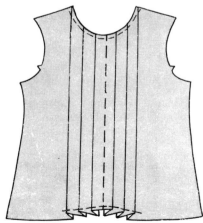

4. Stitching Tucks
Tucks may be sewn by hand or by machine. Some sewing machines will make tucks automatically. Before stitching decide on the direction in which the tucks are to be pressed. Note that tuck edges are not stitched to the garment – the fold is normally pressed into place and secured by the seams at the two ends. Test the pressure, tension and stitch length carefully before use. A straight stitch is normally used, but decorative machine stitches may also be suitable. Choose a matching thread, using Sylko on natural fabrics and Star on man-made fabrics. Pure silk thread gives a pretty pearl effect on silk and artificial silk fabrics.

5. Pressing Tucks
The tucks may all be pressed in one direction, but on a centre front they are often pressed so that each side faces out from the centre.
Pin a tucked section carefully to the ironing board right sides uppermost, stretching it slightly so that the folds stand upright. Using a pressing cloth and an iron at a suitable temperature for the fabric, press the folds lightly in the required direction. Remove the fabric and turn it over. Press the stitching gently over a soft cloth.

6. General Method
(a) Mark the exact lines for the tucks using a template as described above. It may be easier to mark and sew one tuck, before marking the next. For wide tucks tailor's tacks may be used along the length to mark the fold lines. Very fine (pin) tucks may be sewn without marking.
(b) Work from the left-hand side of the fabric towards the right.
(c) Pin and tack each tuck into place along its template length, keeping the grain straight so that a thread runs along the edge of each tuck. Do not use too many pins.
(d) Machine stitch the tuck into place. Use a thread suitable for the fabric because if shrinking occurs during washing the tucks will pucker badly, and look very irregular. Use a needle that is correct for the fabric and make sure that the stitch length pressure and tension are perfect.
(e) Remove tacking and press each tuck lightly along the stitching line from the wrong side of the fabric.
(f) Turn to right side and press tucks using a damp cloth.
(g) When tucks are complete lay out the pattern pieces in the usual manner, pin and cut out pieces.

Tucks

7. Types of Tucks

1. *Blind tucks*
Each tuck overlaps the next so that only one line of stitching is visible.
(a) Mark fold lines.
(b) Mark overlap lines.

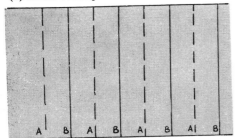

(c) Crease the fold line to the overlap line and press.
(d) Tack the tuck along its length, remembering that the folded edge is *not* stitched down to the garment.
(e) Machine tucks, then remove tacking.
(f) Repeat the process for all tucks.

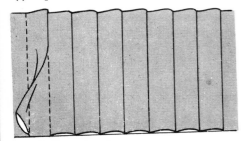

2. *Spaced tucks*
There is an even space between each tuck and the stitches are visible.
(a) Mark fold line.
(b) Mark overlap line.
(c) Mark even spaces.

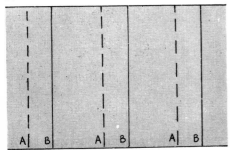

(d) Crease fold line to overlap line and press.

(e) Tack the tuck along its length, remembering that the folded edge is *not* stitched down to the garment.
(f) Machine tuck then remove tacking.
(g) Repeat process for all tucks.

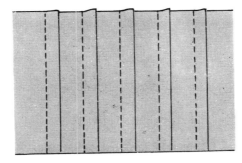

3. *Pin tucks*
These are tiny tucks stitched closely to the edges of folds but with spaces in between them.
(a) Mark fold line.
(b) Mark overlap line.
(c) Mark spaces.

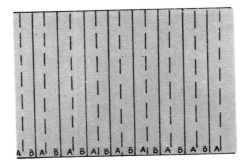

(d) Crease fold line to overlap line and press.
(e) Tack the tuck along its length, remembering that the folded edge is *not* stitched down to the garment.
(f) Machine the tuck very close to the edge of the fold.
(g) Repeat the process for all the tucks and remove tacking.
(h) Press the tucks with a damp cloth to give neat crisp appearance.

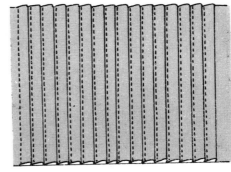

4. *Corded tucks*
(a) Enclose cord in tuck.
(b) Tack along the normal fold line of the tuck.
(c) Machine stitch using zipper foot attachment to allow for passage of cord. Refer to the machine handbook regarding use of zipper foot for cording.
(d) Remove tacking.

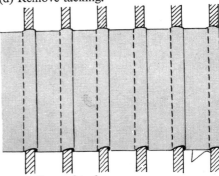

5. *Crossed tucks*
Make tucks to run in one direction as ordinary spaced tucks. Then further tucks are made to run at right angles to, and crossing, the first section of tucks.

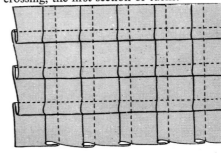

6. *Grouped tucks*
(a) Several lines of tucks should be made close together.

Tucks

(c) Tucks should be stitched across at the top, in one direction.

(d) Turn tucks in opposite direction and stitch across.

(e) Repeat process at intervals, turning the tucks first in one direction and stitching across, then in the opposite direction.

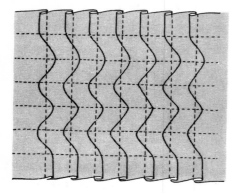

7. Overhand tucks

(a) Mark a design on the fabric.

(b) Over these lines, tiny overhand stitches should be made.

(c) Catch up with the needle just a little bit of the fabric with each stitch made.

(d) Either a contrasting thread can be used or one of a colour similar to the fabric.

8. Machined pin tucks

(a) Refer to your sewing machine manual for instructions in general.

(b) Insert a twin needle and thread as directed. Use either an all purpose foot, or for straight tucks, a tucking foot.

(c) Using either the edge of an all purpose foot as a guide line or the grooves in a tucking foot. Form rows of tucks as required.

(d) For fancy pin tucks the serpentine stitch or the three step zig-zag stitch is very effective. On a fully automatic machine one of the scroll stitches may be used to form more elaborate and decorative cable tucks.

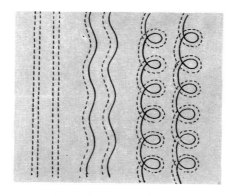

9. Machined shell tucks

(a) Prepare fabric as for spaced tucks.

(b) Using the blind hem stitch, stretch blind stitch or a suitable alternative, sew along tacking line allowing the wide zig-zag part of stitch sequence to fall over edges of fold. This will hold fabric edge at intervals to form "Shells".

(c) A cord may be included along the fold edge for extra decoration.

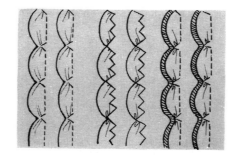

Waistbands and Waistlines

1. **Self Fabric**
2. **Tailored**
   With petersham
   With elastic
3. **Stitched**
4. **Contour**
5. **Waist Edges without Bands**
   With self fabric
   With petersham
6. **Waistlines**
   With plain seam
   Reinforced with ribbon
   Inset waistband
   Elastic on drawstring in a casing
   A casing for one piece of elastic
   A casing for a drawstring

The waist edge of trousers and skirts has to be finished in some way that hides the raw edges and prevents the waistline stretching. Where the top and bottom halves of a garment are joined at the waist, there are several ways of completing the seam.

Waistbands (On skirts or trousers) — must be carefully sewn and fitted so that they fit snugly, without stretching, wrinkling or folding over. The width and type of band used depends on the style of the garment and the fabric used. Most waistbands, particularly on loosely woven fabrics, need the addition of interfacing to prevent stretching. Knitted fabrics need elastic in the waist area for a good fit. Except on gathered skirts, the skirt is eased into the waistband to fit the curve into the waist.

Therefore, the waistband should be 13 – 25 mm larger than the waist measurement. Where the waistband overlaps for fastening allow an overlap of 4 – 5 cm. Side openings — the front overlaps the back.

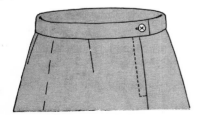

Front openings — the right overlaps the left.

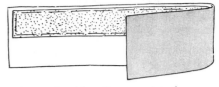

Back openings — the left may overlap the right.

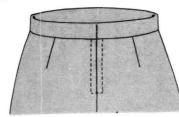

Hooks and eyes or buttons and buttonholes are usually sewn to fasten the overlapping area to the underlap. If the overlap and underlap are much extended on a button-through or wrap-around skirt the two ends may be tied to keep the garment in place round the body.

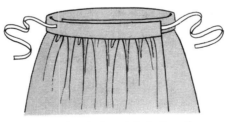

Generally, the zip is put in before the waistband and a lining added afterwards. On special garments a waistband of self fabric is applied so that stitching does not show on the right side. Otherwise top-stitching may be used for strength or decoration.

1. Waistband of Self Fabric

(a) Cut band of fabric to size of waistline, with extra amount for seam allowances and overlap.
(b) The width should be cut to twice the depth of the finished band plus seam allowance.
(c) Cut interfacing to exact length of waistline and half the width of the waistband.

(d) Place the interfacing to the wrong side of the waistband and tack into place.

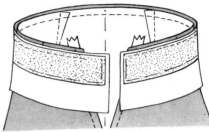

(e) Put right sides of garment and waistband together, easing the skirt into place. Pin, then tack into place.

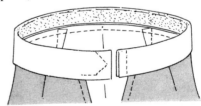

(f) Machine stitch waistband to skirt waist and along the ends of the waistband Remove tacking.
(g) Crease the band in half and press. Stitch the two ends — shaping overlap to a point, if liked.

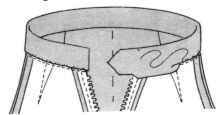

(h) Turn raw edges of the other half of the waistband under to the wrong side of the garment then slipstitch the band into place so that the stitches are not visible on the right side.

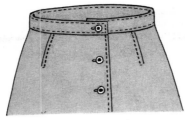

(i) Press the skirt waistband.
(j) Sew hooks and eyes at the ends of the waistband to fasten the skirt top.

Waistbands and Waistlines

2. Tailored Waistband (with Petersham)
(a) Cut a waistband from self fabric, using one long selvedge if possible. (Otherwise neaten one long edge). Make the piece of fabric 7.5 cm longer than the waist, and twice the width of the chosen Petersham ribbon plus two seam allowances.
(b) Cut a piece of Petersham ribbon 3.2 cm shorter than the waistband.

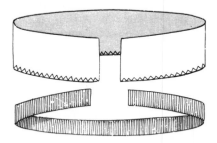

(c) Mark the material along the lengthwise fold with tailor's chalk or long tacking stitches before removing the pattern.
(d) With right sides together, ease the skirt onto the waistband. Remember to leave a 6 cm underlap at one end.
(e) Pin, tack and machine on seam line.

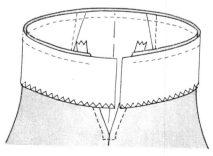

(f) Tack and machine the Petersham in place just above this seam line. Leave a turning of 15 mm at each end of the waistband.

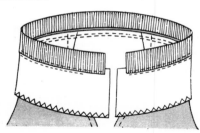

(g) Turn in these turnings and press into place, then fold the waistband over the Petersham to the wrong side of the skirt.

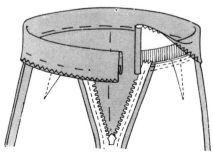

(h) Cut into the seam allowance of the waistband level with the zip tape, then turn under the seam allowance along the underlap extension only. Hem round the extension.

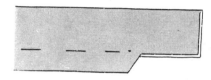

(i) Tack the neatened edge of the waistband into place round the waist.
(j) Stitch along the waist seam line through the skirt and inside waistband but not through the band on the right side. Use stab stitch or straight machine stitching.

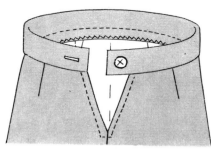

Waistband with elastic section
It is necessary to put a piece of broad elastic into the back of a waistband for knitted fabrics. This gives a smooth, flat front with slight gathers at the back to adjust to the stretch of the fabric. If liked, the back darts can be left out. This method of attaching the waistband is similar to the one above, but the

Petersham at the back is replaced by elastic of the same width.
(a) Measure the Petersham as before but cut a piece only half the length. Cut a piece of elastic of the same width but 5 cm shorter. Join the two together. Now sew a 5 cm piece of Petersham to elastic for the underlap.

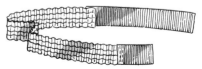

(b) Sew the waistband and Petersham as before but do not stitch the elastic.

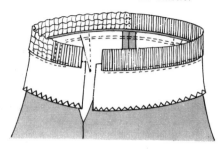

(c) Fold the waistband over and complete, being sure to keep the elastic pulled flat. Note — waistbands, particularly of jersey-knit trousers are sometimes made with a piece of elastic replacing all the Petersham ribbon.

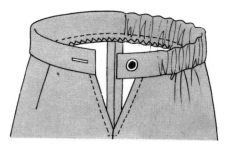

3. Stitched Waistband
This is a quick and strong method used on jeans, children's clothes, etc.
(a) Prepare the waistband with interfacing or Petersham as in the first method.
(b) Fold the band right sides together along its length and machine across the ends (shape one end to a point first, if liked). Trim, turn to the right side, and then press.

Waistbands and Waistlines

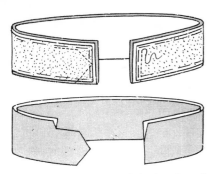

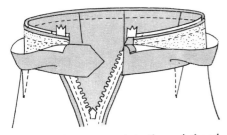

(c) Stitch the right side of the band to the wrong side of the garment, along the seam line, easing as necessary.

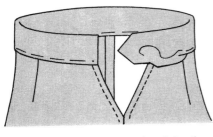

(d) Press the seam up into the waistband.
(e) Turn in the other band seam allowance and tack the folded edge into place on the right side over the seam.

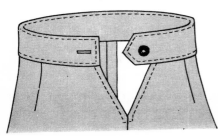

(f) Topstitch all round the band 3 – 6 mm from the edge using a straight or fancy stitch in a matching or contrasting colour.

4. Contour Waistband

Some skirts and trousers have shaped waistbands that are interfaced so that they remain uncreased in wear. It is usual to reinforce the seamline of the long edges with bias binding.

(a) Cut two waistband pieces from the pattern piece.
(b) Interface one piece on the wrong side, trimming away the interfacing seam allowances.
(c) Pin and tack stretched bias binding over the seam lines on the two long edges of the interfaced piece.

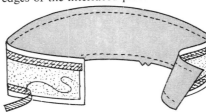

(d) Pin, tack and stitch the two sections together round the two ends and the upper edge. Trim and layer or grade the seam allowances. Press, turn to the right side and press again.

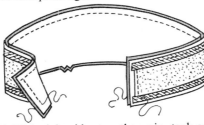

(e) With right sides together, pin, tack and machine the waist edge of the band to the waist edge of the garment. Match balance marks carefully and ease the skirt onto the band.

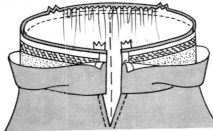

(f) Trim and layer or grade the seam allowances then press them up into the waistband.

(g) Turn under the remaining seam allowance and slipstitch it to the wrong side of the garment, catching up the stitches of the seam underneath. Hem across the underlap. Press.

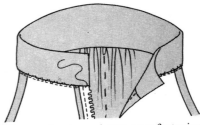

(h) Sew on hooks and eyes as a fastening.

5. Waist Edges without Bands

Some styles of skirts and trousers are finished at the top with a facing only. Fabric or Petersham ribbon may be used.

Waist edge faced with fabric
When a facing of self fabric is used it must be interfaced or the waist edge must be reinforced with seam binding to prevent stretching.
(a) Complete the garment, and tack in a lining if used.
(b) Prepare the facing in the usual way (see chapter on Facings for details).
(c) Cut the facing and interfacing pieces according to the paper pattern. Seam the facing pieces together and interface. Neaten the lower (longer) edge of the facing by overcasting or turning under and stitching.

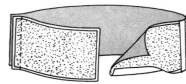

(d) With right sides together, pin, tack and machine facing to garment waist edge. Match balance marks carefully and ease the skirt onto the band.

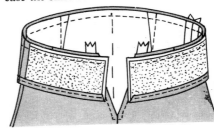

Waistbands and Waistlines

(e) Trim and layer the seam allowances. Clip the edges without cutting the stitches.

(f) Understitch the facing in the usual way, for facings. Turn it to the wrong side of the skirt and press the edge.

(g) Turn the ends under, avoiding the zip, then hem the folds to the zip tape.

(h) Loosely catchstitch the neatened edge of the facing to the seam allowances and darts only, to keep it in place.

(i) Sew a hook and eye at the top of the zip to take the strain.

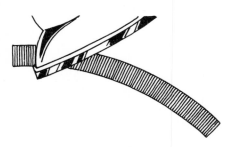

Waist edge faced with petersham
Buy shaped Petersham ribbon, or stretch one side of a straight piece under a fairly hot iron. It must have one edge longer to avoid pulling the waist edge of the garment out of shape.

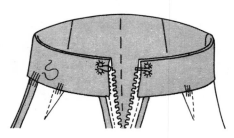

(a) Cut a piece of shaped Petersham 25 mm/2·5 cm longer than the body waist measurement.

(b) Prepare the garment as for a faced edge (see previous method). Trim the seam allowance at the waist to 13 mm and overcast the edge.

(c) With the inside (shorter) curved edge of the ribbon to the right side of the garment edge, pin on the ribbon, easing the skirt if necessary.

(d) Machine along the edge of the ribbon, and a second row 3 mm away. Press.

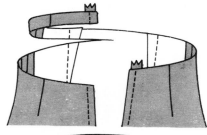

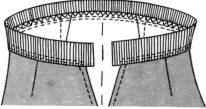

(e) Fold the ribbon to the wrong side of the garment and finish as in the previous method.

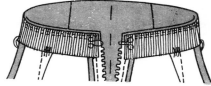

6. Waistlines

Bodices and skirts may be joined in several ways. One of the simplest is to sew them together with a plain, inconspicuous seam which may be reinforced with ribbon.
A waistband may be inset, a shaped belt inserted to fit snugly to the body curves, or a casing filled with elastic or a drawstring.

Waistline with a plain seam

(a) Complete the skirt and staystitch the waist edge just above the seam line.

(b) Complete the bodice and staystitch just *below* the seamline.

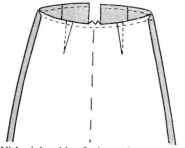

(c) With right sides facing, pin the waist edges of skirt and bodice together. Match the balance marks, notches and opening edges carefully.

(d) Try garment on and adjust the fit if necessary.

(e) Tack and machine along the seam line, easing if necessary.

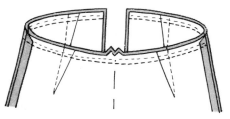

(f) Remove tacking. Pull the bodice upright (still wrong side out) and press the seam allowances upwards.

(g) Trim and neaten the turnings.

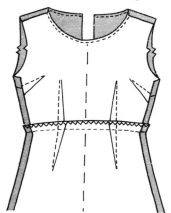

(h) Press carefully on the right side.

Waistline reinforced with ribbon
Add a firm ribbon inside the waistline of stretchy garments, or where the skirt is heavily pleated or gathered.

Waistbands and Waistlines

(a) Join bodice and skirt with the plain seam as in the method above.

(b) Insert the zip, make buttonholes, etc., as required.

(c) With the garment inside out measure round the waist seam line from the edge of one opening to the edge of the other.

(d) Cut a piece of grosgrain ribbon, 15 mm wide, 3·8 cm longer than this measurement. Put in a pin at the halfway mark.

(e) Pin the halfway mark of the ribbon to the centre front (or centre back if the garment opens at the front).

(f) Pin the ribbon round the waist seam and fold the cut ends under — these folded ends must meet exactly.

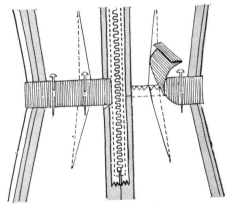

(g) Stitch the ribbon with a few overlapping stitches at the seams, darts, and ends. Try on and adjust if necessary.

(h) Sew hooks and eyes on to the folded ends of the ribbon, so that the edges meet exactly when they are fastened.

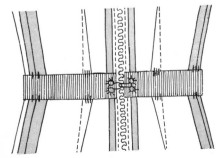

Inset waistband
An inset waistband fits snugly to the body, emphasizing the design. It is important that bodice, waistband and skirt all fit

smoothly — adjust the fit before machining together.

(a) Cut a waistband from the garment fabric according to the pattern piece. Also cut a piece of interfacing and a piece of lining to the same pattern.

(b) Tack or iron the interfacing to the wrong side of the waistband, matching pattern markings. Staystitch the bodice edge.

(c) With right sides together pin and tack one edge of the waistband to the bodice edge, matching notches. (Do not machine at this stage.)

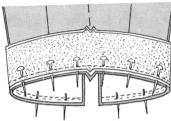

(d) Staystitch the waist edge of the skirt.

(e) Put the bodice inside the skirt with right sides together, and pin the free edge of the waistband to the skirt waist edge. Make sure that the pattern markings match.

(f) Tack along the seam edge. Remove pins.

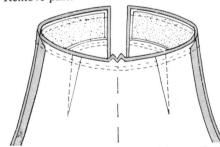

(g) Try on the garment to make sure that it fits snugly.

(h) Machine the waistband to the skirt edge and then to the bodice edge, along the seam lines. Remove tacking.

(i) Trim and layer the seam allowance, the bodice and skirt allowances to 13 mm, the waistband to 6 mm and the interfacing to 3 mm.

(j) Pull the bodice up, with wrong side outside, then press the bodice seam allowances downwards and the skirt seam allowances upwards.

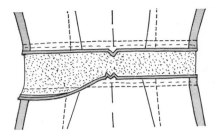

(k) Pin the lining piece over wrong side of the waistband, matching the seam and pattern markings.

(l) Fold under the top and bottom edges of the lining along the seam lines. Slipstitch into place catching the stitches into the two lines of machining. Remove all pins and tacking.

(m) Put in the zip or finish the buttonholes and buttons. Fold under the ends of the lining and slipstitch them to the facing, or zip tapes.

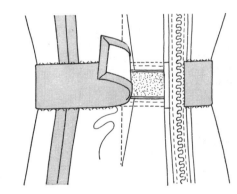

Elastic or drawstring in a casing
A casing, or tunnel of fabric, is made at the waist of simple garments, so that the fabric is drawn into gathers or folds by elastic or a drawstring.

A casing for one piece of elastic
(a) Cut a casing strip of self fabric (if this would be too thick and heavy, use a piece of lightweight fabric instead), using the pattern piece given with the paper pattern.

(b) Pin, tack and machine the ends, right sides together. Remove tacking, trim the seam allowances and press the seam open.

(c) Fold under 6 mm on each side of the casing, and press into place.

Waistbands and Waistlines

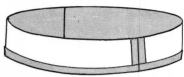

(d) Place this circular casing over the garment, wrong sides together, matching pattern markings.

(e) Pin and tack the folded edges into place along the pattern markings, leaving a few centimetres open for putting in the elastic.

(f) Machine the casing along both sides 3 mm from the edges, still leaving one small area unstitched.

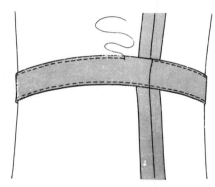

(g) Insert a piece of broad elastic 25 mm/ 2·5 cm longer than the body waist measurement.

(h) Pull both ends of the elastic out far enough to machine the two ends together, with three rows of stitching.

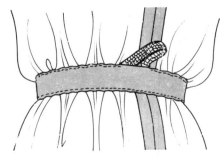

(i) Push the elastic back into the casing and slipstitch the opening closed. Press, and turn right side out.

A casing for a drawstring
A drawstring can be made out of self fabric, rather like a soft tie belt.

Otherwise use ribbon, cord, tubing, braid in a matching or contrasting colour. Use a piece long enough to go round the body and tie in a knot or bow. The opening for pulling out the drawstring to the right side is usually made before the casing is attached. Either:

i. Make two vertical buttonholes in the garment as shown in the pattern.

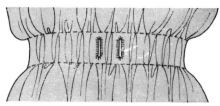

Complete the casing, thread the drawstring through and tie the two ends.

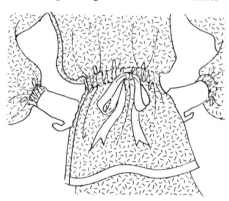

ii. Where there is a suitably placed seam leave open a slot of the right size, and reinforce each end.

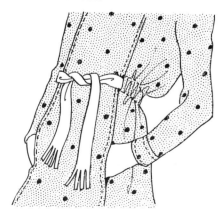

Zipped Fastenings

Zips are a strong, secure and quick method of fastening clothes, and the latest types are lighter and more flexible than earlier models. They are available in many colours, lengths and styles, so choose carefully. Good quality zips have a long life, if cared for and used correctly, and are suitable for all kinds of openings on jackets, dresses, skirts, trousers, sleeves, pockets, soft furnishings, etc. Invisible zips are available to give a concealed finish to openings; alternatively they can be made the focal point of a garment by the use of decorative stitching, braid, etc.

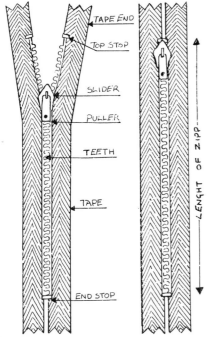

1. Choice

Most zips are available in the following lengths.

Metric	Imperial
10 cm	4 inch
12 cm	5 inch
15 cm	6 inch
18 cm	7 inch
20 cm	8 inch
22 cm	9 inch
25 cm	10 inch
30 cm	12 inch
35 cm	14 inch
40 cm	16 inch
45 cm	18 inch
50 cm	20 inch
55 cm	22 inch
60 cm	24 inch
65 cm	26 inch
70 cm	28 inch
75 cm	30 inch

Always have a zip that is long enough. It is false economy to buy a zip that is too short; taking the garment on and off will break the bottom of the zip quickly. If your measurements and proportions are exactly the same as the pattern buy the length of zip suggested on the pattern packet. If not, wait until the fitting stage with the garment — you may then find that you need a longer opening and therefore a longer zip. Remember that on any zip, the actual opening is almost 13 mm less in length than the zip size. It is possible to arrange for a manufacturer to make a zip of a non-standard length. Aeroluxe zips are made in colours matched to Sylko and Trylko shades, to make your choice easier.

Types of zip

Choose one suitable for the style and weight of the garment.

1. Polyester zips — for man-made and lightweight fabrics. They are machine washable, drip-dry and shrink-resistant, e.g. Aeroluxe.

2. Dress and skirt fasteners — lightweight, closed end, with coloured metal teeth on cotton tape.

3. Invisible zips for skirts and dresses — give a concealed finish to openings, where the teeth are turned inwards by the runner.

4. Open-ended zips for jackets and cardigans, e.g. Aero Open End, medium weight zips with metal teeth.

5. Curved zips for trousers and jeans, in a range of suitable colours.

6. Chunky fashion zips with brass or coloured teeth, plain or fancy tape, and normal runners on large ring pulls.

2. Hints for Use of Zips

(a) Always ensure that the zip is closed before washing or dry cleaning — do not open it when wet.

(b) Pre-shrink, if necessary, by washing before stitching it into a washable garment.

(c) Use the guide lines woven into the zip tape when sewing, as for example on the Aeroluxe polyester zip. The stitching should always be parallel to the zip teeth — never closer than 3 mm, to allow the slider to move freely up and down.

(d) Open the zip right to the bottom when putting on a garment or taking it off; the bottom stop will then take any strain. If it is not completely open the teeth will have to bear this strain and may be damaged.

(e) Be careful that threads and lining do not become caught in the zip teeth when closing and opening it. Stitch tapes and linings securely out of the way, and fasten off all threads.

(f) Preserve the life of the zip by placing a hook and eye at the top, to take the strain.

(g) When ironing a garment, do not bang the iron against the zip slider or teeth — it may cause damage.

(h) Use a pressing cloth when ironing a man made zip fabric and make sure that the appropriate heat setting is used.

(i) Never cut away any part of the zip tapes. They are there to support the zip in use. If cut, fraying will occur and prevent the zip from working efficiently.

(j) If the slider of the zip is difficult to move when the garment has been dry cleaned, a little beeswax, candlewax or even dry soap on the teeth, will help to lubricate them and allow the slider to move freely again.

(k) If wringing is necessary after washing garments, protect the closed zip fastener with folds of the garment. Make sure that it is not twisted, and check that the puller tab lies quite flat.

3. Sewing Tips for Zip Insertion

1. Zips may be applied by machine or by hand. For casual wear, sports wear, children's clothes and any garment that will receive a great deal of washing and wearing, it is advisable to machine stitch the zip into place — this generally gives a more hard-wearing finish. It is also an ideal method where the stitching can act

Zipped Fastenings

as part of the fashion detail. To give a 'couture' finish to a well made garment, however, hand sewing is to be recommended. It is particularly suitable when fabrics are slippery or hard to handle, because the finish is inconspicuous and flexible. The stitch used is a type of backstitch sometimes called a stab stitch. The stitches are smaller than the usual backstitch and do not meet one another — they could be described as quarter back stitches.

(a) After fastening on the thread securely on the wrong side of the fabric bring it through to the right side and take a stitch back for about a thread or two. Bring the needle out about 6 mm in front of the stitch just made. Do *not* pull the thread too tight or the fabric will pucker. The stitch should lie on the surface of the fabric.

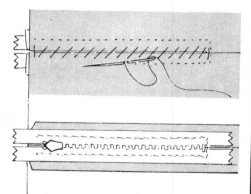

(b) Use the same sewing thread as for the remainder of the garment — natural or man made according to the fabric.

(c) Use a single strand of thread when possible. It gives a finer finish and more even looking stitches.

(d) On heavy fabrics use two rows of stab stitches. The second row of stitches spaced between those of the first row. It helps to lubricate the thread with a little beeswax.

(See also the chapter on Stitches and Threads.)

2. It makes sewing far easier if the zip is inserted before other seams are joined and before waistbands and facings are attached.

3. Press the zip before use to remove creases, should this be necessary.

4. If using the Machine Method of sewing, use a zipper foot. This is an essential aid for a crisp professional-looking finish.

A modern sewing machine will generally have one in the accessory kit supplied. If not, the local sewing machine shop should stock them. Take the normal sewing foot from the machine, so that the retailer can supply one of the correct size.

5. If inserting a zip into a stretchy fabric or a garment cut on the cross, first stay-stitch the edges of the zip opening just inside the stitching line. Use matching thread because this stitching will not be removed.

6. If the slider obstructs sewing whilst machine stitching, snip and remove tacking on the portion already stitched — replace foot and resume sewing.

7. When there is no band in which the zip tapes may be inserted mitre the tape tops as shown in the diagram.

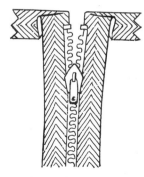

8. When a zip with metal teeth is to be used, a zip shield or underlap will prevent fine undergarments being caught or snagged by the zip teeth. The waistband will need to be cut about 5 cm longer than shown in the pattern so that the top of the shield may be sewn into place.

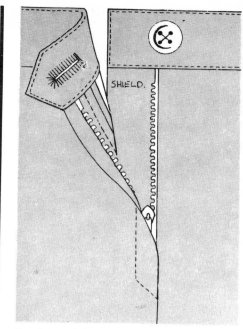

On the straight grain cut a piece of fabric a fraction longer than the zip tapes and three times as wide as the zip. Fold this in half lengthwise and overcast the three raw edged sides together. Stitch the right-hand tape of the zip to the shield on the side opposite the fold, 6 mm in from the edge. Whilst inserting zip, keep shield folded back to prevent it being caught in the left-hand row of stitching — remember to include it when stitching across the bottom of the zip.

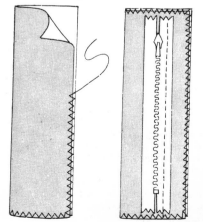

Zipped Fastenings

4. Basic Methods of Inserting a Zip

There are two basic methods of zip insertion for dressmaking but remember that there are no hard and fast rules regarding the positions where either method should be used. Additionally there are various ways in which these applications may be sewn — the two methods that follow are ones that have been found to be very successful. Before any application clearly mark the closure lines with either a line of tacking or tailor's tacks.

Edge-to-edge or slot method

This may be used at the side or back seam of a garment, but it is symmetrical in appearance and therefore also very suitable for a centre front opening. It presents less bulk than the lapped method and is suitable for heavy fabrics.

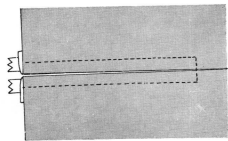

1. Stitch the seam into which the zipper is to be inserted to end of opening. Backstitch at this point for security. Tack the opening together along closure line using long machine tacking stitches. Press the seam open.

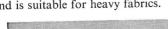

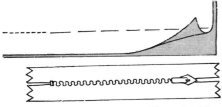

2. Turn garment to wrong side and with right side down place zip along the length of the opening. The slider of the closed zip should be about 25 mm/2.5 cm from top of openings and the bottom stop exactly at the end. The teeth must be centred on the seam. Work from the top of the zip. Centre 2 or 3 cm of the zip at a time, placing the pins at right angles to the tape at 3 cm intervals.

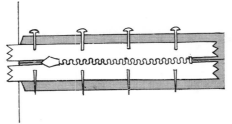

3. Turn back to the right side and tack carefully along both sides of the tape as a guide line for stitching. Remember to keep tacking lines parallel to the teeth using the line woven into the tape as a guide.

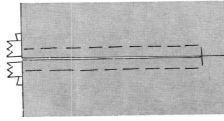

4. Stitch the zip into place. If stitching by machine and the fabric is firm and closely woven, start at the top stitching down one side, pivot the work on the needle and stitch across the bottom. Count the number of stitches to the seamline and make sure to stitch the same number to the other side. This row of stitching may either be stitched straight or to a point.
Pivot the work on the needle again and stitch up the other side. Depending on the width and weight of zipper tape, the stitching should be from 3 – 10 mm from the centre line.

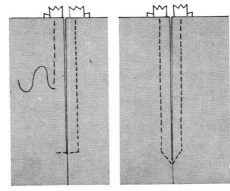

5. Should the fabric tend to slide or give, it is best to sew from the bottom end of the zip to the top, on both sides. When one side has been sewn, stitch across the bottom and then up the other side.
6. Remove the tacking — overcast the tapes to turnings and press.

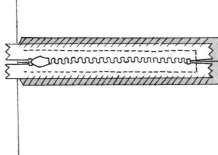

(b) Lapped method

The most common use of this method is for side and back openings on medium and lightweight fabrics. It covers the zip completely and is ideal for snug, closely fitting garments.

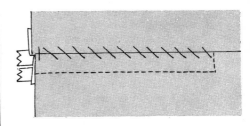

1. Stitch the seam into which the zipper is to be inserted to end of opening, backstitching at end for strength. Press seam open.
2. Turn garment to wrong side and arrange opening as shown in the diagram.
3. Place zipper face downwards on the right-hand seam allowance with the teeth centred on the seamline 15 mm from the edge of fabric.
4. Pin then tack in line with guide line parallel to the teeth all along side of tape. Stitch 3 – 6 mm from zipper teeth depending on fabric thickness, from the bottom stop to the end of the tape at the top.

Zipped Fastenings

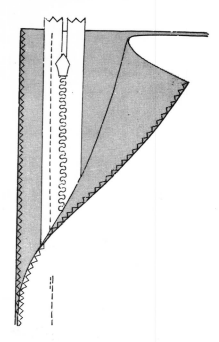

5. Turn the zip to the inside and tack to hold edge ready for pressing. Cover closed zip with pressing cloth and press lightly. No machine stitching is visible on the right side of opening.

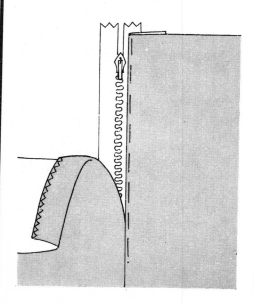

6. Turn the seam allowance on the left hand to the wrong side and tack. Press very lightly using a pressing cloth to flatten the edge. Do not move iron to and fro as this will cause this fold to flute.

7. Lap fold over the zip and extend 3 mm over seamline on the other side. Start at the top of opening and work down to the bottom, pinning flap at 3 cm intervals. This method ensures that the overlap is even all the way down (working upwards from the bottom tends to cause an excess of overlap at the top of the zip). The zip teeth should now be recessed under the flap by 3 mm tapering away at the bottom to avoid a pucker.

8. Cross tack the flap into position as shown in the diagram. *Do not* remove pins until tacking is complete, or flap may "gape" in places.

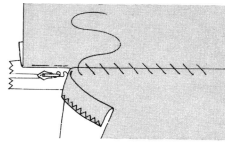

9. Tack a guide line for stitching on the other side of the zipper teeth, remembering to make it exactly parallel with woven guide on tape. Stitch into place by working across the bottom and up the left-hand side of the opening. On light-weight zips the stitching will need to be about 10 mm from the folded edge, on heavier zips about 11 – 13 mm. Stitching any closer than this will prevent the fold covering the slider and it will tend to show.

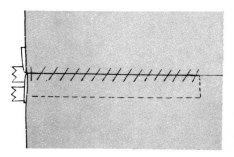

10. Remove tacking. Overcast tapes to raw edges of turnings and carefully press, using pressing cloth.

5. Special Methods

Directions for putting in invisible zips, zips into a fly opening, etc., can be found on the zip packet.

Open end zips

When applying an open ended zip in a blouse or a dress use the instruction for the edge to edge method. It is important to have the end of the tapes exactly level at the bottom.

When applying an open ended zipper to knitted fabric it should be 25 mm/2.5 cm less in length than the opening and the fabric should be carefully eased into place so that it will not be distorted in any way.

The open end fitment on a zip must be treated with respect. When inserting one side into the other the tapes must be absolutely level before attempting to pull the slider.

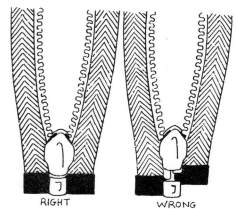

RIGHT   WRONG

6. Zips as a Decoration

Although in most cases every attempt is made to conceal a zip, it CAN be made the focal point on a garment. Decorated with braid or tape, it can completely transform it. There are so very many attractive braids on the market that it is possible to create a really original effect. This method, of course, is really only suitable for a centre front opening.

1. Seam centre front seam to end of opening. Back stitch to secure.
2. Slash into seam allowance horizontally taking slash from 3 to 6 mm into garment fabric, depending on weight of zip to be used.

Zipped Fastenings

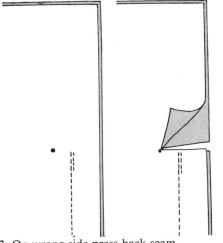

3. On wrong side press back seam allowance on seam and overcast.

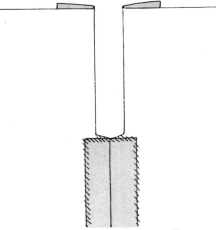

4. On right side fold back seam allowance on opening (from the end of the slash). Tack into place and press.

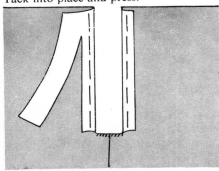

5. Stitch chosen tape to zip 3 mm from teeth making a mitre with the tape at the bottom. Make sure that this is positioned exactly otherwise it will look lopsided. Pin and tack before final stitching.

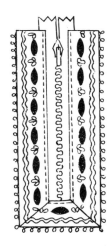

6. Place braided zip unit centrally over opening. Pin carefully and tack into position around edge of braid.
7. Machine stitch zip unit to garment all round outside edge of braid.

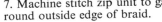
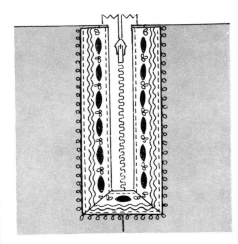

8. Turn to wrong side and neatly slip stitch the folded edges of the turning to the back of the zip tapes. Press very carefully using pressing cloth.

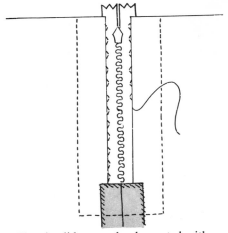

9. The zip slider may be decorated with beads or a fob.